Legal Ethics

BY THOMAS D. MORGAN

George Washington University

Eighth Edition

THOMSON
BAR/BRI

EDITORIAL OFFICES: 111 W. Jackson Blvd., 7th Floor, Chicago, IL 60604
REGIONAL OFFICES: Chicago, Dallas, Los Angeles, New York, Washington, D.C.

PROJECT EDITOR
Linda C. Schneider, B.A., J.D.
Attorney At Law

SERIES EDITOR
Elizabeth L. Snyder, B.A., J.D.
Attorney At Law

QUALITY CONTROL EDITOR
Sanetta M. Hister

Summary of Contents

Text Correlation Chart

Gilbert Law Summary LEGAL ETHICS	Gillers *Regulation of Lawyers: Problems of Law and Ethics* 2002 (6th ed.)	Hazard, Koniak, Cramton *The Law and Ethics of Lawyering* 1999 (3rd ed.)	Morgan, Rotunda *Professional Responsibility Problems and Materials* 2003 (8th ed.)	Schwartz, Wydick, Perschbacher, Bassett *Problems in Legal Ethics* 2003 (6th ed.)
I. REGULATING THE RIGHT TO PRACTICE LAW				
A. Sources of Regulation	Page 1-15	Page 151, 858-861, 959-965	Page 12-16	Page 36-43
B. State Court Regulation of General Admission to Practice Law	682-706	869-889, 1047-1054	31-46, 603-604	31-34
C. Practice in States Where Not Formally Licensed	707-736	1054-1063	603-610	35-36, 142, 155-157
D. Engaging in Federal Court and International Practice	706-707	869-870, 890	45-46, 607-608	36
E. Preventing Unauthorized Practice of Law by Nonlawyers	750-763	992-1013	613-617	157-159
II. THE CONTRACT BETWEEN CLIENT AND LAWYER				
A. Introduction	21-22, 69	449	83	133-137
B. Formation of the Lawyer-Client Relationship— Lawyers' Duties Regarding Accepting Employment	22-38, 213-219, 354, 768-777	457-463, 469-470	84-92	52-68, 76-77
C. Spheres of Authority of Lawyer and Client	72-74, 82-102	469-489	92-95, 318-322	249-250, 255-257, 273
D. Formal Duties that Lawyers Owe to Clients	27-28, 78-80, 743-745, 776-777, 839-846	151-152, 553-557	112-117	133-137, 166-181
E. The Obligation of Client to Lawyer—Fees for Legal Services	143-181, 184-213	489-533	95-112, 120-127	109-132
F. Terminating the Lawyer-Client Relationship	102-106, 599	463-469	112-113, 117-120, 123	68-76
III. DUTY TO PROTECT CONFIDENTIAL INFORMATION OF THE CLIENT				
A. Introduction	28-31	203-206, 261, 269-271	127-128	164
B. Attorney-Client Privilege	34-37, 40-68, 136-139, 545-553	54-55, 205-221, 224, 227-254, 261-267, 274-289, 304-310, 510	128-157, 350-353	164-181
C. Professional Duty of Confidentiality	28-34, 37-40	254-257, 267-274, 282-289, 310-332	132-157, 350-353, 416-420	164-181
IV. DUTY OF UNIMPAIRED LOYALTY—CONFLICTS OF INTEREST				
A. Introduction	229-231, 235-239, 313-322	574-576, 592, 605-606, 622-625	158-171	249, 277
B. Personal Interests that May Affect Lawyer's Judgment	235-249, 254-256	506-507, 557-570, 706-707	126-127, 201-208, 210-212	263-267
C. Concurrent Representation of Clients with Conflicting Interests	260-296, 301-313, 319-322, 325-326	576-591, 595-603, 605, 608-623, 625-626, 628-634	166-168, 171-198, 289-295, 335	261-263, 278, 290-291

Gilbert Law Summary LEGAL ETHICS	Gillers *Regulation of Lawyers: Problems of Law and Ethics* 2002 (6th ed.)	Hazard, Koniak, Cramton *The Law and Ethics of Lawyering* 1999 (3rd ed.)	Morgan, Rotunda *Professional Responsibility Problems and Materials* 2003 (8th ed.)	Schwartz, Wydick, Perschbacher, Bassett *Problems in Legal Ethics* 2003 (6th ed.)
D. Interests of Third Persons Affecting Lawyer-Client Relationships	249-251, 325, 326-333	627-628, 637-640	215-229	250, 257-261
E. Conflict Between Interests of Current and Former Clients	339-350, 352-354	640-667	230-240	278-284
F. Imputed Disqualification of Affiliated Lawyers	251-254, 282-283, 297-299, 311-312, 350-351, 362-380	593-595, 606-607, 667-684	240-260	278-279, 284-289, 292-293
G. Limitations on Representation by Present and Former Government Lawyers	378-389	684-707	260-272	261
V. OBLIGATIONS TO THIRD PERSONS AND THE LEGAL SYSTEM				
A. Lawyer's Role as Counselor	79-85, 611-619	289-302	275-289	188-194
B. Requirement of Honesty in Communications with Others	597-600, 609-610, 621-628	9-10, 303, 445-446, 1146-1159	322-332, 350-352, 362-363, 366-367	188-207
C. Specially Assumed Duty of Candor—Lawyer as Evaluator	824-827	101-118	336-350	298
D. Communicating with Another Person on Behalf of Client	107-133, 628-629	533-553	302-318	212
E. Obligation to Improve the Legal System	972-982	1088-1091	188-189, 635-637, 643-650	341-345
VI. SPECIAL OBLIGATIONS OF LAWYERS IN LITIGATION				
A. Duty to Assert Only Meritorious Claims and Expedite Litigation	492-499	383-432	368-379, 382-386	76-77, 187, 228-231
B. Duty of Honesty	443-448, 457-492, 505-511	9-10, 337-372, 407-420	386-387, 389-392, 401-412, 414-416	186-196, 198-207
C. Other Duties of an Advocate to Nonclients and Tribunals	474-485, 499-505, 513-539	41-61, 148, 267, 434-437, 439-448	386-390, 395-401	214-218, 223-226
D. Limitations on Trial Publicity	943-972	1081-1088	464-473	220-223
E. Limitations on Advancing Money to Client	247, 249	566-568	578-579, 584-586	133
F. Lawyer as Witness and Advocate	234, 333-338	571-573	250, 453-454, 461-464, 479	267-272
G. Improper Contacts with Court Officials and Jurors	634	568-570	453-458, 618-621, 642-643	213-214, 218-220
H. Special Duties of Prosecutors and Other Government Lawyers	123-124	445-446, 552	473-475, 477, 480	226-231
VII. THE BUSINESS OF PRACTICING LAW				
A. Associations of Lawyers for the Practice of Law	219-223, 225, 741-743, 746-750, 901-938	865-867, 938-959, 1008-1013, 1039-1047	77, 511, 530-534, 539-541, 552-562	301-302
B. Regulation of the Manner of Lawyers Seeking Employment—Solicitation and Advertising	985-1040	1013-1038	10, 496-517, 522, 578-581	81-104
C. Specialization and Limitation of Practice	763-764, 1017-1018	1034-1035	517-524	97

Gilbert Law Summary **LEGAL ETHICS**	Gillers *Regulation of Lawyers: Problems of Law and Ethics* 2002 (6th ed.)	Hazard, Koniak, Cramton *The Law and Ethics of Lawyering* 1999 (3rd ed.)	Morgan, Rotunda *Professional Responsibility Problems and Materials* 2003 (8th ed.)	Schwartz, Wydick, Perschbacher, Bassett *Problems in Legal Ethics* 2003 (6th ed.)
D. Division of Fees with Lawyers Outside One's Firm	223-225	507-509	524-530, 555-556	109
VIII. ENFORCEMENT OF LAWYERS' PROFESSIONAL OBLIGATIONS				
A. The Formal Disciplinary Process	834-881	915-934, 1063	46-63	42-46
B. Personal Financial Liability of Lawyer (Malpractice)	765-786, 791-834	79-92, 154-176, 202	63-77	145-151
C. Contempt Sanctions	943-944	1074-1078	77-78	
IX. THE SPECIAL RESPONSIBILITIES OF JUDGES				
A. Introduction	631-632	17	618	41, 328
B. General Norms	674-675		650, 659, 662-664	242-244
C. Judge's Official Actions	634, 664-674		651-659, 661-662	
D. Judicial Disqualification	635-653, 655-664		618-635	329-341
E. Extrajudicial Activities of the Judge	653-655		659-660	
F. Money-Making Activities of the Judge	657-659		664-667	
G. Involvement of Judges and Judicial Candidates in Political Activities			635-643	341-345
H. Standards Applicable to Federal Judges	631-632		651-667	328

Capsule Summary

I. REGULATING THE RIGHT TO PRACTICE LAW

A. SOURCES OF REGULATION

1. State Regulation   §1
The practice of law affects the public interest and is thus subject to regulation by the states.

    a. Inherent judicial power   §2
Unlike other professions, ultimate regulatory power rests with the courts rather than the legislature.

    b. Regulation by state legislature   §5
Many state legislatures also have power to enact statutes regulating the legal profession.

    c. "Integrated" bar   §6
Many states *require* practicing lawyers to join the state bar association and become subject to its rules.

    d. Regulation by multiple states   §9
Lawyers are subject to regulation by *each* state in which they are *admitted* to practice, regardless of where they actually practice, and *also* in any state in which the lawyer violates a regulation.

    e. No preclusion of federal regulation   §10
State regulation does not preclude additional federal regulation of lawyers where the lawyers' activities are within the scope of applicable federal law.

2. American Bar Association as Source of Model Regulation   §11
Many standards for the practice of law come from the organized bar, particularly the American Bar Association ("ABA").

    a. ABA Model Code of Professional Responsibility (1969)   §14
The first ABA standards, the Canons of Professional Ethics, were replaced by the ABA Code, consisting of nine Canons containing axiomatic norms for lawyers. These Canons were supplemented by aspirational Ethical Considerations and mandatory Disciplinary Rules.

    b. Model Rules of Professional Conduct (1983)   §19
In response to criticism of the ABA Code, the ABA approved the *Model Rules*, a set of standards in a "Restatement-type" format. The Model Rules are expressed in "black letter" rules, followed by sometimes extensive Comments.

c. Revision of Model Rules (2002-2003) §20
Extensive changes in the substance of many of the Model Rules were made by the Ethics 2000 Commission. References in this summary to principles of the Model Rules will be made to the relevant Model Rules as revised in 2002-2003.

d. Widespread impact of ABA Code and Model Rules §21
The Model Code was adopted word for word by every state's highest court except in California, which enacted its own code. The 1983 Model Rules have been adopted by more than 40 states, and even in some of the states that have retained the Model Code, the content is close to that of the Rules. As of 2005, only a few states have adopted the 2002-2003 revisions, but many are in the process of doing so.

e. Interpretation of Code and Model Rules §25
Judicial opinions are influential sources for clarifying the meaning of the Code and Model Rules. Other sources include *advisory opinions* from the ABA ("ABA Opn.") and state bar associations.

f. Testing the Model Rules on the Multistate Professional Responsibility Exam ("MPRE") §26
The MPRE tests the current version of the Model Rules and other legal principles governing lawyers. The 2002-2003 amendments have been tested since 2004, whether or not they have been adopted in the state in which the applicant is seeking admission.

3. Indirect Regulation Through Malpractice Liability §27
Malpractice is rarely considered an "ethics" issue, but it is of major concern to lawyers and thus influences lawyer behavior.

4. Contempt Sanctions §28
Courts may immediately regulate a lawyer's conduct by imposing contempt sanctions for misconduct before the court.

5. Restatement of the Law Governing Lawyers §29
In 2000, a Restatement was published that contains rules and case law from all over the country.

B. STATE COURT REGULATION OF GENERAL ADMISSION TO PRACTICE LAW §30
Each state establishes its own standards for admission. These standards must have a *rational connection* to the applicant's *fitness or capacity* to practice law. U.S. citizenship is *not* a constitutionally acceptable requirement for admission, nor is limiting bar admission to a state's own residents.

1. Intellectual Capacity §33
Most states require graduation from an ABA-accredited law school. Nearly all states require passage of a bar examination. The Americans with Disabilities Act has been the basis for the allowance of extra time or other accommodations during the bar examination to an increasing number of bar candidates.

2. **Determination of "Good Moral Character"** §39
States have a valid interest in high moral standards, including mental and emotional stability, of persons admitted.

   a. **Investigative procedure** §40
An applicant usually fills out a detailed questionnaire, lists references, and submits fingerprints and photographs for identification, after which a committee of examiners investigates moral character. If questions arise regarding fitness to practice, a *hearing* is set. The burden of proof is on the applicant, but she is entitled to *procedural due process* and *appellate review*.

   b. **Conduct relevant to determination of "good moral character"** §46
Any past conduct reflecting upon honesty and integrity is relevant.

      (1) **Conviction of crime involving "moral turpitude"** §48
Crimes involving an intent to defraud or intentional dishonesty for personal gain may be enough to show lack of good moral character.

      (2) **Crimes not necessarily establishing lack of character** §49
Crimes not showing moral turpitude, such as adolescent misbehavior and some acts of nonviolent civil disobedience, are not enough by themselves to disqualify an applicant.

      (3) **Effect of concealment** §52
Concealment or a false statement by the applicant is *itself* evidence of lack of character sufficient to deny admission, even if not discovered until after admission to practice.

      (4) **Rehabilitation** §53
An applicant can still gain admission if she can demonstrate sufficient remorse and rehabilitation.

      (5) **Political activity** §54
Refusal to take the *required oath* to support the Constitution may deny admission, but even active membership in the Communist Party is not necessarily sufficient to deny admission.

3. **Duty of Lawyers Not to Aid Admission of the Unqualified** §57
Many states require applicants to submit letters of reference from lawyers. Lawyers must be honest in such letters.

C. PRACTICE IN STATES WHERE NOT FORMALLY LICENSED

1. **Introduction** §58
Each state determines the conditions for admission to its bar, but practicalities have led to lawyers practicing in states in which they have not been admitted. Although requirements vary from state to state, many states admit such lawyers by *reciprocity*, without a bar examination. Most of these states limit such admissions to lawyers from *other states that allow reciprocity*. Other states require an out-of-state lawyer to pass a written examination.

2. **Unauthorized Practice of Law** §62
If a lawyer practices in a jurisdiction in which he is unauthorized, he may be guilty of the unauthorized practice of law.

hac vice to a lawyer seeking to appear in **_federal court_** on a matter involving federal law if the lawyer is admitted to and in good standing with a state bar.

2. **Practice of International Law** §81

A foreign lawyer engaged in international practice has no right to practice in a particular U.S. jurisdiction or forum. However, several states now specially license foreign lawyers as "**_legal consultants_**," to give advice regarding the law of the countries where they are admitted to practice.

 a. **Supreme Court practice** §84

 Supreme Court rules permit a foreign lawyer to appear **_pro hac vice_** at the Court's discretion. If associated with an American lawyer, the foreign lawyer may be admitted to practice before the Court.

E. PREVENTING UNAUTHORIZED PRACTICE OF LAW BY NONLAWYERS

1. **Basic Principles** §85

Laypersons may represent themselves in propria persona, but only lawyers may represent persons other than themselves.

2. **Activities that Constitute the "Practice of Law"** §88

"Practice of law" is not defined by statute or the ABA Code. Courts generally apply one of two tests: (i) the **_history and custom_** test, which relies on whether the activity **_traditionally_** has been handled by lawyers; or (ii) the ABA Code test, which determines whether there is a **_need for professional judgment_**.

 a. **Judicial determinations in specific areas** §92

 Appearing in a judicial proceeding, drafting documents that **_affect substantial legal rights_** or obligations (but **_not merely filling in blanks_** on standard forms), tax planning, giving legal advice (but **_not_** a layperson's **_publication of a book containing general advice_** and forms), and prisoner legal assistance by lay prisoners have all been held to be the "practice of law." However, the Supreme Court has struck down regulations designed to prevent lay prisoner assistance where the state has not provided **_reasonable alternative forms_** of legal aid for prisoners.

3. **Specific Classes of Persons Prohibited from Practicing Law** §104

Many states' laws expressly prohibit the practice of law by certain classes of persons:

 a. **_Judges and court officers_** §105

 b. **_Law students and law clerks_**—However, some states make exceptions for student training programs under a lawyer's supervision. §106

 c. **_Corporations_**—Generally, a corporation may not represent a client directly or furnish representation through its employees who are licensed attorneys; and, in many states, it cannot represent itself. (Exceptions exist for professional law corporations and nonprofit group legal services providers.) §108

to require representation of an indigent client without **compensation**. Furthermore, the Supreme Court has held that, while a federal court may request a lawyer to represent an indigent client in a **civil case**, it cannot order him to do so.

4. Duties to a Prospective Client   §136

Though the lawyer-client relationship is not formed until the parties agree, some duties are owed to a prospective client who consults the lawyer about obtaining legal assistance. These include the duty to **protect confidential information**, which also **prohibits** the lawyer from representing any client with **interests materially adverse** to those of the prospective client if the lawyer has acquired **significantly harmful** information. The lawyer also has a duty to **protect a prospective client's property** and to give **competent legal advice**.

5. Duty to Reject Certain Cases   §143

The ABA Code and Model Rules identify at least seven situations where the lawyer **must refuse** employment; *i.e.*, where:

a.   A **disciplinary standard or other law would be violated**;

b.   The lawyer's **physical or mental condition is impaired**;

c.   The lawyer is **unable to act competently**;

d.   The lawyer's **personal feelings interfere** (as opposed to community pressure);

e.   The client is **already represented**;

f.   The client's **motive is harassment or malicious injury**; or

g.   The client's **legal position is unsupportable**.

6. Agreeing on Scope and Objectives of Representation   §151

A lawyer should act in a way reasonably calculated to advance the client's legal objectives. However, the scope and objectives of the representation may be defined and limited by agreement (*e.g.*, limitation of representation to particular subjects or limitation of remedies to be pursued). Of course, the lawyer must inform the client of advantages and risks of limiting representation, preferably in writing. The burden of proving the contents of an agreement to limit is on the lawyer.

C. SPHERES OF AUTHORITY OF LAWYER AND CLIENT

1. In General   §158

The **client**, with some exceptions, must be allowed to make ultimate decisions on the merits.

2. Matters Within Client's Authority   §159

Decisions on matters that substantially affect the client's rights must be made by the client. These include the **settlement or compromise of an action** (but the client may ratify an unauthorized settlement) and the **dismissal or abandonment of a case** (but there may be an implied authority for the lawyer to dismiss "without prejudice").

3. Duty of Zealous Representation §190

Zealous representation is not defined by the ABA Code or Model Rules. Traditionally, zeal in *litigation* matters has meant that the lawyer must act as an *advocate* and resolve any *doubts in favor of the client*. The lawyer, in the role of an *advisor*, owes the client *greater detachment* in *nonadversary* matters. Moreover, a lawyer need *not* personally adopt the *client's viewpoint* and may take positions on public issues and support reforms that are *contrary* to the client's position.

4. Duty of Communication §195

The Model Rules require a lawyer to explain a matter so that the client can make an informed decision. This requires a lawyer to: (i) keep the client *informed about the status* of a matter; (ii) comply promptly with *reasonable requests for information*; (iii) reasonably consult with the client *about the means* to be used; (iv) promptly inform the client about *circumstances requiring informed consent*; and (v) be certain the client understands any *relevant limitations on the lawyer's conduct* imposed by the rules of conduct.

5. Duty of Confidentiality §198

See *infra*, Chapter III.

6. Duty of Loyalty §199

See *infra*, Chapter IV.

7. Duties with Regard to Client Property §200

A lawyer must keep the funds and property of clients *safe* and *entirely separate* from the lawyer's own assets.

a. Separate bank accounts §201

Funds belonging to clients must be deposited in *separately identified* bank accounts ("trust accounts"). Generally a lawyer may not deposit personal funds in the trust accounts (commingling), which must be in the state of the lawyer's office, absent client consent to the contrary.

(1) Expenses advanced by client §204

Contrary to the ABA Code, the Model Rules require client advances for *costs or expenses* to be deposited in the trust account.

b. Withdrawals from joint funds §205

A lawyer who receives money belonging in part to the client and in part to the lawyer must deposit the *entire* sum in the client's trust account. If the lawyer's share is fixed and *undisputed*, it must be withdrawn *as soon as possible*. *Disputed funds* may *not* be withdrawn until the controversy is resolved. Furthermore, the lawyer cannot disburse funds potentially belonging to a *third party* except as authorized by the client or court order.

c. Client's property (other than funds) §209

The lawyer must label and identify securities and other property and deposit such property at once in a *safe deposit box* or other *suitable storage facility*.

E. THE OBLIGATION OF CLIENT TO LAWYER—FEES FOR LEGAL SERVICES

1. **Timing and Content of Fee Agreement** §211
   With a client not regularly represented by the lawyer, the client must be informed of the basis or rate of the fee *before or within a reasonable time* after agreeing to the representation.

   a. **Required subjects** §212
      The client must be told of the *fee amount* or the *basis* for its calculation, the *scope* of the work, and *likely costs* to the client. The agreement should be *written*, and any *ambiguities* are construed *against the lawyer*. There is a *presumption of undue influence* if the agreement is entered into later than the commencement of representation.

2. **Requirement that Fees Be No More than Reasonable** §216
   Courts may refuse to enforce fee agreements that are "unreasonable," "clearly excessive," or "unconscionable," and such agreements may also subject the lawyer to discipline.

   a. **"Reasonableness"** §217
      The fee's reasonableness depends upon *all relevant circumstances*, including factors such as the *time and labor* required, the *novelty and difficulty* of the issues, the required *skill*, *customary fees* charged in the area, the *amount involved,* the *result obtained*, and the *experience, reputation, and ability* of the lawyer.

   b. **Fee arbitration** §219
      Several states provide arbitration review for dissatisfied clients, usually on a voluntary basis. However, proposals are being made to make them mandatory, and a comment to the Model Rules urges lawyers to submit to arbitration.

3. **Special Problems of Contingent Fee Agreements**

   a. **Propriety of contingent fee agreements** §221
      Contingent fees are permitted, subject to regulation designed to prevent abuses.

      (1) **Specific requirements** §223
         In addition to the requirements for regular fee agreements, the Model Rules require that a contingent fee agreement must:

         (a) Be in *writing signed by the client*;

         (b) State *how* the fee is *to be determined*, including provision for settlement, trial, or appeal;

         (c) *Identify expenses* and the method for their deduction; and

         (d) Be followed up with a *written statement* accounting for *disposition of the recovery*.

      (2) **Maximum limits** §225
         Court rules in a few states fix maximum percentages that a lawyer

may charge under contingent fee contracts. Most states require **court approval** for contingency contracts on behalf of **minors**.

b. Where contingency fees prohibited §227

The Model Rules prohibit contingency fees in **domestic relations** cases (*e.g.*, divorce, alimony, property settlement, or support). However, some courts **permit** such fees in **post-divorce** proceedings (*e.g.*, past due alimony). Contingency fees are also **prohibited** in **criminal cases and for the securing of favorable legislation**.

c. Recovery in quantum meruit §234

If a contingent fee arrangement is void for public policy reasons, courts usually permit the lawyer to recover the **reasonable value** of his lawful services. In the **absence of a fee contract**, the lawyer is also entitled to the reasonable value of his services.

4. Minimum Fee Schedules §236

Fee schedules established by bar associations **violate antitrust laws**. Fees are now established by private contract, by court order, or by controlling legislation.

5. Legislative Regulation of Fees §239

Congress and some state legislatures have set **maximum** fees for some types of services (*e.g.*, workers' compensation claims, representation of indigent criminal defendants). Because of a sometimes harsh effect on a lawyer's fee in certain cases, some statutes provide that the ceiling applies only to a lawyer's "ordinary" services, allowing **additional** reasonable fees for "extraordinary" services.

6. Setting Fees in Class Actions, Derivative Suits, and Certain Civil Rights Actions §242

Courts usually apply the **"lodestar" approach**, using an hourly rate as a basis and adjusting it based on complexity, amount recovered, uncertainty of result, etc. However, the **common fund method** (*i.e.*, awarding the lawyer a percentage of the recovery) is often used when a lawyer recovers a substantial sum for the plaintiff or a class.

a. Negotiating fees as part of settlement §247

The Supreme Court has held that if a defendant offers a generous settlement but insists that the plaintiff's lawyer take less than a reasonable fee, the lawyer may have a duty to accept the settlement. Thus, many lawyers now negotiate fee arrangements with the class in advance.

7. Protecting Lawyer's Right to Compensation

a. Lawyer's duties in collecting fees §248

Lawyers should be "zealous" in efforts to **avoid controversies** with clients over fees. Lawyers must be very careful to avoid overreaching in using self-help remedies and should not sue a client unless necessary to prevent fraud or gross imposition by the client or if the client refuses to pay a fee claim asserted in good faith.

(1)   Credit card financing   §251

As long as there is no increased charge to the client, a lawyer may accept credit card charges for her legal fees, or she may participate in legal fee financing plans.

b.   Retaining (possessory) lien   §252

In many states, lawyers have a possessory lien on all property, documents, and funds belonging to the client that come into the lawyer's possession by reason of employment. Ordinarily, a lawyer need not turn over documents prepared by him and not yet paid for. However, a retaining lien on *files needed* by the client is *void*.

c.   Charging (nonpossessory) lien   §256

In many states, lawyers also have a "charging lien" that gives the lawyer the right to have *any fund or recovery* she obtains for her client serve as security for her fees and disbursements in that matter. The charging lien has the advantages of application to funds not in the lawyer's possession and of *affirmative enforcement*.

(1)   Limitations   §261

The charging lien is limited to fees and costs incurred in that particular action, not for other fees owed by the same client.

(2)   Time lien attaches   §264

Most states permit assertion of a charging lien only upon judgment or settlement. However, provided the lawyer gives *notice* to the defendant and the lien attaches to the cause of action, a client may *not* defeat it by settling *directly* with the defendant. However, some states permit charging liens to attach at *earlier* stages of the proceedings to prevent the client from settling the case without paying the lawyer.

F.   TERMINATING THE LAWYER-CLIENT RELATIONSHIP   §266

Either the lawyer or client may seek to terminate the relationship before completion of the matter.

1.   Withdrawal by Lawyer   §267

A lawyer may not simply terminate the lawyer-client relationship at will. Withdrawal should be made only on the basis of "compelling circumstances" and after careful consideration.

a.   Duty to withdraw   §268

A lawyer *is obliged* to withdraw under the following circumstances:

(1)   The employment is *violative of professional conduct rules*;

(2)   The lawyer is physically or mentally *unable to continue* the employment;

(3)   The client's purpose is *harassment or malicious prosecution*; or

(4)   The lawyer has been *discharged* by the client.

b.   Permissive withdrawal   §273

Where withdrawal is not required, the lawyer has a general duty to continue the employment to its natural conclusion, but the lawyer is **permitted** to withdraw under certain circumstances, such as:

(1) There is **no material adverse effect on the client**, even if the client objects;

(2) The client **involves the lawyer in illegal conduct**;

(3) The client makes **repugnant demands**;

(4) The client **fails to fulfill obligations** to the lawyer (*e.g.*, refuses to pay fee);

(5) The client **has made the relationship unreasonably difficult** (*e.g.*, noncooperation);

(6) The client **freely and knowingly consents**; and

(7) **Other good cause** for withdrawal exists.

c. General obligations of lawyer in withdrawing §281
There is a duty to **safeguard rights and interests** of clients. The lawyer must:

(1) Obtain **court permission** in **litigation** matters;

(2) Give adequate **notice** to the client so other counsel can be retained;

(3) **Refund** unearned fees; and

(4) **Promptly return** all papers and property to which the client is entitled.

2. Discharge by Client §287
The right of a client to terminate the lawyer-client relationship is **virtually unconditional**. The lawyer may be fired **at any time, with or without cause**. Provisions purporting to make the lawyer's employment **irrevocable** are **void**.

a. Continuing fiduciary duty of lawyer §290
Even discharge without cause does **not** relieve the lawyer of all fiduciary duties.

b. Liability of client to lawyer under fee contract §291
The client may remain **contractually liable** to the lawyer (for fees, etc.) if the discharge is **without cause**. Recovery would most often be in quantum meruit.

c. Liability of third parties for inducing discharge §298
The lawyer may have an action for **interference with contractual relations** against third persons who induce discharge without cause.

III. DUTY TO PROTECT CONFIDENTIAL INFORMATION OF THE CLIENT

A. INTRODUCTION

1. Two Basic Legal Doctrines §299
Both the evidentiary **attorney-client privilege** and an ethical **duty of confidentiality** protect the confidential information of clients.

government clients when made to both in-house and independent lawyers. Note that the privilege is **not** lost when nonlegal and legal advice (a mixed communication) are contained in the same communication.

(1) Personal confidences of corporate or government officials   §320
Generally, a corporate or government lawyer is **not** the lawyer for individuals of the entity.

b. Information shared by clients with common interest   §321
If two or more clients have a common interest in a matter, they and their lawyers may share information without losing the privilege. However, the privilege is **not** applicable in subsequent litigation between/among the clients.

3. Exceptions to the Attorney-Client Privilege

a. Consent by client   §324
When the client consents, the lawyer may disclose confidential information.

b. Disclosure of future crime or fraud   §325
The attorney-client privilege **does not cover** a communication in which the client seeks to further the planning or commission of a **future** crime or fraud. The privilege **does protect** revelations of **past** crimes or frauds.

c. Disclosure for lawyer self-protection   §328
A lawyer may reveal sufficient information to defend himself against charges of **negligence or misconduct**, and to **collect fees** owed the lawyer.

4. Responsibilities of Lawyer in Asserting the Attorney-Client Privilege   §329
A lawyer has a duty "to advise the client of the attorney-client privilege and timely to assert the privilege unless it is waived by the client."

a. Wrongful order to disclose   §330
When a court wrongfully orders a lawyer to disclose privileged information, some courts hold that the lawyer **must refuse** to disclose **at all costs** (*e.g.*, jailed on contempt charge). The ABA Code and Model Rules provide that the lawyer **may disclose** when required by court order. The **preferred approach** would be for the lawyer to assert all **nonfrivolous claims for confidentiality**, and then, if the client so directs, allow himself to be held in contempt until the matter is reviewed on appeal. If the order is sustained on appeal, the lawyer should then disclose.

5. Waiver by Disclosure or Failure to Object   §334
Failure to assert the attorney-client privilege, or voluntary disclosure of the privileged information, waives the privilege **forever**. Importantly, waiver with respect to one item may waive **all** items dealing with the **same subject matter**.

a. Inadvertent disclosure   §336
In discovery, if a lawyer inadvertently turns over privileged information along with required material, courts often deem the privilege not waived if the lawyer has taken reasonable measures to prevent such an occurrence and immediately seeks to reclaim the material.

C. PROFESSIONAL DUTY OF CONFIDENTIALITY §338
Besides the attorney-client privilege, lawyers have a **professional duty** not to reveal a much larger body of confidential client information.

1. **Professional Duty Broader than Privilege** §339

   Under the **Model Rules**, a lawyer may **not** reveal **any** information relating to the representation. Under the **ABA Code**, information gained in the professional relationship that would **embarrass the client** or that the **client requests be kept confidential** may not be revealed. Unlike the privilege, the duty is unaffected by third parties being present.

2. **Differences Between Privileged and Confidential Material**

   a. **Identity of client** §341

   Generally, the name of a client is **not** a "communication," and hence is not privileged. However, if revelation of identity would embarrass or **incriminate** the client, it is a "secret" and may not be disclosed. Similarly, the fact that the client consulted a lawyer may be confidential, and the **client's whereabouts** may be both privileged and a secret. However, **disclosure may be required** if a lawyer learns that her client has **violated a court order** obtained by the lawyer **and** she cannot persuade her client to cease the violation.

   b. **Fee arrangement with client** §347

   Although fee arrangements are not protected by the attorney-client privilege, they are **confidential**, and a lawyer is **not ethically** free to disclose them without client consent.

   c. **Presence of strangers** §349

   The duty of confidentiality **applies** to information learned from, or in the presence of, third parties.

   d. **When lawyer may reveal** §350

   A lawyer may reveal sufficient confidential information to defend himself or his associates and employees against **negligence or misconduct** charges or to **collect a fee** owed to him.

   e. **Physical evidence** §351

   Neither the privilege nor the duty requires or permits the lawyer to take possession of or help secrete fruits or instrumentalities of a **crime**. If the lawyer takes possession, he **must** give the physical evidence to the police, even if it incriminates the client, although the lawyer may keep it long enough to do necessary tests.

3. **Use of Information for Lawyer's Benefit** §354

   The **ABA Code prohibits** use of confidential information for a lawyer's own gain. The **Model Rules** prohibit use of the information only if it would be **detrimental** to the client.

4. **Exceptions to Duty of Confidentiality** §357

   The privilege exceptions (client consent, lawyer self-defense) apply to the duty. In addition, a **court may compel** the lawyer's testimony regarding nonprivileged secrets. Also, "generally known" information is not always protected.

third person before accepting a significant gift or bequest from the client. An *instrument* giving the lawyer a gift must be drafted by another lawyer (exception for personal friends or relatives).

6. Negotiating Employment with Opposing Firm §391

Although there is not yet a specific Model Rule provision regarding a lawyer seeking employment with a firm representing an opponent of the lawyer's client, the Restatement covers this situation. When discussions have become *concrete*, and the interests in the move are *mutual*, the lawyer must obtain her client's *informed consent* or end the employment discussions until her client's matter has concluded. The same procedure should apply when a *law firm merger* is involved.

C. CONCURRENT REPRESENTATION OF CLIENTS WITH CONFLICTING INTERESTS §394

The lawyer must exercise independent judgment on behalf of *each* client.

1. General Standards §395

Concurrent conflicts of interest can arise upon *directly adverse representation* in the *same case* or in *unrelated cases*, or when representation of one client is *materially limited by obligations to another client*.

2. Lawyer's Obligation in Such Situations §399

In the above situations, the lawyer must *decline* or *withdraw* from the representation, unless informed consent of each client is possible and obtained.

a. Nonconsentable conflicts §400

A client may not waive: his lawyer's representation of an opposing party in the *same litigation*, the lawyer's *inability* to render *competent and diligent representation* to each client, and representations *prohibited by law*.

b. Informed client consent §404

In most cases, however, a lawyer may proceed after obtaining each client's *informed consent, confirmed in writing*.

3. Application of Standards—Litigation Matters

a. Criminal proceedings §405

Each accused is *constitutionally* entitled to assistance of his own counsel. It is the *duty of the court* to appoint separate counsel whenever differing interests arise.

b. Personal injury litigation §410

Several persons injured in the same mishap may have potentially differing interests, which could make multiple representation improper, absent informed consent.

c. Other civil matters §413

Conflicts of interests among clients may exist in matters such as divorce, where differing interests are present (*e.g.,* property division, child support). Bankruptcies and receiverships also usually involve diverse interests, which often make multiple representation improper.

serving as legislators or public officials must not engage in activities where personal or professional interests are (or *foreseeably may be*) in conflict with official duties.

5. Selecting Judges §568

The lawyer owes a special duty to aid in the selection of qualified persons, and to defend judges against inaccurate or irresponsible charges. Criticism of judges must be aimed at improving the legal system. *Reckless or knowingly false accusations* are grounds for lawyer discipline.

 a. Contributions to judicial candidates §572

 A lawyer may not make campaign contributions for the purpose of obtaining a judge's appointment to handle a matter.

6. Personally Running for Judicial Office §573

Lawyers running for judicial office must comply with the ABA Model Code of Judicial Conduct ("CJC").

VI. SPECIAL OBLIGATIONS OF LAWYERS IN LITIGATION

A. DUTY TO ASSERT ONLY MERITORIOUS CLAIMS AND EXPEDITE LITIGATION

1. Baseless Lawsuits §575

A lawyer may not file suit on behalf of a client unless it has a *nonfrivolous* basis, which includes a *good faith argument* for an *extension, modification, or reversal* of existing law. A filing is *not frivolous* if a lawyer does not have all the facts but expects to determine them *in discovery*. Note that a lawyer may zealously defend a *criminal defendant* whom she believes to be guilty.

 a. Possible sanctions §582

 The filing of a frivolous suit subjects a lawyer to discipline. Further, the lawyer (and her client) may be subject to civil liability for abuse of process or malicious prosecution if the suit was filed for an *ulterior purpose* and caused damage to the opposing party.

2. Abusive Delay in Litigation §584

Delaying a trial to harass or injure the opponent or failure to appear may subject a lawyer to sanctions by the court. The Model Rules impose an *affirmative duty* to expedite litigation.

 a. Federal Rule 11 §586

 The rule requires a lawyer to *sign every pleading*, thus *certifying* that the pleading is not filed for the "purposes of delay." Violations may result in a lawyer or client being required to pay attorney's fees and other expenses incurred by the opponent.

3. Discovery Abuse §589

A lawyer is subject to professional discipline and judicially-imposed compensation to the opponent for making frivolous discovery requests or failing to use diligent efforts to comply with appropriate requests.

B. DUTY OF HONESTY §590

A lawyer must not knowingly make a false statement of law or fact to a tribunal.

1. **In Pleadings** §591
   Pleadings must be truthful and accurate. In many states and federal courts, a lawyer must sign every pleading, thus certifying that there are good grounds to support it and that the pleading is not being submitted for delay purposes.

2. **Ordinarily No Duty to Disclose Harmful Facts** §592
   Generally, a lawyer has *no affirmative duty* to disclose facts harmful to his client's case *except* when necessary to comply with *discovery requirements* or to *correct a previous material misstatement*.

3. **Duty Not to Misstate Law** §595
   A lawyer *must not knowingly mislead* the judge as to the law and *must* also *correct* any *previous misstatement* of law.

4. **Duty to Disclose Adverse Legal Authority** §596
   The lawyer owes an affirmative duty to disclose *applicable law*, including that adverse to the client's case. However, only *directly* contrary authority from the *controlling jurisdiction* need be disclosed.

5. **Duty When a Client or Witness Gives False Evidence** §601
   The lawyer has a duty to the court not to rely on false evidence, but also has a duty to minimize injury to the client.

   a. **False statement in a civil case** §602
      A lawyer must correct, or have the witness correct, any false evidence or material mistakes.

   b. **After false testimony given in a criminal case**

      (1) **ABA Code approach** §605
          The Code differentiates between perjury by a client and by a nonclient. A lawyer *must promptly reveal* perjury by a *nonclient*. If the false evidence comes from a lawyer's client, she must *promptly call upon the client* to correct the record; if the client refuses, the lawyer *must reveal the fraud* to the court unless the information is privileged. Note that the Code includes confidential information to be privileged for this rule.

      (2) **Model Rules approach** §608
          In *all cases* (civil and criminal), a lawyer must *take reasonable remedial measures*. This includes *urging a client* to cooperate in withdrawing or correcting the false evidence. Lacking client cooperation, a lawyer should consider seeking *permission to withdraw*. If not possible or not an effective solution, the lawyer should *disclose* the situation to the judge, even if that would breach client confidentiality.

   c. **Intent to commit perjury in a criminal case** §612
      When a *client or witness* intends to commit perjury, the ABA Code and Model Rules are consistent but not very informative. At a minimum, the lawyer must try to persuade the client or witness either not to testify or not to testify falsely. When a lawyer's efforts (*i.e.,* persuasion, attempt to withdraw) are unsuccessful, she should *reveal* the situation to the judge.

family relationship). Lawyers *may* contribute *campaign funds* to candidates for judicial office.

<table>
<tr><td>2.</td><td colspan="2">Communication with Judge or Hearing Officer
In an adversary proceeding, the lawyer may communicate with a judge regarding the merits of the case only in the course of the proceedings. The limited exceptions to this rule require that copies of written communications and prior notice of proposed oral communications be given to opposing counsel.</td><td>§698</td></tr>
</table>

3. Contacts with Jurors §702

A lawyer owes a duty to the legal system to avoid improper contact with jurors.

a. Communications before trial §703

Lawyers *must not communicate* with persons known to be members of the panel for the case, *but* a lawyer may investigate members of the panel if the investigation is conducted with "circumspection and restraint."

b. Contacts during trial §704

Only "official" communications (*e.g.,* voir dire) are permitted.

c. Communications after trial §705

These are proper to: (i) determine a basis for *challenging the jury verdict*; or (ii) to *improve advocacy skills* (becoming informed of factors that led to the verdict).

(1) Limitations §708

A lawyer may not *harass or embarrass* the jurors or try to influence their conduct in future jury service.

d. Communications with members of juror's family §709

The same restraint on communications with jurors and prospective jurors applies to contacts with jurors' family members.

H. SPECIAL DUTIES OF PROSECUTORS AND OTHER GOVERNMENT LAWYERS §710

The "client" of government lawyers is the state. A prosecutor's duty is to *seek justice* rather than to convict.

1. Special Limitations on Prosecutorial Function §711

The prosecutor must: (i) use *restraint* in the exercise of governmental power (*e.g.,* charges filed must be supported by *probable cause*; no urging an unrepresented accused to *waive important pretrial rights*); (ii) help the accused *retain counsel*; and (iii) perform the *dual role* of advocate and representative of the broad public interest at trial.

2. Duties Respecting Witnesses and Evidence §717

The prosecutor must make timely disclosure to the defense of any available evidence known to the prosecutor that may negate guilt, mitigate the degree of the offense, or reduce the appropriate punishment. Other duties include the obligation to pursue *evidence harmful* to the government's case and to allow defense counsel *access* to government witnesses.

a. Defense records §721

Prosecutors are normally *prohibited* from *subpoenaing defense records* (or calling defense lawyers before a grand jury) unless the information is not privileged and is essential to the investigation or prosecution, and there is no other feasible way to obtain the information.

3. **Obligations of Government Lawyers Generally**   §722
Many of the above duties are incumbent upon *all* government lawyers. Thus government lawyers should not institute or continue obviously unfair civil actions, and the government lawyer is obliged to develop a full and fair record.

VII. THE BUSINESS OF PRACTICING LAW

A. ASSOCIATIONS OF LAWYERS FOR THE PRACTICE OF LAW

1. Law Firm

a. Roles in a traditional law firm

(1) Partners   §727
Partners are the principals in a traditional firm.

(2) Associates   §730
Normally, associates perform legal services as salaried employees of the firm.

(3) "Of counsel"   §732
This signifies a lawyer's continuing relationship with a firm other than as partner or associate.

(4) Paralegals   §733
These are nonlawyer legal assistants.

b. Practice through professional law corporations   §734
In most states, lawyers may form a corporation or limited liability company to carry on the practice of law.

c. Supervisory relationships   §735
Under the Model Rules, reasonable efforts must be made to assure that all lawyers in the firm conform to ethical standards. The Model Rules also direct a subordinate lawyer to act ethically, even when directed to act contrary to ethical standards by a supervisor.

(1) Responsibility for another lawyer's conduct   §738
A lawyer is responsible for another lawyer's ethical violation if the lawyer *ordered*, or with knowledge, *ratified* the conduct, or if she is a *partner* in the firm or a *direct supervisor* of the other and *failed* to take reasonable *remedial action*.

d. Name of firm or corporation   §742
Under the Model Rules, trade names are now allowed if they are *not misleading* and do *not imply connection with a government agency* or legal services organization. The firm name may contain the names of deceased or retired members, but the name of a lawyer who has left the firm for public service for a substantial period must be removed.

e. Association with nonlawyers in practice

(1) Partnerships with nonlawyers prohibited   §748
These are *prohibited* if *any* of the partnership activities includes the *practice of law*.

(1) ABA Code §775

The ABA Code was amended to accommodate *Bates,* but still contained numerous restrictions. Because the Model Rules were then under consideration, the ABA Code has not been further amended. Thus, it does *not* reflect the current status of the law.

(2) Model Rules approach to advertising §777

The Model Rules *prohibit only false and misleading advertising* and permit advertising through any public medium or written communication that does not involve in-person solicitation. The advertising must contain the name of the lawyer responsible for its content.

c. Additional limits on state regulation—*Zauderer* §781

The Supreme Court in *Zauderer* upheld the Model Rules ban on false and misleading advertising and protected the use of accurate illustrations as well as text in lawyer advertising.

d. *Went For It* case §784

The Court, in a split decision, *upheld state limits* on lawyer advertising in the *Went For It* case by letting stand a state law barring direct mail advertising within 30 days of an accident or disaster. The regulation was valid based, in part, on a state's substantial interest in protecting the "flagging reputation" of the legal profession.

3. Solicitation §787

Solicitation is *direct contact* with a potential client that is not protected as advertising.

a. Model Rules §788

The Model Rules prohibit in-person or live telephone contact with strangers where a *significant motive* is the *lawyer's personal gain*. The Model Rules also forbid contact if a person has informed the lawyer that he does *not desire to be solicited* or if the solicitation involves duress, and the Rules require that written materials or recorded messages directed at persons known to be in need of services be *labeled "advertising."*

b. Constitutionality §791

The Supreme Court has upheld regulation of in-person solicitation, at least where a fee will be charged and deception or improper influence is involved.

c. Exceptions to general prohibition on solicitation §792

There are certain situations where contact otherwise prohibited as solicitation is allowed:

(1) Advice to *close friend, relative, or present or former client*;

(2) Request for referrals from *lawyer referral service or legal aid organization*;

(3) Free services offered to *persons in need*; and

(4) *Certain class action situations*.

VIII. ENFORCEMENT OF LAWYERS' PROFESSIONAL OBLIGATIONS

A. THE FORMAL DISCIPLINARY PROCESS

1. **General Grounds for Discipline** §824
   A lawyer may be disciplined for:

   a. *Violation of the rules of professional conduct;* §825

   b. *Commission of a crime* that casts doubt on the lawyer's fitness to practice—*i.e.,* under the Model Rules, a crime that reflects adversely on the lawyer's honesty, trustworthiness, or fitness as a lawyer, or, in some states, conduct that offends the generally accepted moral code; §831

   c. *Engaging in conduct involving dishonesty, fraud, deceit, or misrepresentation*, but note that *no conviction* is required; §837

   d. *Engaging in conduct prejudicial to administration of justice;* §838

   e. *Stating or implying ability to improperly influence officials;* §839

   f. *Assisting a judge in violation of judicial code* or other law; and §840

   g. *Violating specific statutory grounds for discipline* (some states enumerate specific grounds). §841

2. **Sanctions** §844
   In general, these are *disbarment*, *suspension from practice*, *reprimand*, *admonition*, or, in some states, other sanctions (*e.g.,* restitution, probation). Factors considered are the *seriousness* of the offense, the lawyer's *mental state*, the *injury* caused by the offense, *aggravating or mitigating factors* (*e.g.,* chronic alcoholism), and *rehabilitation* evidence.

3. **Stages in Disciplinary Proceedings**

   a. **Complaint to state bar** §851
      Most complaints come from aggrieved clients, but they may also come from lawyers, judges, or any other persons with knowledge of the alleged misconduct.

   b. **Screening of complaint by state bar** §854
      If the charge presents a prima facie case of misconduct, the lawyer may be asked to submit an explanation to the committee. The complaining party has no right of review once a charge is dismissed by the committee.

   c. **Hearing before grievance committee** §857
      The accused lawyer is entitled to *procedural due process* (proper notice, a right to be heard and to introduce evidence, a right to counsel, and a right to cross-examine adverse witnesses) but is not provided all of the due process protections of a criminal case.

   d. **Decision by grievance committee** §868
      The committee either dismisses the charges or recommends sanctions.

rules of law which may readily be found by *standard research techniques*.

    (b)   No liability for errors in judgment   §899

However, lawyers do not guarantee the soundness of their opinions or the validity of instruments they are engaged to draft.

b.   Causation—harm to client must be shown   §902

Traditionally, there is no malpractice liability *unless harm to the client has proximately resulted*.

c.   Damages   §906

Damages (*e.g.,* the value of a lost cause of action) must be proved.

d.   Liability for acts of others   §907

The general standard of care may render lawyers liable for the acts of co-counsel, partners, employees, and any lawyer to whom he has referred a client. Note the increased use of limited liability partnerships that expressly limit liability to the negligent partner and the entity itself.

4.   Other Theories for Malpractice Liability   §913

Intentional torts (*e.g.,* fraud, misrepresentation, misuse of funds), breach of contract, and breach of fiduciary duty may also be grounds for a malpractice action.

5.   Malpractice Liability to Third Parties   §921

Although a lawyer is usually liable only to the lawyer's client, exceptions impose liability to nonclients when:

    a.   The lawyer's conduct involves a *prospective client* (*e.g.,* misuse of confidential information);

    b.   The lawyer *invites a nonclient to rely* on her legal opinion (*e.g.,* meaning of contract terms);

    c.   The lawyer is employed by the client to render services *intended to benefit an identified third person* (*e.g.,* intended will beneficiary); and

    d.   The lawyer represents a trustee or similar fiduciary who owes duties to *beneficiaries*, and the lawyer knowingly assists the trustee-client in the breach of a fiduciary duty.

6.   Limitations on Liability Prohibited   §926

The ABA Code expressly prohibits any attempt by lawyers to exculpate themselves or otherwise limit their liability to clients for malpractice. The Model Rules permit a contractual waiver of malpractice liability, *if the client is separately represented* in making it.

C.   CONTEMPT SANCTIONS

1.   Direct Criminal Contempt   §931

This is any conduct *within the personal knowledge of the judge* that tends to obstruct the court in the administration of justice or that brings it into disrepute. If a direct contempt is committed in open court, the trial judge may punish the contemnor **summarily**. If the contempt is not so punished, it must be referred to another judge for a hearing. A jury trial is required if the proposed punishment exceeds six months in jail.

2. **Indirect Criminal Contempt** §935

When the relevant facts are **outside the personal knowledge of the judge**, the contempt is indirect and a **hearing** must be held.

IX. THE SPECIAL RESPONSIBILITIES OF JUDGES

A. INTRODUCTION §937

The ABA Model Code of Judicial Conduct ("CJC"), as amended in 1990, establishes the special rules pertaining to state judges and becomes legally binding on judges as it is adopted by individual states. It does not apply to third-party neutrals. The content of the CJC is tested on the Multistate Professional Responsibility Examination.

B. GENERAL NORMS

1. **Maintain High Standards of Conduct** §942

A judge must establish, maintain, enforce and observe high standards of personal conduct.

2. **Promote Public Confidence in Judiciary** §943

Judges must **obey the law** and behave in a manner promoting public confidence in the **integrity and impartiality** of the judiciary.

3. **Avoid Using Influence or Being Influenced** §944

A judge must not let anyone influence judicial conduct; he may not advance others' interests in his judicial capacity, nor may he be a **character witness unless subpoenaed**.

4. **Avoid Memberships in Discriminatory Organizations** §948

Judges are barred from membership in organizations that invidiously discriminate on the basis of race, sex, religion, or national origin. Upon learning of discrimination, a judge must **promptly resign** or endeavor to **end the discriminatory practice**. On the other hand, a judge may belong to a **completely private** organization whose membership limitations cannot be constitutionally prohibited **or** to one that is "**dedicated to the preservation of religious, ethnic, or cultural values**."

C. JUDGE'S OFFICIAL ACTIONS

1. **Priority of Judicial Duties** §951

Judges should put judicial duties ahead of other activities.

2. **Behavior on the Bench** §952

A judge must be **faithful to the law, remain competent**, and be **unswayed** by outside pressures. He must hear all cases assigned (unless disqualified), give every person with a legal interest in a proceeding the right to be heard, maintain order in the court, and be courteous to others. He must not exhibit bias or prejudice, nor allow lawyers to manifest such bias.

e. The judge's ***relative's involvement in the case*** (as a likely witness, a party, an officer or director of a party, or a lawyer) or a relative having an interest that could be substantially affected; and §991

f. ***Contributions from a party or a party's lawyer*** to the judge's election campaign if the contributions were made within a designated number of years and exceed the jurisdiction's specified amount. §994

2. Disclosure by Judge §995
Even if a judge believes there is no reasonable ground for disqualification, she should disclose, on the record, information that she believes the parties or their lawyers might consider relevant to the issue of impartiality.

3. Remittal of Disqualification §996
If a judge is disqualified for any reason "***other than personal bias or prejudice*** concerning a party," the parties and their lawyers may ***waive*** the disqualification if ***all*** agree that the interest has an insubstantial effect and ***each*** person then indicates in writing a waiver of the disqualification.

4. Rule of Necessity §999
The rule of necessity, created by case law, ***overrides disqualification rules***. It applies when a judge would otherwise be disqualified on a conflict of interest basis, but there is no other way for the case to be heard.

E. EXTRAJUDICIAL ACTIVITIES OF THE JUDGE

1. In General §1000
A judge's extrajudicial activities ***must not***: (i) cast doubt on the judge's impartiality, (ii) demean the judicial office, or (iii) interfere with proper performance of judicial duties.

2. Speak, Write, Lecture, and Teach §1001
These are proper on both legal and nonlegal subjects.

3. Consult with Legislators and Executive Officials §1002
A judge may do so only on subjects of the ***law, the legal system, or administration of justice***.

4. Serve on Government Commissions §1003
Such service is ***limited*** to the ***law, legal system, or administration of justice***, but a judge may serve as an official representative at certain ceremonial occasions.

5. Officer of Organizations §1004
A judge ***may*** be a member, officer, trustee, director, or nonlegal advisor to ***non-profit*** agencies or educational, religious, charitable, fraternal, or civic groups. But service on the board of a public educational institution other than a law school is prohibited, while service on the board of a private educational instituion is generally permitted.

a. Restrictions §1005
A judge ***may not serve*** as an officer of an organization that ***frequently litigates*** in her court, nor may she personally ***raise money*** for organizations, although she may participate in investment decisions.

F. MONEY-MAKING ACTIVITIES OF THE JUDGE

1. In General   §1008

Financial activities of a judge must not affect her impartiality, interfere with judicial duties, exploit the office, or involve her with persons likely to come before the court.

2. Investments   §1009

Subject to the above qualifications, a judge *may* hold and manage investments, including real estate.

3. Participation in a Business   §1010

A judge *may not* be an officer, director, manager, advisor, or employee of any business (*except* a closely-held family business or investment trust).

4. Gifts, Bequests, Favors, or Loans   §1011

A judge and family members residing in his household must be careful about accepting gifts, etc. The CJC enumerates the types of gifts a judge may accept.

5. Fiduciary Activities   §1012

A judge *may not* serve as a fiduciary (*e.g.*, executor, guardian) *except for family members*, and even this is forbidden if the matter is likely to proceed in the judge's court or under its appellate jurisdiction.

6. Arbitrator or Mediator   §1015

Unless sanctioned by law, a judge *may not* serve as an arbitrator or mediator.

7. Practice Law   §1016

A judge *may not* practice law (but he may give uncompensated legal advice to family members without compensation).

8. Receiving and Reporting Compensation   §1017

All judges *must report* compensation and reimbursement of expenses as required by law, and compensation must be *reasonable* in amount. The CJC requires at least an annual public reporting. Other disclosures of assets need only be made as required by law or specific provisions of the CJC.

G. INVOLVEMENT OF JUDGES AND JUDICIAL CANDIDATES IN POLITICAL ACTIVITIES

1. General Principles Applicable to Judges and Judicial Candidates   §1022

Subject to a few exceptions, the following rules apply to judges and also to lawyers running for judicial offices:

a. *No office in political organizations;*

b. *No endorsements of political candidates;*

c. *No speeches for political organizations;*

d. *No political fund-raising;*

e. *No running for nonjudicial office* (a judge must resign if running);

    f.   ***No other political activity***—An incumbent judge (but not a judicial candidate) must avoid all other political activity **except** those (i) designed to improve the law, the legal system, or the administration of justice; (ii) specifically authorized by law; or (iii) permitted under the CJC; and

    g.   ***No misrepresentations or campaign promises.***   §1029

2.   Judicial Candidates Subject to Public Election

    a.   **All judicial candidates subject to public election**   §1033
All such candidates (or a judge subject to election for a nonjudicial position) **may buy tickets** for political functions, **attend** political events, **identify** their political party, and **contribute** to a political organization.

    b.   **Judicial candidates running for public election**   §1034
When actually running for public election, a judge or candidate **may** also **speak to gatherings** on her own behalf, appear in **media advertising** and distribute her **promotional literature** supporting her candidacy, and **publicly endorse or oppose candidates** for the same office.

    c.   **Solicitation of campaign contributions**   §1035
Candidates **may not personally** solicit campaign contributions. Properly constituted committees may solicit contributions during a period one year before and up to 90 days after the election.

3.   Candidates Seeking Appointment to Judicial Office

    a.   **No personal solicitation of funds**   §1038
A person seeking appointment to judicial office **may not solicit** or accept funds—even through a committee.

    b.   **Other political activity**   §1039
Political activity to secure appointment is barred, except: (i) **communicating with the nominating authority**; (ii) **seeking endorsements from organizations** that regularly make recommendations for such appointments; (iii) **providing information** about qualifications to the appointing authority; and (iv) if the person is **not currently a judge**, he may continue to be active and **hold office** in his political party.

    c.   **Judge seeking other government office**   §1040
The **same rules** apply to an incumbent judge who is seeking another government office.

4.   Sanctions for Violations   §1041
A **successful** judicial candidate who violates the political activity rules is subject to **judicial discipline**. An **unsuccessful lawyer** candidate who violates the rules is subject to **lawyer disciplinary rules**.

H.   STANDARDS APPLICABLE TO FEDERAL JUDGES

1.   No Practice of Law   §1042
Federal statute holds a federal judge or justice who engages in the practice of law guilty of a "high misdemeanor."

2. Circumstances in Which Disqualification Required §1043

Most of the disqualification standards for federal judges are **substantially the same** as rules under the CJC (*e.g.*, personal bias, financial interest in the matter). However, a few rules are different or are stated differently:

a. A federal judge must recuse himself upon a **litigant's filing** of a "timely and sufficient affidavit" asserting **personal bias or prejudice**.

b. A federal judge, including a Supreme Court justice, must recuse herself whenever her "**impartiality** might reasonably be questioned."

c. Disqualification is required whenever a federal judge **participated**, as counsel, adviser, or witness, in the case **or expressed an opinion** concerning the merits of the case; and

d. If a **disqualifying financial interest** is discovered only after a judge has spent substantial time on a case, he may **avoid disqualification by disposing** of the interest.

3. Discipline of Federal Judges §1048

Federal judges are appointed for life but can be removed from office through impeachment by the House of Representatives and conviction by the Senate. Also, the judicial council of each circuit may impose less severe discipline on federal judges.

Approach to Exams

A. INTRODUCTION

Legal Ethics concerns the law governing legal practice. To protect the public and maintain the integrity of the legal profession, rules have been established to prohibit the unauthorized practice of law, set standards for admission to the practice of law, and regulate the conduct of lawyers after admission. Most states have adopted some version of the American Bar Association ("ABA") Model Rules of Professional Conduct. Thus, the ABA Model Rules form an *indirect* basis for regulation of much of the legal profession, and they are the subject of the Multistate Professional Responsibility Exam ("MPRE").

B. APPROACH

In analyzing Legal Ethics problems, begin by asking whether the question relates to the lawyer's responsibilities to a client, a person with whom the lawyer deals on the client's behalf, the court, or others. Then consider what duties the lawyer owes to the other person and whether the lawyer violated the rules detailing those duties. This will help you to determine whether the lawyer may be subject to discipline and to identify the remedies.

C. LAWYER'S DUTIES TO CLIENTS—IN GENERAL

A lawyer must protect a *prospective* client's confidential information and property and must use reasonable care in giving the person any legal advice. *After termination* of the lawyer-client relationship, the lawyer still must not reveal confidential information of the former client or represent interests that conflict with the former client's interests in a substantially related matter. Moreover, a lawyer owes these additional duties to *current* clients:

1. Competence

A lawyer must act with the knowledge, skill, thoroughness, and preparation reasonably necessary for the representation.

2. Diligence

A lawyer should pursue a matter on the client's behalf with zeal and promptness.

3. Communication

A lawyer must explain the matter to the client and keep the client informed.

4. Confidentiality

A lawyer must not reveal client information.

5. Loyalty

A lawyer must avoid conflicts of interest.

6. Protection of Client Property

A lawyer must safeguard the client's money and property and keep them entirely separate from the lawyer's assets.

D. DUTY TO PROTECT CLIENT'S CONFIDENTIAL INFORMATION

The two most important doctrines that govern a lawyer's dealing with confidential information are the attorney-client privilege and the duty of confidentiality.

1. Attorney-Client Privilege

The attorney-client privilege is the narrower of the two doctrines. It is a rule of evidence that prevents a court from compelling the revelation of confidential communications between a lawyer and a client that were made in order to give or obtain legal advice or assistance.

2. Duty of Confidentiality

The duty of confidentiality prohibits a lawyer from disclosing any information related to the representation of a client, a prospective client, or a former client. It also prohibits a lawyer from using this information to the disadvantage of the client.

E. DUTY OF UNIMPAIRED LOYALTY—CONFLICT OF INTEREST

A lawyer must not represent a client if there is an *actual or potential* conflict of interest, unless the client gives informed consent. The four major conflicts are:

1. Conflicts between the lawyer's *personal interest* and the interest of the client;

2. Conflicts between the interests of *two or more clients* that the lawyer is concurrently representing;

3. Conflicts between the client's interest and that of a *third party*; and

4. Conflicts between the lawyer's duties to a present client and the lawyer's continuing duties to a *former client*.

F. DUTIES TO THIRD PERSONS

A lawyer must represent the client zealously, but the law imposes important limitations on what a lawyer may do on the client's behalf.

1. Duty as Counselor Not to Assist Client in a Crime or Fraud

A lawyer may advise a client as to the legal consequences of the client's intended conduct and may assist a client to commit an act that will, in good faith, test the validity, scope, meaning, or application of the law. However, a lawyer must not counsel or assist a client to engage in conduct that the lawyer knows is illegal or fraudulent.

2. Duty of Honesty

The lawyer must be honest with others and sometimes must also affirmatively disclose matters to the court or the other party.

3. Duty to Communicate with Adverse Party's Lawyer

A lawyer must not communicate about the subject of a controversy with a person the lawyer knows is represented by counsel, unless that person's counsel consents or the communication is authorized by law.

G. DUTIES OF LAWYERS IN LITIGATION

A lawyer must not abuse the litigation process, and thus:

1. A lawyer has a duty not to bring *frivolous claims.*

2. A lawyer has a duty to *expedite litigation.*

3. A lawyer has a duty of *candor to the tribunal* and must *disclose directly adverse legal authority from the controlling jurisdiction.*

4. A lawyer has a duty to *deal with the opposing party and counsel with integrity.*

5. A lawyer has a duty to *preserve the impartiality and decorum of the tribunal.*

6. A lawyer must *restrict out-of-court comments about a case* that are likely to be widely disseminated.

7. A lawyer *may not lend money* to the client except for litigation expenses.

8. A lawyer ordinarily *must not act as both an advocate and a witness.*

9. A lawyer *must not make gifts or loans to court personnel, contact the judge* without notice to the other party, or *contact jurors* during the trial.

10. A *public prosecutor or government attorney* has a duty, beyond those above, to *seek justice* in the proceeding, not just to represent the state or government.

H. DUTIES RELATED TO THE PRACTICE OF LAW

1. Duties of Partners and Supervisory Lawyers
Partners and supervisory lawyers must make reasonable efforts to ensure that other lawyers in their organization adhere to the Model Rules.

2. Duties of Subordinate Lawyers
A subordinate lawyer will be subject to discipline if he carries out a supervisory lawyer's order that is a clear ethics violation.

3. Duties Regarding Nonlawyers
Partnerships between lawyers and nonlawyers are prohibited if any of the partnership activities include the practice of law. When a lawyer employs nonlawyer assistants, the lawyer must instruct the nonlawyers about legal ethics and should ensure that they act in conformity with professional standards.

4. Advertising and Solicitation
As a general rule, advertising is permitted as long as it is not false or misleading.

On the other hand, solicitation (*i.e.*, direct contact with a potential client for the lawyer's personal gain) is generally not allowed unless the potential client is a close friend, a relative, a current or former client, or another lawyer.

5. Specialization
A lawyer may not identify herself as a specialist unless she is a patent or admiralty lawyer or a certified specialist.

6. Fee Sharing
When two or more lawyers from different firms work together on a case, they may split the fee if the total fee is reasonable, the lawyers assume joint responsibility, and the client agrees to the split in writing. Sharing fees with a nonlawyer is prohibited unless shared on a flat salary basis, in a retirement or profit-sharing plan, as payments to the estate of a deceased lawyer, or as court-awarded fees shared with the nonprofit organization that hired or recommended the lawyer as counsel in the matter.

I. REMEDIES
The remedies for lawyer misconduct are:

1. Professional Discipline by the State
A lawyer may be subject to disbarment, suspension, reprimand, or admonition for a violation of professional ethics.

2. Malpractice Liability
A lawyer may have to pay damages for harm to a client due to negligence, intentional tort, breach of contract, or breach of fiduciary duty.

3. Contempt Sanctions
A lawyer may be punished for failure to adhere to proper standards of courtroom conduct through direct contempt (if the conduct is within the personal observation of the judge) or indirect contempt (if the conduct is outside the courtroom or not within the judge's personal observation).

J. JUDICIAL ETHICS

1. Code of Judicial Ethics
The ABA's Code of Judicial Conduct ("CJC") serves as a model for the ethical conduct of judges. As with the Model Rules, the content of the CJC is tested on the MPRE. The CJC is intended to ensure the *integrity and independence* of the judiciary. Its standards apply to a judge's official actions, unofficial and money-making activities, and political activities.

2. Judge's Official Actions
Judicial duties should take precedence over all of a judge's other activities. A judge must maintain competence, be faithful to the law, and be unswayed by

outside influences. If the judge's impartiality might reasonably be questioned, she must recuse herself.

3. Judge's Extrajudicial Activities

A judge's extrajudicial activities may not cast doubt on her impartiality, demean the judicial office, or interfere with her official duties.

4. Judges and Politics

Generally, a judge must avoid involvement in politics. However, a judge may participate if the political activities are specifically authorized by law or permitted by the CJC.

5. Federal Judges

Federal judges are subject to rules that are similar, but not identical, to those for state judges. Federal judges hold office for life, during good behavior, but can be removed by impeachment. Also, the judicial council of each circuit may discipline federal judges in less severe ways (*e.g.*, by admonishment).

Chapter One:
Regulating the Right to Practice Law

CONTENTS

Chapter Approach

Attorneys act on behalf of clients who need help but who often are not in a position to know whether they have been well or badly represented. Thus, the practice of law is a classic subject for regulation. To protect the public, states regulate who can become licensed to practice in the state, and they attempt to prevent such practice by those not licensed.

As you look at the material in this chapter, think about the following issues:

1. *Who regulates lawyers* and the role of the American Bar Association in that process;

2. Standards for *admission to the bar*, including the right to practice in jurisdictions in which the lawyer is not licensed; and

3. The *unauthorized practice of law* by nonlawyers.

A. Sources of Regulation

1. **State Regulation [§1]**
   Like other professions or businesses, the practice of law affects the public interest and is therefore subject to regulation by the states. [**Bates v. State Bar of Arizona,** 433 U.S. 350 (1977)]

   a. **Inherent judicial power to regulate [§2]**
      Unlike other professions, however, the ultimate regulatory power over the legal profession rests with the courts rather than with the legislature. The practice of law is so intimately concerned with the administration of justice that in most states the judicial branch is deemed to have *inherent* regulatory power over the practice of law (whether in or out of court). [**Shaulis v. Pennsylvania State Ethics Commission,** 833 A.2d 123 (Pa. 2003)]

      (1) **Lawyers as officers of the court [§3]**
          In recognition of the judicial source of their authority, lawyers are often called *"officers of the court."* This designation does not significantly alter a lawyer's substantive obligations, but courts invoke the principle to hold lawyers to standards of honesty and fair dealing in the judicial process. [**Newby v. Enron Corp.,** 302 F.3d 295 (5th Cir. 2002)]

      (2) **Regulation by state's highest court [§4]**
          The most pervasive form of regulation is that imposed by the highest court

of the state in which a lawyer is licensed to practice. [**Hoover v. Ronwin,** 466 U.S. 558 (1984)]

b. Regulation by state legislature [§5]

In many states, legislatures also have power to enact statutes regulating the legal profession. [*See, e.g.,* Cal. Bus. & Prof. Code §6146] Statutory regulation is most often upheld where lawyers are not singled out but are simply included within the reach of a general regulation. [**Maunus v. State Ethics Commission,** 544 A.2d 1324 (Pa. 1988)]

c. Regulation by "integrated" bar [§6]

A majority of states today have "integrated" bar systems created by state statute or judicial decision. In an integrated bar system, all lawyers licensed by the state are *required* to join the state bar association and become subject to its rules (including its rules of professional conduct). Membership in an integrated state bar association is mandatory, while membership in any other bar association (including the American Bar Association and all city and county bar associations) is voluntary.

(1) Constitutionality [§7]

The compulsory membership requirement of integrated bar systems has been upheld against attacks that it violates rights of free association. [**Lathrop v. Donahue,** 367 U.S. 820 (1961)]

(2) Use of membership dues [§8]

However, mandatory membership dues may be used only to support legislative proposals of direct interest to the bar. They may not be used to support legislation favored by a majority of the bar but unrelated to the practice of law. [**Keller v. State Bar of California,** 496 U.S. 1 (1990)]

d. Regulation by multiple states [§9]

A lawyer is subject to regulation by *each* state in which the lawyer is *admitted* to practice, regardless of where the lawyer has an office or commits a regulatory violation. A lawyer is *also* subject to regulation by any state in which the lawyer commits a *regulatory violation* while providing legal services, even if the lawyer is not admitted to practice there. [ABA Model Rule 8.5(a)]

e. No preclusion of federal regulation [§10]

The fact that a lawyer is qualified to practice under state law does not preclude *additional* federal regulation where the lawyer's activities are within the scope of applicable federal law. Lawyers who wish to practice before some federal agencies or tribunals are required to have special qualifications, and increasingly, federal agencies are imposing regulatory requirements on lawyers who "appear and practice" before them. [*See, e.g.,* 17 C.F.R. §§205.1-.7—SEC regulations issued pursuant to the Sarbanes-Oxley Act]

2. **American Bar Association as a Source of Model Regulation [§11]**

   Voluntary bar associations have no formal role in lawyer regulation, but many standards for the practice of law come from the American Bar Association ("ABA").

   a. **Composition of the ABA [§12]**

      The ABA is a voluntary association, but its members are almost 50% of all practicing lawyers in the United States and include lawyers from all geographic areas and types of practice.

   b. **Articulating standards of conduct [§13]**

      Since it first published its Canons of Professional Ethics in 1908, the ABA has been active in the field of legal ethics and has formulated standards of conduct which serve as a guide to the state supreme courts in adopting professional regulations.

   c. **ABA Model Code of Professional Responsibility (1969) [§14]**

      In 1969, the ABA replaced the Canons of Ethics with a comprehensive Model Code of Professional Responsibility. Hereafter, whenever this Summary speaks of the "ABA Code," it should be understood to mean the ABA Model Code of Professional Responsibility (1969), as amended.

      (1) **Canons of Ethics [§15]**

          The ABA Code contained nine brief Canons that established "axiomatic norms" for a lawyer's responsibilities.

      (2) **Amplification of Canons [§16]**

          Each of the Canons was supplemented by two sets of principles, *Ethical Considerations* ("EC") and *Disciplinary Rules* ("DR"). These were substantially more detailed than the Canons and were designed to implement the general concepts expressed in the Canons and relate them to the situations encountered in everyday practice.

          (a) **Ethical Considerations [§17]**

              The EC were *"aspirational"* — *i.e.*, they represented objectives that a lawyer should *strive* to meet in specific situations.

          (b) **Disciplinary Rules [§18]**

              The DR were *mandatory* and stated the minimum level of conduct below which a lawyer could not fall without being *subject to disciplinary action*.

   d. **ABA Model Rules of Professional Conduct (1983) [§19]**

      In response to criticism of the ABA Code, in 1983, the ABA approved a new, "Restatement-type" format for what is called the ABA Model Rules of Professional Conduct. Model Rules are stated in "black letter," followed by sometimes extensive "Comments" that explain the black-letter provisions and sometimes apply them to specific examples.

e. **ABA Model Rules as revised by the Ethics 2000 Commission (2002-2003) [§20]**
The ABA again considered revisions to its model standards when it received the report of its "Ethics 2000 Commission" in 2002. This time, there was no change in the format of the Model Rules, but extensive changes were made in the substance of many rules. Where principles discussed in this Summary are reflected in the ABA Model Rules of Professional Conduct, reference will be made to the relevant "Model Rules" as they stand after the revisions made in 2002-2003.

f. **Widespread impact of ABA Code and Model Rules on state regulation of practice [§21]**
Neither the ABA Model Code nor Model Rules regulates the legal profession in the various states until adopted by each state's highest court, but both Models were designed to be so adopted.

(1) **ABA Model Code originally adopted in most states [§22]**
Shortly after its effective date in 1970, the ABA Model Code was adopted word for word in almost every state in the country but California.

(2) **ABA Model Rules almost as influential [§23]**
The 1983 version of the ABA Model Rules has been adopted by over 40 states. And even in some of the states that have not adopted the Rules, although the ABA Model Code format has been preserved, the content is close to that in the Model Rules (*e.g.*, New York). As of 2004, only a few states have adopted the 2002-2003 revisions, but it is likely that many will do so in the future. In any event, there is now more variation among published state professional standards than ever before.

(3) **California approach [§24]**
The California Rules of Professional Conduct largely go it alone and make no mention of the ABA Code or Model Rules. However, they do say that "ethics opinions and rules and standards promulgated by other jurisdictions and bar associations may also be considered." [Cal. Rule 1-100] This may allow some citation to the ABA Code and Model Rules even in California.

g. **Interpretation of ABA Code and Model Rules [§25]**
The meaning of the ABA Code and Model Rules can most authoritatively be determined from *judicial opinions* imposing discipline for the conduct of particular lawyers. However, the ABA Standing Committee on Ethics and Professional Responsibility also issues *advisory opinions* as a guide to applying the Model Rules in particular fact situations. State bar associations (and sometimes state courts) often provide similar opinions construing a particular state's rules. All references in this Summary to *"ABA Opn."* will be to *Formal Opinions* published by the ABA.

h. **Testing the Model Rules on the Multistate Professional Responsibility Exam [§26]**
As a practical matter for law students, it is significant that the ABA Model Rules

are the subject of the Multistate Professional Responsibility Exam ("MPRE"). Applicants for the bar in many states must get a satisfactory score on that exam in order to be admitted. The MPRE tests the current version of the Model Rules and other principles of the law governing lawyers. It tests amendments to the Model Rules one year after they become effective, so the Model Rules as amended in 2002-2003 began to be tested in 2004 regardless of whether they were adopted in the state to which an applicant sought admission.

EXAM TIP **gilbert**

Remember that, in most states, the professional ethics rules governing the conduct of lawyers are patterned after models created by the ABA, but the ABA standards of conduct do **not regulate** the legal profession in a state **unless adopted by that state's highest court**. However, because a large majority of states have adopted some version of the ABA Model Rules of Professional Conduct, the ABA Model Rules form an **indirect** basis for regulation of much of the legal profession, and they are tested on the Multistate Professional Responsibility Exam, which is a component of many states' bar admission process.

STATE REGULATION OF PRACTICE OF LAW **gilbert**

SOURCE	SCOPE OF AUTHORITY
STATE COURTS	Ultimate and inherent regulatory power
STATE LEGISLATURES	May establish standards to aid judiciary
INTEGRATED BAR SYSTEMS (IN MAJORITY OF STATES)	May assist courts in regulation and discipline
AMERICAN BAR ASSOCIATION	Its standards often are adopted as a basis for state regulation, but until they are adopted by a state's highest court, they do not regulate lawyers in that state.

3. **Indirect Regulation Through Malpractice Liability [§27]**

   Malpractice liability is a major concern for the practicing lawyer and is, for practical purposes, a major influence "regulating" lawyer conduct and conforming it to professional standards. At the present time, malpractice is rarely taught as separate from issues of "legal ethics." It will be considered in this Summary only where malpractice standards or procedures differ from those relating to professional discipline. (*See infra*, §§885 *et seq.*)

4. **Contempt Sanctions—Immediate Regulation by the Courts [§28]**

   One of the most direct forms of lawyer regulation is a court's imposition of a contempt sanction on a lawyer for misconduct in a case before the court. This sanction may be in addition to formal disciplinary proceedings. (*See infra*, §§930 *et seq.*)

5. Restatement of the Law Governing Lawyers [§29]

In 2000, after a lengthy process, the American Law Institute ("ALI") published its *Restatement of the Law (Third): The Law Governing Lawyers* to stand alongside other ALI Restatements, such as those on Torts and Contracts. Unlike the ABA Model Rules, the Restatement is not intended to help "regulate" lawyers. Instead, it collects rules and cases from all over the country, whether involving professional regulation, malpractice liability, or contempt, and distills them into 135 black letter sections with related comments. References in this Summary to the "Restatement" will be to this useful ALI document upon which courts increasingly rely.

B. State Court Regulation of General Admission to Practice Law

1. Introduction [§30]

As a method of maintaining the integrity and competence of the legal profession, states require certain standards for admission to the bar. Each state establishes its own criteria, which must be met by persons seeking to practice law within the state. The usual constitutional standard is only that the requirements imposed have some *rational connection* with the applicant's *fitness or capacity* to practice law. [**Schware v. Board of Bar Examiners**, 353 U.S. 232 (1957)]

a. Citizenship not a valid requirement for admission [§31]

A state may *not* constitutionally require that a person be a United States citizen in order to be admitted to practice law within the state. [*In re* **Griffiths**, 413 U.S. 717 (1973)]

(1) Rationale

The fact that a person is an alien bears *no rational relationship* to that person's fitness to practice law. Moreover, any discrimination against aliens as a class is "inherently suspect" under the Fourteenth Amendment Equal Protection Clause, and thus can be justified only by a "compelling" state interest; there is no such interest in excluding aliens from practicing law if they meet all other admission requirements.

b. Residency not a valid requirement for admission [§32]

The requirement that a bar applicant be a resident of the state in order to be admitted to the bar has also been struck down, this time on the ground that it violated the Privileges and Immunities Clause of the Constitution. [**Supreme Court of New Hampshire v. Piper**, 470 U.S. 274 (1985)]

2. Determination of Intellectual Capability

a. Educational requirements [§33]

Practically all states require an applicant to complete a prescribed period of college work, followed by a period of law school study, as a means of demonstrating sufficient training to practice law.

(1) Accreditation [§34]

Many states also require graduation from a law school *accredited* by the ABA. This requirement has been upheld by state and lower federal courts as bearing a "rational relationship" to fitness to practice. [**Massachusetts School of Law at Andover v. American Bar Association,** 107 F.3d 1026 (3d Cir. 1997); *In re* **Brooks,** 11 S.W.3d 25 (Ky. 2000)]

(2) Specific courses [§35]

In two states, Indiana and South Carolina, supreme court rules require that law students take courses in specific fields in order to be admitted to the bar.

b. Examination by state bar [§36]

In addition to formal training, nearly all states require the candidate to pass an examination prepared and administered by the state bar. Each state adopts its own test, although the National Conference of Bar Examiners recommends standards to be followed in such examinations and also prepares the Multistate Bar Exam as part of the examination in a majority of states today.

(1) Constitutionality [§37]

The constitutionality of fairly administered exams has been repeatedly upheld by the courts. [*See, e.g.,* **Jones v. Board of Commissioners of Alabama State Bar,** 737 F.2d 996 (11th Cir. 1984)]

(2) Effect of Americans with Disabilities Act [§38]

An increasing number of bar candidates have successfully relied upon the Americans with Disabilities Act to get extra time or other accommodations while taking the bar examination. [**Bartlett v. New York State Board of Law Examiners,** 226 F.3d 69 (2d Cir. 2000)]

3. Determination of "Good Moral Character" [§39]

A more troublesome step in the admission process involves the investigation of an applicant's moral character. The state clearly has a valid interest in insuring that persons admitted to practice possess high moral standards, including mental and emotional stability. [*See* Model Rule 8.1; EC 1-2, 1-6; DR 1-101(B)] On the other hand, the constitutional rights of applicants must also be protected against *unwarranted* infringement by the state.

a. Investigative procedure [§40]

The investigation of a candidate's moral fitness to practice law is generally conducted by a committee of bar examiners on behalf of the state's highest court. Usually the applicant is required to fill out a detailed questionnaire, list a number of references, and submit fingerprints and photographs for identification purposes. The information obtained is then checked by letter or personal investigation.

b. Hearing before committee [§41]

If the committee feels that a question exists regarding moral fitness, the applicant is requested to appear at a hearing before the committee.

(1) Issue same as for disbarment [§42]

The question before the committee of bar examiners has been *equated with* the question before a *discipline* committee—namely, "is the applicant a fit and proper person to practice law?" [**Hallinan v. Committee of Bar Examiners,** 65 Cal. 2d 447 (1966)]

(2) Burden of proof on applicant [§43]

The burden of coming forward with evidence and establishing good moral character is on the applicant, who is deemed to be in the best position to know the pertinent facts. The applicant owes a *duty to cooperate* in reasonable investigations by the state bar and *to make disclosures* relevant to fitness to practice. [*In re* **Anastaplo,** 366 U.S. 82 (1961)]

(3) Applicant's procedural rights [§44]

At the same time, the applicant is entitled to procedural due process in committee proceedings—which includes the right to know the charges, to explain away derogatory information, and to confront critics or objectors. [**Wellner v. Committee,** 373 U.S. 96 (1963)]

(4) Judicial review of adverse determination [§45]

An applicant who is denied admission on the ground of bad moral character is also entitled to judicial review, usually by the highest court of the state.

c. Conduct relevant to determination of "good moral character" [§46]

The bar committee has the right (indeed the obligation) to investigate all aspects of an applicant's past conduct that may reflect upon the applicant's honesty and integrity. [**Konigsberg v. Board of Bar Examiners,** 353 U.S. 262 (1957)]

(1) Any past conduct relevant [§47]

The committee's investigation of the applicant is not limited to criminal convictions. Rather, the committee may consider *any conduct* of the applicant.

Example: Filing for bankruptcy so as to default on student loans three days before law school graduation was found to show a student's lack of sensitivity to his "moral responsibility to his creditors" and thus led to denial of his admission to the bar. [*Re* **G.W.L.,** 364 So. 2d 454 (Fla. 1978)]

---

(2) Conviction of crime involving "moral turpitude" [§48]

Conviction of certain crimes may be enough by itself to show lack of good moral character. Such crimes include those involving an *intent to defraud* or *intentional dishonesty for the purpose of personal gain*—*e.g.*, forgery, bribery, perjury, theft, robbery, extortion, etc. [*In re* **Krule**, 741 N.E.2d 259 (Ill. 2000)—insurance fraud; *and see* discussion of moral turpitude in discipline cases *infra*, §§831-833]

(3) Conviction of crimes not necessarily establishing lack of good moral character [§49]

Many crimes do not involve "moral turpitude," and conviction of such crimes is *not* enough by itself to disqualify the applicant. Whether moral turpitude exists will depend on both the *nature* of the offense and the *motivation of the violator*.

(a) Application—"adolescent misbehavior" [§50]

Arrests for fistfighting and the like during youth may *not* be enough to establish "moral turpitude" sufficient to disqualify an applicant. Rather, this can be viewed as "adolescent behavior" which does not necessarily bear on the applicant's present fitness to practice law. [**Hallinan v. Committee of Bar Examiners**, *supra*, §42]

(b) Application—civil disobedience [§51]

Nonviolent civil disobedience may also be insufficient grounds for denying admission to practice, since such conduct often may be committed by "persons of the highest moral courage," and therefore may not affect their qualification to practice law. [*See* **Hallinan v. Committee of Bar Examiners**, *supra*]

(4) Effect of concealment [§52]

Even when conduct by the applicant does not itself demonstrate a lack of good moral character, it still must be disclosed in response to inquiry by the bar examiners. *Concealment or false statements* by the applicant in response to such inquiry is *itself* evidence of sufficient lack of moral character to justify denial of the application. It makes no difference that the concealment is not discovered until after the applicant is admitted to practice, because a lawyer is subject to disciplinary sanctions (*e.g.*, disbarment) for making a *materially* false statement or for deliberately failing to disclose a *material* fact in her application for admission. [Model Rule 8.1; DR 1-101; **Radtke v. Board of Bar Examiners**, 601 N.W.2d 642 (Wis. 1999)]

(5) Rehabilitation as mitigating factor [§53]

An applicant whose past record does contain acts of moral turpitude may still gain admission by demonstrating *sufficient rehabilitation* of character. The courts seem inclined to reward self-improvement by the applicant—

especially where other evidence indicates that the applicant is presently fit to practice law. [**March v. Committee of Bar Examiners**, 67 Cal. 2d 718 (1967)]

(6) Political activity [§54]

A lawyer is sworn to uphold the Constitution and laws of the United States and the state in which the lawyer is admitted to practice.

(a) Refusal to take oath to support Constitution [§55]

An applicant who refuses to take the *required oath* to support the federal and state constitutions may be *denied admission*, since there has been held to be a rational connection between this requirement and the practice of law. [**Law Students Research Council v. Wadmond**, 401 U.S. 154 (1971)]

(b) Distinguish—membership in Communist Party [§56]

However, even *actual* membership in the Communist Party was held not to be a sufficient inference of "bad moral character" per se to permit exclusion from the practice of law. [**Schware v. Board of Bar Examiners**, *supra*, §30]

EXAM TIP   **gilbert**

When answering a question involving an investigation of an applicant's moral character during the admission process, remember that:

- *Any past conduct* that reflects on an applicant's *honesty and integrity* is relevant to an evaluation of moral character. This includes charges of which the applicant was acquitted and any litigation to which the applicant was a party.

- On the other hand, mere conviction of a crime is *not* necessarily sufficient to deny the applicant admission to practice law. To cause disqualification of an applicant, the crime in question must involve *moral turpitude*, such as a crime involving intentional dishonesty for the purpose of personal gain.

- Despite past conduct involving moral turpitude, an applicant may still gain admission to the legal profession if he can *demonstrate sufficient rehabilitation* of his character and a present fitness to practice law.

---

d. Duty of lawyers not to aid admission of the unqualified [§57]

Many states require an applicant to submit letters of reference from lawyers as part of the application for admission to the bar. The Model Rules prohibit a lawyer writing a letter of reference from:

(i) Knowingly *making a false statement* of material fact;

(ii) *Failing to disclose a fact* necessary to correct a misapprehension known to have arisen in the matter; or

(iii) Knowingly *failing to respond to a lawful demand for information* about an applicant that is not privileged or otherwise confidential under Model Rule 1.6.

[ABA Model Rule 8.1]

C. Practice in States Where Lawyer Not Formally Licensed

1. Introduction [§58]

Each state determines the conditions for admission to its bar. There is no constitutional duty to permit out-of-state lawyers to practice within the state, but the needs of clients and ease of transportation and communication have led to lawyers engaging in the practice of law even in jurisdictions in which they have not become formally licensed.

2. Admission to General Practice [§59]

Requirements for an out-of-state lawyer to be admitted to general practice within another state vary widely.

a. Admission by reciprocity [§60]

A number of states admit practicing lawyers from other states without a bar exam, provided the lawyer has actively practiced in the first state for a certain period of time (usually four to six years). Most of these states limit such admission to lawyers from *other states that allow reciprocity,* disqualifying lawyers from states that do not grant such rights. Such a limitation does not violate the Equal Protection Clause. [**Schumacher v. Nix,** 965 F.2d 1262 (3d Cir. 1992)]

b. Separate examination [§61]

Other states require lawyers to pass a written examination in addition to having practiced in the first state for the requisite period. [*See* Cal. Bus. & Prof. Code §6062(d)]

3. Unauthorized Practice of Law [§62]

A lawyer may be guilty of the unauthorized practice of law if the lawyer practices in a jurisdiction in which the lawyer is unlicensed. [Model Rule 5.5(a)]

Example: In the case in which this principle was made most real to lawyers, a New York law firm was denied the right to collect its fee for initiating arbitration proceedings and negotiating a settlement in California at the request of its California client. [**Birbrower, Montalbano, Condon & Frank, P.C. v. Superior Court,** 17 Cal. 4th 119 (1998)]

4. **Temporary Multi-Jurisdictional Practice [§63]**

Because many clients ask law firms to conduct such activities on a limited basis in other jurisdictions, newly revised ABA Model Rule 5.5 now provides that lawyers may "provide legal services on a temporary basis" in jurisdictions in which they are not licensed under four circumstances:

a. **Association with local lawyer [§64]**

Temporary practice is allowed if the lawyer associates with "a lawyer who is admitted to practice in the jurisdiction and who actively participates in the matter." [Model Rule 5.5(c)(1)]

b. **Litigated matter [§65]**

Temporary practice is also allowed if the services "are in or reasonably related to a pending or potential proceeding before a tribunal . . . if the lawyer, or a person the lawyer is assisting, is authorized by law or order to appear in such proceeding, or reasonably expects to be so authorized." [Model Rule 5.5(c)(2)]

(1) **Admission pro hac vice [§66]**

This part of the rule simply adopts the longstanding principle that an out-of-state lawyer may obtain permission to appear in the courts of a sister state in connection with a *particular* case ("pro hac vice").

(2) **Normally granted as matter of comity [§67]**

While such permission is technically discretionary, most courts will allow an out-of-state lawyer to appear and litigate a particular case as a matter of reciprocity or comity with the courts of the state in which the lawyer is admitted.

(3) **Inadequate local counsel [§68]**

The discretion to limit appearances pro hac vice was sometimes used to block adequate representation in local civil rights cases, and *where adequate local counsel is unavailable* due to racial bias or prejudice, the courts have invalidated local rules that would exclude out-of-state lawyers from appearing in such cases. [*See, e.g.,* **Sanders v. Russell**, 401 F.2d 241 (5th Cir. 1968)]

c. **Arbitration or other alternative dispute resolution proceeding [§69]**

The out-of-state lawyer may provide services if they are in or are reasonably related to an alternative dispute resolution proceeding that is reasonably related to the lawyer's practice in a state where he is admitted and if the forum does not require pro hac vice admission for those services. [Model Rule 5.5(c)(3)]

d. **Reasonable relation to lawyer's usual practice [§70]**

The lawyer may provide services that "arise out of or are reasonably related to the lawyer's practice in a jurisdiction in which the lawyer is admitted to practice." [Model Rule 5.5(c)(4)]

CHECKLIST FOR TEMPORARY MULTI-JURISDICTIONAL PRACTICE **gilbert**

A LAWYER MAY PROVIDE LEGAL SERVICES ON A TEMPORARY BASIS IN A JURISDICTION IN WHICH THE LAWYER IS NOT ADMITTED IF:

☑ The out-of-state lawyer *associates with* a lawyer who is admitted to practice in the jurisdiction and who is actively participating in the matter;

☑ The out-of-state lawyer, or a person the lawyer is assisting, received or expects to receive *special permission* from a local court, administrative agency, or other tribunal to handle that *particular matter* in that tribunal ("pro hac vice");

☑ The out-of-state lawyer is engaging in *alternative dispute resolution* that arises out of or is reasonably related to his practice in a state in which he is admitted; or

☑ The services are *reasonably related to the lawyer's home-state practice*.

---

5. **Prohibition of Permanent Practice [§71]**

   In spite of the authority to conduct a temporary practice, a lawyer may not "establish an office or other systematic and continuous presence . . . for the practice of law" in a jurisdiction in which the lawyer is unlicensed. [Model Rule 5.5(b)(1)]

   a. **Corporate counsel exception [§72]**

   Because an in-house lawyer for a corporation, government, or other organization has a single client that can presumably assess the lawyer's competence, such lawyers usually may work permanently, even in states in which they are not licensed. [Model Rule 5.5(d)(1)]

   b. **Prohibition of holding out [§73]**

   In addition, a lawyer may not "hold out to the public or otherwise represent that the lawyer is admitted to practice" in a jurisdiction in which that is untrue. [Model Rule 5.5(b)(2)]

D. Engaging in Federal Court and International Practice

1. **Admission to Practice in the Federal System**

   a. **Separate requirements for admission [§74]**

   Admission to the bar of a state does not confer the right to practice in federal courts. Rather, *each* court at *each level* of the federal judicial system independently grants admission pursuant to its own rules.

(1) No separate examination [§75]

Most federal courts do not require passage of a federal bar examination in order to practice in the system. They simply require that the candidate be a member of the bar of the state in which the court sits—although a separate application for admission still must be made.

(2) Course requirements [§76]

In response to concerns about the competency of trial lawyers, however, a few federal courts now require that applicants complete certain courses relevant thereto (*e.g.*, trial advocacy, professional responsibility, and federal civil and criminal procedure). [*See* **Brown v. McGarr,** 583 F. Supp. 734 (N.D. Ill. 1984)]

b. Validity of state regulation applied to those engaged exclusively in "federal" practice [§77]

The question has arisen whether a person who is engaged exclusively in a "federal" practice (*e.g.*, bankruptcy, antitrust) must be admitted to the bar in the state in which she practices.

(1) Where specific federal regulation of practice exists [§78]

If federal legislation provides for admission to and regulation of a particular area of practice, federal law *preempts* any state regulation of that practice.

Example: State statutes barring "nonlawyers" from practicing law within the state cannot be applied to a nonlawyer *patent agent* who is admitted to practice before the United States Patent Office and who *limits practice* to patent law. [**Sperry v. State of Florida** *ex rel.* **Florida Bar,** 373 U.S. 379 (1963); *and see* Model Rule 5.5(d)(2)]

---

(2) Where no federal regulation exists [§79]

The rule is less clear where no federal regulation specifically authorizes the practice, but there is authority for saying that states may not prevent out-of-state lawyers from practicing federal law in the jurisdiction. [*In re* **Desilets,** 291 F.3d 925 (6th Cir. 2002)—bankruptcy practice]

c. Appearances pro hac vice [§80]

Where an out-of-state lawyer seeks to appear in *federal court* on a particular matter involving federal law, the state in which the federal court is located may *not* deny admission pro hac vice to a lawyer *admitted* to and in good standing with a *state bar*, absent a showing of misconduct that would justify disbarment of one already admitted to practice before the court. [*In re* **Admission of Lumumba,** 526 F. Supp. 163 (S.D.N.Y. 1981)]

(1) Rationale

The Privileges and Immunities Clause of the U.S. Constitution guarantees a citizen with a federal claim or defense the right to employ an out-of-state lawyer to assist in the case.

2. Practice of International Law [§81]

A foreign lawyer engaged in international practice has *no* general right to practice in a particular U.S. jurisdiction or forum.

a. Maintaining a law office [§82]

Therefore, a state may properly enjoin a foreign lawyer from maintaining an office within the state and giving advice on foreign legal proceedings. [**Bluestein v. State Bar,** 13 Cal. 3d 162 (1974)]

b. Foreign legal consultant rules [§83]

However, several states (*e.g.*, New York) now specially license foreign lawyers as "legal consultants" to enable them to render advice as to the law of countries in which they are admitted to practice. [*See, e.g.*, N.Y. Ct. Appeals R. 521]

c. Supreme Court practice [§84]

The United States Supreme Court rules provide that a foreign lawyer may appear before it *pro hac vice* at the discretion of the Court, and if associated with an American lawyer, may be admitted to practice before the Supreme Court. [Sup. Ct. R. 6]

E. Preventing Unauthorized Practice of Law by Nonlawyers

1. Basic Principles

a. Lay persons may represent themselves [§85]

A lay person is not required to seek legal assistance and may appear in court "in propria persona." The lay person is said to be "ordinarily exposing only himself to possible injury." [EC 3-7]

(1) Criminal cases—constitutional right [§86]

Moreover, in criminal cases, the Supreme Court has held that defendants have a constitutional right to represent themselves. [**Faretta v. California,** 422 U.S. 806 (1975)]

b. Only lawyers may represent persons other than themselves [§87]

However, lawyers are given the exclusive privilege of practicing law on behalf of others. This privilege is said to be based upon the two attributes for which persons admitted to the legal profession are examined: (i) *competence*—"the educated ability of the lawyer to relate the general body and philosophy of law to a specific legal problem," and (ii) *integrity*—the ethical standards of the profession which are vital because of the fiduciary nature of the attorney-client relationship. [EC 3-1, 3-5; **Lawline v. American Bar Association,** 956 F.2d 1378 (7th Cir. 1992)]

2. **Activities that Constitute the "Practice of Law" [§88]**

The term "practice of law" is not defined by statute, and the ABA Code declares a definition to be "neither necessary nor desirable." [EC 3-5; *compare* Model Rule 5.5, comment 2] The courts have therefore had to attach meaning to the term in specific situations.

a. **Tests applied—in general [§89]**

Courts have generally applied one of two tests in determining whether a particular service or activity by nonlawyers constitutes the practice of law.

(1) **"History and custom" [§90]**

Decisions often turn on whether the activity *traditionally* has been handled by lawyers. [**State Bar v. Arizona Land Title & Trust Co.,** 366 P.2d 1 (Ariz. 1961)]

(a) **Criticism**

This test ignores changing conditions and supports lawyers' vested interests more than client needs.

(2) **ABA Code test—"need for professional judgment" [§91]**

The ABA Code says that each activity should be judged in terms of the need for a lawyer's "professional legal judgment"—*i.e.*, bringing judgment to bear on *specific facts* based on a knowledge of the general body and philosophy of law. [EC 3-5]

EXAM TIP   **gilbert**

If you get an exam question that requires you to determine whether the practice of law is involved, ask yourself: (i) whether the activity is one *traditionally performed by lawyers,* and (ii) whether the activity involves *legal knowledge* beyond that which the average layperson possesses, and involves applying the law to a *specific situation* (as opposed to writing a book, for example).

---

b. **Judicial determinations in specific areas**

(1) **Appearance in judicial proceedings [§92]**

The complexities of court procedure and the importance of having proceedings run smoothly and efficiently have been stated as the reasons for making representation in court proceedings the *sole* privilege of lawyers. [**Bilodeau v. Antal,** 455 A.2d 1037 (N.H. 1983)]

(a) **Distinguish—appearance in administrative proceedings [§93]**

However, state and federal administrative agencies and boards often permit specially qualified laypersons to appear before them representing clients (*e.g.*, accountants are often permitted to represent clients before taxing authorities).

(2) Drafting documents [§94]

The drafting of documents that *affect substantial legal rights or obligations* of others is generally considered the practice of law.

(a) Distinguish—filling in blanks on forms [§95]

While drafting agreements may be the practice of law, filling in blanks on standard forms is typically seen as a clerical function (for "scriveners"), and as such may be performed by laypersons. The difficult issue, of course, is the point at which "scrivening" by laypersons becomes "drafting."

1) Real estate brokers [§96]

It is customary for real estate brokers to fill in the blanks in offers to purchase land that their clients want to buy. Such activities ordinarily do *not* constitute the practice of law as long as the contract forms are simple or standardized and the broker charges *no separate fee* (other than a commission) for such work. [**Chicago Bar Association v. Quinlan & Tyson**, 214 N.E.2d 771 (Ill. 1966)]

2) Title insurance escrow companies [§97]

Again, to the extent that standardized forms are used, most courts today permit title insurance and escrow companies to fill in the blanks in mortgages, deeds, etc., according to information furnished by the parties to the sale.

(3) Tax planning [§98]

Giving advice on tax *law* and resolving *legal* tax questions involve the practice of law.

(a) Distinguish—preparing tax returns [§99]

However, an accountant or other layperson may prepare tax returns and answer questions *incidental* to the preparation of the returns.

(4) Giving advice [§100]

Giving individualized advice about legal rights and obligations is usually regarded as the practice of law, whether or not a fee is charged for such advice. Similarly, it is unauthorized practice of law for a layperson to draft a will or prepare an estate plan for another person. [**Oregon State Bar v. Miller & Co.**, 385 P.2d 181 (Or. 1963)]

(a) Distinguish—general publications [§101]

On the other hand, the publication by a layperson of *a book or pamphlet* containing *general* advice and forms (*i.e.*, not calculated to apply to a particular individual) does not constitute the practice of law. [*See* **New York County Lawyers Association v. Dacey**, 21 N.Y.2d 694 (1967)—"do-it-yourself" probate kit permissible because all persons have the right to represent themselves if they choose to do so]

(b) Computer-assisted drafting programs [§102]

One case held that the Quicken Family Lawyer CD-ROM constituted the unauthorized practice of law because the user could interact with it in developing written forms. [**Unauthorized Practice of Law Committee v. Parsons Technology**, 1999 WL 47235 (N.D. Tex. 1999)] But the holding was almost immediately reversed by the Texas legislature.

(5) Prisoner legal assistance by lay prisoners [§103]

The activities of "jailhouse lawyers" to assist fellow inmates in seeking post-conviction relief are clearly the unauthorized practice of law. However, in several cases, the Supreme Court has struck down state regulations designed to suppress this assistance, where *the state has not provided reasonable alternative forms of legal aid for prisoners.* [**Wolff v. McDonnell**, 418 U.S. 539 (1974); *and see* Constitutional Law Summary]

UNAUTHORIZED PRACTICE OF LAW—EXAMPLES OF WHEN PROFESSIONAL JUDGMENT REQUIRED	**gilbert**
PERMISSIBLE LAY ACTIVITIES	**IMPERMISSIBLE LAY ACTIVITIES**
Real estate broker/agent filling in blanks on standard sales contract	Real estate broker/agent drafting sales contract
Tax adviser preparing tax returns	Tax adviser giving advice on tax law and resolving legal tax questions
Estate planner disseminating general information to the public on estate planning	Estate planner drafting wills or preparing estate plans for specific individuals

3. Specific Classes of Persons Prohibited from Practicing Law [§104]

Statutes in many states expressly prohibit the practice of law by certain classes of persons.

a. Judges and court officers [§105]

Judges, court commissioners, and court clerks are usually prohibited from practicing law, ***whether or not*** they are also licensed attorneys. In the case of judges, the prohibition may be constitutional as well as statutory. (*See infra*, §1016—Code of Judicial Conduct prohibition.)

b. Law students and law clerks [§106]

Clerks and students not admitted to practice may perform research or administrative tasks in a law firm, but they may not do any acts that would constitute the practice of law (such as advising clients or appearing in court).

(1) Exception for student training programs [§107]

Several states have authorized law students to engage in a variety of legal activities. These often include preparation of pleadings or briefs, interviewing clients and witnesses, participation in negotiations, and appearances in court. [*See, e.g.,* Ill. Sup. Ct. R. 711] However, such activity must take place under the *guidance and supervision* of a licensed lawyer, and the lawyer must assume *personal* responsibility for the student's work.

c. Corporations [§108]

The general rule in most states is that a corporation may not practice law; *i.e.,* it cannot represent a client directly or furnish representation through its employees who are licensed attorneys.

(1) Rationale

The reason for this limitation is said to be the *relationship of trust and confidence* essential between lawyer and client. When the lawyer owes primary allegiance to the corporation (as the lawyer's immediate employer), there is a substantial risk that the lawyer's loyalty to the client may be incidental or divided.

(2) No corporate self-representation [§109]

In many states, a corporation may not even represent *itself*; *i.e.,* it may not appear in court through nonlawyer officers and directors. Thus, for example, a corporation must hire a lawyer to file suit to collect its bills. [**Remole Soil Service v. Benson,** 215 N.E.2d 678 (Ill. 1966); *but see contra,* Cal. Civ. Proc. Code §116.530—small claims court]

(3) Split of authority—insurance companies [§110]

The courts split on whether an insurance company may employ lawyers full time to represent a company's policyholders. [*See* **Gardner v. North Carolina State Bar,** 341 S.E.2d 517 (N.C. 1986)—saying no; *In re* **Allstate Insurance Co.,** 722 S.W.2d 947 (Mo. 1987)—saying yes]

(4) Exception—professional law corporations [§111]

The absolute prohibition of the corporate practice of law has now been significantly modified as most states' statutes expressly allow lawyers and law firms to practice as professional corporations. (*See infra,* §734.)

(5) Exception—group legal services [§112]

Another important exception to the general rule allows legal clinics and similar organizations to deliver group legal services. (*See infra,* §§759-768.)

4. Efforts to Prohibit Practice of Law by Nonlawyers [§113]

Sanctions against a nonlawyer who practices law include *injunctions, criminal prosecution, or denial of the right to fees* for the unauthorized services.

a. Obligations of attorney in preventing unauthorized practice [§114]

ABA Model Rule 5.5 and ABA Code Canon 3 both require lawyers not to aid a nonlawyer in the unauthorized practice of law. [Model Rule 5.5(a); DR 3-101(A)]

EXAM TIP	gilbert

Note that the above rule does not prohibit a lawyer from delegating tasks to a paralegal, law clerk, student intern, or other such person; but the lawyer must *supervise* the delegated work carefully and must be *ultimately responsible* for the results.

---

(1) Not share legal fees with a nonlawyer [§115]

In furtherance of this principle, a lawyer may not (with certain limited exceptions) *share legal fees with a nonlawyer.* [Model Rule 5.4(a); DR 3-102; *and see infra*, §§751-755]

(2) Not enter into a partnership with a nonlawyer [§116]

Likewise, a lawyer may not enter into a partnership with a nonlawyer if any of the partnership activities include the practice of law. [Model Rule 5.4(b); DR 3-103; *and see infra*, §748]

b. Bar opinions on what constitutes unauthorized practice [§117]

Traditionally, the bar's unauthorized practice committees have stipulated what is and is not the unauthorized practice of law, and lawyers have felt constrained to follow these decisions.

c. Need to expand availability of legal services [§118]

However, related to the expansion of activity by nonlawyers is the increasing public demand for services historically considered to be the "practice of law." Such services may range from appearances before courts or administrative agencies to counseling on leases, contracts, and other legal instruments. The bar has been criticized for devoting more attention to unauthorized practice issues than to the need for legal help among large groups of citizens.

Chapter Two:
The Contract Between Client and Lawyer

CONTENTS

Chapter Approach

This chapter provides an overview of a lawyer-client relationship from its beginning to its end.

1. It begins with how the relationship is formed and the duties a lawyer owes even to prospective clients.

2. It then moves to the respective authority of client and lawyer and reviews the duties that a lawyer owes a client.

3. Next comes the client's duty to pay the lawyer's fee.

4. The chapter closes with a consideration of how the lawyer-client relationship ends and what duties extend beyond that time.

A. Introduction

1. In General [§119]
The relationship between client and lawyer is best understood as based on a contract between them. Many of the terms of that contract are implied by custom and profesional rules, but with few exceptions, the terms may be varied by agreement between client and lawyer.

2. The Lawyer as Agent [§120]
It is often helpful to see a lawyer as an agent of the client and thus subject to the standards imposed by the law of agency. Thus, for example, a lawyer may not be hired to perform an illegal act for a client any more than the client could lawfully hire any other agent to do something illegal.

3. The Lawyer as Fiduciary [§121]
Like any other agent, a lawyer stands in a fiduciary relationship to a client. Indeed, many of the traditional duties owed by a lawyer to a client are derived from general fiduciary standards. Fiduciary duties do not change the contractual character of their relationship, but they mean that departures from the customary contract are likely to be construed against the lawyer and closely scrutinized for fairness.

B. Formation of the Lawyer-Client Relationship—Lawyers' Duties Regarding Accepting Employment

1. **When a Lawyer-Client Relationship Is Formed [§122]**
    A lawyer-client relationship can be formed in three ways:

    a. **By consent [§123]**
        Typically, a lawyer-client relationship is formed when a prospective client indicates a wish to retain the lawyer and the lawyer indicates consent. [Restatement §14(1)(a)]

    b. **Client's reasonable belief [§124]**
        A lawyer-client relationship can also be created when a prospective client indicates a wish to retain the lawyer, the lawyer does not indicate a lack of consent, and the prospective client reasonably believes the lawyer has agreed to the relationship. [**Togstad v. Vesely, Otto, Miller & Keefe,** 291 N.W.2d 686 (Minn. 1980); Restatement §14(1)(b)]

        Example: In **Togstad v. Vesely, Otto, Miller & Keefe,** *supra,* a woman whose husband was left paralyzed after a medical procedure consulted with a lawyer about whether to bring a medical malpractice suit. After interviewing the woman, the lawyer told her that she probably did not have a case but that he would discuss it with another attorney. The woman believed that a lawyer-client relationship had been established, but the lawyer did not contact her after the initial interview. When the woman consulted another lawyer one year later, the statute of limitations for medical malpractice had already run. The court found that there was sufficient evidence to establish the existence of a lawyer-client relationship and awarded malpractice damages to the plaintiffs.

EXAM TIP	gilbert

        Remember that a lawyer's consent to represent a prospective client is implied if the lawyer fails to *clearly decline* representation and the prospective client *reasonably relies* on the representation. The reasonableness of the reliance depends on the circumstances and is a question of fact. The lawyer bears the risk of uncertainty as to whether a lawyer-client relationship has been formed and should avoid any ambiguity.

    c. **Court appointment [§125]**
        A lawyer-client relationship can also be created when a court appoints a lawyer to represent the client. [Restatement §14(2)]

2. **No Obligation to Accept Every Case [§126]**
    Unlike English barristers (who must accept most cases within their areas of experience upon tender of a proper fee), American lawyers need not take every matter presented to them. [EC 2-26—"A lawyer is under no obligation to act as adviser or advocate for every person who may wish to become his client."]

3. Ethical Duty to Provide Representation Where Needed [§127]

Nevertheless, the freedom of lawyers to select their clients does not override the interest of each person in obtaining legal representation when needed.

a. ABA standards [§128]

Both the ABA Code and the Model Rules assert that each lawyer has a personal obligation to serve persons who could not normally afford legal services. However, failure to meet the obligation is *not a disciplinable offense* under either standard. [Model Rule 6.1; EC 2-25]

(1) Voluntary contribution of 50 hours annually [§129]

The Model Rules provide that a lawyer should "aspire to render" at least 50 hours of pro bono service each year, the "substantial majority" of which should be rendered to "persons of limited means" or organizations serving such persons. [Model Rule 6.1(a)]

(2) Other forms of service [§130]

ABA Model Rule 6.1 acknowledges the value of civil rights work and other community service but sees that as coming only after direct service to the poor. [Model Rule 6.1(b)]

b. State standards [§131]

Some state regulations go further and assert a positive *duty* for lawyers to represent "the causes of the defenseless or the oppressed," the breach of which could theoretically result in suspension or disbarment. [*See, e.g.,* Cal. Bus. & Prof. Code §§6068(h), 6103]

c. Accepting appointment as counsel [§132]

A lawyer's duty to represent a client when the lawyer would not choose to do so is most apparent where the client has a *constitutional right to counsel (e.g.,* in a criminal trial) but cannot afford to hire a lawyer. Most courts now have paid public defenders or panels of lawyers who volunteer for such cases, but in their absence, it is the *moral obligation* of every lawyer to accept court appointment to represent an indigent client. [Model Rule 6.2; EC 2-29; **State v. Richardson**, 631 P.2d 221 (Kan. 1981)]

(1) Grounds for rejecting an appointment [§133]

Despite the general obligation to accept court appointment, and lawyers' general reluctance to offend a judge who seeks to appoint them, sometimes it is appropriate for a lawyer to refuse the appointment. ABA Model Rule 6.2 identifies three situations in which an appointment may be refused; *i.e.,* where there is:

(a) *A violation of a Model Rule*—*e.g.,* where the representation would involve a conflict of interest;

(b) *An unreasonable financial burden*—*i.e.,* a burden "so great as to be unjust" (this standard is affected by §134, *infra*); or

(c) *A personal feeling of repugnance* at the client that would affect the lawyer's ability to represent the client adequately.

(2) Right of lawyer to payment if appointed to represent client [§134]

Contrary to prior tradition, some cases have now held that it is unconstitutional to require a lawyer to represent an indigent client without compensation by some public agency. [*See* **Stephan v. Smith,** 747 P.2d 816 (Kan. 1987); **DeLiso v. Alaska Superior Court,** 740 P.2d 437 (Alaska 1987)]

(3) Duty in civil cases [§135]

While a federal court may "request" a lawyer to represent an indigent client in a civil case, the Supreme Court has held that 42 U.S.C. section 1915 does not permit the court to order that the lawyer do so. [**Mallard v. United States District Court,** 490 U.S. 296 (1989)]

4. Duties to a Prospective Client [§136]

Between the time a person discusses the possibility of forming a lawyer-client relationship with a lawyer and the time the relationship is formed (or not formed), the lawyer owes duties to the person who at that time is called a "prospective client." [Model Rule 1.18(a); Restatement §15]

a. Duty to protect confidential information [§137]

As explained more fully later in this Summary, a lawyer must protect the confidential information revealed by a prospective client as fully as that revealed by a client. [Model Rule 1.18(b); Restatement §15(1)(a); *and see infra*, §302]

(1) Lawyer who acquires "significantly harmful" information [§138]

As a way of protecting a prospective client's confidential information if no lawyer-client relationship is formed, a lawyer who had discussions with the prospective client that could be "significantly harmful" to that person in the matter is *prohibited from representing any client* "with interests *materially adverse* to those of the prospective client in the same or a substantially related matter." [Model Rule 1.18(c); Restatement §15(2)]

(a) Caution in scope of initial discussion warranted [§139]

Some law firms have found themselves disqualified from acting on behalf of other clients in later matters because of what they were told in meetings with prospective clients. Therefore, the ABA advises lawyers to require prospective clients to reveal as little confidential information as possible in the initial interview with a lawyer. [ABA Opn. 90-358]

(2) Exception allows lawyer's firm to participate in matter [§140]

Many reasons explain the failure ultimately to form a lawyer-client relationship. At the time of the initial discussion, for example, the lawyer may not know that the adverse party in the matter is a client of the firm. In such cases, if the lawyer who talked to the prospective client "took reasonable measures to avoid exposure to more disqualifying information than was reasonably necessary to determine whether to represent the prospective client," that lawyer must be screened from participation in the matter, but the firm may represent an adverse party. [Model Rule 1.18(d); Restatement §15(2)]

b. Duty to protect prospective client's property [§141]

If a prospective client entrusts documents or other property to the lawyer before a lawyer-client relationship is formed (*e.g.,* for the lawyer to use to understand what the representation would be about), the lawyer must guard the property in the same manner required for property entrusted by a client. [Model Rule 1.15(a); Restatement §15(1)(b); *and see infra,* §209]

c. Duty to give competent legal advice [§142]

A lawyer does not have to give a prospective client any legal advice at all, but if the lawyer negligently gives the prospective client inaccurate information about the law or the prospective client's need for legal services, the lawyer may be liable for professional malpractice. [Restatement §15(1)(c); *see infra,* §§885 *et seq.*]

EXAM TIP   **gilbert**

Keep in mind that the lawyer's duties to "clients" begin before the attorney-client relationship is established—*even if the lawyer is never hired* to represent the person. At the very least, the lawyer must protect the prospective client's confidential information and property, and if the lawyer chooses to give legal advice, it must be competent.

---

5. Duty to Reject Certain Cases [§143]

The ABA Code and the Model Rules specify several situations in which the lawyer *must refuse* employment:

a. Where disciplinary standard would be violated [§144]

If representation of a client would force the lawyer to violate a disciplinary standard or other law (*e.g.,* violate a prohibition against a conflict of interest), the lawyer must decline the case. [Model Rule 1.16(a)(1)]

b. Where lawyer's physical or mental condition is impaired [§145]

If the lawyer's physical or mental condition is impaired and would materially impair the lawyer's ability to represent the client, the lawyer must decline the case. [Model Rule 1.16(a)(2)]

c. Where lawyer is unable to act competently [§146]

A lawyer may not accept a case that the lawyer is too *busy* or too *inexperienced* to handle competently. [Model Rule 1.1; EC 2-30]

d. Where lawyer's personal feelings interfere [§147]

If a lawyer's personal feelings (as distinguished from community pressure) about a prospective case or client are so strong that they might *impair her effective representation* of that client, then the lawer should decline the case. [EC 2-30; *compare* Model Rule 6.2(c)—ground for declining appointment by a court; *and see supra*, §133]

e. Where client is already represented [§148]

Traditionally, a lawyer who knows that the client has already retained counsel may accept the case only if the other counsel *approves, withdraws, or has been discharged* by the client. [EC 2-30]

f. Where client's motive is harassment [§149]

A lawyer should not accept representation if "it is obvious that" the prospective client wishes to "bring a legal action, conduct a defense, assert a position in litigation," or take other steps where the client's motive is to *harass or maliciously injure* any person. [DR 2-109(A)(1); *compare* Model Rule 4.4—where client's purpose is to embarass, delay, or burden another or violate another's legal rights]

g. Where client's legal position is unsupportable [§150]

Similarly, a lawyer should not accept representation if "it is obvious that" the prospective client wishes to present a claim or defense in litigation that is neither warranted under *existing law* nor supportable by *"good faith argument" for a change* in the law. [DR 2-109(A)(2); Model Rule 3.1]

6. Agreeing on Scope and Objectives of Representation [§151]

Once retained, a lawyer's obligation to a client is to act in a manner reasonably calculated to advance the client's lawful objectives as defined by the client. [Restatement §16(1)]

a. Definition of scope and objectives of representation [§152]

Consistent with the contractual nature of the lawyer's relationship with a client, the scope and objectives of a given representation may be defined and limited by agreement between lawyer and client as long as reasonable under the circumstances. [Model Rule 1.2, comments 6, 7; DR 7-101(A)(1)]

(1) Limitation of representation to particular subjects [§153]

A lawyer and client may agree that the lawyer will undertake to address some, but not all, legal needs of the client. For example, the lawyer may undertake to incorporate the client's business, but not to give the client income tax advice. [Model Rule 1.2(c); Restatement §19, comment c]

(2) Limitation on legal remedies to be pursued in representation [§154]

A lawyer and client may similarly agree that the lawyer will seek to resolve a matter short of litigation or will not pursue remedies against particular persons.

b. **Informed consent of client required to limit scope or objectives [§155]**

In general, the law assumes that a client wants to pursue all lawful objectives in all lawful ways. Thus, informed client consent is required for decisions to limit the scope and objectives of representation.

(1) **Lawyer's role in counseling about alternatives [§156]**

One of a lawyer's roles is to ensure that the client understands the advantages and risks associated with any limitations on the representation. [Model Rule 1.2(c)]

(2) **Lawyer should document agreement with client [§157]**

The lawyer must communicate the agreed-upon scope of the representation to the client, "preferably in writing," before or within a reasonable time after beginning the representation. Because in any later litigation, the burden of proving the contents of the agreement with the client will be on the lawyer, a written agreement is advisable. [Model Rule 1.5(b)]

C. Spheres of Authority of Lawyer and Client

1. In General [§158]

The fact that a lawyer is retained to represent the client does *not* mean that the lawyer assumes complete control over the case. The client remains the party in interest and, with a few exceptions, must be allowed to make all ultimate decisions about the case. [Model Rule 1.2(a); EC 7-7]

2. Matters Within Client's Authority [§159]

The decision on any matter that will substantially affect the client's rights must be made by the client. When such matters arise, the lawyer has a duty to advise the client on particular courses of action, but the decision itself *rests with the client.* [Model Rule 1.2(a); EC 7-7; Restatement §22]

a. **Settlement or compromise of action [§160]**

The client must agree to any settlement or compromise of a civil action. *A fortiori,* the client also has the sole power to authorize dismissal or otherwise to end a case on its merits. [Model Rule 1.2(a); Restatement §22(1)]

(1) **Effect of unauthorized settlement or compromise [§161]**

While a client can give a lawyer actual authority to conclude a settlement on the client's behalf, a lawyer does not inherently have apparent authority to do so, and a client can disclaim a settlement that is unauthorized. [**Luethke v. Suhr,** 650 N.W.2d 220 (Neb. 2002); Restatement §27, comment d]

(2) Ratification by client [§162]

If the lawyer without authority agrees to a compromise or settlement, the client may still *ratify* it. Ratification will be found if the client seeks to claim the benefits of the agreement. [**Daniel v. Scott,** 455 So. 2d 30 (Ala. 1984); Restatement §26(3)]

(3) Client may dismiss at any time [§163]

The client may dismiss a case at any time regardless of the lawyer's wish to proceed, but the client's dismissal of the case or direct settlement with the opposing party may entitle the lawyer to whatever fee was provided for in the retainer agreement in event of settlement. (*See infra,* §§248-265.)

(4) Dismissals "without prejudice" [§164]

A lawyer may have implied authority to dismiss a case "*without* prejudice" (*i.e.,* no bar to relitigation) if the dismissal is *in the client's interest*—e.g., when some tactical advantage may be gained by refiling the suit elsewhere, and the dismissal would not jeopardize the client's case (no problem of statute of limitations, etc.).

b. Important decisions in criminal cases [§165]

A lawyer should counsel the client about what plea to enter, whether to waive jury trial, and whether to testify. However, the lawyer may not make these decisions and must accept and implement what the client decides as to each. [Model Rule 1.2(a); Restatement §22(1)]

EXAM TIP   **gilbert**

Remember that the implication of Model Rules 1.2(a) and 1.4(a) is that the lawyer must promptly convey any offer to *settle* a civil case, or offer of a *plea bargain* in a criminal case, to his *client*, unless the *client* has previously instructed the lawyer that an offer on those terms is acceptable or unacceptable. Even if a settlement offer is unreasonably low, the lawyer must convey it to the client before rejecting it, or the lawyer will be subject to discipline.

---

c. Whether to appeal [§166]

In addition, a lawyer must leave to the client the decision whether to appeal an adverse decision in a civil or criminal case. [Restatement §22(1)]

3. Matters Within Lawyer's Authority [§167]

While decisions about the objectives or "ends" of a representation are the client's to make, the "means" are more often within the authority of the lawyer. Even as to means, however, issues affecting cost and the impact on third parties are often reserved to the client. [Model Rule 1.2(a), comments 1, 2]

a. Matters required by law [§168]

A lawyer has authority to comply with all requirements of law or of a court and authority to refuse to follow a client direction that the lawyer reasonably believes to be illegal. This authority may not be waived by contract. [Restatement §23]

b. Procedural matters [§169]

With respect to most procedural matters during a judicial proceeding, the client has little expertise and therefore the lawyer is presumed to have authority to act in the client's interest. [Model Rule 1.2(a), comment 1]

c. "Judicial admissions" [§170]

Admissions of fact made by a lawyer in the pleadings or in the course of narrowing the issues for trial (*e.g.,* at the pretrial conference) are deemed "judicial admissions." As such, they are *conclusive* and bind the client, unless the court permits them to be amended or withdrawn. (*See* Evidence Summary.) If the court refuses such relief, the client's only remedy would be a *malpractice* action against the lawyer for any harm or loss resulting from the admission.

(1) Distinguish—other admissions [§171]

Other admissions of fact made by the lawyer (*e.g.,* in negotiations or correspondence) are ordinarily *not conclusive* as to the client, but are admissible in evidence against the client *if* the lawyer was authorized to speak for the client with respect to the subject in question. (*See* "vicarious admissions" in Evidence Summary.)

SCOPE OF REPRESENTATION—EXAMPLES gilbert	
DECISIONS TO BE MADE BY CLIENT (Decisions Affecting Merits)	**DECISIONS TO BE MADE BY LAWYER** (Procedural Tactics)
Acceptance or rejection of settlement offers	Choice of motions to file
Plea to be entered in a criminal case	Scope of discovery to take
Waiver of jury trial in a criminal case	Questions to ask in direct and cross-examinations
Whether to testify in a criminal case	What evidence to introduce

4. Special Problems in Representing Clients with "Diminished Capacity" [§172]

Lawyers sometimes represent clients with "diminished capacity," *i.e.,* those whose "ability to make adequately considered decisions" is impaired, typically by old age. Insofar as possible, the lawyer must maintain a *normal relationship* with such clients, including *consulting with them about major decisions.* [Model Rule 1.14(a); EC 7-12; Restatement §24(1)]

a. **Appointment of guardian [§173]**

If the lawyer concludes that the client "cannot adequately act in the client's own interest," the lawyer may take "reasonably necessary protective action," including consulting with family members and others who can protect the client. If necessary, the lawyer may seek appointment of a legal guardian to act for the client. [Model Rule 1.14(b); Restatement §24(4)]

EXAM TIP | **gilbert**

It is important to note that just because a client is under a disability, it does not mean that the attorney can ignore the client's wishes. The Model Rules *require* the attorney to *maintain a normal relationship* as much as possible and to *consult* with the client about major decisions. Obviously if the client is unable to make decisions (*e.g.*, is in a coma), a guardian would have to make the decisions, but if the client has at least some capacity, he should be advised and consulted, and should assist in making decisions of which he is capable.

---

b. **Application—representation of minors [§174]**

Because the law often treats minors as if they were incompetent to act on their own behalf, these principles may apply to their representation as well. A lawyer must consult with a minor client and let the minor decide most matters within a client's authority to decide, but the lawyer may have to see that a guardian is appointed to decide matters where the law so requires.

D. Formal Duties that Lawyers Owe to Clients

1. **Introduction [§175]**

Legal ethics has traditionally broken out categories of duties that lawyers owe to clients. Most are derived from principles that apply to fiduciaries generally, and in this part of the Summary, the duties are discussed one by one.

2. **Duty of Competence [§176]**

The duty to represent a client competently has at least two components: (i) the *ability*—the knowledge and skill to perform the required services for the client, and (ii) *care*—the necessary thoroughness and preparation in performing the services. These combine as the first principle of the Model Rules. [Model Rule 1.1; DR 6-101]

a. **Ability to represent client [§177]**

A lawyer may not attempt to handle a legal matter that she knows *or should know* she is not competent to handle, without *associating* a lawyer who is competent in the matter. [Model Rule 1.1; DR 6-101(A)(1); Restatement §52(1); **Lewis v. State Bar of California,** 28 Cal. 3d 683 (1981)]

(1) Exception—where competency anticipated [§178]

A lawyer *may* accept such employment if that lawyer in good faith expects to become qualified to perform the necessary services. The lawyer must diligently undertake whatever work or study is required to attain proficiency in the matter and not cause the client *unreasonable delay or expense*. [Model Rule 1.1; EC 6-3, 6-4]

(2) Association of competent counsel [§179]

When a lawyer faces a problem outside that lawyer's own area of competence, the lawyer should associate another lawyer who is already proficient in the area. Association of co-counsel, of course, requires the client's consent. [Model Rule 1.1; EC 6-3; **Horne v. Peckham,** 97 Cal. App. 3d 404 (1979)]

EXAM TIP | **gilbert**

A fairly common exam question involves a newly admitted attorney who has just put out her shingle when a client with a lucrative case walks in the door. The new attorney really wants to take the case because she has student loans to pay, mouths to feed, etc., but she knows she isn't competent to handle it. Recall that the general rule is *no competency, no case,* but the new attorney has two options: (i) *find a qualified lawyer to associate* (and get the client's consent); or (ii) figure out a way to *become proficient quickly*. If she can do one of those two things, she may ethically take the case.

---

(3) Emergency matters [§180]

The Model Rules recognize that times will arise when a client needs immediate action from a trusted lawyer and there is no time to become competent or associate another lawyer. A lawyer *may act* in such cases, but *should limit* the action to only what is reasonably required, because "ill-considered action under emergency conditions can jeopardize the client's interest." [Model Rule 1.1, comment 3]

EXAM TIP | **gilbert**

Keep in mind that in an emergency (*e.g.,* the dreaded call in the middle of the night from a real estate client who has been arrested for battery), a lawyer *may assist* a client even if the lawyer lacks competence in that particular area. However, the assistance cannot exceed what is *reasonably necessary to meet the emergency*.

---

b. Duty of care in representing a client [§181]

Even where the lawyer is capable of performing required services for the client, or where competent counsel is associated, the services must be performed with "thoroughness and preparation reasonably necessary for the representation." [Model Rule 1.1]

(1) Standard depends on circumstances [§182]

Lawyers' services are costly and are borne by the client, so the attention and preparation the lawyer must put into a case varies with how much is at stake for the client. [Model Rule 1.1, comment 5]

(2) Aspirational goal higher [§183]

The Ethical Considerations of the ABA Code urge greater care than the bare minimum of "nonnegligence." The lawyer should be motivated by *professional pride,* rather than by fear of malpractice suits or discipline. [EC 6-5]

c. Remedies for breach of the duty of competence

(1) Malpractice liability [§184]

While it is possible for an attorney who has incompetently represented a client to be subject to professional discipline, by far the most common remedy is a suit for professional malpractice against the lawyer. [Restatement §52(1); *see infra,* §§885 *et seq.*]

(2) Setting aside a criminal conviction [§185]

Relatively few cases have set aside a criminal conviction because of incompetency of counsel, and then only where the errors of defense counsel were so shocking that they deprived the accused of the constitutional right to *effective assistance of counsel.* A defendant must show that counsel's acts or omissions "were outside the wide range of professionally competent assistance," and they must have caused *"actual prejudice,"* not just some "conceivable effect" on the outcome. [*See* **McMann v. Richardson,** 397 U.S. 759 (1970); **Strickland v. Washington,** 466 U.S. 668 (1984)]

(3) Setting aside a civil default judgment [§186]

Courts have been more reluctant to set aside *civil* judgments on the basis of negligence of counsel, but where the lawyer's negligence results in entry of a default judgment against the client (*e.g.,* the lawyer failed to answer within statutory period), courts are frequently willing to set aside the default judgment if there is a *reasonable excuse* for the lawyer's error. Here, the policy in favor of resolving litigation on the merits outweighs the policy that binds a client by the lawyer's errors. [**Coerber v. Rath,** 435 P.2d 228 (Colo. 1967)—setting aside default judgment where default had resulted from *inexcusable* neglect by counsel]

3. Duty of Diligence [§187]

The Model Rules also require a lawyer to act with *reasonable diligence and promptness* in representing a client. [Model Rule 1.3] The Model Rules note that "no professional shortcoming is more widely resented than procrastination." [Model Rule 1.3, comment 3]

a. **Not precluded from agreeing to postponement [§188]**

A requirement of diligence might seem to require resolving matters quickly, but the Model Rules make clear that a lawyer is not required to use "offensive tactics" and may show everyone in the legal process "courtesy and respect." [Model Rule 1.3, comment 1] For example, a lawyer may agree to "a reasonable request for a postponement that will not prejudice the lawyer's client." [Model Rule 1.3, comment 3]

b. **ABA Code provision [§189]**

Ethical Consideration 6-4 of the ABA Code required lawyers to "give appropriate attention to" legal work, so the Model Rules do not constitute a change in policy, but a lawyer's lack of diligence is now a basis upon which professional discipline may be imposed.

4. **Duty of Zealous Representation [§190]**

There is a long tradition of saying that a lawyer must "zealously" represent a client. In fact, however, neither the ABA Code nor the Model Rules define "zealous representation." The Restatement says that "zealousness" is captured by the terms "competence" and "diligence." [DR 7-101(A); Restatement §16, comment d]

a. **In litigation matters—doubts to be resolved in favor of client [§191]**

Traditionally, the requirement of "zeal" has meant at least that in litigation matters, the lawyer must act as an *advocate* and resolve any doubts about the facts of the case or the bounds of the law in favor of the client. As long as a good faith argument for the client's position can be made, the lawyer may make it even if the lawyer does not personally believe that it will or should prevail. [Model Rule 3.1; EC 7-3, 7-4]

b. **Greater detachment owed in nonadversary matters [§192]**

By contrast, in *nonlitigation* matters, even a zealous lawyer owes the client the greater detachment of an *adviser*. In that role, the lawyer should inform the client of possible adverse consequences of the facts and give the client the benefit of the lawyer's professional judgment in charting the client's *future* dealings or conduct. In short, the adviser should make known possible pitfalls in advance so that the client may act accordingly. [Model Rule 2.1; EC 7-5]

c. **Lawyer need not adopt client's viewpoint personally [§193]**

The duty to provide "zealous" representation as an advocate never obligates a lawyer personally to adopt a client's viewpoints. Thus, a lawyer may properly take positions on public issues and espouse legal reforms that are *contrary* to the client's position, although the lawyer should do this "with circumspection" so as not to prejudice the client's rights. [Model Rule 1.2(b); EC 7-17]

d. **Additional implications of zealousness [§194]**

Because most practical implications of the duty of zealousness arise in litigation, additional issues will be considered in Chapter VI of this Summary. (*See infra,* §§574 *et seq.*)

5. **Duty of Communication [§195]**

The ABA Model Rules also require a lawyer to "explain a matter" to the client "to the extent reasonably necessary to permit the client to make informed decisions" about the representation. [Model Rule 1.4(b)]

a. **Specific requirements [§196]**

The communication requirement demands that the lawyer:

(i) *Keep each client informed* about the status of the client's matters;

(ii) *Comply promptly with reasonable client requests for information;*

(iii) Reasonably *consult* with the client *about the means* the lawyer is to use to accomplish the client's objectives;

(iv) Let the client know promptly about *circumstances* as to which the *client's informed consent is required;* and

(v) Be sure the client understands any *relevant limitations on the lawyer's conduct* imposed by the Rules of Professional Conduct.

[Model Rule 1.4(a)]

b. **Right to withhold certain information [§197]**

If disclosure of certain information would be likely to be "imprudent" (*e.g.,* where the information is a diagnosis that the client is mentally ill), such disclosure may be "delayed." However, the lawyer may not withhold information to serve the lawyer's own interest or convenience. [Model Rule 1.4, comment 7]

6. **Duty of Confidentiality [§198]**

The duty of confidentiality is such a central obligation of a lawyer that it is considered in detail in Chapter III of this Summary. (*See infra,* §§299 *et seq.*)

7. **Duty of Loyalty [§199]**

The duty of loyalty—*i.e.,* the duty to avoid conflicts of interest—is of such importance that it too merits a full chapter. It is described in detail in Chapter IV of this Summary. (*See infra,* §§366 *et seq.*)

8. **Duties with Regard to Client Property [§200]**

As another part of the broad fiduciary duties owed each client, a lawyer must keep the funds and property of clients *safe and entirely separate* from the lawyer's own assets. [Model Rule 1.15; DR 9-102; Cal. Rule 4-100]

a. **Separate bank account [§201]**

All funds belonging to the client that are received by the lawyer must be deposited in one or more *separately identified* bank accounts (usually called "trust accounts" or "clients' funds accounts"). The lawyer may use a single trust account to hold money of many clients, but a careful accounting must be made of the funds of each client. [Model Rule 1.15(a); DR 9-102(A)]

(1) No commingling [§202]

In general, the lawyer must not deposit any personal funds in these bank accounts, although a lawyer may deposit small amounts into the trust account to pay the *bank charges* thereon. [Model Rule 1.15(b); DR 9-102(A)(1)]

(2) Location of accounts [§203]

Absent client consent, the accounts must be maintained in the state where the lawyer's office is located. [Model Rule 1.15(a); DR 9-102(A)(1)]

(3) Expenses advanced by client [§204]

Under the ABA Code, a lawyer did not have to deposit monies advanced by the client to cover *costs or expenses* into a trust account. [DR 9-102(A)] However, the Model Rules are more restrictive and require such advances to be deposited in the trust account. [Model Rule 1.15(c); Cal. Rule 4-100]

b. Withdrawals from joint funds [§205]

A lawyer who receives money that belongs in part to the client and in part to the lawyer (*e.g.*, a settlement in a contingent fee case) must deposit the *entire* sum in the client's trust account.

(1) Undisputed fee [§206]

If the lawyer's portion is undisputed and the amount is fixed, the lawyer *must withdraw it as soon as possible* (to prevent commingling with clients' funds) and promptly turn the client's share over to the client. [Model Rule 1.15(d); Cal. Rule 4-100; **Black v. State Bar**, 57 Cal. 2d 219 (1961)]

(2) Disputed funds [§207]

But if the client disputes the lawyer's right to receive all or any portion of the funds, the disputed portion may *not be withdrawn* until the controversy is resolved. [Model Rule 1.15(d); DR 9-102(A)(2)]

(3) Funds potentially belonging to a third party [§208]

A lawyer holds the client's funds in a fiduciary capacity and cannot distribute them except as authorized by the client or ordered by a court. Thus, without authorization, the lawyer cannot disburse funds even if the lawyer personally concludes that the client owes the money involved to a third party (*e.g.*, the client's doctor or other creditors). [Model Rule 1.15(e); **Jackson v. State Bar**, 15 Cal. 3d 372 (1975)]

c. Duties regarding custody of clients' property (other than funds) [§209]

As a fiduciary, the lawyer must identify and label securities and other property of the client upon receipt thereof, and must deposit such property at once in a *safe deposit box or other suitable storage facility*. [Model Rule 1.15(a); DR 9-102(B)]

EXAM TIP   **gilbert**

Note that there are two requirements regarding client property: (i) the property must be kept *safe*, and (ii) it must be kept *separate*. For exam purposes, the safety requirement is fairly easy—the lawyer has to store the property in a safe place—for money, that's in the bank and for other property, in a safe deposit box or other safe place—so that it doesn't get stolen, destroyed, etc. It also means the lawyer can't use the property or borrow against it. A more likely exam topic will involve keeping the property separate from the lawyer's property. Recall that although the lawyer can commingle several *clients'* funds in a trust account, he *cannot put any of his own money* in there except to pay the bank fees. Also, if the lawyer receives a settlement check or other payment to the client from which his fee is to be paid, he can take his fee out of the fund only if there is no dispute about rights to the money in the account. If there is a dispute, the lawyer cannot withdraw it until the issue is resolved.

CHECKLIST OF LAWYER'S DUTIES TO CLIENT   **gilbert**

A LAWYER OWES THE FOLLOWING DUTIES TO THE CLIENT:

☑ Duty of *competence*—act with knowledge, skill, thoroughness, and preparation;

☑ Duty of *diligence*—pursue the matter with zeal and promptness;

☑ Duty of *communication*—keep client informed;

☑ Duty of *confidentiality*—not reveal client information;

☑ Duty of *loyalty*—avoid conflicts of interest;

☑ Duties with regard to *client property*—keep safe and separate from lawyer's own assets.

E. The Obligation of Client to Lawyer— Fees for Legal Services

1. In General [§210]

While lawyers have several important obligations to clients, the converse is not true. The ABA Code and Model Rules are silent on the client's obligations, and the Restatement identifies only: (i) a duty to indemnify the lawyer for liability to which the client exposed the lawyer without the lawyer's fault, (ii) the duty to fulfill any contractual obligations to the lawyer, and (iii) the most important client obligation, the duty to pay the lawyer's fee. [Restatement §17]

2. Timing and Content of the Fee Agreement [§211]

When the lawyer has not regularly represented a client, the Model Rules require that the client be told the basis or rate of the fee *before or within a reasonable time* after commencing the representation. [Model Rule 1.5(b); Restatement §38(1)]

a. Required subjects to be agreed [§212]
Three matters must be specified in the fee arrangement [Model Rule 1.5(b)]:

(1) Amount or basis
The amount of the fee or the basis for its calculation (*e.g.,* hourly rate of the lawyer, contingent fee) must be set out.

(2) Scope of work
The agreement must specify what the lawyer will be expected to do for the client to earn the fee (*see supra,* §§151-157).

(3) Expenses
Costs likely to be incurred and charged to the client must also be specified.

b. Written agreement preferable [§213]
A fee agreement, unless for a contingent fee, is enforceable *whether oral or written.* Technically, under the Model Rules, it need only be "communicated to the client" and the client's silence will be deemed consent. However, good practice dictates that the agreement be in writing and signed by both parties. [Model Rule 1.5(b); EC 2-19; Restatement §38; for contingent fees, *see infra,* §223]

c. Ambiguities construed against lawyer [§214]
Because the lawyer initiates the fee agreement and is presumed capable of saying things clearly, in the event of a dispute about the fee, any ambiguity or uncertainty will be *construed against the lawyer.* [Restatement §18(2), comment h]

d. Presumption of undue influence where fee agreement entered into later [§215]
If no fee arrangement is made at the outset of the representation, the burden will be on the lawyer to show that any later contract and the circumstances of its formation were fair and reasonable to the client. [Restatement §18(1)(a)]

3. Requirement that Fees Be No More than Reasonable [§216]
Courts may refuse to enforce a fee agreement against a client and may impose professional discipline upon a lawyer if the fees charged are found to be "unreasonable." [Model Rule 1.5(a)] The corresponding terms in other lawyer codes are "clearly excessive" [DR 2-106(A)] or "unconscionable" [Cal. Rule 4-200].

a. Determining "reasonableness" [§217]
The "reasonableness" of a fee agreement depends upon *all relevant circumstances.* In this respect, the interests of both clients and lawyers must be considered; *i.e.,* excessive fees would deter the use of legal services, while inadequate compensation might undermine effective representation. [EC 2-17, 2-18]

b. Relevant factors [§218]
The following factors have regularly been cited as keys to the determination of reasonableness, although they are not the only ones that a court may consider:

(i) The *time and labor* required, the *novelty and difficulty* of the issues, and the *skill* needed to perform the legal services;

(ii) The likelihood, if apparent to the client, that taking the case will mean the lawyer will be *precluded from other employment*;

(iii) The *fee customarily charged* for the services in the locality;

(iv) The *amount involved* and the *results obtained*;

(v) *Time limitations imposed* by the client or the circumstances;

(vi) The *nature and length of the attorney-client relationship*;

(vii) The *experience, reputation, and ability* of the lawyer; and

(viii) Whether the fee is *fixed or contingent*.

[Model Rule 1.5(a); DR 2-106(B); Restatement §34, comment c]

c. Fee arbitration [§219]
Several states allow clients who are dissatisfied with their bills for legal services to have them reviewed by an arbitrator. Most such plans are voluntary, but proposals are being made to make them mandatory, and the comment to Model Rule 1.5 exhorts lawyers to submit to arbitration.

4. Special Problems of Contingent Fee Agreements [§220]
Contingent fees depend upon success in the case; *i.e.,* by agreement, the lawyer is to receive a percentage of whatever the client recovers at trial or by settlement—and nothing if the client loses.

a. Propriety of contingent fee agreements [§221]
In this country, the problem of contingent fees has been resolved in favor of permitting their use, subject to regulation designed to prevent abuses. [*See* Model Rule 1.5; EC 2-20; DR 5-103(A)(2); Restatement §35]

(1) Factors supporting use of contingent fees [§222]
Contingent fees have the advantage of enabling poor clients with meritorious claims to enforce them without compromising for a small fraction of their total value. It is also urged that such arrangements help to support and encourage a body of independent lawyers ready to challenge wrongs done to their clients from any source.

(2) Specific regulatory requirements [§223]

In addition to the requirements for any fee agreement, the Model Rules state that a contingent fee agreement must:

(i) *Be in writing* and the writing must be *signed by the client*;

(ii) *State the method by which the fee is to be determined,* including the lawyer's percentages in the event of settlement, trial, or appeal;

(iii) *Identify expenses to be deducted* from the recovery and whether they are before or after the lawyer's percentage is calculated; and

(iv) *Be followed up with a written statement* accounting for disposition of the recovery.

[Model Rule 1.5(c)]

(3) Reasonableness requirement [§224]

A contingent fee may be higher than a fixed or hourly fee because of the increased risk the lawyer assumes. However, contingent fees are subject to the reasonableness requirement applicable to all fees. [Restatement §35, comment c]

EXAM TIP   **gilbert**

If faced with a question involving a contingent fee, keep in mind that the amount of a contingent fee must be *reasonable at the time the contingent fee agreement is made*. However, the fee may appear to be reasonable to a client who anticipates a lengthy trial, not realizing that most cases settle. The lawyer is in a better position to assess the merits of the case and the likelihood that the case will settle. Thus, the lawyer should inform the client of the strength of the case and the prospects for a quick settlement before the fee agreement is executed and discuss fee options with the client. Furthermore, the lawyer should not use a contingent fee when the facts of the case make it unreasonable to do so.

---

(4) Maximum limits on contingency fees [§225]

In a few states, *court rules* fix maximum percentages that may be charged by lawyers under contingent fee contracts. (Usually, the maximum declines as the size of the recovery increases—*e.g.,* 50% of the first $1,000, 40% of the next $2,000, 30% of the next $5,000, etc.) Such schedules have been upheld against attacks that they constitute unconstitutional interference with lawyers' freedom to contract. [**American Trial Lawyers Association v. New Jersey Supreme Court,** 316 A.2d 19, *aff'd,* 330 A.2d 350 (N.J. 1974)]

(5) Minors' claims [§226]

In most states, any contract with a minor for litigation services is void unless approved by the court, and the same applies to any contract with the parents "on behalf of" the minor. The proper procedure is for the parents to be appointed "guardians ad litem" by the court and then to seek *court approval* of a contingency fee contract.

b. Kinds of cases in which contingent fees are prohibited

(1) Domestic relations cases [§227]

Because of the relationships involved in domestic relations proceedings, contingent fee arrangements are prohibited in most domestic relations cases (divorce, custody, etc.). [EC 2-20; Restatement §35(1)(b)]

(a) Model Rules [§228]

The Model Rules specifically prohibit a lawyer from accepting a fee *contingent upon obtaining a divorce, alimony, property settlement, or support*. The rationale is that the contingent fee might interfere with the possibility of reconciliation. [Model Rule 1.5(d)(1)]

(b) Distinguish—post-divorce matters [§229]

Once a divorce has been *granted,* and the current proceedings involve only collection of a debt (*e.g.,* past due alimony), some courts permit contingent fee arrangements. [**Krieger v. Bulpitt,** 40 Cal. 2d 97 (1953); Restatement §35, comment g]

(2) Criminal cases [§230]

A lawyer is prohibited from taking a criminal case on a contingent fee. [Restatement §35(1)(a)]

(a) Criminal defense [§231]

A lawyer may not represent a criminal defendant on a contingent fee basis. The rationale sometimes given for this rule is that legal services in such cases do not yield the client a fund or property with which to pay the fee, but the better argument is that such a fee might discourage the lawyer from encouraging the client to accept an otherwise desirable plea agreement that might lower what the lawyer received. [Model Rule 1.5(d)(2); EC 2-20; DR 2-106(c)]

(b) Criminal prosecution [§232]

Likewise, a lawyer may not prosecute a case on a contingent fee basis because it might interfere with a prosecutor's duty to do justice even if it involves dismissing a case. [**People** *ex rel.* **Clancy v. Superior Court,** 39 Cal. 3d 740 (1985); Restatement §35, comment f(ii)]

(3) Securing favorable legislation [§233]

Likewise, contingent fees are unlawful where their payment depends upon the lawyer's securing passage of legislation or other governmental action.

The rationale is that possible harm might result from the lawyer's use of extreme measures to achieve success. [**Trist v. Child,** 88 U.S. 441 (1874)]

c. Recovery permitted in quantum meruit [§234]

Where a contingent fee arrangement is void for reasons of public policy (*e.g.,* in a criminal or domestic relations case), the courts usually permit the lawyer to recover the *reasonable value* of his services (assuming the services rendered were otherwise lawful); *see infra,* §235. [**Hay v. Erwin,** 419 P.2d 32 (Or. 1966)]

5. Fee in the Absence of a Fee Contract [§235]

If a lawyer and client have not agreed on a fee, or the fee agreement is invalid, the lawyer is entitled to recover the *reasonable value* of services rendered. [Restatement §39]

6. Minimum Fee Schedules [§236]

In the past, some state and local bar associations published schedules of minimum fees for various kinds of legal services. In some instances, the fees in the schedules were offered merely as a "suggestion" of the "going rate" for particular services, but in other instances, lawyers were threatened with discipline if they regularly undercut the fees stated in the schedules.

a. Violation of antitrust laws [§237]

In **Goldfarb v. Virginia State Bar,** 421 U.S. 773 (1975), the United States Supreme Court held that a fee schedule that had the *effect* of creating uniform fees for legal work connected with interstate commerce was illegal as price fixing under section 1 of the Sherman Act.

b. Fees a matter of private contract or legal decree [§238]

The result of *Goldfarb* is that specific fees are no longer a matter for bar association determination or review. Fees are either the product of private negotiation between lawyer and client, as discussed above, or they are established by court order or controlling legislation, as discussed below (*infra,* §§239 *et seq.*).

7. Legislative Regulation of Fees [§239]

Congress and some state legislatures have set *maximum* fees for certain types of legal services. Typical examples include legal services rendered in connection with probate of a decedent's estate, guardianships, workers' compensation claims, Social Security claims, and representation of indigents in criminal proceedings. In general, state courts adhere rigorously to these legislative ceilings on fees, and disciplinary action may be taken against lawyers who attempt to avoid the limitation.

a. Effect on right to counsel [§240]

The impact of these limits can be severe. For example, Congress limits lawyers in Prison Litigation Reform Act cases to 150% of actual damages recovered. Thus, where a prisoner won the case but recovered only $1 in nominal damages, his lawyer's fee was capped at $1.50. [**Bovin v. Black,** 225 F.3d 36 (1st Cir. 2000)]

b. **"Ordinary" vs. "extraordinary" services [§241]**

Some statutes are drafted to mitigate the above problem by specifying a ceiling only for the lawyer's "ordinary" services in handling the case. Such statutes empower the tribunal hearing the claim to award *additional* reasonable fees for "extraordinary" services. [**Bias v. Oklahoma**, 568 P.2d 1269 (Okla. 1977)]

8. **Setting Fees in Class Actions, Derivative Suits, and Certain Civil Rights Actions [§242]**
   In cases involving multiple plaintiffs or fees paid by the losing party, the rules often provide for judicially established attorneys' fees.

   a. **Lodestar approach [§243]**

   Under the most common approach now used, the court establishes a "lodestar," *i.e.*, the number of hours reasonably expended multiplied by the lawyer's reasonable hourly rate. [**Hensley v. Eckerhart**, 461 U.S. 424 (1983)] The lodestar amount is presumed to be a reasonable fee. [**Pennsylvania v. Delaware Valley Citizens' Council for Clean Air**, 478 U.S. 546 (1986)]

   (1) **Prevailing rates [§244]**

   The reasonableness of the lawyer's rate is determined by comparing it to the prevailing market rate in the community. Thus, even if the actual lawyer works for a labor union or is otherwise actually paid less that those rates, she is entitled to the market rate. [**Raney v. Federal Bureau of Prisons**, 222 F.3d 927 (Fed. Cir. 2000)]

   (2) **Proportionality not required [§245]**

   Also, the attorney's fee may be substantially in excess of the amount the plaintiff recovered if necessary to reward the lawyer for efforts on the plaintiff's behalf. [**City of Riverside v. Rivera**, 477 U.S. 561 (1986)]

   b. **Common fund method [§246]**

   In cases where the lawyer recovers a substantial sum for the plaintiff or class, many courts now award the lawyer a percentage of the recovery, as if there had been a contingent fee agreement. [**Vizcaino v. Microsoft Corp.**, 290 F.3d 1043 (9th Cir. 2002)]

   Example: In **Vizcaino v. Microsoft Corp.**, *supra*, the court determined that the percentage-of-recovery approach was appropriate where the attorneys for a class of employees successfully pursued a claim for employee benefits. In applying the percentage-of-recovery approach rather than the lodestar method in this class action, the court found that an award of attorneys' fees over $27 million (28% of an approximately $97 million settlement fund) was reasonable.

   c. **Negotiating attorney's fees as part of overall settlement [§247]**

   A difficult conflict of interest can arise if the defendant offers to make a generous settlement in favor of the plaintiff class but conditions it on the plaintiff's lawyer taking a less than reasonable fee. The Supreme Court has held that accepting such a settlement may be part of a lawyer's duty, so many lawyers now negotiate a fee agreement with the class in advance. The lawyer will be paid out of a court award of fees if it is sufficient, but out of the clients' award if not. [**Evans v. Jeff D.,** 475 U.S. 717 (1986); **Venegas v. Mitchell,** 495 U.S. 82 (1990)]

9. Protecting Lawyer's Right to Compensation

a. Lawyer's duties in collecting fees [§248]

According to the ABA standards, lawyers are obliged to be "zealous" in their efforts to *avoid controversies with clients over fees* and should attempt to resolve amicably any differences that arise. [EC 2-23]

(1) Self-help remedies [§249]

A lawyer who uses self-help remedies in collecting a fee must be very careful not to overreach the client. For example, a lawyer can be disciplined for withholding necessary documents in a case until the client pays the fees. [**State v. Mayes,** 531 P.2d 102 (Kan. 1975)]

(2) Litigation to be avoided if possible [§250]

EC 2-23 states that a lawyer should not sue a client for a fee "unless necessary to prevent fraud or gross imposition by the client." As a practical matter, however, courts do not require lawyers to abstain from litigation over fees. As long as the fee claim is asserted in good faith, and prior demand for payment has been made, it is not improper for a lawyer to file suit against the client to collect the fee. [Restatement §41]

(3) Credit card financing [§251]

Provided there is no increased charge to the client, it is not improper for a lawyer to accept credit card charges for legal fees or to participate in legal fee financing plans (*e.g.,* where the fees receivable are assigned to local banks where client's credit has been established). [ABA Opn. 338]

b. Retaining (possessory) lien [§252]

In many states (but not California), a lawyer has, by statute or judicial decision, a *possessory lien* on property, documents, and funds belonging to the client that come into the lawyer's possession by reason of the employment. The basic value of the retaining lien lies in the *inconvenience* that the client or the client's successors experience in being denied access to the property. Ordinarily, a retaining lien *cannot* be sued upon by the lawyer (although it can be asserted as a *defense* to a suit by the client demanding return of his property).

(1) Documents prepared by the lawyer [§253]

A lawyer ordinarily need not turn over documents prepared by the lawyer and not yet paid for by the client (*e.g.,* a will or contract drafted for the client). [Restatement §43(1)]

(2) Limited to property acquired as attorney [§254]

With respect to other property of the client that the lawyer holds, a retaining lien attaches *only* to property that comes into the lawyer's possession in the lawyer's capacity *as attorney* for the client. Hence the lien does *not* apply to documents or other materials received by a lawyer while acting as trustee, escrow holder, director, etc., for the client. [**Brauer v. Hotel Associates, Inc.,** 192 A.2d 831 (N.J. 1963)]

(3) Note—retaining lien on needed files void [§255]

Even if there is a written agreement by which the lawyer has a retaining lien on a client's papers and files as security for the fees, such lien will *not* be upheld as applied to files the client needs to pursue her case. [**People v. Altvater,** 78 Misc. 2d 24 (1974)]

c. Charging (nonpossessory) lien [§256]

In many states, in addition to the retaining lien, a lawyer has, by statute or judicial decision, a "charging lien." This lien gives the lawyer the right to have *any fund or recovery* obtained for the client serve as security for the attorney's fees and disbursements in that matter. For example, a lawyer who prosecutes a contingent fee case to judgment is recognized as having a lien on the judgment for the amount of the contingent fee and expenses. [Restatement §43(2)]

(1) Charging lien created by contract [§257]

In some states, including California, the common law charging lien is *not* recognized. In those states, however, the lawyer and client may, by *express* agreement, create a lien on the client's prospective recovery to secure the attorney's fees and expenses. In general, the express lien is subject to the same rules and limitations as the common law lien.

(2) Advantages over retaining lien [§258]

The charging lien has several advantages over the general retaining lien:

(a) Charging lien is nonpossessory [§259]

This lien applies even though the lawyer does not have possession of any fund. In contrast, the retaining lien reaches only things that come into the lawyer's "possession," and hence would not apply to a judgment rendered by a court.

(b) Enforcement [§260]

The major advantage of the charging lien over the retaining lien is that the charging lien can be *affirmatively enforced.* If the client fails or refuses to pay the agreed fee, the lawyer can file a legal action to foreclose the lien on the client's judgment (or whatever fund or recovery has been obtained).

(3) Limitations on charging liens [§261]

At the same time, the charging lien is subject to limitations:

(a) Limited to fees in particular case [§262]

The lien is limited to the fees and costs incurred by the client in connection with the particular action in which the judgment or settlement is obtained. It does *not* secure other fees owed by the same client on other matters. [Restatement §43(2)(c)]

(b) No lien for fees in defense [§263]

In addition, a lawyer does not have a charging lien on property involved in litigation where the lawyer merely *defeats* a claim against the client. The lien applies only where there is some recovery or affirmative relief.

(4) Time at which charging lien attaches [§264]

Most states permit the lawyer to assert a charging lien against the client's interest only when a judgment or settlement is obtained. However, provided the lawyer gives the defendant *notice* of the contingent fee interest and the lien is held to attach to the *cause of action* (*see supra*, §262), the client may not defeat a charging lien by settling the claim *directly* with the defendant. Furthermore, a number of states have *expanded* the scope of charging liens and permit them to attach at earlier stages in the proceeding, thus preventing the client from settling the case without paying the lawyer.

(a) No right to continue case [§265]

The lien merely assists the lawyer in recovering her fee. Even if the client settles the claim directly with the defendant, the settlement itself is *effective*. Most courts hold that the lawyer has *no right to continue the case to judgment* (in hopes of getting a larger recovery and hence a bigger fee). [Restatement §43(2)(d)]

COMPARISON OF ATTORNEYS' LIENS — gilbert

RETAINING LIEN	CHARGING LIEN
• *Possessory lien*—client property, documents, and funds that come into the lawyer's possession in the lawyer's capacity as attorney for the client	• *Nonpossessory lien*—any fund or recovery obtained for the client in that matter
• *General lien* for the balance the client owes to the lawyer	• *Specific lien* covering only the lawyer's services in the action in which the recovery was obtained
• *Not affirmatively enforceable* in court	• *Can be affirmatively enforced*
• Lien on needed files is *void*	• Can be created *by express agreement* if not recognized by state statute

F. Terminating the Lawyer-Client Relationship

1. Introduction [§266]

The attorney-client relationship typically concludes when a matter is resolved and the lawyer has performed all necessary legal services. However, either the lawyer or the client may also seek to terminate the relationship *before* completion of the matter.

2. Withdrawal by Lawyer [§267]

Once a lawyer undertakes to represent a client, the lawyer may not simply terminate their relationship at will. A lawyer's decision to withdraw should be made only on the basis of "compelling circumstances," and the lawyer should make all "reasonably practicable" efforts to minimize possible adverse effects on the client. [Model Rule 1.16(d); EC 2-32]

a. Duty to withdraw [§268]

Under certain circumstances, the lawyer has an *obligation* to withdraw from employment.

(1) Employment violative of rules of professional conduct [§269]

A lawyer has a duty to withdraw from a representation when she knows (or should know) that continued employment will result in violation of a standard of professional conduct, *e.g.*, where the lawyer would be involved in assisting the client to commit a crime or fraud. [Model Rule 1.16(a)(1); DR 2-110(B)(2); Restatement §32(2)(a)]

(2) Personal inability to continue employment [§270]

Likewise, the lawyer must withdraw if the lawyer's mental or physical condition makes it *"unreasonably* difficult" to provide effective representation. [Model Rule 1.16(a)(2); DR 2-110(B)(3); Restatement §32(2)(b)]

(3) Client's purpose is harassment or malicious prosecution [§271]

The ABA Code provides that a lawyer must withdraw if the lawyer knows or it is obvious that the client wishes to use the lawyer's services merely to harass or maliciously injure another. [DR 2-110(B)(1)]

(4) Discharge by client [§272]

The lawyer must of course withdraw if discharged by the client. [Model Rule 1.16(a)(3); DR 2-110(B)(4); Restatement §32(2)(c); *and see* below]

b. Permissive withdrawal [§273]

Where withdrawal is *not required,* the lawyer is under a general duty to continue the employment to its natural conclusion. However, there are specific exceptions that *permit* a lawyer to withdraw from a matter.

Must the attorney withdraw?

- Employment will violate rules of professional conduct;

- Attorney is physically or mentally unable to continue employment;

- Client's purpose is harassment or malicious prosecution; or

- Client has fired attorney.

YES

NO

May the attorney withdraw?

- There will be no material adverse effect on client;

- Client involves attorney in illegal conduct;

- Client makes repugnant demands on attorney;

- Client fails to pay fee or comply with some other obligation;

- Relationship between attorney and client has become unreasonably difficult;

- Client freely and knowingly consents; or

- There is some other good cause.

YES

Has the attorney done **all** of the following?

- Obtained court permission to withdraw (if pending case);

- Given client sufficient notice;

- Refunded any fees paid in advance; and

- Delivered all papers and property to client.

NO

YES

NO

Attorney
may
withdraw.

Attorney may **not**
withdraw.

(1) No material adverse effect on client [§274]

A lawyer may withdraw, even over the client's objection, if the withdrawal can be accomplished without material adverse effect on the client. It is not clear, however, when there will ever be such a finding if the client strenuously objects to the withdrawal. [Model Rule 1.16(b)(1); Restatement §32(3)(a)]

(2) Client involves lawyer in illegal conduct [§275]

The lawyer may also withdraw if the client has employed, plans to employ, or persists in employing the lawyer in what the lawyer reasonably believes to be criminal or fraudulent conduct. [Model Rule 1.16(b)(2), (3); Restatement §32(3)(d), (e)]

(3) Repugnant demands by client [§276]

A lawyer may withdraw if the client insists on taking action that the lawyer "considers *repugnant* or with which the lawyer has a *fundamental disagreement*." [Model Rule 1.16(b)(4); Restatement §32(3)(f)]

(4) Client fails to fulfill obligation to the lawyer [§277]

The lawyer may withdraw if the client fails to pay the required fee or fails to comply with some other obligation to the lawyer, but the lawyer must give reasonable warning that withdrawal will follow unless the obligation is met. [Model Rule 1.16(b)(5); Restatement §32(3)(g)]

(5) Relationship unreasonably difficult [§278]

A lawyer may withdraw if the client has rendered the obligation "unreasonably difficult" for financial or other reasons (*e.g.,* client will not cooperate with attorney). [Model Rule 1.16(b)(6); DR 2-110(C)(1)(d); Restatement §32(3)(h)]

(6) Consent of client [§279]

A lawyer may withdraw when the client *freely and knowingly consents* to the termination of employment. [DR 2-110(C)(5)]

(7) Other good cause for withdrawal [§280]

Finally, a lawyer may withdraw when other good cause for withdrawal exists. [Model Rule 1.16(b)(6); DR 2-110(C)(6); Restatement §32(3)(i)]

c. General obligations of lawyer in withdrawing from employment [§281]

Whether withdrawal is mandatory or permissive, the lawyer has a duty to *safeguard the rights and interests* of the client. [Restatement §33(1)]

(1) Approval of court in litigation matters [§282]

When a matter is pending before a court or other tribunal, the lawyer may have to obtain *permission from the court* to withdraw. [Model Rule 1.16(c); Restatement §32(5)]

(2) Notice to client [§283]

The lawyer may not withdraw until the client has been given sufficient notice so that other counsel can be retained. [Model Rule 1.16(d); DR 2-110(A)(2)]

(3) Refund of unearned attorney's fees [§284]

Upon withdrawal from employment, the lawyer must *refund* any fees the client paid in advance which the lawyer has not earned. [Model Rule 1.16(d); DR 2-110(A)(3)]

(a) Distinguish—retainer fees [§285]

A true retainer fee is different from a payment of a fee in advance. A true retainer fee is money that is paid solely to ensure the availability of the lawyer, and the lawyer who is fired or withdraws generally need not refund the retainer fee. On the other hand, if a lawyer requires his fee to be paid in *advance*, he *must refund* any unearned part of the advance if he is fired or withdraws.

(4) Delivery of clients' materials [§286]

The lawyer must also promptly return to the client *all papers and property* to which the client is entitled. [Model Rule 1.16(d); DR 2-110(A)(2)]

3. Discharge by Client [§287]

Unlike the limitations on a lawyer's freedom to withdraw from employment, the right of a client to terminate the attorney-client relationship is *virtually unconditional*. Termination may come *at any time, with or without just cause*. [Model Rule 1.16(a)(3); DR 2-110(B)(4); Restatement §32(1)]

a. Provision for "irrevocability" invalid [§288]

It follows that any provision in a retainer agreement that purports to make the lawyer's employment irrevocable is *void*. [**Richette v. Solomon**, 187 A.2d 910 (Pa. 1963)]

b. Judicial refusal to allow discharge in exceptional cases [§289]

In some instances, courts may *refuse* to permit the discharge of a lawyer because it would disrupt a trial. For example, where a client seeks to discharge a lawyer during trial in order to make a "flaming" personal address to the jury, the court may refuse to honor such a request. [**Dennis v. United States**, 183 F.2d 201 (2d Cir. 1950); Restatement §32(5)]

EXAM TIP   **gilbert**

Keep in mind that although the general rule is that a client may fire his lawyer at any time with or without cause, most courts require the court's permission for a substitution of attorneys *after a lawsuit has been filed*. Courts usually grant the necessary permission, but permission may be denied if a substitution of attorneys would cause *undue delay or disruption*. A lawyer must also obtain permission of the court to withdraw from a matter that is pending before the court, but if permission is denied, the lawyer *must continue* the representation even if there is good cause for withdrawal.

c. **Continuing fiduciary duty of lawyer [§290]**
The fact that a lawyer is discharged without cause does *not* relieve the lawyer of fiduciary obligations to the client. As in the case of withdrawal, the lawyer is still prohibited from revealing confidential information or from representing conflicting interests [Restatement §33(2); *see infra* §§299 *et seq.*]

d. **Liability of client under fee contract [§291]**
While the client is free to discharge the lawyer for any reason, the client may still be *contractually* liable in the event the client terminates the relationship *without cause.* [Restatement §40]

(1) **Fixed fee [§292]**
If a fixed fee agreement was involved (a set amount for the particular case or transaction), the lawyer may be entitled to recover on a quantum meruit basis for the work done but may not recover more than the amount set in the agreement.

(2) **Nonrefundable retainer fee ineffective [§293]**
A lawyer may not avoid the consequences of discharge by charging a "non-refundable retainer." Such agreements typically provide that once the lawyer has taken the case, even if the lawyer is later terminated, the client owes the entire fee. Because such agreements limit the right to terminate the lawyer and are likely to constitute an unreasonably excessive fee, they are usually unenforceable and a basis for sanctioning the lawyer. [*In re* **Cooperman,** 83 N.Y.2d 465 (1994)]

(3) **Contingent fee—measure of recovery [§294]**
There is a split of authority as to the proper measure of recovery where the case was being handled on a contingent fee basis.

(a) **Recovery of full contingent share [§295]**
Some courts hold that the discharged lawyer is entitled to the *full share* of any recovery ultimately obtained by the client, particularly if the lawyer was discharged on the eve of the verdict after rendering all services. [**Dombey v. Detroit Toledo & Ironton Railroad,** 351 F.2d 121 (6th Cir. 1965)]

(b) **Recovery of reasonable value of services [§296]**
The more common view is that the contingent fee contract is *not enforceable* where the client discharges the lawyer, because to enforce the contract would significantly deter clients from exercising *their essential right to change lawyers.* These courts permit the discharged lawyer to recover only the *reasonable value of services actually rendered.* [**Fracasse v. Brent,** 6 Cal. 3d 784 (1972); Restatement §40(2)]

(c) Recovery requirement [§297]

Under either approach, however, the lawyer usually gets *nothing* unless and until the client *recovers* on the claim, either by settlement or judgment. [*See* **Plaza Shoe Store v. Hermel,** 636 S.W.2d 53 (Mo. 1982)]

e. Liability of third parties for inducing discharge [§298]

A lawyer is also afforded protection against third parties who induce the client to discharge the lawyer without good cause. In this situation, the lawyer may seek damages from the third person for *interference with contractual relations.* (*See* Torts Summary.)

Chapter Three: Duty to Protect Confidential Information of the Client

CONTENTS

Chapter Approach

A general rule of agency law is that no agent may reveal confidential information of the principal without the principal's consent. This rule is especially important in the practice of law, given the sensitivity of issues with which lawyers often deal and the importance of getting the client to give the lawyer truthful information necessary for effective representation.

This chapter considers the two most important doctrines that govern a lawyer's dealing with confidential client information—the *attorney-client privilege* and the *professional duty of confidentiality*. A third doctrine, work product immunity, is traditionally considered in the course of evidence rather than legal ethics and is not covered in this Summary.

A. Introduction

1. **Two Basic Legal Doctrines [§299]**

   There are two related but quite different doctrines that govern a lawyer's dealing with confidential client information:

   (i) *The attorney-client privilege,* a rule of *evidence* that protects certain information from disclosure by a lawyer *even* in *judicial proceedings.* Such privileged information is sometimes referred to as a client's *"confidences"* [DR4-101(A)]; and

   (ii) *The professional duty of confidentiality,* a rule of *legal ethics* requiring that a lawyer not disclose a much larger body of information that the lawyer learns in the course of the representation. The unprivileged part of this information is sometimes called *"secrets"* of the client [DR 4-101(A)].

EXAM TIP	gilbert

   Note and remember the differences between the attorney-client privilege and the duty of confidentiality. The **attorney-client privilege** applies only to **communications made during the course of the relationship** and covers only the attorney's formal **testimony**. The **duty of confidentiality** protects from **any** disclosure **all information** related to the representation, however and whenever derived.

2. **Focus in Model Rules and in Courts [§300]**

   The *Model Rules* concentrate on the professional duty of confidentiality. However, the *courts* draw a sharp distinction between privileged and unprivileged confidential information even in states that have adopted the Model Rules, because courts *may not* order that *privileged* information be disclosed but *may* order that *unprivileged confidential* information be disclosed. [*See* Model Rule 1.6]

3. Period During Which Duty and Privilege Apply [§301]

Both the privilege and the duty of confidentiality are *not limited* to the time of a lawyer's employment.

a. Before employment [§302]

Confidential information disclosed to a lawyer by a potential client in discussions *preliminary* to any actual employment is protected by the attorney-client privilege *and* the ethical obligation of confidentiality. This is true even if no agreement is reached regarding representation or if the lawyer refuses to take the case (*i.e.,* even if no "client" relationship developed). [Model Rule 1.18(b); EC 4-1; Restatement §§15(1)(a), 70; *and see supra* §§137-140]

(1) Rationale

This encourages potential clients to discuss the facts of their cases freely when they first consult a lawyer without concern that the lawyer may later testify against them or use information so obtained in representing an adversary. Furthermore, it helps the lawyer get all the facts needed to decide whether to take the case. [**Taylor v. Sheldon,** 173 N.E.2d 892 (Ohio 1961)]

(2) May affect right to accept employment from opposing side [§303]

Where preliminary discussions disclose confidential information, the lawyer will thereafter be prevented from representing the opposing side (although the lawyer's firm might not be prevented). [Model Rule 1.18(c); Restatement §15(2); *and see infra,* §461]

b. After employment ceases [§304]

The duty to preserve confidential information also *continues after* the lawyer is no longer employed by the client. [Model Rules 1.6(a); EC 4-6]

c. After client's death [§305]

The attorney-client privilege continues even after the death of the client, except that some courts have allowed privileged information to be revealed to verify to whom the client meant to leave a gift under a will. [**Swidler & Berlin v. United States,** 524 U.S. 399 (1998); Restatement §81]

EXAM TIP   **gilbert**

Sometimes the facts of an exam question will indicate that the representation is over (*e.g.,* the client fired the attorney, the trial is over and there is no appeal, or even that the client died). Or the question may show that the representation never really began (*e.g.,* the client consulted the attorney but never hired her). Don't let these facts lead you astray; remember that the attorney-client privilege and duty of confidentiality *start even before the actual representation begins* and *continue after it is over.*

4. Permitted Disclosures Within Law Firm [§306]

Unless the client specifies otherwise, a lawyer may properly discuss the client's affairs with partners or associates, as this conforms to ordinary law firm procedures in which members usually work together in representing a client. Furthermore, the lawyer may make such disclosures to secretaries, investigators, and other employees of the firm as reasonably required. [Model Rule 1.6(a); EC 4-2; Restatement §61]

a. Disclosure to outside personnel [§307]

The lawyer may even give limited information from her files to persons outside the law firm for *bookkeeping, accounting,* or other legitimate purposes, provided the client does not object. [Model Rule 1.6(a); EC 4-3; Restatement §61]

b. Duty to safeguard in general [§308]

However, the lawyer owes a duty to exercise reasonable care to prevent employees and associates from disclosing confidential information obtained from a client. Specifically, the lawyer is charged with *selecting and training* responsible persons and with *supervising their access* to clients' files. [Model Rules 5.1, 5.3(a); DR 4-101(D); EC 4-2, 4-5; Restatement §60(1)(b)]

B. Attorney-Client Privilege

1. Introduction [§309]

The *legal* privilege against compelled disclosure governs the extent to which a lawyer may be required by legal process to disclose what a client has revealed to the lawyer in confidence. The privilege is based on the need to insure that every person may freely and fully confide in his lawyer so as to be adequately represented. [**Upjohn Co. v. United States,** 449 U.S. 383 (1981)]

2. Subject of the Privilege [§310]

The privilege is discussed in detail in the Evidence Summary. Briefly, however, four basic elements are necessary for the attorney-client privilege to apply:

(i)   There must have been a *communication*;

(ii) The communication must be between someone who was (or wanted to be) a client to an *attorney acting as such at the time;*

(iii) The communications must be made *in confidence* (without strangers present); and

(iv) The communications must be made *for the purpose of obtaining legal assistance.*

[Restatement §68]

a. **Requirement of a communication—the problem of physical evidence [§311]**

The privilege applies only to *"communications"* from the client; *i.e.*, information transmitted orally or in writing from the client to the attorney and from the attorney to the client. It also covers information passed to or from the agents of either the attorney or the client. It does *not* protect incriminating documents or physical evidence turned over to the lawyer by the client, or evidence discovered by the lawyer on his own while investigating the case (*e.g.*, the murder weapon or the stolen property). [**Morrell v. State**, 575 P.2d 1200 (Alaska 1978); Restatement §119; *see infra* §§351, 352]

EXAM TIP   gilbert

Watch for an exam question in which the client turns over to the attorney documents or other evidence relevant to the case. An item does *not* become privileged merely because it was given to an attorney. The privilege extends only to *communications*. Thus, if the item would be discoverable in the client's hands, it is equally discoverable in the attorney's hands.

---

b. **Requirement that communication be made "in confidence" [§312]**

The usual communication between lawyer and client takes place in the lawyer's office with the door closed. If the communication takes place under less than such confidential circumstances, however, the entire privilege may be lost.

(1) **Third party in a position to overhear [§313]**

The presence of a third party may destroy the privilege. If the client's statement is made when it is clearly possible for someone other than the lawyer or lawyer's employee to hear it, the statement is *not* privileged. [**People v. Harris**, 57 N.Y.2d 335 (1982)]

Example: Shortly after being arrested, Harris wanted to talk to a lawyer. The call was placed and a police officer showed Harris to the phone. Another person was already in that room, and before the police officer could leave, Harris told the lawyer, "Oh, my God, I think I've killed [victim]." The court held that this statement was not privileged because it was made in the presence of third parties, whose presence was known to the defendant. [**People v. Harris**, *supra*]

EXAM TIP   gilbert

An exam question in this area will often have a client make a statement in the presence of other people. Check to see exactly who these people are. If they are (i) *agents of the attorney* (e.g., a secretary or law clerk) *or the client* (e.g., an accountant to help explain his books or a minor's parents) or (ii) someone there *to further the attorney-client relationship* (e.g., a translator or investigator), the privilege is *not* lost. But if a conversation occurs in front of friends at a party or even in the middle of the lawyer's crowded waiting room, it is not privileged.

(a) Distinguish—eavesdroppers

In the past, the presence of an unsuspected eavesdropper was sometimes held to destroy the confidentiality of a communication. Under modern evidence law, that is no longer true; an eavesdropper can be prohibited from testifying about a confidential communication.

(2) Waiver by subsequent disclosure [§314]

The privilege may later be lost if the client does not treat the communication as confidential, such as where the client discloses the lawyer's opinion in the course of business negotiations with a third party. [**Jonathan Corp. v. Prime Computers, Inc.**, 114 F.R.D. 693 (E.D. Va. 1987)]

EXAM TIP   **gilbert**

Keep in mind that the attorney-client privilege exists for the benefit of the client, not for the benefit of the lawyer. Therefore, the *client is the "holder" of the privilege* and is the one who can claim or waive the privilege. However, if the client has not waived the privilege, and if someone tries to obtain privileged information when the client is not present, the lawyer must claim the privilege on the client's behalf.

---

3. Special Cases to Which the Privilege Applies

a. Corporation or government as "client" [§315]

The privilege against disclosure of confidential communications extends to *corporate and government* clients as well as to personal clients. [**Radiant Burners v. American Gas Association**, 320 F.2d 314 (7th Cir. 1963); **Upjohn Co. v. United States**, *supra*, §309; Restatement §§73, 74]

(1) Privilege applicable to all legal counsel [§316]

The attorney-client privilege of corporations applies to confidences made both to in-house counsel and to independent attorneys retained by the corporation.

(2) Not available to avoid legitimate discovery [§317]

However, like a personal client, a corporation may not use the attorney-client privilege as a means of avoiding discovery. Thus, where the corporation simply "funnels" papers and files to its lawyers, the privilege does not apply. [**Radiant Burners v. American Gas Association**, *supra*]

(3) No privilege for nonlegal communications [§318]

As with individual clients, the professional relationship necessary to invoke the privilege does not exist when a corporate client seeks *business or personal* advice as opposed to legal assistance. [Restatement §73(3)]

(a) Distinguish—"mixed" communications [§319]

Nevertheless, the privilege is *not* lost simply because relevant nonlegal advice is contained in communications that involve legal advice.

Otherwise, the corporate client would be under an impossible burden in deciding what it could or could not disclose to its lawyers. [**Satcom International Group PLC v. Orbcomm International Partners, L.P.,** 1999 WL 76847 (S.D.N.Y. 1999)]

(4) No individual privilege for personal confidences of corporate or government officials [§320]

The lawyer for a corporation or the government is normally *not* the lawyer for corporate or government officials, even if they think such is the case. Thus, a corporate officer's confession of wrongdoing to the corporate lawyer might be privileged in a case where the *corporation* is the defendant, but *not* where the officer is tried *as an individual*. [*In re* **Lindsey,** 158 F.3d 1263 (D.C. Cir. 1998)—White House counsel talking to President about possible personal criminal liability]

b. Information shared by co-clients or clients with a common interest [§321]

If two or more clients are represented by the same lawyer, or have separate lawyers but a common interest in a matter, they and their lawyers may share the information each provides in the course of preparing their common case without losing the privilege. [**Eisenberg v. Gagnon,** 766 F.2d 770 (3d Cir. 1985); Restatement §§75, 76]

(1) Privileged against third parties [§322]

Any of the clients may assert the privilege against the government or any other third party who attempts to compel disclosure of the communication. [**Hunydee v. United States,** 355 F.2d 183 (9th Cir. 1965)]

(2) Not privileged in later dispute among clients [§323]

However, if the clients later have a falling-out, each may use the disclosure of the others against them in the subsequent litigation. [**Ohio-Sealy Mattress Manufacturing Co. v. Kaplan,** 90 F.R.D. 21 (N.D. Ill. 1980)]

4. Exceptions to the Attorney-Client Privilege

a. Consent by client [§324]

When the client *consents* to the disclosure of confidential information, the privilege no longer protects such information. [Restatement §78(1)]

b. Disclosure of future crime or fraud [§325]

The attorney-client privilege *does not cover* a communication in which the client seeks the services of a lawyer to further the planning or commission of a *future crime or fraud*. [Restatement §82; Cal. Evid. Code §956]

Example: Client asks Lawyer to help her prepare false documents to defraud X. Client's request is not covered by the privilege; both Client and Lawyer could be compelled to testify about the request.

---

(1) Distinguish—past crime or fraud [§326]

The attorney-client privilege *does protect* confidential communications in which the client reveals the *previous* commission of a crime or other unlawful act.

(2) Distinguish—crime or fraud prevented [§327]

If the lawyer tells the client that the planned conduct is illegal and the client abandons the plan, information about the original communication remains privileged. [Restatement §82(a)]

c. Disclosure for lawyer self-protection or to collect a fee [§328]

A lawyer may also reveal sufficient privileged information to defend himself, his associates, or his employees against charges *of negligence or misconduct*, or to collect a fee owed to the lawyer. [**Meyerhofer v. Empire Fire & Marine Insurance Co.**, 497 F.2d 1190 (2d Cir. 1974); Restatement §83]

CHECKLIST OF EXCEPTIONS TO ATTORNEY-CLIENT PRIVILEGE

A COURT *MAY* COMPEL DISCLOSURE OF THE FOLLOWING CLIENT INFORMATION:

☑ In a later dispute among *co-clients*, information that had been shared by them in their common case;

☑ Information for which disclosure is expressly or impliedly *authorized by client* (e.g., by not treating it as confidential);

☑ Information relevant to a *dispute involving attorney fees or the attorney's conduct* (e.g., malpractice case, misconduct charges);

☑ Communication seeking lawyer's help in committing a *future crime or fraud*.

---

5. Responsibilities of Lawyer in Asserting the Attorney-Client Privilege

a. Duty to assert privilege [§329]

A lawyer has a duty "to advise the client of the attorney-client privilege and timely to assert the privilege unless it is waived by the client." [EC 4-4; Restatement §78]

b. Response to wrongful order to disclose [§330]

A court should not require a lawyer to disclose privileged information. To do so would render the privilege meaningless. Nevertheless, sometimes courts do order disclosure of privileged information, and the question arises as to what the lawyer should do.

(1) Resist at all costs [§331]

Some courts hold that an *attorney must refuse to disclose* information believed to be privileged *regardless of the personal consequences.* For example, it has been suggested that a lawyer ordered to testify under threat of a citation for contempt should *go to jail* rather than disclose confidential information without the consent of the client. [Cal. Bus. & Prof. Code §6068(e); **People v. Kor,** 129 Cal. App. 2d 436 (1954)—lawyer should accept punishment and "take his chances on release by a higher court"]

(2) Comply with court order [§332]

However, the ABA seems to impose a *less rigorous duty* upon the lawyer in this situation. Both the ABA Code and Model Rules say that a lawyer *may* reveal the confidences and secrets of a client when "required by . . . *court order.*" [Model Rule 1.6(b)(6); DR 4-101(C)(2)]

(3) Preferred approach [§333]

Where the propriety of the court's disclosure order is questionable, the best solution for the lawyer would seem to be to *assert all nonfrivolous claims on behalf of confidentiality* and then, if the client so directs, respectfully allow himself to be placed in contempt by the trial court so as to get the matter tested on appeal. If the order is sustained on appeal, then the lawyer should disclose it. [*See* Model Rule 1.6, comment 13]

6. Waiver by Disclosure or Failure to Object [§334]

It is important to assert the attorney-client privilege because a failure to do so, or a voluntary disclosure of the privileged information, causes the privilege to be *lost forever.* [Restatement §§78, 79]

a. Subject matter waiver [§335]

Another reason the issue of waiver is so important for lawyers and clients is that waiver of the privilege with respect to one item may be held to be a waiver with respect to *all* items dealing with the *same* subject matter. [*In re* **Sealed Case,** 877 F.2d 976 (D.C. Cir. 1989); Restatement §79, comment f]

b. Inadvertent disclosure [§336]

In discovery, it sometimes happens that a lawyer inadvertently turns over more material than is required, and among the documents is privileged material. If the lawyer has taken reasonable measures to prevent that from happening and seeks to reclaim the material within a short time, courts often excuse the inadvertence and deem the privilege not waived. [Restatement §79, comment h; *compare* Model Rule 4.4(b)—duty to notify opponent of receipt of inadvertently disclosed material]

c. Waiver by putting communication in issue [§337]

Another way to waive the privilege is to assert the fact of the communication by way of claim or defense (*e.g.,* a claim of acting on advice of counsel waives the privileged character of the lawyer's opinion). [Restatement §80]

C. Professional Duty of Confidentiality

1. **Professional Duty of Confidentiality Broader than Attorney-Client Privilege [§338]**
   The description of the professional duty is stated slightly differently in the ABA Code and Model Rules, but in both, the duty of nondisclosure covers considerably more information than is protected by the attorney-client privilege.

PROTECTION OF CLIENT'S INFORMATION		gilbert
SOURCE OF PROTECTION	**SCOPE**	**EXAMPLES**
ATTORNEY-CLIENT PRIVILEGE	• Only *communications* between client and attorney are covered • Must be *confidential* (no third party present) • Protected against *compelled testimony*	Conversation between attorney and client Letters between attorney and client
DUTY OF CONFIDENTIALITY	• *Any information* relating to representation is covered • Protected from *voluntary disclosure* and from *use harmful to client*	Relevant preexisting documents and things (but *not* fruits or instrumentalities of crime) Communication between attorney and client with third party present Information about fees or other mechanical details of attorney-client relationship

   a. **ABA Code [§339]**
   According to the ABA Code, the duty of confidentiality turns on how the lawyer learns the information, the client's wishes, and the likely impact that disclosure could have on the client. The lawyer must *not* disclose information gained in the *professional relationship* that would *embarrass* the client or that the client *requests* be kept confidential. [DR 4-101(A)]

   b. **Model Rules [§340]**
   The Model Rules require a lawyer not to disclose *any* information relating to the representation, no matter from whom learned or under what circumstances. [Model Rule 1.6(a)]

2. **Differences Between Privileged and Confidential Material—Illustrations**

a. **Identity of client [§341]**

In most cases, the identity of a client is *not* itself a "communication" and hence is generally not privileged. However, the fact that the client had consulted a lawyer is "related to the representation" and may be required to be kept confidential.

(1) **Identity privileged where it might incriminate client [§342]**

It has been held that the government may not compel a lawyer to disclose the name of the client on whose behalf the lawyer was acting in paying a large sum of unreported income taxes, because the ability to consult a lawyer would be impaired by such disclosure. The effect of compelling the lawyer to disclose the client's identity would be to *incriminate* the client for nonpayment of the taxes. [**Baird v. Koerner**, 279 F.2d 623 (9th Cir. 1960)]

(2) **Identity confidential where it might endanger client [§343]**

A lawyer reporting information regarding political corruption and graft to an investigating commission should withhold the informant's identity. In such instances, the client's identity is a "secret" and should not be disclosed. [*In re* **Kaplan**, 8 N.Y.2d 214 (1960)]

b. **Whereabouts of client**

(1) **Whereabouts as privileged [§344]**

Absent other circumstances, a lawyer is *privileged* not to disclose a client's address, if supplied by the client in confidence and for the *purpose* of allowing the lawyer to *communicate* with the client. [*Ex parte* **Schneider**, 294 S.W. 736 (Mo. 1927)]

(2) **Whereabouts as confidential [§345]**

Whether or not the client's address is privileged, the lawyer must treat it as confidential if disclosure could harm or embarrass the client.

(3) **Compelled disclosure where violation of court order [§346]**

When a lawyer applies for a court order on behalf of a client, the lawyer impliedly represents to the court that the client will abide by the terms and conditions of the order. Therefore, as an officer of the court, the lawyer *must* advise the court of the client's whereabouts (*i.e.,* there is neither privilege nor confidential information) if the lawyer learns that the *client has violated* the order *and* cannot persuade the client to cease the violation. [**Dike v. Dike**, 448 P.2d 490 (Wash. 1968)—lawyer must disclose address of client who took child away after receiving visitation rights from the court]

c. **Fee arrangements with client**

(1) Generally not privileged [§347]

Information regarding the fees paid or owed by a client to a lawyer is generally *not* protected by the attorney-client privilege. [**United States v. Haddad,** 527 F.2d 537 (6th Cir. 1975)]

(2) Confidentiality applies [§348]

While fee information is generally not legally privileged, it is confidential information "relating to the representation." Thus, a lawyer is *not ethically free to disclose fee arrangements*, without client consent.

d. **Effect of strangers' presence [§349]**

While the attorney-client *privilege does not apply* to communications made in the presence of third parties (and thus not "in confidence"), the professional *duty of confidentiality applies* even to information learned from third parties or where third parties were present.

Example: Information about a client's net worth is disclosed by the client's banker in the presence of a friend of the client. The lawyer is required to treat it as within the professional obligation of confidentiality.

---

e. **No difference as to lawyer self-protection or to collect a fee [§350]**

A lawyer may reveal sufficient confidential information to defend himself, his associates, or his employees against charges of *negligence or misconduct,* or to collect a fee owed to the lawyer. [Model Rule 1.6(b)(5)]

f. **No difference as to physical evidence [§351]**

Neither the attorney-client privilege nor the duty to preserve client secrets requires or permits a lawyer to take possession of or help secrete fruits or instrumentalities of a *crime*.

(1) Duty to turn over to police [§352]

When the lawyer takes possession of physical evidence, he *must* turn it over to the police even if it thereby incriminates the client, although it may be kept long enough to run necessary tests on the evidence. [**State v. Olwell,** 394 P.2d 681 (Wash. 1964); Restatement §119]

(2) Mere information handled differently [§353]

If the lawyer merely knows the whereabouts of physical evidence but has not taken possession of it, the information is protected as a privilege *or* secret. [**People v. Beige,** 83 Misc. 2d 186 (1975)]

3. Prohibition of Use of Confidential Information for Lawyer's Benefit [§354]

It is a standard principle of agency law that an agent must not use confidential information for the agent's own gain, even if that use would not be adverse to the interest of the principal. That rule is applied to lawyers by the ABA Code. [DR 4-101(A)(2)]

a. Model Rules distinction [§355]

The Model Rules retain the prohibition of a lawyer's personal use of confidential client information when it would be *detrimental* to the interest of the client. However, the Model Rules permit the lawyer to use the information for the lawyer's benefit where the use would not adversely affect the client. [Model Rule 1.8(b)]

b. Restatement distinction [§356]

The Restatement acknowledges the Model Rules position but notes that, under agency law, the lawyer would be obliged to turn over to the client any profit made using the client's information. Thus, the Model Rules position applies for purposes of lawyer discipline, but not as a matter of financial liability. [Restatement §60(2)]

4. Exceptions to the Duty of Confidentiality [§357]

Some exceptions to the duty to protect a client's secrets are identical to exceptions to the attorney-client privilege (*e.g.*, client consent, use in fee collection or lawyer's self-defense, and sharing of one co-client's information with another co-client). [Model Rule 1.6(b); Restatement §§62, 64, 65] But there are some significant differences in the scope and character of some exceptions.

a. Court-compelled testimony about secrets [§358]

By definition, a court will not compel a lawyer to disclose information protected by the attorney-client privilege even if it is highly relevant to the resolution of a contested issue in a case. However, relevant information subject to the lawyer's professional duty of confidentiality, but not legally privileged, *may be compelled* to be disclosed in a deposition or at trial. [**Fellerman v. Bradley**, 493 A.2d 1239 (N.J. 1985)]

b. Generally known information [§359]

Because the scope of information required to be protected is otherwise so broad, a lawyer probably does not need to protect information once it has become generally known. [Model Rule 1.9(c); Restatement §59]

c. Securing advice about compliance with professional standards [§360]

Under the 2002 amendments to Rule 1.6, a lawyer may now reveal confidential client information to another lawyer in an effort to get advice about the first lawyer's professional duties. [Model Rule 1.6(b)(4)]

d. Revelation of future crime or fraud [§361]

While information about a client's plans to commit a future crime or fraud is not privileged, and testimony about it could be compelled, the information is rarely known by a third party who could compel such testimony. Instead, the practical question is whether or when a lawyer may come forward to warn potential victims about the client's plans.

(1) ABA Code—intention of client to commit a crime [§362]

The ABA Code *permits* (but does not require) a lawyer to reveal the intention of the client to commit *any* crime (*e.g.*, shoplifting) and the information necessary to prevent that crime. [DR 4-101(C)(3)]

(2) Model Rules—to prevent reasonably certain death or substantial bodily harm [§363]

The Model Rules *permit less* disclosure of crimes. Only if the proposed criminal act threatens someone with *reasonably certain death or substantial bodily harm* may the lawyer reveal the client's intention to commit it. [Model Rule 1.6(b)(1); Restatement §66]

(a) But note

Unlike the standard prior to the 2002 amendments to the Model Rules, the lawyer may reveal the act even if the client is not the one likely to commit it, even if the likely death or injury is not "imminent," and whether or not the act is a crime.

---

e.g. **Example:** A lawyer learns that the client's brother's business has polluted the local water supply in a way that will cause the premature death of 50 people over the next 10 years. The lawyer's client does not want to expose his brother's act. Even though the offender was not the client and the deaths may not occur soon, the lawyer may disclose the increased risk.

---

(3) Model Rules—to prevent substantial financial injury [§364]

A 2003 amendment to the Model Rules allows a lawyer to reveal client information to prevent, mitigate, or rectify *substantial* financial injury *reasonably certain* to result from a client's past or future crime or fraud *using the lawyer's* services. This amendment brings the Model Rules in line with Restatement section 67 and the law in a majority of states. The circumstances under which these disclosures may be made are narrow. The client must have used the lawyer's services in committing the crime or fraud, and the threatened injury must be (i) *substantial* and (ii) *reasonably certain*. But the lawyer no longer must always be silent while a client perpetrates a financial fraud. [Model Rule 1.6(b)(2), (3)]

(4) Model Rules—possible mandatory disclosure under Rule 4.1(b) [§365]

A possible stealth effect of the 2003 amendment to Rule 1.6 could transform the discretionary character of disclosure under Rule 1.6(b)(2) and (b)(3) into *mandatory disclosure* under Model Rule 4.1(b) in cases where the attorney is unable to withdraw or otherwise avoid assisting an illegal act. The latter rule requires disclosure of material facts "necessary to avoid assisting a criminal or fraudulent act by a client, unless disclosure is prohibited by Rule 1.6." Insofar as Rule 1.6(b)(2) and (b)(3) no longer prohibits disclosure, the mandatory character of Rule 4.1(b) seems to apply with full force. [Model Rule 4.1(b)]

CHECKLIST OF EXCEPTIONS TO THE DUTY OF CONFIDENTIALITY — gilbert

A LAWYER *MAY* REVEAL THE FOLLOWING CLIENT INFORMATION:

☑ Information for which disclosure is expressly or impliedly *authorized by client*;

☑ Information relevant to a *dispute involving attorney fees or the attorney's conduct* (e.g., malpractice case, misconduct charges);

☑ Information *compelled by court* or other governmental tribunal;

☑ Some *generally known* information;

☑ Information necessary for the lawyer *to obtain legal ethics advice*;

☑ Information necessary to prevent *reasonably certain death or substantial bodily harm*;

☑ Information revealing intent to commit future *crime or fraud reasonably certain to result in substantial financial harm if lawyer's services used* (or to prevent, mitigate, or rectify financial harm if client has *already* acted).

Chapter Four: Duty of Unimpaired Loyalty—Conflicts of Interest

---

CONTENTS

Chapter Approach

In addition to duties such as competence, communication, and confidentiality, a lawyer owes a client a duty of unimpaired loyalty. Thus, the lawyer may not represent a client when the lawyer has a conflict of interest, unless the client gives informed consent.

The four major kinds of conflicts of interest discussed in this chapter are:

1. Conflicts between the *lawyer's personal interest and the interest of the client (e.g.,* the lawyer wishes to enter into business transactions with the client, receive a gift from the client, etc.).

2. Conflicts between the interests of *two or more clients that the lawyer is concurrently representing.* This is especially a problem in litigation matters but can also arise in nonlitigation situations.

3. Conflicts between the *client's interest and that of a third party to whom the lawyer owes obligations.* Here you should watch out for facts showing a third party paying the lawyer's fee, *e.g.,* a lawyer for the insurer representing the insured.

4. Conflicts between the *lawyer's duties to a present client and the lawyer's continuing duties to a former client.*

Also keep in mind that when a lawyer is disqualified due to a conflict of interest, it is likely that others associated with the lawyer will also be disqualified.

A. Introduction

1. **Basic Standard for Identifying a Conflict of Interest [§366]**
   Both the ABA Code and Model Rules provide overall standards for determining when a lawyer has a conflict of interest. The four specific kinds of conflicts discussed in this chapter are derived from these basic principles.

   a. **ABA Code—adverse effect on lawyer's independent professional judgment [§367]**
      The key principle underlying the ABA Code's approach to conflicts of interest is that what a lawyer offers to any client is *professional judgment*. A client can get appropriate representation only if the lawyer's judgment is *independent* of the lawyer's other responsibilities or interests. [DR 5-101(A); DR 5-105(A), (B)]

   b. **Model Rules—material limitation on lawyer's representation of client [§368]**
      The Model Rules make the same point in a different way. They state the rule against conflict of interest as a prohibition of a lawyer's representing one client when the representation will be *materially limited* by the lawyer's other interests

or responsibilities. One such conflict arises when a representation would be *directly adverse* to another of the lawyer's clients. [Model Rule 1.7(a); *and see* Restatement §121]

2. **Representation in Spite of a Conflict—Informed Consent [§369]**

Under either statement of the rule, a lawyer *may* represent a client *in spite of a conflict* only if:

(i) The conflict is *consentable*—*i.e.*, it is objectively possible to represent the client effectively; and

(ii) The client gives *informed consent* (*i.e.*, with *adequate information* about the *material risks* of, and *available alternatives* to, such representation), confirmed in writing (*i.e.*, at least recorded in writing by the lawyer and sent to the client). [Model Rule 1.7(b), 1.0(e)—definition of informed consent; DR 5-105(A), (C); Restatement §122; *and see infra*, §404]

a. **Decision of client final and binding [§370]**

In analyzing the interests of two or more clients (in either a litigation or nonlitigation matter), the lawyer may conclude that she could effectively represent all interests. Even so, the lawyer should disclose and discuss multiple representation with the clients. If a client decides (for whatever reason) that the arrangement is undesirable, the lawyer must defer to that opinion and withdraw, despite the lawyer's own belief that the representation could be handled properly. [EC 5-19]

3. **Consequences of Failing to Deal Properly with a Conflict of Interest**

a. **Discipline [§371]**

If the lawyer does not obtain consent, or if disclosure to the clients was less than candid, the lawyer is subject to discipline. [Model Rule 1.7; DR 5-105; Cal. Rule 3-310]

b. **Malpractice liability [§372]**

In addition, a lawyer who undertakes multiple representation without making full disclosure runs a risk of civil liability to a client who suffers a loss caused by such lack of disclosure. [**Crest Investment Trust, Inc. v. Comstock**, 327 A.2d 891 (Md. 1974)]

c. **Fee forfeiture [§373]**

Furthermore, courts are increasingly forcing lawyers to forfeit their fees for work done despite a conflict of interest, even in the absence of actual damage suffered by the clients. [Restatement §37; **Hendry v. Pelland**, 73 F.3d 397 (D.C. Cir. 1996); *and see infra*, §§919, 920]

B. Personal Interests that May Affect Lawyer's Judgment

1. **Introduction [§374]**

Whether the interest predates the representation or arises later, a lawyer must not allow a personal interest to detract from the lawyer's duty of loyalty to the client. [Model Rule 1.7(b); DR 5-101(A); Restatement §125] Some of the interests that may affect a lawyer's judgment are discussed below.

2. **Financial Interest Adverse to Client [§375]**

The most basic kind of personal interest conflict arises when the lawyer would profit if the client does not prevail. For example, this can occur if the lawyer owns a significant financial interest in the party opposing the client. Thus, it is improper for a lawyer to purchase or otherwise knowingly have a property or financial interest adverse to the client, unless the client expressly consents after full disclosure. [Model Rule 1.7(a)(2); DR 5-101(A); Restatement §125]

3. **Prohibition on Acquiring Interest in Subject Matter of Employment [§376]**

A slightly different problem is presented when the lawyer has or acquires an interest in the claim or property that is the subject matter of litigation being conducted for the client. Thus, a lawyer conducting patent litigation for a client may not become part owner of the patent. [Model Rule 1.8(i); DR 5-103(A); Restatement §125]

   a. **Rationale**

   It is sometimes said that this prohibition is to eliminate the lawyer's incentive to stir up litigation. A better rationale is that if the lawyer is personally interested in the litigation, the lawyer might be tempted to give less weight to the client's judgment of an acceptable settlement.

   b. **Exception—security for fees [§377]**

   Both the ABA Code and Model Rules specifically recognize that a lawyer may acquire a financial interest in the subject of litigation to *secure fees and costs*; *e.g.*, the lawyer may charge a contingent fee and may enforce an attorney's lien (*see supra*, §§220-234).

4. **Publication Rights Concerning Subject Matter of Employment [§378]**

Prior to the conclusion of all aspects of a case, a lawyer generally may not acquire publication rights from the client as to the subject matter of the lawyer's employment. [Model Rule 1.8(d); DR 5-104(B); Restatement §36(3)] This prohibition is based on the possibility that the ownership of such rights might have an adverse effect on the lawyer's exercise of independent professional judgment. For example, great media interest in a sensational case might influence the lawyer, consciously or unconsciously, to conduct the case in a manner that would enhance the value of the publication rights but prejudice the client's position. [EC 5-4]

---

e.g. **Example:** In a notorious California criminal case, an attorney and his client entered into a fee agreement that provided that, in return for his legal services, the attorney was granted the exclusive literary and dramatic rights to the client's life story, including the account of the trial. The court held that the attorney's financial stake in the literary contract motivated him to take a position adverse to his client and created a prejudicial conflict of interests. [**People v. Corona,** 80 Cal. App. 3d 684 (1978)]

---

cf. **Compare:** In another California case involving a similar fee agreement, although the defendant was willing to waive the potential conflict of interests, the trial judge disqualified his attorneys. The California Supreme Court found that the defendant had competently and knowingly waived the conflict and that the disqualification denied the defendant his right to counsel of his choice. The supreme court granted the defendant's petition for a writ of mandate and directed the trial court to reinstate the defense attorneys. [**Maxwell v. Superior Court,** 30 Cal. 3d 606 (1982)]

---

5. **Business or Financial Transactions with Client [§379]**

When a lawyer enters into a business transaction with a client, the law fears that the lawyer may breach the fiduciary duty to avoid *overreaching or undue influence.* Thus, *e.g.,* where the lawyer invests in the client's business, the courts examine such transactions with great care. [Model Rule 1.8(a); DR 5-104(A); Restatement §126; **Committee on Professional Ethics v. Mershon,** 316 N.W.2d 895 (Iowa 1982)]

   a. **Presumption of undue influence [§380]**

   Even apart from the ethics rules, courts generally hold that a lawyer who enters into a business transaction with a client must overcome a presumption of overreaching or undue influence by *affirmative evidence* to the contrary. Failure to present such evidence is grounds for *setting aside the transaction,* regardless of the legal sufficiency of the consideration. [**Benson v. State Bar,** 13 Cal. 3d 581 (1975)]

   b. **ABA Code standard [§381]**

   The ABA Code flatly states that a lawyer may not, absent client consent following full disclosure, enter into a business transaction with a client in which their interests *differ,* if the client expects the lawyer to protect the client's interest. [DR 5-104(A)]

   c. **Model Rules approach [§382]**

   The Model Rules define specific circumstances that must exist to permit any business transaction between lawyer and client, other than a standard commercial transaction, *e.g.,* one in which the lawyer buys a dinner at the client's restaurant. The Model Rules requirements are:

   (i) *The terms must be fair and reasonable* and have been *transmitted in writing* to the client in an *understandable* form;

   (ii) *The client must be advised in writing* that it would be desirable to *get independent counsel* and given reasonable opportunity to do so; and

   (iii) *The client must consent in writing* to the terms of the transaction and the lawyer's role in it, including whether the client expects the lawyer to protect the client's interest.

[Model Rule 1.8(a); Cal. Rule 3-300; Restatement §126; *and see* **In re Brown,** 559 P.2d 884 (Or. 1977)]

d. Related issue [§383]

Likewise, a lawyer *may not purchase property* (directly or through any intermediary) at a probate, foreclosure, or judicial sale in an action in which the lawyer or any member of her law firm appears as attorney for a party, or in which the lawyer is acting as executor, trustee, etc. Again, the potential for overreaching disqualifies the lawyer as a purchaser. [*See* Cal. Rule 4-300]

6. Gifts or Bequests to Lawyer [§384]

A related issue of undue influence or overreaching is raised when a lawyer or his relative receives a gift or bequest from a client. In this situation, "relative" includes a spouse, child, parent, grandparent, grandchild, and other persons with whom the lawyer has a close, familial relationship. [Model Rule 1.8(c)]

a. No solicitation of gift [§385]

It is improper under *any* circumstances for a lawyer to *ask* that any *substantial* gift be made to the lawyer or for the lawyer's benefit. [Model Rule 1.8(c); EC 5-5]

---

e.g. Example: Lawyer is a loyal alumnus of Port Arthur School of Law. The school asked Lawyer to serve as a pro bono legal advisor to a committee that was drafting a new affirmative action policy for the school. Lawyer gladly agreed and worked many hours on the project for no fee. When the work was done, Lawyer told the school's dean that his daughter would love to attend the school, but that she could not afford the high tuition. The dean then arranged for Lawyer's daughter to be admitted on a full scholarship. Lawyer is subject to discipline for soliciting a substantial gift from the school to his daughter.

---

b. Requirement before accepting a gift [§386]

Even where the client voluntarily offers to make a substantial gift to the lawyer or someone related to the lawyer, the lawyer should have the client obtain the *disinterested advice of a competent third person.* [EC 5-5] However, a lawyer may accept a small gift from a client (*e.g.,* an appropriate wedding present or a small token of appreciation). [Model Rule 1.8, comment 6]

c. Beneficiary under an instrument [§387]

A lawyer must insist that *any instrument* (typically a will) giving the lawyer a substantial gift be prepared by a different lawyer. [Model Rule 1.8(c); Restatement §127; **State v. Horan,** 123 N.W.2d 488 (Wis. 1963)]

(1) Presumption of undue influence [§388]

Apart from the ethical issue, a probate court may presume undue influence if a gift under a will is made to the lawyer who drafted the will; *i.e.,* the lawyer may not be entitled to receive the gift unless she can produce *independent evidence* showing that the testator chose to make the gift freely and independently. (*See* Wills Summary.)

(2) Exception—drafting wills for personal friends or relatives [§389]

Most courts *do* permit a lawyer to prepare wills for the lawyer's family, friends, or relatives even though the will names the lawyer (or members of the lawyer's family) a beneficiary, *provided* that there is no hint of over-reaching and that the bequest is reasonable under the circumstances. [*See* Model Rule 1.8(c); Restatement §127(2)(a); **State v. Collentine**, 159 N.W.2d 50 (Wis. 1968)]

d. Executor, trustee, counsel [§390]

Along the same lines, a lawyer should not knowingly influence a client to name her executor, trustee, or counsel in an instrument, although the lawyer is not prohibited from so acting if the client asks and the lawyer's actions are not tainted by self-interest. [Model Rule 1.8(c), 1.7; EC 5-6; **State v. Gulbankian**, 196 N.W.2d 733 (Wis. 1972)]

EXAM TIP	gilbert

Sometimes an exam question will present a longtime client who wants to leave the lawyer something in her will in appreciation of assistance over the years, or a client who wants to name the lawyer executor because she trusts the lawyer to handle the estate. Remember that *neither* the gift nor the appointment *is automatically prohibited*, but that the lawyer should advise the client to hire an *independent attorney* (not the lawyer's partner) to draft the will. If the client refuses to seek independent counsel, you need to analyze the facts to determine whether there is an ethical problem. Facts such as the client having had a long and ongoing relationship with the lawyer, having been a friend or family member, or the reasonableness of the gift or appointment, all tend to show there was not over-reaching by the lawyer. But circumstances such as a large gift to the lawyer, the lawyer suggesting the gift, etc., point to a conflict of interest situation. (And remember, in addition to the ethics rules, probate law may provide for a rebuttable presumption of undue influence in these cases.)

---

7. Negotiating Employment with Opposing Firm [§391]

A problem of increasing importance can arise when a lawyer seeks to take a job with another firm but is currently representing a client in a matter in which that firm has a client on the other side. The issue has not yet become the subject of a specific Model Rule Provision.

a. Recommended action [§392]

The Restatement says that when the discussions have become *concrete* and the interest in the move is *mutual*, the lawyer must tell the client about the situation and seek *informed consent* to continue the representation. In the absence of such disclosure, the lawyer must *end the employment discussions* until the matter is over. [Restatement §125, comment d; ABA Opn. 96-400 (1996); **Kala v. Aluminum Smelting & Refining Co.**, 688 N.E. 2d 258 (Ohio 1998); *compare* Model Rule 1.12(b)—procedures under which judge's law clerk may negotiate for employment]

b. Law firm mergers [§393]

The same requirements and procedures should apply where law firm merger discussions have reached the concrete and mutual stage. [Restatement §125, comment d; **Stanley v. Richmond**, 35 Cal. App. 4th 1070 (1995)]

C. Concurrent Representation of Clients with Conflicting Interests

1. Introduction [§394]

The lawyer's obligation to exercise independent professional judgment on behalf of *each* client can be severely tested where the interests of more than one client are involved in a given matter. Problems arise whenever a lawyer seeks to represent *two or more* clients with *differing* interests in an outcome, whether the interests are "conflicting, inconsistent, diverse, or otherwise discordant." [EC 5-14]

2. General Standards [§395]

What Model Rule 1.7 calls a *"concurrent conflict of interest"* exists in three basic situations:

a. Directly adverse representation in the same case [§396]

This is the unusual situation in which the lawyer finds herself representing both the plaintiff and defendant in the same case. More often, it might arise when one defendant represented by the lawyer becomes a third-party plaintiff suing another of the defendants the lawyer represents in the matter. Typically, any relief the lawyer gets for one of the clients would be at the expense of the other.

b. Directly adverse representation in unrelated cases [§397]

This more common situation arises when the client the lawyer is representing in the current matter opposes a client the lawyer represents in some other, wholly unrelated matter. Again, the benefit to one client will be at the other's expense, but, at least within the particular matter, the other client will presumably be represented by counsel not similarly burdened by a conflict.

c. Representation materially limited by obligations to another client [§398]

Cases falling under this standard do not involve matters in which the two clients are opposing parties, but rather the result reached on behalf of Client A will have a significant impact on Client B that might limit the lawyer's willingness to pursue the interest of Client A fully and effectively.

3. Lawyer's Obligation in Such Situations [§399]

When any of the above three situations arise, the lawyer must *decline* or *withdraw*

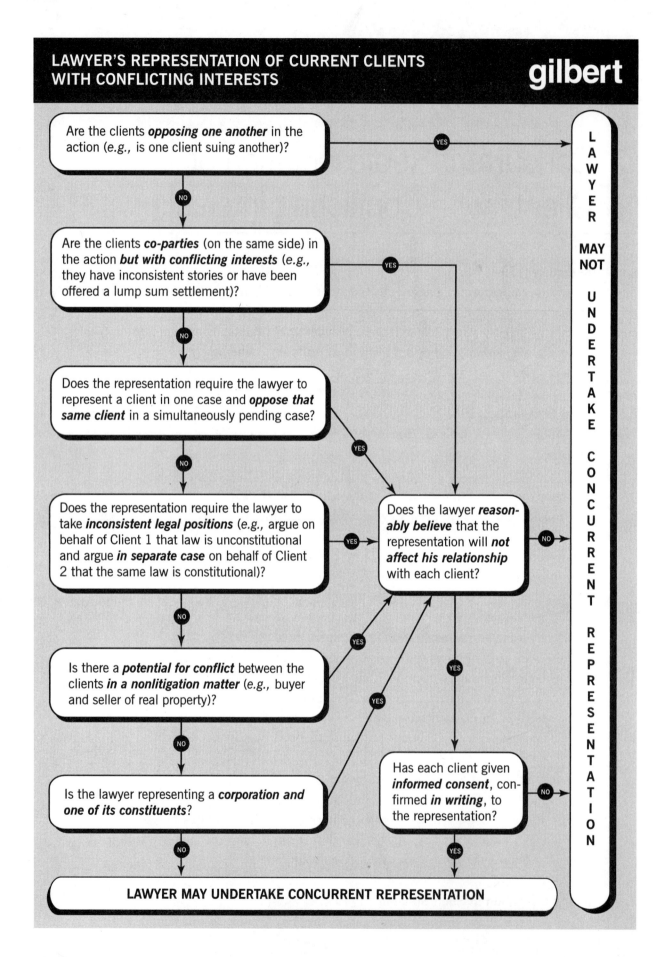

LAWYER'S REPRESENTATION OF CURRENT CLIENTS WITH CONFLICTING INTERESTS

gilbert

Are the clients *opposing one another* in the action (*e.g.,* is one client suing another)?

YES →

Are the clients *co-parties* (on the same side) in the action *but with conflicting interests* (*e.g.,* they have inconsistent stories or have been offered a lump sum settlement)?

YES →

Does the representation require the lawyer to represent a client in one case and *oppose that same client* in a simultaneously pending case?

YES →

Does the representation require the lawyer to take *inconsistent legal positions* (*e.g.,* argue on behalf of Client 1 that law is unconstitutional and argue *in separate case* on behalf of Client 2 that the same law is constitutional)?

YES →

Does the lawyer *reasonably believe* that the representation will *not affect his relationship* with each client?

NO →

Is there a *potential for conflict* between the clients *in a nonlitigation matter* (*e.g.,* buyer and seller of real property)?

YES

Is the lawyer representing a *corporation and one of its constituents*?

YES

Has each client given *informed consent*, confirmed *in writing*, to the representation?

NO →

LAWYER MAY NOT UNDERTAKE CONCURRENT REPRESENTATION

LAWYER MAY UNDERTAKE CONCURRENT REPRESENTATION

from the representation(s), unless informed consent of each affected client is possible and obtained. [Model Rule 1.7; DR 5-105]

a. Nonconsentable conflicts [§400]

Although the client's informed consent can waive many conflicts of interest, there are some conflicts that cannot be waived:

(1) Representing opposing parties in same litigation [§401]

Cases like that in §396 above, in which the lawyer represents both sides in the same case, are deemed not subject to client consent, even if informed clients want to give that consent. In part, this is because a lawyer on both sides of a case would confuse the court and jury, regardless of the clients' preferences. [Model Rule 1.7(b)(3); Restatement §122(2)(b)]

(2) Inability to give adequate representation to each client [§402]

A second kind of conflict not subject to consent conflict arises when a reasonable lawyer would conclude that *competent and diligent representation* could *not* be afforded each client. Such a situation might exist, *e.g.,* if the lawyer's clients are bidding against each other for the same piece of property and the lawyer cannot benefit one client other than at the expense of the other. [Model Rule 1.7(b)(1); Restatement §122(2)(c)]

(3) Representation prohibited by law [§403]

In a few circumstances (*e.g.*, some cases involving government entity clients), state law renders the conflict not waiveable by client consent. [Model Rule 1.7(b)(2); Restatement §122(2)(a)]

b. Obtaining informed client consent [§404]

In the great majority of cases, however, a lawyer faced with a conflict of interest may proceed after obtaining *informed consent* from each affected client, *confirmed in writing*. Informed consent requires that the lawyer have communicated "adequate information and explanation about the material risks of and reasonably available alternatives to the proposed course of conduct." [Model Rule 1.7(b)(4), 1.0(e); DR 5-105(C); Restatement §122(1)]

EXAM TIP | **gilbert**

Always keep in mind that "informed" consent means just that—that the client has been given *sufficient information* about the risks and the alternatives to make her decision. If the lawyer has not given the client important information, the consent is *invalid*.

---

4. Application of Standards to Common Situations—Litigation Matters [§405]

The likelihood of impaired judgment and prejudice to the client is greatest when the lawyer seeks to represent several clients in the same litigation.

a.   **Criminal proceedings—constitutional considerations [§406]**
The problem of differing interests frequently arises when a lawyer is appointed to represent several indigent defendants in the same criminal proceeding. If the defendants' interests are in fact divergent, there is more than an ethical problem. Each accused is *constitutionally* entitled to the assistance of his own counsel, and it is the *duty of the court* to appoint separate counsel whenever differing interests appear. [**Holloway v. Arkansas**, 435 U.S. 475 (1978); **Cuyler v. Sullivan**, 446 U.S. 335 (1980); Restatement §129]

(1) **Accusations by one client against another [§407]**
If one defendant accuses a co-defendant of the crime, their interests are clearly adverse, and representation of both by the same appointed counsel is unconstitutional. This is true regardless of whether the accusing defendant denies guilt or admits it. [**White v. United States**, 396 F.2d 822 (5th Cir. 1968); **Commonwealth v. Westbrook**, 400 A.2d 160 (Pa. 1979)]

(2) **Differences in strength of case [§408]**
Common representation may also be unconstitutional where the defenses available to one client defendant are *stronger* than those available to the others. The defendant with the stronger case may be prejudiced by failure of the shared lawyer to establish or emphasize relevant defenses, and vice versa. [**Campbell v. United States**, 352 F.2d 359 (D.C. Cir. 1965)]

(3) **Privately retained counsel [§409]**
If the two defendants are not indigent and have jointly retained *private* counsel, it is their shared counsel's duty to advise them of any potential conflict of interest. On appeal, the test of their joint counsel's representation will be whether it amounted to actual prejudice. [**People v. Cook**, 13 Cal. 3d 663 (1975); *but see* **Aetna Casualty & Surety Co. v. United States**, 438 F. Supp. 886 (W.D.N.C. 1977)]

b.   **Personal injury litigation [§410]**
Several persons injured in the same mishap may seek to retain a single lawyer to represent them in jointly litigating their respective claims. Such claimants may have potentially differing interests which could make multiple representation improper, absent informed consent. [EC 5-17; Restatement §128]

(1) **Plaintiff and cross-defendant [§411]**
If one of several plaintiffs is *also* named as a cross-defendant (*e.g.*, plaintiffs A and B sue D; D cross-complains against A claiming that A was jointly liable in causing injury to B), a lawyer *cannot* represent the co-plaintiffs, even with client consent. The lawyer would in effect be representing both sides in an adversary action, where interests must necessarily differ. [**Jedwabny v. Philadelphia Transportation Co.**, 135 A.2d 252 (Pa. 1957); *and see supra*, §401]

(2) Driver and passenger [§412]

Similarly, it may be improper for a lawyer to represent *both driver and passenger* in a negligence action against a common defendant, at least if the passenger contends that the accident resulted from the concurrent negligence of the driver and the defendant. If the lawyer contests the driver's contributory negligence, he will prejudice the interest of the passenger. [**DuPont v. Southern Pacific Co.,** 366 F.2d 193 (5th Cir. 1966)]

Example: In **DuPont v. Southern Pacific Co.,** *supra,* the trial court ordered that lead counsel represent all plaintiffs, the survivors of the driver of a car and the survivors of the passengers, in a wrongful death action against a railroad company. The survivors of the passengers contended that the concurrent negligence of the driver of the car and the operators of the defendant's train caused the accident. The survivors of the driver claimed that only the railroad was negligent, since contributory negligence would bar their action. On appeal, the court found that there was a conflict of interest, because the plaintiffs' lawyer could not contest the driver's contributory negligence without prejudicing the interests of the survivors of the passengers.

---

c. Divorce proceedings [§413]

If a state's divorce proceedings require a judicial hearing in which the spouses will be designated as opposing parties in litigation, the conflict is obvious and nonconsentable.

(1) No fault dissolution [§414]

Even where such proceedings are no longer adversary in nature (*e.g.,* the California dissolution proceeding, which eliminates any determination of fault), potentially differing interests over subjects like *property and child custody* make separate representation essential in most cases.

(2) Distinguish—prelitigation matters [§415]

However, a lawyer sometimes may *counsel* spouses who are contemplating a separation or dissolution as to their mutual rights and obligations, but only after *full disclosure* of the conflicting interests and with the *informed consent* of both spouses.

(3) Document preparation [§416]

Again, if informed consent is obtained, a lawyer ordinarily may prepare a written agreement providing for division of property, support, and child custody, which the parties acting *pro se* can then submit to the court in an *uncontested* proceeding. [**Klemm v. Superior Court,** 75 Cal. App. 3d 893 (1977)]

d. Liquidation and reorganization proceedings [§417]

Regardless of whether individual bankruptcies or major corporate receiverships are involved, liquidation and reorganization proceedings usually involve diverse and conflicting interests which make only some multiple representations proper.

(1) Basic categories of parties [§418]

There are usually three main classes of parties to such proceedings: *creditors, stockholders, and management groups,* each with its own particular interests. And within each class there may also exist various subclasses whose interests are similarly divergent (*e.g.,* secured and unsecured creditors, preferred and common stockholders).

(2) Joint representation strictly scrutinized [§419]

Courts have insisted upon the unimpaired loyalty of lawyers who represent parties to such proceedings. Sometimes a lawyer may be permitted to represent several small claimants in a given group simply because none could afford to hire a lawyer otherwise, but a lawyer for "junior" claimants (*e.g.,* general creditors or common stockholders) may *not* also represent "senior" claimants (*e.g.,* bondholders or preferred stockholders). [**Woods v. City National Bank,** 312 U.S. 262 (1941)]

e. Representing opposing clients in unrelated matters [§420]

The prohibition on representing opposing sides in adversary proceedings applies even where the adversary proceedings are unrelated. Absent both clients' informed consent, a lawyer employed by a client to provide legal services in a lawsuit may *not* simultaneously agree to represent another party in a different lawsuit against that same client. [Restatement §128(2); **Grievance Committee v. Rottner,** 203 A.2d 82 (Conn. 1964)]

---

e.g. **Example:** In *Rottner, supra,* the court held that it was a breach of loyalty for a law firm that was representing a client in a collection matter to institute an unrelated personal injury suit against that client on behalf of another client.

---

(1) Avoiding appearance of divided loyalty [§421]

No actual conflict of interest is necessary. The prohibition is designed to maintain *public confidence in the bar* by assuring existing clients that they will have the *undivided loyalty* of their lawyers throughout the duration of employment. [**Jeffrey v. Pounds,** 67 Cal. App. 3d 6 (1977)]

(2) Application to members of a corporate family [§422]

A lawyer prohibited from filing suit against a client may also be prohibited from maintaining an action against a parent, subsidiary, or sibling corporation of that client. The ABA has said that kinds of corporate family relationships are too varied to state a bright-line rule forbidding such suits. The lawyer must ask whether: (i) the corporations are in effect *one entity*; (ii) the lawyer has agreed to treat the corporate family as a *single client*; or (iii) the lawyer's obligations to one of the entities will *impair* pursuit of the claim against the other. [Model Rule 1.7, comment 34; ABA Opn. 95-390]

f. Representing two clients with inconsistent legal positions in two unrelated cases [§423]

Absent informed, written consent from both clients, a lawyer must not represent two clients in separate, unrelated matters when they have inconsistent legal positions if there is a substantial risk that the representation of one client will be materially limited by the lawyer's responsibilities to the other client.

(e.g.) **Example:** Lawyer represents two clients in different cases that are pending in different tribunals. On behalf of Client One, Lawyer needs to argue that a certain statute is unconstitutional. On behalf of Client Two, Lawyer needs to argue that the same statute is constitutional. Aside from that legal issue, the cases are unrelated. However, Client One's case will be heard next week in the intermediate appellate court that hears cases from Judicial District Six. Client Two's case will be tried seven months from now in a trial court in Judicial District Six. Thus, the appellate court's decision in Client One's case is likely to become the controlling precedent in Client Two's case. This presents a substantial risk that Lawyer's representation of one client will be materially limited by her responsibilities to the other client. Therefore, Lawyer must fully disclose the situation to both clients and seek their informed, written consent. If either or both clients will not consent, Lawyer must seek the court's permission to withdraw from one or both cases. [*See* Model Rule 1.7, comment 24]

---

g. Lump sum settlement for several clients [§424]

A lawyer who, with informed consent, represents more than one client in litigation may face divergent interests when a lump sum settlement is offered by the other side. Here, again, the lawyer must carefully preserve independent judgment and loyalty to *each* client.

(1) Consent of each client after full disclosure [§425]

To prevent conflicting interests, *each client must consent* to the aggregate settlement after being advised of: (i) the *existence and nature of all claims* involved in the proposed settlement, (ii) the *total amount* of the settlement, and (iii) the *participation of each person* in the settlement. [Model Rule 1.8(g); DR 5-106; Restatement §128]

(a) Distinguish—unnamed members of a class [§426]

However, in class action litigation, the unnamed members of a class ordinarily are *not* regarded as clients for conflict of interest purposes.

(2) Application to criminal defendants [§427]

The Model Rules extend the requirement of informed consent to situations where a lawyer represents multiple criminal defendants considering nolo contendere or guilty pleas that might have an impact on the other defendants. [Model Rule 1.8(g)]

5. Application of Standards to Common Situations—Nonlitigation Matters

a. Real estate transactions [§428]

A lawyer for the seller of real property may not also represent the buyer in closing title without the informed consent of both clients. Indeed, some major real estate deals may be so contentious and complex that the conflict may not be consentable at all. [**Baldasarre v. Butler,** 625 A.2d 458 (N.J. 1993)]

b. Borrower and lender [§429]

The same problems may arise where a lawyer purports to represent both borrower and lender on a mortgage or other security. Again, such representation is improper without full disclosure to both sides of the potential conflicts and the parties' informed consent. [*In re* **Greenberg,** 121 A.2d 520 (N.J. 1956)]

c. Testator and fiduciary [§430]

Provided the testator fully understands the relationship and its implications (*e.g.,* fees), a lawyer who also represents a bank may properly draw a will for a testator that names that bank as executor and trustee. [ABA Opn. 243]

6. Special Problems of Corporate Counsel [§431]

The lawyer for a corporation or other complex organization faces a situation in which the interests of *stockholders, officers, directors, and employees* of the corporation are to some degree inherently in conflict. The lawyer may not be able to serve each totally in a given situation.

a. Entity theory of representation [§432]

Both the ABA Code and Model Rules take the traditional view that the *corporate entity is the client*, and its own interests are to be favored over those of any constituent part. [Model Rule 1.13(a); EC 5-18; Restatement §131]

b. Representing both the corporation and one or more constituents [§433]

A lawyer representing the corporation may also represent one or more of its individual constituents (*e.g.,* represent the corporation and the driver of its truck that allegedly hit the plaintiff). However, such situations must be treated as any other conflict of interest and each client must give informed consent, confirmed in writing. [Model Rule 1.13(g); Restatement §131]

EXAM TIP   **gilbert**

Keep in mind that the lawyer must act in the best interests of the *organization* and not any particular officer, employee, or other person associated with the organization. Beware of exam questions where a lawyer is asked to act in the interests of the corporation's president or other official when that *conflicts with the best interests of the organization*.

---

c. **Representing corporation when a constituent violates duties to it [§434]**

Special obligations are imposed upon a corporation's lawyer who learns that someone is acting in a way that will significantly injure the corporation.

(1) Basic obligation—reporting up [§435]

If a lawyer learns that someone within the organization is violating or intends to *violate a legal obligation* to the organization or one that may be imputed to the organization, and which is likely to result in *substantial injury* to the organization, the lawyer shall proceed as *reasonably necessary* in the best interests of the organization. Measures presumptively include referral of the matter higher in the organization, even ultimately to the corporation's board of directors. [Model Rule 1.13(b); *compare* 17 CFR §§205.3 *et seq.*—Sarbanes-Oxley Act regulations]

(2) Reporting out [§436]

If the lawyer is *unsuccessful* in getting the matter resolved by the highest authority in the organization and the matter is *clearly a violation of law* and *reasonably certain* to result in substantial injury to the corporation, the lawyer may refer the matter to others outside the organization insofar as *reasonably necessary* to avoid the threatened injury. [Model Rule 1.13(c)]

(3) Exception—lawyer hired to defend against charges [§437]

The Model Rules expressly withhold the authority to "report out" from lawyers retained to investigate or defend the corporation against the charges that would otherwise be reported. [Model Rule 1.13(d)]

7. **Special Rule for Legal Aid Work [§438]**

A lawyer's pro-bono service may involve the lawyer in giving advice for a few hours a month in a nonprofit legal clinic or as part of a similar call-in help line. Clients may have problems that need immediate attention, and there will be no time to determine whether the lawyer may have a conflict of interest under traditional standards.

a. **Short-term and limited services [§439]**

The Model Rules were amended in 2002 to provide that a lawyer may give short-term limited legal services of the kind described, *i.e.*, "without expectation . . . that the lawyer will provide continuing representation," unless the lawyer has actual knowledge of a conflict of interest (*e.g.*, that the lawyer or the lawyer's firm represents someone opposing the client). [Model Rule 6.5(a)]

b. **No imputation of conflict [§440]**

Furthermore, the work done by the lawyer at the legal aid clinic will not disqualify other members of the lawyer's firm from work they might be doing or might be asked to do by someone opposing the legal aid client. [Model Rule 6.5(b)]

D. Interests of Third Persons Affecting Lawyer-Client Relationships

1. **Introduction [§441]**

   The lawyer is under a duty to disregard the desires or interests of any third person that would *impair the lawyer's independent judgment and loyalty* to the client. [Model Rule 1.7(b); EC 5-11; DR 5-107(B)] The major situations where this may occur are discussed below.

2. **Compensation from Third Parties for Representing Client [§442]**

   A lawyer may not accept any form of compensation from a third person for services to the client unless: (i) the client *gives informed consent*, (ii) the third person *does not interfere with the lawyer's independence* or the representation of the client, and (iii) the arrangement *does not compromise the client's confidential information*. [Model Rule 1.8(f); DR 5-107(A)]

   EXAM TIP   **gilbert**

   A common question in this area sets up a person who needs legal assistance but with someone else ready to pay the legal fees. It might be, for example, a parent paying the child's legal fees or a corporation paying the fees for its officer or employee. Note that this type of situation is *not automatically prohibited*, but it should raise a red flag for you. You should check the facts of the question carefully to be sure that the lawyer *remembers who the client is*—the person with the legal problem, not the person with the checkbook—and that the lawyer's *independence and loyalty are not affected*. If it seems that the person paying the fee is able to exert influence on the lawyer (*e.g.*, the parent or the corporation is telling the lawyer how to proceed), then the representation is not proper.

   ---

3. **Employment by Lay Intermediary [§443]**

   Nor may a lawyer accept employment by a corporation or anyone else who would have the *right to direct or control* the lawyer's professional judgment in representing clients. [Model Rule 5.4(c); DR 5-107(B); **Matter of Abrams**, 266 A.2d 275 (N.J. 1970)]

4. **Representing Liability Insurer and Insured [§444]**

   Liability policies usually provide that the insurance company will indemnify the insured against liability to third persons up to the monetary limits of the policy, and that the company will provide a lawyer (selected and paid by the company) to represent the policyholder in any lawsuit filed against her. These policies also provide that the insured agrees to cooperate in defending against claims covered by the policy.

   a. **Nature of problem [§445]**

      When a claim is brought against an insured under the liability policy, differing interests may arise. The insured wants the dispute settled without personally incurring liability, whatever the cost may be to the insurance company. On the other hand, the company wishes to pay as little as possible in resolving the case—whether in the form of payment to the opposing party *or* in its costs of litigation.

   b. **Propriety of representation [§446]**

      Despite these potential conflicts, the insurance company's providing a lawyer to defend the insured is an essential ingredient of liability insurance, and it is both proper and common for a lawyer selected by the insurance company to represent both the company and the policyholder in defending claims brought against the insured. [Restatement §134, comment f]

c. Duty of lawyer to avoid conflicting interest [§447]
However, areas of conflict can arise that the lawyer must avoid.

(1) Policy coverage in dispute [§448]
Insurance policies often cover certain situations (*e.g.,* negligence) but not others (*e.g.,* intentional harm). The insured naturally wishes any liability to be covered under the policy, while the insurer is best served if liability is found to be in the excluded area. If a dispute arises between the insured and the insurance company as to whether the claim is covered under the policy, the lawyer clearly may *not represent both* the insurer and insured. (As a practical matter, the insurance company often agrees to defend the action "with a reservation of rights"—meaning that it will defend the claim without waiving any policy defenses it may have against the insured for payment of the damage award.) [**Parsons v. Continental National American Group,** 550 P.2d 94 (Ariz. 1976)]

---

e.g. **Example:** Natasha drove her car over her boyfriend Boris in circumstances that make it unclear whether she acted intentionally or only negligently. Boris sued Natasha, alternatively alleging negligence and intentional conduct. Natasha's auto liability policy covers negligence, but not intentional conduct. Her insurance company hired lawyer Rocket to defend the case, but it sent Natasha a "reservation of rights" letter, informing her that it might ultimately contend that she acted intentionally, thus freeing the company from liability. During pretrial preparation, Natasha told Rocket in confidence that she ran over Boris intentionally. Rocket must not disclose that confidential information to the insurance company. Moreover, if Natasha's confidential statement means that Rocket cannot defend her effectively, Rocket must withdraw. [Restatement §134, comment f]

---

(2) Settlement proposals—policy limits cases [§449]
The interests of the insurance company and the insured may also conflict where a settlement demand is made by the plaintiff that is *within or close to the policy limits.*

(a) Obligation of the insurer [§450]
The insurance company must take care to protect the interests of the insured. When a settlement offer close to the policy limits is made, the insurer must evaluate the offer as though its liability exposure was for the whole of plaintiff's claim, not just part of it. If the insurer rejects the offer negligently or in bad faith, it will be liable for *all* of a subsequent judgment—even the part above the policy limits. [**Crisci v. Security Insurance Co.,** 66 Cal. 2d 425 (1967)]

> **e.g.** **Example:** Plaintiff sued Defendant (insured), claiming personal injury damages of $100,000. Defendant's liability insurance was limited to $10,000. Later Plaintiff offered to settle the case for $10,000 (policy limits). Naturally, Defendant wanted the insurance company to accept the settlement offer and avoid the risk of a judgment against him personally, in excess of the policy limits. On the other hand, the insurance company thought it might have nothing to lose and everything to gain by litigating the matter and possibly getting a lower verdict. However, after the jury awarded Plaintiff $100,000, the court imposed liability on the insurance company in excess of the policy limits for failure to meet its duty to consider Defendant's interest in accepting the proposed settlement. [**Crisci v. Security Insurance Co.,** *supra*]

(b) Obligation of lawyer [§451]

A lawyer representing both the insurer and insured who is faced with such a settlement offer should advise both clients of the conflict of interest involved. The lawyer is obliged not only to *inform the insurer of its duty to the insured* regarding settlement but also to use all best efforts to *see that the interests of the insured are protected*. Lawyers who regard themselves as primarily lawyers for the insurance company, and act accordingly, risk liability to the policyholder.

(3) Collusion or failure to cooperate by insured [§452]

In certain instances, especially those involving liability claims against the insured by members of her own family, the policyholder refuses to give adequate cooperation in defending against the claim. (For example, Son claims he slipped and fell in driveway as result of insured Mother's negligence in failing to remove grease.)

(a) Withdrawing from the case [§453]

If a lawyer suspects collusion or lack of cooperation by the insured, the lawyer may: (i) recommend to the insured that she seek independent counsel, and (ii) withdraw from the proceedings altogether. [Model Rule 1.16(b)(2)]

(b) Duty in course of withdrawal [§454]

If a suit is pending, however, the lawyer may withdraw only with leave of court and after giving the insured reasonable time to obtain a new lawyer. [Model Rule 1.16(c), (d); **Thomas v. Douglas,** 2 A.D.2d 885 (1956)]

5. Juvenile Court Proceedings [§455]

A lawyer retained or appointed to defend a juvenile in delinquency or criminal proceedings owes a duty to act as *advocate* for the juvenile. It is the court's function, not the lawyer's, to decide whether the child needs punishment, rehabilitation, parental care, or the like.

a. Disclosure and decisionmaking [§456]

As with any other client, the lawyer owes a duty to disclose all relevant considerations and submit all important decisions to the juvenile. [*Compare* Model Rule 1.14—decisionmaking by someone with diminished capacity]

b. No client responsibility to parent [§457]

Even if the fee is being paid by the parents, the lawyer's obligation is to the child (the client). Thus, for example, the lawyer must refuse to disclose to the parents information revealed in confidence by the child, and the attorney-client privilege pertains to the child and not the parents. Likewise, the lawyer must follow the child's decisions as to the case, rather than the parents' (*see supra,* §174).

c. Potential conflicts of interest with parents [§458]

There may be cases where the parents' interests actually conflict with those of the child (*e.g.,* where a child is cited for delinquency because of parental neglect). In such cases, the lawyer may *not* represent *both* the parents and the child.

6. Service on Board of Legal Services Organization [§459]

A lawyer who serves on the board of a legal services organization has fiduciary duties to persons represented by that organization. Service on such a board is not per se prohibited, but the lawyer may not knowingly participate in a decision or action of the organization that would: (i) conflict with the lawyer's duty to a private client, or (ii) have an adverse effect on an organization client whose interests are adverse to the lawyer's other clients. [Model Rule 6.3]

E. Conflict Between Interests of Current and Former Clients

1. . Introduction [§460]

The final traditional conflict of interest is not really a problem of divided loyalties. Here, the former client is simply someone who is owed some residual duty by the lawyer. At the very least, the lawyer has a continuing duty to *protect the former client's confidential information.*

2. Prohibition on Representation in Same Matter [§461]

The lawyer may *not* successively represent opposing parties in the *same* litigation. Thus, *e.g.,* it is *improper* and a denial of *due process* for a lawyer hired to represent an *accused in a criminal case* thereafter to accept an appointment as prosecutor and represent the state against the accused on the same charge. [Model Rule 1.9(a); Restatement §132; **Corbin v. Broadman,** 433 P.2d 289 (Ariz. 1967)]

3. **Prohibition on Representation in Substantially Related Matters [§462]**

The bar to a lawyer's later representation applies more often where the lawyer would be taking a position that is materially adverse to a former client in a matter that is *substantially related*. The critical issue in such cases is typically whether there is a substantial risk that the lawyer will *use confidential information* obtained in the prior representation against the former client. [Model Rule 1.9(b)]

a. **Cases factually related [§463]**

A lawyer who has defended medical malpractice cases for a hospital may not thereafter represent a patient in a malpractice suit against the hospital, at least where the facts arose during the period when the lawyer was representing the hospital. [**Crawford Long Hospital of Emory University v. Yerby**, 373 S.E.2d 749 (Ga. 1988)]

b. **Cases involving contract lawyer drafted [§464]**

A lawyer who has drafted employment contracts for a client may not thereafter represent an employee suing to construe or challenge the contract. [**NCK Organization, Ltd. v. Bregman**, 542 F.2d 128 (2d Cir. 1976)]

c. **Former client now a witness in present case [§465]**

Because the interest to be protected is that of the former client, even if that client is not a party to the new case, the lawyer will be disqualified if the former client will be an essential witness for the other side and confidential information might be used by the lawyer to impeach the former client. [**United States v. Iorizzo**, 786 F.2d 52 (7th Cir. 1986)]

d. **Actual disclosure of confidential information not required [§466]**

The court is not required to determine what confidential information might have been disclosed or used against the former client. To make that inquiry would require the former client to disclose that which it had a right to protect. [**T.C. Theatre Corp. v. Warner Bros. Pictures, Inc.**, 113 F. Supp. 265 (S.D.N.Y. 1953)—case in which the "same or substantially related" test was first announced]

e. **Former client's expectation that information would be held confidential is required [§467]**

For information to be confidential, there must be some expectation that it will be kept confidential. Thus, where a lawyer had represented two clients in a joint venture and there had been complete sharing of business information, there was no expectation of confidentiality and it was not improper for the lawyer to represent one of the clients in the bankruptcy of the other. [**Allegaert v. Perot**, 565 F.2d 246 (2d Cir. 1977)]

4. **Consent of Affected Clients Can Waive Conflict [§468]**

As in the case of other kinds of conflicts of interest, a lawyer may undertake "conflicted" representation if both the current and former client gives *informed consent*, confirmed in *writing*. [Model Rule 1.9(a)]

PERSONAL INTERESTS OF LAWYER

- *Financial interests adverse* to client

- *Proprietary interest in the subject matter* of employment

- *Publication rights in the subject matter* of client's case

- *Business or financial transactions* with client

- *Gifts or bequests* to lawyer

- Interest in *employment with opposing firm*

INTERESTS OF CLIENTS

- Clients with *directly adverse* interests in *same case*

- Clients with *directly adverse* interests in *unrelated cases*

- Criminal *co-defendants*

- *Co-parties* in civil litigation

- Multiple clients in *nonlitigation matters* (e.g., seller and buyer of real estate)

- *Current client* with interest *adverse to former client in same case*

- *Current client* with interest *adverse to former client in substantially related matter*

INTERESTS OF THIRD PERSONS

- *Compensation from third person* for representing client

- *Lay employer's right to control* lawyer's professional judgment in representing clients

- Representation of liability *insurer and insured*

- Parental interference in *juvenile court* proceedings

F. Imputed Disqualification of Affiliated Lawyers

1. In General [§469]

Except in the case of wholly personal conflicts, the prohibition on representing clients because of a conflict of interests extends to persons affiliated with the lawyer. Thus, if one lawyer in a practice organization has a conflict of interest, all affiliated lawyers do. [Model Rule 1.10(a); DR 5-105(D); Restatement §123]

2. Private Law Firms [§470]

The most common application of this principle is to persons affiliated as partners, associates, and other lawyers in a private law firm.

a. Offices in multiple cities [§471]

The rule even applies where one firm has offices in different cities. Thus, if a client is represented by lawyer A in one city, A's partners in another city are disqualified from representing clients in an unrelated suit against A's client. [**Cinema 5, Ltd. v. Cinerama, Ltd.,** 528 F.2d 1384 (2d Cir. 1976); **Westinghouse Electric Corp. v. Kerr-McGee Corp.,** 580 F.2d 1311 (7th Cir. 1978)]

b. Affiliated persons or firms [§472]

Even different firms that have been working on a case with a disqualified firm may themselves be disqualified pursuant to this rule. The factual question will be whether the relationship between the firms was *close enough* to warrant concern that prohibited confidential information may have passed between them. [**Fund of Funds, Ltd. v. Arthur Andersen & Co.,** 567 F.2d 225 (2d Cir. 1977)—firm disqualified; **American Can Co. v. Citrus Feed Co.,** 436 F.2d 1125 (5th Cir. 1971)—no disqualification]

c. Persons other than lawyers with disqualifying information [§473]

Similar problems can arise if a law firm hires a nonlawyer, *e.g.,* a secretary or a law student, who had worked for the firm on the other side of a major case, but imputed disqualification is less automatic in such cases. Ordinarily, such persons may be screened (*i.e.,* isolated through the firm's timely imposition of procedures to protect confidential information [Model Rule 1.0(k)]) from participation in the matter. [Model Rule 1.10, comment 4; Restatement §123, comment f; **Herron v. Jones,** 637 S.W.2d 569 (Ark. 1982)]

d. When disqualified person has left law firm [§474]

If a lawyer who would have had a personal conflict of interest has permanently ceased association with a law firm, leaving no records and no person in the firm who would be similarly disqualified, the firm is no longer prohibited from undertaking a representation. [Model Rule 1.10(b)]

---

e.g. **Example:** Partner of Law Firm One represents client A in the *A v. B* case. She obtains reams of confidential information from A. Then she leaves Law Firm One to start her own law firm, taking all of A's records with her. If no other lawyer at Law Firm One had access to the confidential information received from A, then any lawyer at Law Firm One may represent B in the *A v. B* case.

---

cf. **Compare:** If Partner had worked with Associate at Law Firm One in the *A v. B* case, and Associate remained at that firm after Partner's departure, no lawyer at Law Firm One may represent B in the *A v. B* case unless A gives informed, written consent. Also, no lawyer at that firm may represent C in the case of *C v. A* if that case is substantially related to the *A v. B* case and if the confidential information Associate obtained is material to the *C v. A* case.

---

e. When person leaves disqualified law firm [§475]

The converse is also true. If a person who would have been vicariously disqualified at a law firm in which one member had a conflict of interest then leaves the law firm without having learned any disqualifying information about the matter, that lawyer will no longer be prohibited from working on the matter at a new firm. [Model Rule 1.9(b)]

3. Other Practice Organizations [§476]

The imputed disqualification rule in the Model Rules is stated in terms of a "firm," but that term is defined very broadly to include "lawyers employed in a legal services organization or the legal department of a corporation or other organization." [Model Rule 1.0(c), 1.10(a); Restatement, §123] However, application to organizations with no common economic interest is less clear.

a. Lawyers sharing office space [§477]

When lawyers share office space but otherwise do not work on each other's cases or share revenue from them, imputed disqualification will not be imposed if each lawyer's confidential information is adequately protected. [Restatement §123, comment e; **United States v. Bell,** 506 F.2d 207 (D.C. Cir. 1974)]

b. Government legal offices [§478]

In general, government legal offices are treated as a "firm" for purposes of imputation. But the practical effect of potentially making it impossible for an entire government legal office to act has caused courts to be more cautious about disqualifying such offices. [Model Rule 1.0(c), comment 3; 1.11(d), comment 2; Restatement §123, comment d; **State v. Jones,** 429 A.2d 936 (Conn. 1980)—refusal to disqualify entire prosecutor's office]

4. Lawyers Related as Spouses [§479]

When one spouse is on one side of a case and the other spouse who works for a different firm is on the other side, there is a danger that each might receive the other's telephone messages or otherwise make inadvertent disclosures and might compromise the interests of clients. Thus, the two related lawyers may not themselves represent clients who are directly adverse unless their clients give informed, written consent. [Model Rule 1.7, comment 11]

a. Other related lawyers [§480]

The Model Rules impose the same prohibition in the case of parent-child and sibling relationships, although the assumption about sharing income and telephone calls is often much less likely in such cases. [Model Rule 1.7, comment 11]

b. No imputation within law firm [§481]

The concern about this problem is considered entirely personal to the lawyers, so the firms for which spouses work are not automatically barred from representing opposing interests. [Model Rule 1.7, comment 11; Restatement §123, comment g]

5. Interlocutory Appeals of Disqualification [§482]

A practical issue in the disqualification/imputation area has been the right to an interlocutory appeal of a grant or denial of a motion to disqualify. It is clear at least in the federal courts that *neither* a grant nor denial of such a motion may be appealed until the case reaches final judgment. [**Firestone Tire & Rubber Co. v. Risjord**, 449 U.S. 368 (1981)—denial of motion in civil case; **Richardson Merrill, Inc. v. Koller,** 469 U.S. 915 (1985)—grant of motion in civil case; **Flanagan v. United States,** 465 U.S. 259 (1984)—grant in criminal case; **United States v. White**, 743 F.2d 488 (7th Cir. 1984)—denial in criminal case]

6. Screening as a Remedy for Imputed Disqualification [§483]

In general, with the exceptions discussed in this Summary and exceptions created by statute in a few states, a law firm *may not screen* a disqualified lawyer and continue its representation in the case. Courts have been concerned that there will be no way to assure that law firms will respect the screens they are required to impose. [Model Rule 1.0(k), comments 8 - 10; *but see* Restatement §124—limited screening where "no substantial risk" confidential information will have "material adverse effect"]

7. Use of Work Product [§484]

However, if one firm is *disqualified* from acting as counsel in a matter after beginning work, its work product *may be used* by successor counsel to the extent it is not tainted by the use of confidential information. [**First Wisconsin Mortgage Trust v. First Wisconsin Corp.**, 584 F.2d 201 (7th Cir. 1978)]

G. Limitations on Representation by Present and Former Government Lawyers

1. **Introduction [§485]**

   When a lawyer leaves or enters government, special conflicts questions are presented.

2. **ABA Code [§486]**

   The ABA Code deals only with the issue of the lawyer leaving government. It prohibits a lawyer from accepting private employment in any matter in which that lawyer had *substantial responsibility* while a public employee. [DR 9-101(B)]

   a. **"Matter" defined [§487]**

      For purposes of this rule, the same "matter" is the "same lawsuit" or "representation concerning some issue of fact involving the same parties." [ABA Opn. 342]

   b. **No claim of improper influence [§488]**

      In addition, no lawyer may claim or imply an ability to improperly influence government officials. [DR 9-101(C)]

3. **Model Rules [§489]**

   The Model Rules distinguish four different problems involving present and former government lawyers.

   a. **Lawyer having personal and substantial involvement [§490]**

      Consistent with DR 9-101(B), a former government lawyer may not represent a private client in any matter in which the lawyer participated *personally and substantially* while in government, unless the appropriate government agency consents. [Model Rule 1.11(a); *compare* Model Rule 1.12(a)—former judge or law clerk; Restatement §133(1)]

       Example: Attorney is the District Attorney of Colma County. She is in charge of 16 deputies working out of five different offices spread throughout the county. Her rubber-stamped signature appears on every paper that goes out of the five offices. In theory, she is personally responsible for every detail of every case; in fact, most of Attorney's day is consumed in supervision and administration. The disqualification rule would cover only the few, exceptional cases in which Attorney does become personally and substantially involved.

      ---

      (1) **"Matter" defined [§491]**

         Here again, the word "matter" means any "judicial . . . proceeding, application, request for a ruling, . . . contract, claim, controversy, . . . or other particular matter involving a specific party or parties." [Model Rule 1.11(e)] Among the things *excluded* from this definition is the drafting of legislation or regulations of *general* applicability. [Restatement §133]

          Example: When Lawyer worked for the State Consumer Protection Agency, she was assigned to draft some regulations to govern the conduct of door-to-door salespeople. The regulations that she drafted were ultimately adopted, almost verbatim, by the agency. A year later, Lawyer left government service and entered private practice. She was asked to represent American Encyclopedia Company (a door-to-door sales company) in a dispute with the State Consumer Protection Agency. The essence of the dispute is the proper application of the regulations that Lawyer herself drafted. She may represent American because the drafting of regulations is not a "matter"; it does not involve specific facts and specific parties.

---

cf. **Compare:** When serving as Oakville City Attorney, Lawyer drafted a city ordinance for the rezoning of a particular tract of land owned by Developer. The drafting of the ordinance is a "matter" because it involved one narrow, specific situation. Thus, when Lawyer later enters private law practice, she may not work on a case that involves that ordinance. [*See* Restatement §133]

EXAM TIP	gilbert

Be sure that you understand the meaning of the word **"matter"** as it is used in the rule applied to lawyers leaving government jobs to enter private law practice. As used in this rule, "matter" has a narrow, technical meaning. It does not mean a general topic or broad subject area. It means a **specific dispute** involving **specific facts and parties**. Likewise, the term **"personal and substantial"** has a narrow meaning. It means that the lawyer worked on the matter **herself** and that her work was more than trivial.

(2) Imputation to partners and associates [§492]

A former government lawyer's *firm* is *not* disqualified if: (i) the tainted lawyer is *screened from any participation* in the matter, (ii) the tainted lawyer *shares no fees* earned from the case, and (iii) *written notice* is promptly given to the appropriate government agency. [Model Rule 1.11(b); *and compare* Model Rule 1.12(c)—former judge or law clerk]

b. Lawyer having confidential government information [§493]

Even if the lawyer's work on a matter was not personal and substantial while in government, the lawyer may not represent a private client adverse to another private party about whom the lawyer learned confidential government information without the consent of that adverse party. [Model Rule 1.11(c); Restatement §133(2)]

(1) "Confidential government information" defined [§494]

"Confidential government information" is information obtained under government authority and which, at the time the rule is invoked, the government may not disclose or which is otherwise not available to the public. [Model Rule 1.11(c)]

(2) Imputation [§495]

Once again, the tainted lawyer's firm may only handle the matter if the tainted lawyer is adequately screened and notice is given to the lawyer's former agency. [Model Rule 1.11(c)]

c. Lawyer coming to government from private practice [§496]

A lawyer in government service is subject to Model Rules 1.7 (concurrent conflict of interest) and 1.9 (duties to former clients) and may not participate in work on any matter in which the lawyer was *personally and substantially* involved while in nongovernmental employment, unless other law expressly permits. [Model Rule 1.11(d)(1), (2)(i)]

d. Lawyer negotiating for private employment [§497]

A government lawyer may not negotiate for private employment with any person involved in a matter on which the government lawyer is working. [Model Rule 1.11(d)(2)(ii); *compare* Model Rule 1.12(b)—judge or law clerk negotiating employment]

4. Federal Statute [§498]

The Federal Conflict of Interest Act, originally passed in 1963, imposes substantial *criminal sanctions* for certain representation of private parties after government service, whether or not the government service was as a lawyer.

a. Permanent bar [§499]

A lawyer who has participated *personally and substantially* in a matter is *barred forever* from *contacting the government about it* on behalf of a private client. [18 U.S.C. §207(a)(1)]

b. Two-year bar [§500]

A lawyer is barred for *two years* from *contacting the government* about any matter within the lawyer's *official responsibility* while in government, even if the lawyer did no personal work on it at all. [18 U.S.C. §207(a)(2)]

c. No imputation [§501]

Unlike the ABA Code and Model Rules provisions, these disqualifications are *personal* and not imputed to the lawyer's firm. Indeed, the former government lawyer *may* personally work on the cases as long as she *does not contact* the government orally or in writing. [18 U.S.C. §207(a)]

Chapter Five: Obligations to Third Persons and the Legal System

CONTENTS

Chapter Approach

Although the duties of a lawyer to the client are the beginning of any analysis of legal ethics, the law imposes important *limitations* on what a lawyer may do on the client's behalf and imposes *affirmative duties* to others. The important limitations and duties include:

1. **Giving Advice Without Assisting Illegal or Fraudulent Conduct**

   The lawyer has a duty to give candid advice. However, the lawyer must not help a client commit a crime or fraud, or help the client cover it up or avoid detection, but the lawyer *may discuss* the legal consequences of proposed conduct.

2. **Being Honest in Communicating with Others**

   Although the lawyer must represent the client zealously, this does not allow the lawyer to make false statements of *material fact or law*. Sometimes the lawyer must also affirmatively disclose matters to the court or other party.

3. **Communicating with Persons Through Counsel**

   If the adverse party is represented by counsel, the lawyer must communicate *directly with counsel* on any subject of the controversy. If the adverse party has no counsel, the lawyer must be careful not to advise the party or to take *unfair advantage* of him.

4. **Improving the Legal System**

   Lawyers have a duty to *support and improve* the legal system (*e.g.,* by becoming involved in public service and by supporting judges and the judicial system). Also, a lawyer representing a client before a legislative body has duties both to the client and to the legislative body.

Note that these limitations and duties apply regardless of whether the matter is in litigation.

A. Lawyer's Role as Counselor

1. **Duty to Give Candid Advice [§502]**

   In advising a client, a lawyer must "exercise independent professional judgment and render candid advice." [Model Rule 2.1]

   a. **Duty not to sugarcoat reality [§503]**

   A lawyer must give the client *straightforward* advice that may involve "unpleasant facts and alternatives that a client may be disinclined to confront." A lawyer should not withhold advice from a client because it may be unpalatable. [Model Rule 2.1, comment 1; EC 7-8; Restatement §94, comment h]

b. Right or duty to counsel about nonlegal considerations [§504]

The Model Rules expressly authorize a lawyer to "refer not only to law" but also to things such as *"moral, economic, social and political factors"* that may lead to a wise course of action for the client. Indeed, failure to include such factors may sometimes constitute inadequate advice. [Model Rule 2.1, comment 2; *and see* Restatement §94(3), comment h]

2. Duty Not to Counsel or Assist Illegal or Fraudulent Conduct [§505]

A lawyer may not counsel or assist a client to engage in conduct that the lawyer knows is illegal or fraudulent. [Model Rule 1.2(d); DR 7-102(A)(7), (8); Restatement §94(1), (2)]

Examples: Advising and assisting clients to make *illegal bribes* to union agents can subject lawyers to both personal criminal liability and disbarment. [**Disciplinary Counsel v. Stem**, 526 A.2d 1180 (Pa. 1987)] Similarly, a lawyer who knowingly assists in preparation of a client's *fraudulent income tax returns* both violates the criminal law and is subject to professional discipline as a lawyer. [**West Virginia State Bar Association v. Hart**, 410 S.E.2d 714 (W. Va. 1991)]

---

a. Violation of court order [§506]

Although not directly mentioned in the Model Rules, lawyers are equally prohibited from counseling or assisting a client to violate a court order. [*In re* **Robinson**, 639 A.2d 1384 (Vt. 1994); *compare* Model Rule 8.4(d)—conduct prejudicial to administration of justice]

b. Advice about enforcement policy [§507]

A lawyer also may not counsel a client to engage in an act the lawyer knows to be illegal simply because it is unlikely the client will get caught or be punished. [Restatement §94, comment f]

c. Distinguish—good faith testing of bounds of the law [§508]

A lawyer *may* assist a client to commit an act that will, in good faith, test the validity, scope, meaning, or application of the law. [Model Rule 1.2(d); Restatement §94(2)(a); *compare* DR 7-106(a)—good faith testing of court order]

3. Discussing Legal Consequences of Conduct [§509]

Lawyers are sometimes asked about conduct that if undertaken would be illegal. In such cases, a lawyer *may discuss* the legal consequences of proposed conduct with a client as long as the lawyer *does not advocate* the client's undertaking it or counsel the client on how to avoid detection or escape arrest. [Model Rule 1.2(d); EC 7-5; Restatement §94(2)]

EXAM TIP	**gilbert**

Be sure that you understand the distinction between providing a legal analysis of a client's questionable conduct and aiding a client in the commission of a crime. A lawyer *may* discuss a proposed course of conduct with a client, explain that the conduct would be unlawful, and give an opinion regarding the likely consequences of such conduct. However, the lawyer *must not* knowingly advise a client to commit a crime or assist a client in any illegal conduct.

4. Refusal to Assist Arguable Crime or Fraud [§510]

A lawyer may refuse to assist a client in conduct the lawyer believes to be illegal even if the conduct is arguably legal. [DR 7-101(B)(2); *compare* Model Rule 1.16(b)(2)—lawyer's right to withdraw in such a case]

B. Requirement of Honesty in Communications with Others

1. Basic Obligation of Truthfulness [§511]

A lawyer may not knowingly make a *false statement of material fact or law* to a third person in the course of representing a client, even if that might seem to serve the client's interest. [Model Rule 4.1(a); DR 7-102(A)(5); Restatement §98]

---

e.g. Example: A lawyer who misleads doctors by saying that the client lacks the money to pay their bills is subject to professional discipline. [**Florida Bar v. McLawhorn,** 505 So. 2d 1338 (Fla. 1987)]

---

a. Comment

This obligation is consistent with the lawyer's broad duty to avoid "conduct involving dishonesty, fraud, deceit, or misrepresentation." [Model Rule 8.4(c); DR 1-102(A)(4)]

2. Duty to Come Forward with Information [§512]

A lawyer sometimes even has an obligation to correct a *misapprehension of material fact* by a third person, but the scope of this obligation is much more controversial than the lawyer's duty to tell the truth. [Model Rule 4.1(b); DR 7-102(A)(3); Restatement §98(3)]

a. Model Rules requirement [§513]

The Model Rules say that a lawyer may not "knowingly fail to disclose a material fact to a third person when disclosure is necessary to avoid assisting a criminal or fraudulent act by a client, unless disclosure is prohibited by Rule 1.6" (the duty to protect confidential client information). [Model Rule 4.1(b); *and see supra,* §365—duty to disclose to prevent client fraud]

b. ABA Code provision [§514]

The ABA Code and the Restatement are more general and leave open what the law requires to be revealed. The ABA Code states that a lawyer may not "conceal or knowingly fail to reveal that which he is required by law to reveal." [DR 7-102(A)(3); Restatement §98(3)]

c. Noisy withdrawal [§515]

Before the 2003 amendment to Model Rule 1.6 (*see supra,* §364), a particularly difficult disclosure issue was presented when a lawyer learned that his services had been used to perpetrate a fraud. The lawyer was *required* to withdraw from the matter by Model Rule 1.16(a). Comments to Model Rule 1.6 said that the lawyer *may* withdraw noisily, even though that may have the effect of revealing client confidences. As amended, Model Rule 1.6 allows a lawyer to reveal client information to prevent, mitigate, or rectify substantial financial injury reasonably certain to result from a client's past or future crime or fraud using the lawyer's services. In states that allow this disclosure (expected to be the majority of states), noisy withdrawal is no longer needed.

3. **Lawyer's Duty in Negotiations [§516]**

Issues of honesty and affirmative disclosure often arise in the context of negotiations. In general, a lawyer has *no duty* to do the other side's fact research *nor any right* to reveal facts that would undermine the client's position.

a. **Puffing and other subjective assertions [§517]**

It is part of the essence of negotiation that a lawyer may magnify the strength of the client's position, and a reasonable hearer would not take many of a lawyer's statements as literally true. [*See* Restatement §98, comment c]

Example: In a personal injury negotiation, a lawyer's statement to defense counsel that "any jury would award my client at least a million dollars" would ordinarily constitute permitted puffing, not prohibited dishonesty.

EXAM TIP   **gilbert**

It is important to remember that although puffing is allowed in negotiations, a lawyer must **not** make a false statement of **material fact**. The key factor in determining whether a statement contains a material fact is whether the opponent would be **reasonable in relying** on the statement. If so, the statement is not mere puffery.

---

b. **No duty to correct misapprehensions not involving act by lawyer or client [§518]**

Furthermore, a lawyer who believes that an opponent is underestimating the strength of its position has no duty to correct that belief unless the lawyer or client has caused the underestimation. [**Brown v. County of Genessee**, 872 F.2d 169 (6th Cir. 1989)—opponent miscalculated amount of her lost pay]

c. **Distinguish—when disclosure is required [§519]**

In some cases, a lawyer has been required to disclose information. Although a failure to disclose might not literally assist a fraud, the opponent's lack of knowledge of pertinent facts may be so important that disclosure is necessary.

Example: Settlement of a case was *set aside* when the plaintiff's lawyer failed to disclose to the defendant that the plaintiff, for whom damages had been negotiated based on life expectancy, had already died. [**Virzi v. Grand Trunk Warehouse**, 571 F. Supp. 507 (E.D. Mich. 1983)]

> **Example:** A prosecutor was held to have a *duty to tell* a criminal defendant, prior to accepting a guilty plea, that physical evidence of the defendant's guilt had been accidentally destroyed. [**Fambo v. Smith,** 433 F. Supp. 590 (W.D.N.Y. 1977)]

C. Specially Assumed Duty of Candor—Lawyer as Evaluator

1. Giving Opinions to Nonclients [§520]

In the interest of time or reducing cost, a lawyer may be asked by the party on the other side of a transaction to **certify facts or issues of legal authority** on which the other party may rely. Unless contrary to the interest of the lawyer's client, the lawyer may do so. [Model Rule 2.3; Restatement §95] Lawyers frequently agree to make such certifications. Sometimes they take the form of formal opinion letters (*e.g.,* "the client is validly incorporated"); other times they take the form of title examinations as to property the client wants to sell or mortgage.

a. Model Rule requirements [§521]

The Model Rules call this making an "evaluation for use by third persons" and permit it whenever it is "*compatible* with other aspects of the lawyer's relationship with the client." [Model Rule 2.3(a); *and see* Restatement §95(1)]

b. Duty of care in making evaluation [§522]

Because the evaluation is made with the knowledge that a third party will rely on it, the lawyer will be *liable to the third party* for any negligence in determining the facts. [**Greycas, Inc. v. Proud,** 826 F.2d 1560 (7th Cir. 1987)—lawyer certified client's title to farm equipment without checking records; in fact, all was previously mortgaged]

c. When opinion may adversely affect client [§523]

Because the lawyer must be accurate and candid in the opinion, if investigation of the facts reveals information that would have to be disclosed which would embarrass or otherwise *adversely affect* the client, the lawyer must *obtain the client's consent* before going ahead with the opinion. [Model Rule 2.3(b)]

d. Confidential information not required to be disclosed [§524]

Facts disclosed in the opinion are, of course, thereafter not privileged. Thus, the client may limit the scope of the evaluation, but the lawyer should describe any material limitation in his report. Any facts learned by the lawyer that are *not* required to be disclosed, must continue to be treated by the lawyer as *confidential* and are protected by Model Rule 1.6. [Model Rule 2.3(c)]

2. **When Lawyer's Opinion Is to Be Widely Disseminated [§525]**

Consistent with the above rules, when a lawyer agrees to certify facts to a large number of persons who can be expected to rely on the lawyer, the lawyer has a special obligation to be *complete, accurate, and candid*.

a. **Application—securities cases [§526]**

This special obligation is most often implicated when the lawyer has prepared an opinion letter to be used in disclosure documents for securities investors. The lawyer may be held responsible for *both* misstatements and omissions of material facts. [**Securities and Exchange Commission v. National Student Marketing Corp.**, 457 F. Supp. 682 (D.D.C. 1978)]

(1) **Due diligence required [§527]**

A lawyer is not a guarantor of every fact in disclosure materials about a company or transaction, or even those upon which the lawyer relies in rendering an opinion. However, if facts the lawyer learns seem inconsistent, or the lawyer has any other reason to doubt their accuracy, the lawyer has a *duty to inquire* to determine what the correct facts are. [ABA Opn. 335]

b. **Application—tax shelter opinions [§528]**

When a lawyer gives a widely disseminated legal opinion about the tax treatment likely to be afforded an investment, the lawyer must candidly disclose and estimate the degree of risk that the IRS will not allow the tax deductions being sought, even if such disclosure will be contrary to the interest of the lawyer's client in maximum sales of the investment. [ABA Opn. 346]

3. **Regular Audit Letters [§529]**

A standard part of corporate practice is responding to letters (typically annually) from auditors inquiring about the status of the client's litigation to determine what loss reserves, if any, the client should be required to establish. Responses to these letters are "evaluations" within the meaning of Model Rule 2.3, but the legal and accounting professions have established a "treaty" prescribing certain ground rules for such letters. [Restatement §95, comment f]

a. **Likelihood client will prevail in pending cases [§530]**

Auditors would like lawyers to tell them precisely what the chances are that the client will prevail in pending cases, and lawyers are equally reluctant to do so. In part, that is because litigation is uncertain and, in part, because an admission that the client has a 75% chance of losing would have value to the client's opponent. Thus lawyers need only say if the chance the opponent will win is *probable* (*i.e.*, extremely high) or *remote* (*i.e.*, extremely remote). No estimate need be given of cases that fall between those extremes.

b. Unasserted possible claims [§531]

A harder issue is presented when the lawyer knows that someone might have a claim against the client but no suit has been filed yet.

(1) Information confidential [§532]

Such information about client contingent liabilities is clearly *confidential* (*see supra,* §338-340), because disclosure might be embarrassing to the client or might even *cause* the potential claimants to assert the claims.

(2) Opine only on extreme cases [§533]

Under the lawyer-accountant treaty, lawyers need only disclose claims that: (i) are *probable* of assertion, (ii) if asserted, the client faces a reasonable possibility of *losing*, and (iii) are large enough to be *material.*

D. Communicating with Another Person on Behalf of Client

1. Person Represented by Counsel [§534]

A lawyer who *knows* that another person is represented by counsel in a particular matter *must not communicate* with that person on any subject of the controversy, unless that person's counsel is present or has given prior consent or the communication is authorized by law or court order. [Model Rule 4.2; DR 7-104(A)(1); Cal. Rule 2-100(A); Restatement §99(1)]

a. Scope of prohibition [§535]

Any communication touching on the subject of controversy is prohibited. The purpose of the ban is to prevent *any possibility* of interference with the lawyer-client relationship on the other side. [**Mitton v. State Bar,** 71 Cal. 2d 525 (1969)]

(1) No contact with any represented person [§536]

Note that Model Rule 4.2 prohibits contact with *any* person represented by counsel, not just an adverse party. Thus, the rule covers individuals before a suit or charge is actually filed, as well as people such as victims in a criminal case or witnesses who may have counsel in the matter.

EXAM TIP	gilbert

It is important to keep in mind that although Model Rule 4.2 prohibits a lawyer's communication with represented witnesses, a lawyer *may communicate* with an *unrepresented* person who will be called as a witness by the adverse party.

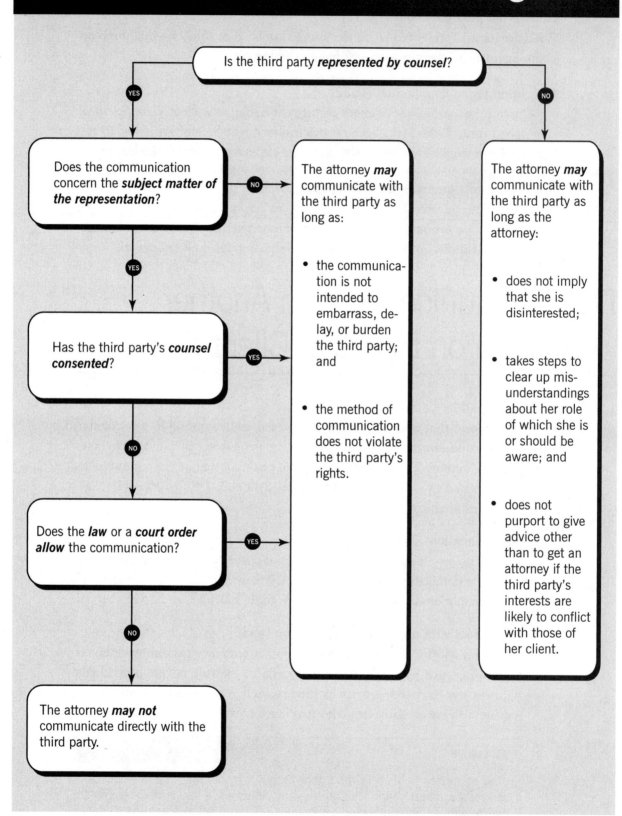

Is the third party **represented by counsel**?

YES

NO

Does the communication concern the **subject matter of the representation**?

NO

YES

Has the third party's **counsel consented**?

YES

NO

Does the **law** or a **court order allow** the communication?

YES

NO

The attorney **may not** communicate directly with the third party.

The attorney **may** communicate with the third party as long as:

- the communication is not intended to embarrass, delay, or burden the third party; and

- the method of communication does not violate the third party's rights.

The attorney **may** communicate with the third party as long as the attorney:

- does not imply that she is disinterested;

- takes steps to clear up misunderstandings about her role of which she is or should be aware; and

- does not purport to give advice other than to get an attorney if the third party's interests are likely to conflict with those of her client.

(2) Improper intent not required [§537]

If the lawyer knows that someone has counsel in the matter, it is improper for the lawyer to even respond to contact initiated by the represented person, except to suggest that the person could have his attorney contact the lawyer. [Model Rule 4.2, comment 3; *In re* **News America Publishing, Inc.,** 974 S.W.2d 97 (Tex. 1998)]

(3) Represented persons may meet [§538]

Represented persons may communicate without their lawyers and even settle the matter on their own. A lawyer may help prepare the client for such a meeting. [Restatement §99(2), comment k]

b. Application of the rule to corporations and other organizations [§539]

When the "person" protected by Rule 4.2 is an impersonal organization, the lawyer is barred from talking to only some of the individuals who work for the organization:

(1) Individuals treated as part of the organizational "person" [§540]

Persons to whom opposing counsel may not speak are: (i) those who have authority to settle the matter for the organization, (ii) those who regularly talk with the organization's counsel about the matter, and (iii) those whose conduct or statements in the matter may be imputed to the organization for purposes of liability. [Model Rule 4.2, comment 7; Restatement §100]

(2) Special rule for government agencies [§541]

Although government agencies are treated as other organizations for purposes of Rule 4.2 in most ordinary litigation, the Rule does *not prevent* a lawyer from communicating with an agency policymaker about an issue of *general public policy*. [Restatement §101]

(3) Former employees [§542]

Generally, a lawyer *may* contact *former* employees of an organization, even if they had one of the identified roles at the time they were employed. However, such contact is *prohibited* if the employee *continues* to regularly communicate with the organization's counsel about the matter. [ABA Opn. 91-359; Restatement §100, comment g] Furthermore, when talking with either a present or former employee, a lawyer must take care not to violate the organization's legal rights, such as the attorney-client privilege. [Model Rule 4.2, comment 7]

Example: Lawyer represents Plaintiff in a defamation action against the Herald Newspaper Corp. Without getting the permission of the Herald's counsel, Lawyer interviewed the newspaper's former editor-in-chief and convinced him to disclose some privileged communications he had with the newspaper's lawyer about the case. Lawyer acted improperly in prying into the privileged communications. [Model Rule 4.2, comment 7; *and see* Model Rule 4.4, comment 1]

---

c.   Communication authorized by law or court order [§543]

Some communication with a represented person is inevitable (*e.g.*, the law may require service of process on an opposing party, not the person's lawyer). Such contact is authorized by law and is not prohibited by the rule. [Model Rule 4.2; DR 7-104(A)(1); Restatement §99(1)(c)]

(1)   Represented criminal defendant [§544]

Particular controversy has arisen over whether a prosecutor may talk with a criminal defendant, at the request of that defendant, in the absence of the defendant's counsel. This situation often arises when the defendant wants to enter into a plea agreement but his lawyer refuses to go to the prosecutor. A majority of courts confronted with this situation have held that a prosecutor's duty to refrain from communicating with an indicted defendant known to be represented by counsel cannot be waived by the defendant. [*See* **United States v. Lopez,** 4 F.3d 1455 (9th Cir. 1993)]

(a)   Justice Department efforts [§545]

Two U.S. Attorneys General tried to authorize such contacts "by law," but the courts rejected their efforts. Nevertheless, the words "or court order" were added to Model Rule 4.2 to permit lawyers to seek a court ruling interpreting the scope of Rule 4.2 or justifying contact in exceptional circumstances.

2.   Person Unrepresented by Counsel [§546]

When a person is not represented by counsel, the lawyer may communicate directly.

a.   Must not imply disinterest [§547]

In the course of communication with the unrepresented person, however, the lawyer must make clear that she represents someone else and thus is *not disinterested* or representing the person being interviewed. If the lawyer knows or reasonably should know that the person misunderstands the lawyer's role in the matter, the lawyer should try to correct the misunderstanding. [Model Rule 4.3; DR 7-104(A)(2); Restatement §103]

b.   Must not give person advice [§548]

Furthermore, if the person's interests have a reasonable possibility of being *in conflict* with those of the lawyer's client, the lawyer *may not advise* the person beyond suggesting that he secure counsel to represent his own interests. [Model Rule 4.3; DR 7-104(A)(2)]

EXAM TIP   **gilbert**

If a question involves a lawyer's communication with an *unrepresented person*, remember that the lawyer *may communicate* directly with the person but that he must be careful in doing so. If the lawyer *knows, or reasonably should know,* that the unrepresented person *misunderstands* the lawyer's role in the matter, the lawyer must make reasonable efforts to correct the misunderstanding. Likewise, if the lawyer knows or should know that her client's interests are likely to be in conflict with those of the unrepresented person, she must not give legal advice to that person (other than to get a lawyer).

3. **Acquisition of Evidence from a Third Party [§549]**

The Model Rules also forbid the lawyer "to embarrass, delay, or burden a third person, or use methods of obtaining evidence that violate the legal rights" of another person. [Model Rule 4.4(a)]

a. **Obligation not to record conversations in violation of law [§550]**

A lawyer *should not record* any conversation where such recording would *violate the law*. This applies to conversations with clients, other lawyers, or any other member of the public (including witnesses and public officials). The ABA has reversed its former position, however, and *no longer prohibits* tape recording that is *not illegal* (*e.g.,* to document obscene phone calls or threats). [ABA Opn. 01-422]

b. **Prosecutorial duty to supervise police [§551]**

It has also sometimes been held that actions of police officers who violate the rights of suspects will be treated as actions of the prosecutor. Thus, if an officer is considered an agent of the prosecutor, he must not interview a defendant in the absence of the defendant's lawyer. [*See* **United States v. Thomas,** 474 F.2d 110 (10th Cir. 1973)—statement obtained during Special Agent's interview with defendant was not allowed into evidence because defendant's lawyer was not notified of the interview]

4. **Threats of Criminal Prosecution [§552]**

A lawyer is prohibited from filing or threatening to file criminal charges solely to obtain an advantage for a client in a civil case. For example, a lawyer for an accident victim may not threaten to go to the police and accuse the driver of drunk driving if he does not agree to a settlement. [DR 7-105(A); *and see* **People ex rel. Gallagher v. Hertz,** 608 P.2d 335 (Colo. 1979)]

a. **Rationale**

The *civil adjudicative process* is designed to *settle disputes* between parties, whereas the *criminal process* is designed to *protect society* as a whole. Threatening to use the criminal process in order to coerce settlement of private civil matters tends to diminish public confidence in the legal system. [EC 7-21]

b. **Not limited to criminal charges [§553]**

It is equally improper for a lawyer to file or threaten to file charges that would expose the other party to *administrative or disciplinary* sanctions (*e.g.,* threatening another lawyer with disbarment). [Cal. Rule 5-100]

c. **Omission of prohibition in Model Rules [§554]**

The Model Rules expressly *omit* this principle, apparently in the belief that it is primarily a subject of tort and criminal law rather than a matter of legal ethics, but it is not clear that the law is really different in Model Rules states. [Restatement §98, comment f]

d. **Potential penalties [§555]**

Under many penal codes, the threat of criminal proceedings to obtain a settlement constitutes the crime of *extortion*.

E. Obligation to Improve the Legal System

1. Representing Client Seeking Legislation [§556]

A lawyer representing a client before a legislative or rulemaking body has duties to both the client and the public.

a. Duty of zeal generally [§557]

A lawyer appearing before an administrative rulemaking body or a legislative committee owes the same obligation of zealous representation of the client's interests as in an adversary proceeding. Thus, a lawyer can properly argue and press a client's claims or viewpoints without disclosing weaknesses or possible defenses. It is the lawyer's duty to act as an **advocate**; it is the legislature's function to evaluate the merits of the claims presented. [EC 7-15, 7-16]

b. Duty to disclose representative capacity [§558]

In any such appearance or communication with a public body, the lawyer **must disclose** that the lawyer is representing interests that may be affected by the action or legislation under consideration. [Model Rule 3.9; EC 7-15, 7-16; Restatement §104]

2. Support of Legislation in Public Interest [§559]

The lawyer should participate actively in proposing and supporting legislation and programs to improve the system, rather than leaving needed reforms only to public-spirited laypersons.

a. Particular legislation [§560]

Because of their unique qualifications, lawyers should, whenever possible, encourage **simplification of laws** and **improvements in legal procedures.** [EC 8-2, 8-9]

b. Views of clients largely irrelevant [§561]

A lawyer may take personal positions on legislation without regard to the general interests or desires of clients or former clients, **unless** to do so will **materially and adversely** affect work the lawyer is doing for the client on the issue. Thus, a lawyer may not lobby for legislation for a client in the morning and lobby against the same bill as a citizen in the evening. [EC 8-1; Restatement §125, comment e]

3. Membership in Legal Services or Law Reform Organizations [§562]

It follows that a lawyer may be a member, officer, or director of an organization that serves the needs of persons whose interests are adverse to the lawyer's regular clients. [Model Rule 6.3]

a. Exception—decisions that conflict with client's interests [§563]

If the lawyer knows that a decision or action of a legal services organization would *conflict* with the interest of a client of the lawyer, the lawyer *must not participate* in that particular decision or action. [Model Rule 6.3(a)]

b. Actions that benefit client [§564]

If the lawyer knows that such a decision would materially *benefit* one of the lawyer' clients, the lawyer may participate in the decision after *disclosing* the fact of the benefit without identifying the client. [Model Rule 6.4]

4. Lawyers in Public Service [§565]

Service by lawyers in a public capacity is encouraged as a significant method of improving the legal system. [EC 8-8] However, lawyers who serve as legislators or other public officials must *not* engage in activities in which their personal or professional interests are, or foreseeably may be, *in conflict* with their official duties. [EC 8-8; Restatement §135]

a. Use of public position to advance client's interests prohibited [§566]

Lawyers holding public office owe their primary duty to the public and, therefore, may *not* use public office to obtain special advantages for themselves or a client. [Model Rule 8.4, comment 5; DR 8-101(A)(1), (2)]

b. Appearances before other public bodies [§567]

The right of a lawyer holding public office to appear as counsel on behalf of clients before a public body is *narrowly limited*. For example, it is a crime for a member of Congress to receive compensation for representing a client before a federal agency. [18 U.S.C. §203(a); **Office of Disciplinary Counsel v. Eilberg**, 441 A.2d 1193 (Pa. 1982)]

5. Involvement in Selection of Judges [§568]

Lawyers are uniquely capable of evaluating the qualifications of those seeking or being considered for judgeships and, therefore, owe a special duty to aid in the selection of qualified persons. A lawyer should protest against the appointment or election of those who are not qualified and do everything possible to prevent political considerations from outweighing judicial fitness in the selection process. [EC 8-6]

a. Defending the judiciary [§569]

Judges are not wholly free to defend themselves against unjust criticism. Thus, it is also the responsibility of the organized bar, and of lawyers individually, to defend judges and the judiciary against *inaccurate or irresponsible* charges. [EC 8-6]

b. Criticizing the judiciary [§570]

The duty to defend the judiciary does not mean that lawyers cannot criticize judges in public statements. However, *reckless or knowingly false* accusations are grounds for discipline. [Model Rule 8.2(a); DR 8-102(B); EC 8-6; Restatement §114]

(1) Rationale

Unrestrained or intemperate criticism of judges by lawyers tends to lessen public confidence in the legal system and may weaken the impact of *legitimate* complaints about the judiciary. [**Kentucky Bar Association v. Heleringer,** 602 S.W.2d 165 (Ky. 1980)]

(2) Sanctions [§571]

Charges going to the *integrity* of the courts are particularly dangerous. A lawyer who makes such charges against a judge or the judicial system is subject to serious disciplinary sanctions if the charges prove untrue.

---

e.g. **Example:** A lawyer accused the judges of the state supreme court of having accepted a bribe. The lawyer was disbarred, even though the accusation was partially true—some of the judges had accepted a bribe. [*In re* **Grimes,** 364 F.2d 654 (10th Cir. 1966)]

---

c. Contributions calculated to obtain favoritism prohibited [§572]

A lawyer who makes or solicits a political contribution for a judge for the purpose of later getting legal engagements or appointments from that judge is prohibited from later accepting such engagements or appointments. [Model Rule 7.6]

6. Personally Running for Judicial Office [§573]

Where the lawyer is seeking election or appointment to a judgeship (either against another candidate or in a merit system election), the lawyer must comply with the applicable provisions of the ABA Model Code of Judicial Conduct ("CJC") (*see infra,* §§937 *et seq.*). [Model Rule 8.2(b); DR 8-103(A)]

Chapter Six:
Special Obligations of Lawyers in Litigation

CONTENTS

Chapter Approach

Chapter Approach

As has been discussed throughout this Summary, a lawyer has duties to persons other than the client. The last chapter discussed duties that apply regardless of whether the subject of the representation is in litigation. This chapter presents the special duties of lawyers involved in litigation.

Some things to keep in mind are:

1. A lawyer *must not assert a frivolous claim or defense* and *must not delay proceedings for improper purposes.*

2. A lawyer *must not knowingly make a false statement of material fact* to the court, and *must disclose adverse legal authority.*

3. A lawyer *may present the client's case in the best possible light,* but the lawyer must not disregard her duty to the court and to opposing parties; *e.g.,* the lawyer *must not suppress evidence* when there is a legal duty to reveal or produce it, *must not use untruthful testimony or false evidence, and must not ignore professional standards or court rules* in presenting evidence.

4. A lawyer must not try the case in the media; *i.e.,* the lawyer *must restrict out-of-court comments* about a case, especially in criminal proceedings.

5. A lawyer *must not lend money to the client except for litigation expenses.* (Note that the ABA Code requires the client to remain liable for those expenses, but the Model Rules allow repayment to be contingent on the outcome of the case.)

6. A lawyer ordinarily *must not act as both an advocate and a witness.*

7. A lawyer *must not take actions that could affect the impartiality of the court; i.e.,* the lawyer may not make gifts or loans to court personnel, contact judges without notice to the other party, or contact jurors during the trial.

8. A *public prosecutor or government attorney* has a duty, beyond those above, to *seek justice* in the proceeding, as well as represent the state or government.

A. Duty to Assert Only Meritorious Claims and Expedite Litigation

1. Introduction [§574]

A lawyer has a duty to the court, the client, and opposing parties not to assert frivolous claims or defenses or delay proceedings for improper purposes.

2. Baseless Lawsuits [§575]

A lawyer may not file suit on behalf of a client unless there is a *nonfrivolous* basis for doing so, which includes a *good faith argument* for an *extension, modification, or reversal* of existing law. [Model Rule 3.1; DR 7-102(A)(2); Restatement §110(a)]

a. Distinguish—expectation of developing facts in discovery [§576]

A filing is *not frivolous* if the lawyer does not have all the facts but reasonably expects to be able to determine them in discovery. [Model Rule 3.1, comment 2]

b. Distinguish—defense of a criminal case [§577]

There is a strong public interest in seeing that *all* persons accused of a crime have the services of counsel, and a criminal defendant has a constitutional right to effective assistance of counsel. The fact that counsel is court-appointed, rather than privately retained, does not reduce the lawyer's obligation to provide *zealous* representation to an accused in a criminal case. Moreover, a lawyer *may defend* a criminal client *whom the lawyer believes to be guilty* and *may require the prosecution to prove every necessary element* of the crime. [Model Rule 3.1; Restatement §110(2)]

(1) Plea bargaining [§578]

Even if there appears to be no effective defense, a criminal defendant may reject a plea bargain. Thus, if the lawyer concludes after a full investigation that conviction of the client is likely, zealous representation requires seeking permission of the client to engage in plea bargaining and going forward with trial if the client rejects the plea bargain. [ABA Standards Relating to the Defense Function §6.1]

(2) Doubts about client's innocence [§579]

If the lawyer for an accused has personal doubts about the innocence of the client and allows such feelings to affect the presentation of the client's case, the lawyer will be unable to provide zealous representation. Thus, the client will be denied his constitutional right to effective assistance of counsel. [**Johns v. Smyth,** 176 F. Supp. 949 (E.D. Va. 1959)]

Example: In *Johns, supra,* a court-appointed attorney for a defendant in a murder trial doubted his client's statement regarding provocation for the killing. Because the lawyer believed that his client was guilty of first degree murder, he did not submit jury instructions to the trial judge as to involuntary manslaughter, and he did not argue the case before the jury. In a hearing on the defendant's habeas corpus petition, the federal district court found that the defendant was denied effective representation and did not receive a fair trial.

---

(3) Questionable grounds for appeal [§580]

Problems may also arise when counsel is appointed for an appeal requested by the defendant. The lawyer must recognize that his duties are those of an *active advocate supporting the appeal* to the best of his ability, as opposed to those of an "amicus curiae" advising the court on the merits of the appeal. [**Anders v. California**, 386 U.S. 738 (1967)—if lawyer appointed for criminal defendant's appeal finds the case to be frivolous, she must request permission to withdraw and supply a brief covering all grounds that might arguably support an appeal; *but see* **Jones v. Barnes**, 463 U.S. 745 (1983)—lawyer need not press all nonfrivolous issues]

EXAM TIP   **gilbert**

Note that an exam question raising the issue of frivolous claims or defenses often actually requires you to discuss what is *not* frivolous. For example, if the question indicates that the claim or defense cannot be supported by existing law, check the facts to see if the lawyer can make a *good faith argument that the law should be changed*. If so, the claim or defense is *not frivolous*. And note that the lawyer doesn't have to believe that the argument is necessarily a winning one; it just has to be a sound argument that can be made in good faith. Also watch for facts about a *criminal lawyer* who believes her client is guilty of the crime charged. Recall that it is not frivolous for her to conduct the case so that the *prosecutor must prove every necessary element* of the crime.

---

  c.   **Distinguish—duty to assert "technicalities" [§581]**

To the extent that the client's interests are *advanced* or protected by reliance on "technicalities," the lawyer usually *owes a duty* to assert them. However, it is not improper to waive or fail to assert a technicality where, in the lawyer's professional judgment, it is in the client's best interests. Such a waiver is not a ground for a malpractice action against the lawyer. [DR 7-101(B)(1)]

  d.   **Possible sanctions**

    (1)   **Professional discipline [§582]**

A lawyer is subject to professional discipline for filing a suit or claim that is *obviously without factual or legal merit*. [**Gullo v. Hirst**, 332 F.2d 178 (4th Cir. 1964)—discipline imposed against lawyer who filed for declaratory relief as to a domestic relations matter that was not only outside federal jurisdiction, but already res judicata]

    (2)   **Civil liability for abuse of process [§583]**

In addition, if the suit or court process was filed for an *ulterior purpose* and has resulted in damage to the opposing party, the lawyer (as well as the client for whom the lawyer was acting) may be subject to tort liability for malicious prosecution or abuse of process. (*See* Torts Summary.)

3.   **Abusive Delay in Litigation**

  a.   **ABA Code [§584]**

The ABA Code states the traditional prohibition of a lawyer's delaying a trial "merely to harass or maliciously injure another." [DR 7-102(A)(1)]

b. Model Rules—duty to expedite [§585]

One of the major departures of the Model Rules from the ABA Code is the *affirmative requirement* that lawyers *expedite litigation*. Benefits to the client from improper delay may not be taken into account by a lawyer. [Model Rule 3.2 and comment]

c. Federal Rule 11 [§586]

Federal Rule of Civil Procedure 11 requires that a lawyer *sign every pleading* and stipulates that the lawyer's signature constitutes a *certification* that the pleading "is not being interposed for the purpose of delay." For abuse or violation of this rule, a lawyer or client may be forced to pay attorney's fees and other expenses incurred by the opponent in dealing with a pleading interposed for delay.

d. Courts' inherent power to sanction [§587]

Courts have been held to have *inherent power* to punish lawyers for using delay to get an advantage in the litigation process. [*See* **Chambers v. NASCO, Inc.,** 501 U.S. 32 (1991)]

(1) Failure to appear [§588]

The sanction most frequently imposed against lawyers for delay caused by failing to appear at a scheduled hearing or trial is a *citation for contempt of court.* [**Kandel v. State,** 250 A.2d 853 (Md. 1969)]

4. Discovery Abuse [§589]

A lawyer is subject to professional discipline and judicially-imposed compensation to the opponent for (i) making a frivolous request in discovery, or (ii) failing to make a diligent effort to comply with a legally proper discovery request by opposing counsel. [Model Rule 3.4(d); Restatement §110(3); **Roadway Express, Inc. v. Piper,** 447 U.S. 752 (1980)]

B. Duty of Honesty

1. General Rule [§590]

Although a lawyer acts as a partisan representative of the client, the lawyer must not "knowingly make a false statement of fact or law to a tribunal." [Model Rule 3.3(a)(1); DR 7-102(A)(3), (5); Restatement §120(1)(b)]

2. Duty as to Pleadings [§591]

Pleadings prepared by a lawyer are, in effect, representations to the court and thus must be truthful and accurate. In federal practice and in many states, a lawyer must sign every pleading, and this signature operates as a certification that there are good grounds to support it, as well as that it is not being interposed for purpose of delay (*see supra,* §586). [Fed. R. Civ. P. 11]

An attorney may be subject to discipline for:

LAW

Knowingly making a false statement of law to the tribunal

or

Failing to correct a false statement of ***material*** law previously made by the attorney to the tribunal

or

Failing to disclose ***directly adverse*** law of the ***controlling jurisdiction***

FACTS

Knowingly making a false statement of fact to the tribunal

or

Failing to correct a false statement of ***material*** fact previously made by the attorney to the tribunal

or

Failing to volunteer to the tribunal known harmful facts if the proceeding is ***ex parte***

EVIDENCE

Knowingly offering false evidence

3. **Ordinarily No Duty to Disclose Harmful Facts [§592]**

   In general, a lawyer is under *no affirmative duty to disclose facts* that would be *harmful* to the client's case. Such facts are protected by the lawyer's professional duty of confidentiality. Under our adversary system of justice, it is left to opposing counsel to bring such matters to the court's attention. [Model Rule 1.6; DR 4-101]

   a. **Exception—compliance with discovery requirements [§593]**

      Today's broad discovery rules, which impose disclosure obligations, constitute a large exception to the practical effect of this ethical principle.

   b. **Exception—correction of previous material misstatement [§594]**

      If a lawyer has made (presumably by mistake) a false statement of fact to a tribunal, she must correct the statement if it is *material*. [Model Rule 3.3(a)(1)]

4. **Duty Not to Misstate Law [§595]**

   A lawyer likewise *must not knowingly mislead* the judge as to the law. The lawyer must not misquote the language of any statute or decision, nor knowingly cite as authority any decision that has been overruled or any statute that has been repealed. As with misstatements of fact, the lawyer *must* also correct any *material misstatement of law* the lawyer has previously made. [Model Rule 3.3(a)(1); Cal. Rule 5-200(c); Restatement §111(1)]

   EXAM TIP   **gilbert**

   Regarding misstatements of fact or law, note that the lawyer's duty differs depending on whether she is first making the statement or attempting to correct a previously made misstatement. The lawyer must not knowingly *make any* false statement of fact or law, but her duty to *correct* previously made false statements extends *only to those that are material*.

   ---

5. **Duty to Disclose Adverse Legal Authority [§596]**

   As an officer of the court, the lawyer owes an *affirmative duty to disclose the law* applicable to the matter at hand—whether such law supports or is adverse to the client's case.

   a. **What must be disclosed [§597]**

      The lawyer must disclose:

      (i) Legal authority

      (ii) In the *controlling jurisdiction*

      (iii) Known by the lawyer

      (iv) To be *directly adverse* to the position of the client and

      (v) Not disclosed by opposing counsel.

      [Model Rule 3.3(a)(2); DR 7-106(B)(1); Restatement §111(2)]

(1) Application [§598]

The adverse decision does not have to be on "all fours." It is sufficient that it be the kind of precedent that a *reasonable judge might wish to consider* in dealing with the case at hand. If it is, the lawyer owes a duty to disclose it. [**Katris v. Immigration & Naturalization Service**, 562 F.2d 866 (2d Cir. 1977)]

EXAM TIP | **gilbert**

Sometimes an exam question involving the duty to disclose adverse legal authority will mention that a case is directly adverse to the client's position. If so, be sure to check that the case is *from the controlling jurisdiction*. Thus, if the lawyer's case is in state court, the lawyer needs to disclose only adverse decisions of the higher courts *of that state*—not decisions from other states or even from the federal courts in that state, as they are not controlling.

---

b. Right to challenge soundness of adverse authority [§599]

The obligation to disclose adverse law does not override the duty of zealous representation. Once the adverse authority is disclosed, the lawyer should attempt to distinguish it or present reasons why it is unsound and should not be followed in the present case. [EC 7-23]

c. Manner of presenting adverse authority [§600]

If the lawyer concludes that adverse authority should be cited, but believes that such decisions are distinguishable from or tangential to her basic position, the lawyer *need not diffuse* the main point of her argument by dealing with the adverse authority exhaustively. The use of footnotes or parenthetical asides may be useful *stylistic devices* by which a lawyer can fulfill the duty of disclosure while still presenting the client's position in its best light.

6. Duty When a Client or Witness Gives False Evidence [§601]

A lawyer faces a dilemma when it becomes clear that someone has given or plans to give false evidence favorable to the lawyer's client. In such a case, the lawyer has a duty to the court not to rely upon false evidence, but also has a corresponding duty to minimize injury to the client.

a. False statement in a civil case [§602]

If a client or witness has given false evidence or has made a material mistake (*e.g.*, got a date or other fact wrong in a deposition in a civil case), the lawyer's obligation to correct the record is clear. Even though the lawyer was not the one who made the false statement, the lawyer is said to have "offered" the false statement and thus must correct it or have the witness correct it. [Model Rule 3.3(a)(3)]

b. False testimony in a criminal case [§603]

The issues take on constitutional dimensions when a criminal proceeding is involved and the lawyer has a duty to provide the client effective assistance of counsel.

(1) When false testimony has already been given [§604]

The ABA Code and the Model Rules take different approaches regarding the lawyer's duty when false evidence has been given.

(a) ABA Code approach [§605]

The ABA Code directs the lawyer to act differently depending on whether the perjury, false document, etc., came from the lawyer's client or from another witness.

1) False evidence by witness other than the client [§606]

If a lawyer discovers that someone other than the client has made a mistake in testimony or has committed perjury, the lawyer *must promptly reveal* that "fraud" to the court. [DR 7-102(B)(2)]

2) False evidence by the client [§607]

If the false evidence has come from the lawyer's client, the lawyer must:

(i) *Promptly call upon the client to correct* the record; and if the client does not,

(ii) *Reveal the fraud* to the court, *except where the information is protected as privileged.* [DR 7-102(B)(1)]

But note: As interpreted by the ABA, the exception for privileged information swallows up the rule; "privileged" means not only information protected by the attorney-client evidentiary privilege, but includes all information that the lawyer is required to hold confidential. [ABA Opn. 341]

(b) Model Rules position [§608]

The Model Rules do not draw a distinction based on who gave the false evidence. In *all* cases, the lawyer is required to "*take reasonable remedial measures.*" [Model Rule 3.3(a)(3); Restatement §120(2)]

1) Urge client to cooperate [§609]

The lawyer must speak confidentially with her client and urge the client to cooperate in withdrawing or *correcting the false evidence.* [Model Rule 3.3, comment 10]

2) Ask permission to withdraw [§610]

If the client will not cooperate, the lawyer should consider asking the court's permission to *withdraw.* Ordinarily, withdrawal is not mandatory, unless the lawyer's discovery of the false evidence creates such a rift between the lawyer and client that the lawyer can no longer represent the client effectively. [Model Rule 3.3, comments 10, 15]

UNDER THE MODEL RULES, IF A CLIENT INTENDS TO COMMIT PERJURY, THE LAWYER SHOULD TAKE THE FOLLOWING STEPS:

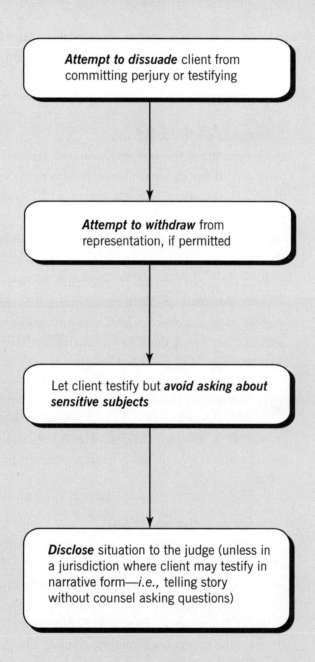

Attempt to dissuade client from committing perjury or testifying

Attempt to withdraw from representation, if permitted

Let client testify but *avoid asking about sensitive subjects*

Disclose situation to the judge (unless in a jurisdiction where client may testify in narrative form—*i.e.,* telling story without counsel asking questions)

3) Disclose situation to judge [§611]

If withdrawal is not permitted or will not solve the problem, the lawyer probably must *disclose* the situation to the judge, even if that means disclosing the client's information that would otherwise be protected under the duty of confidentiality. [Model Rule 3.3, comment 10]

(2) When client or witness intends to commit perjury [§612]

When the client or another witness has not yet committed perjury but has an *intention* to do so, the ABA Code and Model Rules are *consistent,* but not very informative.

(a) Attempt to dissuade [§613]

At a minimum, the lawyer must seek to persuade the client or witness not to testify at all, or at least not to commit perjury. [Model Rule 3.3, comment 6; Restatement §120, comment g]

Example: In the leading Supreme Court case dealing directly with this problem, the lawyer effectively dissuaded his criminal defendant client into telling the truth by threatening to impeach the client's intended lie. Without deciding that this was the best way to handle such a situation, the Court unanimously held that the lawyer's action was not a denial of effective assistance of counsel. [**Nix v. Whiteside,** 475 U.S. 157 (1986)]

Compare: The Supreme Court later held in **Rock v. Arkansas,** 483 U.S. 44 (1987), that a defendant has a constitutional right to testify in his own defense. The *Rock* case did not authorize perjured testimony, but the dilemma inherent in this area of the law is clear.

(b) Attempt to withdraw [§614]

The lawyer next might attempt to withdraw from the representation. This often will not be permitted, especially if the trial is imminent, and it is also likely to make the judge suspicious of the client. However, these problems ordinarily do not make a lawyer's attempt to withdraw improper. [**People v. Schultheis,** 638 P.2d 8 (Colo. 1981)] In fact, the threat itself might persuade the client not to testify.

(c) Avoid sensitive subjects [§615]

Sometimes, a lawyer can let the defendant testify without asking questions about subjects on which the client intends to lie. The Model Rules *require* a lawyer not to offer evidence the lawyer *knows* is false, and *permit* a lawyer in a civil matter not to offer what she *reasonably believes* is false, but the latter rule does not apply in a criminal matter. [Model Rule 3.3(a)(3); *but see* Restatement §120(3)— not invoking the exception]

(d) Disclose situation to judge [§616]

If the lawyer's attempt to withdraw and attempt to dissuade the client from committing perjury have been unsuccessful, the lawyer probably must reveal the situation to the judge, even if that means disclosing the client's confidential information. [Model Rule 3.3(a)(3)]

1) Exception—use of narrative testimony [§617]

Some jurisdictions require that if withdrawal is not permitted, the lawyer should let the client take the stand and tell his story in narrative form. Under this approach, the lawyer may not rely on the false testimony in arguing the case. [*See* **Lowery v. Cardwell**, 575 F.2d 727 (9th Cir. 1978); *and see* Model Rule 3.3, comment 7]

2) Argument for letting client testify [§618]

Reasoning that a defendant's constitutional right to testify should be the controlling principle, some argue that a defense lawyer should be allowed to present perjurious testimony and leave its truth or falsity to the jury. [Monroe Freedman, *Understanding Lawyers' Ethics* (1990)]

7. Disclosure of Crime or Fraud upon the Court [§619]

If a lawyer learns that her client intends to act, is acting, or has acted to criminally or fraudulently corrupt a proceeding, the lawyer must take *"reasonable remedial measures,"* which may include *disclosure to the tribunal*. [Model Rule 3.3(b)] This requirement applies to crimes such as jury tampering, rather than the issues of perjured testimony discussed above. Fortunately, the situation rarely arises.

8. Scope and Duration of the Requirements [§620]

The Model Rules provide their own statute of limitations for the requirements under Model Rule 3.3(a) and (b), just discussed, and their own exception to the duty of confidentiality.

a. When duty ends [§621]

The lawyer's duty ends at "the conclusion of the proceeding." For example, the lawyer need not correct a false statement of fact or law after a final judgment has been *"affirmed on appeal* or the time for review has passed." [Model Rule 3.3(c) and comment 13]

EXAM TIP   **gilbert**

Beware of an exam question in which the client prevails in a proceeding, the opposing party does not file an appeal, and the client *then* tells the lawyer in confidence that he lied. Remember that the lawyer is under *no obligation* to reveal the perjury to anyone because the proceeding is over.

b. Confidential information may be disclosed [§622]
The duty to make disclosures to the tribunal under these provisions—including disclosures about client perjury—expressly overrides the duty of confidentiality under Model Rule 1.6. [Model Rule 3.3(c)]

9. Special Candor Required in *Ex Parte* Proceedings [§623]
When the court is asked to enter a preliminary injunction or considers some other *ex parte* motion, it must rely upon the facts as presented by counsel, untested by the usual adversary process. For this reason, counsel for the moving party must "inform the tribunal of *all material facts* known to the lawyer" that are likely to be *relevant* "whether or not the facts are adverse." [Model Rule 3.3(d); Restatement §112]

C. Other Duties of an Advocate to Nonclients and Tribunals

1. Conduct Affecting Witnesses and Evidence

a. Suppression of evidence [§624]
A lawyer *may not obstruct* any party's *access* to, nor unlawfully *alter or destroy,* relevant evidence. [Model Rule 3.4(a); DR 7-109(A); Cal. Rule 5-220; Restatement §118]

b. Obstructing access to potential witnesses [§625]
A lawyer may not ask a person other than the client not to give relevant information to an opposing party *unless* (i) the person is a *relative, employee, or agent* of the client, and (ii) the lawyer reasonably believes that refraining from giving information *will not affect the person adversely.* [Model Rule 3.4(f); Restatement §116(4); *compare* DR 7-109(B)—must not hide a witness]

c. Inducing favorable testimony [§626]
A lawyer should counsel witnesses to testify truthfully and may not seek to influence their testimony by money or any other means. [Model Rule 3.4(b); EC 7-28]

(1) Prohibition on excessive payments to witness [§627]
Thus, a lawyer may not pay, nor allow the client to pay, a fact witness more than *reasonable* reimbursement for the witness's *expenses* and *loss of time.* [Model Rule 3.4(b); DR 7-109(C); Restatement §117(1)]

(2) Experts [§628]
Of course an expert witness may be paid a reasonable fee for services, both in testifying and pretrial preparation. [Model Rule 3.4(b); DR 7-109(C); Restatement §117(1)]

(3) Fees contingent on outcome of case [§629]

The lawyer *may not* agree to pay even an expert witness a fee *contingent* upon the content of the witness's testimony and/or the outcome of the proceeding. [DR 7-109(C); Cal. Rule 5-310(B); Restatement §117(2); **Person v. Association of the Bar of the City of New York**, 554 F.2d 534 (2d Cir. 1977)—upholding constitutionality of this prohibition]

EXAM TIP	gilbert

If on an exam you see a payment being made to a witness, do not assume it is automatically improper. Remember that a lawyer may: reimburse a witness for *reasonable expenses* (e.g., travel, hotel, meals), compensate a witness for *loss of time*, and pay an *expert witness a reasonable fee* for services. However, a lawyer *must not pay* a fee that is *contingent* on the content of the testimony or the outcome of the case.

---

d. Coaching witnesses [§630]

Discussions with a witness before putting the witness on the stand are normally essential to pretrial preparation and presentation of the evidence. However, such discussions must not turn into "coaching" sessions whereby the witness is improperly influenced to give certain testimony.

(1) Application

It is clearly improper for the lawyer to bend the testimony or put words in the witness's mouth. However, it is *not improper* for the lawyer to *probe the witness's recollection*, to *point out fallacies or inconsistencies* in the witness's version of the facts, and even to *refresh* and *remind* the witness of key points in the evidence that the witness has trouble recalling. [*See, e.g.,* **People v. McGuirk**, 245 N.E.2d 917 (Ill. 1969)—not improper for prosecutor to help nine-year-old rape victim frame her testimony before trial]

(2) Note

It is very difficult to draw a line between improper coaching and proper preparation of a witness. The important point is that the *essential nature* of the witness's testimony *may not be altered* or colored by the lawyer's emphasis or suggestions prior to trial.

e. Treatment of adverse witnesses at trial [§631]

The rules of evidence give a lawyer considerable leeway in cross-examining a hostile witness, including the right to impeach the witness and undermine the witness's credibility with the jury. Nevertheless, there are certain restraints on the zeal with which such examinations can be conducted.

(1) Examining to degrade or harass a witness [§632]

It is misconduct for a lawyer to use cross-examination simply to degrade or harass a witness, or for the purpose of prejudicing the jury. [Model Rule 4.4; DR 7-106(C)(2); Restatement §106, comment c]

(2) Expressing personal opinion on witness's credibility [§633]

It is likewise improper for a lawyer to express a *personal opinion* as to the *credibility* of the testimony. [Model Rule 3.4(e); DR 7-106(c)(4); Restatement §107(1)]

CONDUCT WITH WITNESSES—EXAMPLES   gilbert

WHEN PREPARING A WITNESS FOR TRIAL AND WHEN CROSS-EXAMINING AN ADVERSE WITNESS, A LAWYER MUST BE CAREFUL NOT TO CROSS THE ETHICAL LINE.

PROPER CONDUCT	IMPROPER CONDUCT
• Probing a witness's memory	• Coaching a witness
• Refreshing a witness's recollection	• Putting words in a witness's mouth
• Pointing out fallacies or inconsistencies	• Bending the witness's testimony
• Impeaching an adverse witness	• Harassing or degrading an adverse witness
• Undermining an adverse witness's credibility	• Expressing personal opinion as to witness's credibility

---

f. Receipt of an inadvertently sent document [§634]

A problem created by broad discovery and new technology is the inadvertent transmission of a privileged or otherwise sensitive document to someone not entitled to it. For example, confidential e-mail might mistakenly be sent to *all* counsel instead of just to counsel in a privileged relationship to the client.

(1) Original ABA advice—send it back [§635]

The first ABA response to this problem was to say that, as a matter of professional courtesy, the receiving lawyer should refrain from reading it and should destroy the document or send it back. [ABA Opn. 94-382]

(2) New requirement—notify the sender [§636]

Later reflection by the ABA, however, recognized that the former rule put the recipient lawyer in a difficult position through no fault of her own. It required the lawyer to forget what could not be forgotten. Thus, the Model Rules were amended in 2002 to say that the recipient must "promptly notify the sender" of the mistaken transmission, but the burden is then on the sender to get a judicial declaration that the item must be returned, remains privileged, etc. [Model Rule 4.4(b)]

2. Strategy and Tactics in Trial [§637]

Although the lawyer is expected to be a partisan advocate for the client, there are limits to the tactics the lawyer may employ in the courtroom. Procedural and evidentiary rules are means of insuring that the proceedings are conducted in the interests of justice; professional standards also impose restrictions on the lawyer. [EC 7-25]

a. **Reference to matters unsubstantiated by evidence [§638]**

In court appearances, a lawyer must not state or allude to any matter that the lawyer has no reasonable basis to believe will be supported by admissible evidence. [Model Rule 3.4(e); DR 7-106(c)(1); Restatement §107(2)]

(1) **Opening statement by counsel [§639]**

A lawyer should not make references in the opening statement to purported facts in the case without having a *good faith belief* that they will be *supported by admissible evidence.* [EC 7-25]

(2) **Unsubstantiated testimony from witness [§640]**

It is likewise *improper* for the lawyer to imply, in the way the lawyer frames questions to a witness, the existence of *facts not in the record or incapable of being proved.*

(3) **Improper arguments [§641]**

It is misconduct for a lawyer to suggest or imply in argument to the jury the existence of *facts not proved.*

b. **Personal knowledge or opinion of lawyer [§642]**

The lawyer is also *prohibited* from asserting *personal knowledge* of the facts in issue (except when testifying as a witness), or presenting a *personal opinion* on the justness of a claim, the credibility of a witness, the culpability of a civil litigant, or the guilt or innocence of an accused. [Model Rule 3.4(e); DR 7-106(C)(3), (4); Cal. Rule 5-200(E); Restatement §107(1); **Hawk v. Superior Court,** 42 Cal. App. 3d 108 (1974)]

EXAM TIP   **gilbert**

Don't get confused about this rule. Although a lawyer *cannot give his personal opinion* about the credibility of a witness, he can certainly make the point that the witness is not credible by referring to the evidence. Thus, the lawyer *cannot* say, "Defendant told you that the light was green, but I don't believe him and you shouldn't either," but he *can* say, "Defendant says the light was green, but he stands to lose a lot of money in this case. Two eyewitnesses, who have nothing to gain or lose, testified that it was red. You decide whom to believe."

---

c. **Appeals to emotion or prejudice [§643]**

Some appeal by an advocate to the emotion of jurors is inevitable. However, it is misconduct for a lawyer to arouse the emotions or prejudices of jurors as to matters that are not supported by admissible evidence and thus are legally irrelevant. [Model Rule 3.4(e); DR 7-106(c)(1); Restatement §107(2)]

(1) **References to defendant's insurance or lack thereof [§644]**

In most jurisdictions, it is improper for plaintiff's counsel to make any reference to the fact that the defendant is covered by liability insurance to prove negligence or other wrongdoing. Its mention is calculated solely to encourage the jury to award a greater sum. In some jurisdictions, it is equally improper for defense counsel to tell the jury that the defendant is **not** insured. [*See* Fed. R. Evid. 41]

(2) "Golden rule" argument [§645]

Jurors are required to act as objective triers of fact and to exclude personal feelings in arriving at their verdict. Hence, it is *improper* for counsel to ask the jury to "bring back a verdict that you would expect if *you* were the plaintiff." [**Miku v. Almen,** 193 So. 2d 17 (Fla. 1966)]

d. Violation of rules of evidence or procedure [§646]

A lawyer must not knowingly violate an established rule of procedure or evidence. [Model Rule 3.4(c); Restatement §105; *and see* DR 7-106(c)(7)—violation may not be "intentional or habitual"]

(1) Distinguish—may test validity of particular rule [§647]

It is *not improper* for a lawyer to *openly refuse* to comply with a court order or rule of procedure in order to *test the validity* of the order or rule—provided this is done in good faith. [Model Rule 3.4(c); EC 7-25]

(2) Sanctions [§648]

The sanctions that may be imposed against lawyers (and/or their clients) for violation of procedural and evidentiary rules depend upon the nature of the violation. Courts may impose *sanctions against the lawyer personally* where it appears that the violations are *deliberate*. Such intentional conduct may be punished as a *contempt of court* (*i.e.,* by fine or imprisonment), and may lead to *professional discipline* (*i.e.,* suspension or disbarment).

(a) Distinguish—constitutional limitation [§649]

Sanctions may *not* be imposed when the lawyer in good faith advises the client not to comply with an *unconstitutional* court order, when ordinary methods of challenge and review would not sufficiently protect the client's rights. [**Maness v. Meyers,** 419 U.S. 449 (1975)—client advised not to produce documents where privilege against self-incrimination could not otherwise be fully protected; lawyer's contempt conviction set aside]

3. Requirement of Dignity in Adversary Proceedings [§650]

A lawyer's duty to represent the client with zeal must also be balanced against the lawyer's obligation of courtesy and proper behavior toward *all persons* involved in the legal process.

a. Advocate must not disrupt tribunal [§651]

In handling a case, the lawyer must not engage in conduct intended to *disrupt* the tribunal. [Model Rule 3.5(d); *and see* DR 7-106(c)(6)—avoid undignified or discourteous conduct]

(1) Distinguish—objections to questions or comments by the judge [§652]

It is *not improper* for a lawyer to *object* to any *questions* the trial judge may ask of a witness (whether the witness was called by the court or by another party).

Example: Where the jury had been deliberating in a murder trial for over three weeks, and the judge interrupted their deliberations with a "dynamite" charge and comments regarding credibility of witnesses that was heavily slanted against his client, the defendant's lawyer was entitled to object. [**Cooper v. Superior Court**, 55 Cal. 2d 291 (1961)]

---

(2) Respect for court rulings in proceedings [§653]

Respect for judicial rulings is essential to the administration of justice. Thus, a lawyer may not disregard (nor advise the client to disregard) rulings made by the court in the proceeding. But a lawyer *may* properly take steps in *good faith* to test the correctness of any ruling or action by the court. [Model Rule 3.4(c); DR 7-106(A); Restatement §105]

b. Conduct toward opposing counsel [§654]

A standard of dignity and courtesy is required in all dealings with opposing counsel. Each lawyer must abstain from offensive conduct toward adversaries, and a lawyer who indulges in personal abuse or vilification is subject to discipline. [EC 7-37]

(1) Compliance with local customs and practice [§655]

A lawyer must comply with "known local customs of courtesy or practice of the bar or a particular tribunal," unless the lawyer gives opposing counsel timely notice of his intention not to comply. [DR 7-106(C)(5)]

(2) Compliance with reasonable requests [§656]

Likewise, a lawyer should accede to reasonable requests from opposing counsel regarding court proceedings, settings, continuances, waiver of procedural formalities, or similar matters that do not prejudice the client's rights or interests. [Model Rule 3.2, comment 1; EC 7-38]

c. Physical appearance of lawyer in court [§657]

As part of the lawyer's duty to maintain the dignity of court proceedings, a lawyer should refrain from sensationalism or exhibitionism in personal appearance or attire in court. [**State v. Cherryhomes**, 840 P.2d 1261 (N.M. 1992)]

d. Undue solicitude toward court [§658]

While the dignity of judicial proceedings is adversely affected by discourteous behavior on the part of counsel, it may also be compromised by flattery or other actions designed to obtain favorable treatment from the court. [EC 7-36]

4. Settlement Restricting Lawyer's Right to Practice [§659]

The law expressly prohibits an agreement made as part of settling a client's claim that restricts the lawyer's future practice. [Model Rule 5.6(b); DR 2-108(B); Restatement §13(2)] For example, if a lawyer has done a particularly good job investigating a product for her client's product liability claim, the defendant may want to settle the matter and include a provision that the lawyer will not file any future cases on behalf of future plaintiffs. The lawyer may not enter into such an agreement.

D. Limitations on Trial Publicity

1. Introduction [§660]

Impartial adjudication of disputes can be adversely affected when advocates make public comments about their cases, unrestrained by the rules of evidence. Thus, a series of restrictions are imposed on out-of-court statements in connection with pending criminal and civil proceedings. [Model Rule 3.6; DR 7-107; Restatement §109]

2. General Rule [§661]

A lawyer may not make an out-of-court statement likely to be reported by the news media if the lawyer knows or reasonably should know that the statement would have a *"substantial likelihood of materially prejudicing an adjudicative proceeding."* [Model Rule 3.6(a)]

a. Tension with the First Amendment [§662]

The public's important right to know about government acts such as criminal trials makes it important that restrictions on comments be no greater than necessary. In extreme cases, however, the Court has held that prejudicial publicity denied the defendant due process of law. [*See, e.g.,* **Sheppard v. Maxwell,** 384 U.S. 333 (1966)]

b. Constitutionality of Model Rule standard upheld [§663]

The Supreme Court has upheld the constitutionality of the "substantial likelihood of material prejudice" standard as applied to pretrial statements by lawyers. However, the Court held that a state standard permitting lawyers to describe only the "general nature" of a defense "without elaboration" was void for vagueness. [**Gentile v. Nevada State Bar,** 501 U.S. 1030 (1991)]

3. Criminal Proceedings

a. Information that may be disclosed [§664]

A lawyer associated with the investigation of a criminal matter (*e.g.,* a district attorney) is forbidden to make any out-of-court statement capable of public dissemination that does more than state *without elaboration:*

(i) The *crime* being investigated;

(ii) Information in a *public record*;

(iii) The fact that an *investigation is in progress*;

(iv) A request for *assistance* in apprehending a suspect or other assistance;

(v) A *warning* of any danger to the public;

(vi) The *identity* of the accused; and

(vii) *Arrest information*, if any.

[Model Rule 3.6(b); DR 7-107(A), (C); *compare* Restatement §109—caution about lists such as these]

b. Matters that should not be disclosed [§665]
Particularly sensitive matters identified by the rules include: (i) the *prior arrest record* of the accused, (ii) the existence of a *confession* or the *possibility of a guilty plea*, (iii) *results of tests* performed or the *refusal to submit to such tests*, (iv) any *opinion as to the guilt* of the accused, and (v) information that would be *inadmissible at trial*. [DR 7-107(B); Model Rule 3.6, comment 5]

c. Lawyers affected [§666]
These restrictions apply to any lawyer—whether part of the prosecution or defense—and any lawyer associated with the office or agency prosecuting the case. [Model Rule 3.6(a), (d); DR 7-107(B)]

d. Special duty of prosecutors [§667]
In addition, the Model Rules now say that prosecutors, "except for statements that are necessary to inform the public of the nature and extent of the prosecutor's action and that serve a legitimate law enforcement purpose," must "refrain from making extrajudicial comments that have a *substantial likelihood of heightening public condemnation* of the accused." [Model Rule 3.8(f)]

e. Latitude given defense lawyers [§668]
Under what is informally called the "anti-leak rule," defense lawyers now may "make a statement that a reasonable lawyer would believe is required to protect a client from the substantial undue prejudicial effect of recent publicity not initiated by the lawyer or the lawyer's client." However, such a statement must "be limited to such information as is necessary to mitigate the recent adverse publicity." [Model Rule 3.6(c)]

f. Professional or juvenile disciplinary proceedings [§669]
All of the above limitations on statements during criminal actions apply as well to professional disciplinary proceedings or juvenile proceedings, to the extent they are consistent with other rules applicable to such matters. [Model Rule 3.6, comment 2; DR 7-107(F)]

4. **Civil and Administrative Proceedings [§670]**

By their terms, most of the above limitations on pretrial publicity apply equally to civil litigation. [*But see* **Hirschkop v. Snead,** 594 F.2d 356 (4th Cir. 1979)—rule of Virginia Code of Professional Responsibility held unconstitutional as applied to other than criminal cases] However, it is likely that the number of civil cases in which publicity will be found to violate the "substantial likelihood of material prejudice" standard will be far fewer than the number of criminal cases.

E. Limitations on Advancing Money to Client

1. **Introduction [§671]**

A controversial but longstanding limitation on a trial lawyer's conduct forbids the lawyer from giving financial support to a client during litigation. Such support was traditionally prohibited along with solicitation because of the tendency to stir up litigation, but today, the concern is that the more financially involved the lawyer becomes, the more difficult it is to exercise independent judgment in handling the case.

2. **ABA Code Standards [§672]**

When *litigation is pending or contemplated,* the ABA Code *prohibits* the lawyer from lending money (or guaranteeing a loan) to the client, except that the lawyer may lend the client money for litigation expenses, *"provided the client remains ultimately liable for such expenses."* [DR 5-103(B)]

a. **Litigation expenses [§673]**

"Litigation expenses" include such things as court costs, expenses of investigation and discovery, expenses of medical examinations in preparation for trial (but not expenses for treatment), and expenses of obtaining and presenting evidence (*e.g.,* expert witness fees).

b. **Client's obligation to repay loan [§674]**

The client must remain ultimately liable for any expenses advanced by the lawyer. However, nothing in the ABA Code requires the lawyer to sue if the client fails to repay the funds.

3. **Model Rules Approach [§675]**

The Model Rules take a somewhat more permissive attitude toward financial assistance.

a. **Litigation expenses [§676]**

The Model Rules *permit* a lawyer to advance court costs and other litigation expenses, repayment of which *may be contingent* on the outcome of the case. [Model Rule 1.8(e); Restatement §36(2)]

b.   **Indigent client [§677]**

If the client is indigent, the lawyer need make no provision for repayment of the expenses. [Model Rule 1.8(e)]

4.   No Other Financial Support [§678]

However, the law has consistently forbidden paying living expenses or meeting other financial needs of the client, even when the payments are based on genuine compassion. [*See* **State of Oklahoma v. Smolen,** 17 P.3d 456 (Okla. 2000)—lawyer loaned client $1,200 after client's house burned down]

a.   **Criticism of traditional rule [§679]**

Prohibiting a lawyer who is handling a case from lending money to cover the client's living expenses may leave the client without means of support. As a result, the client may be forced to accept an inadequate settlement. This would defeat both the client's interest and that of the lawyer who is handling the matter on a contingent fee basis.

b.   **Some evidence the law is changing [§680]**

In at least a few cases, courts have suggested that there is little justification for this prohibition. [*Compare* **Osprey v. Cabana Limited Partnership,** 532 S.E.2d 269 (S.C. 2000)—allowing lender to advance living expenses in exchange for interest in judgment]

F. Lawyer as Witness and Advocate

1.   Nature of the Problem [§681]

When a lawyer representing a client in litigation also may be a witness in the case, the lawyer may have to assume inconsistent roles. The function of the lawyer as *advocate* is to advance and *argue* the client's case, whereas the function of a *witness* is to state facts *objectively*. The advocate-witness may be forced to argue his own credibility, may be more easily impeached, and therefore may be less effective both as counsel and as witness. [EC 5-9]

2.   Prohibition on Appearance in Both Capacities [§682]

The general rule is that a lawyer may *neither accept nor continue employment* in litigation if the lawyer knows (or if it is likely) that the lawyer may be called as a witness during the proceedings. [Model Rule 3.7; DR 5-101(B), 5-102(A); Restatement §108; *but see* Cal. Rule 5-210(c)—permitting client consent to dual role]

a.   **Doubts resolved in favor of lawyer withdrawing from case [§683]**

The lawyer does not have a choice of which role to assume. The lawyer must act *as a witness* in the matter if that testimony would be material to establishing the client's claim or defense. [EC 5-10; Rule 3.7(a); Restatement §108(1)(b)]

b. Representation by another lawyer in witness-lawyer's firm [§684]

The force of this rule is significantly moderated by the fact that the Model Rules provide that the disqualification is *not imputed*; *i.e.,* another lawyer in the witness's firm *may* act as advocate in the trial. [Model Rule 3.7(b); *but see* DR 5-105(D)—not permitting the related lawyer to act]

3. Exceptions to General Rule [§685]

In some situations, the lawyer may appear as a witness on behalf of the client while continuing to serve as advocate.

a. Testimony on uncontested matter [§686]

A lawyer who intends to testify solely on *an uncontested matter* (*i.e.,* one as to which there is no reason to expect substantial evidence in opposition, *e.g.,* as witness to execution of an instrument or to establish receipt of correspondence) may properly act as both witness and counsel. [Model Rule 3.7(a)(1); DR 5-101(B)(1), (2); Restatement §108(2)(a); **Haack v. Great Atlantic & Pacific Tea Co.,** 603 S.W.2d 645 (Mo. 1980)]

---

e.g. **Example—will execution:** It is permissible for a lawyer to testify as a witness to the *execution of a decedent's will* and to express an opinion as to the decedent's testamentary capacity, freedom from undue influence, etc., where those issues are not in real dispute.

---

cf. **Compare—will contest:** In the event of a *will contest* in which testamentary intent or capacity is at issue, the lawyer who drafted the will *cannot* appear as an attorney for any party to the will contest. The lawyer is a crucial witness on the issue of testamentary intent or capacity, and therefore, appearing as an advocate would be improper.

---

b. Testimony on nature and value of legal services [§687]

The lawyer is *not barred* from representing a client as both counsel and witness when testimony is required about the nature and value of legal services rendered by the lawyer or his law firm (*e.g.,* where the client sues a third party to recover legal expenses as a result of third party's breach of contract). [Model Rule 3.7(a)(2); DR 5-101(B)(3); Restatement §108(2)(a)]

c. Preventing hardship to client [§688]

The law also permits the lawyer to testify with respect to even a contested matter if failure to do so, or the need to withdraw as counsel, would "work as a substantial hardship on his client because of the distinctive value of the lawyer or his firm as counsel in the particular case." [Model Rule 3.7(a)(3); DR 5-101(B)(4); Restatement §108(2)(b)]

(1) Relevant factors [§689]

In determining whether a "hardship" situation exists, the following factors are relevant: (i) the *personal or financial sacrifice* caused the client if the lawyer refuses, or withdraws from, employment; (ii) the *materiality* of the lawyer's testimony; and (iii) the *effect* of such testimony on the lawyer's advocacy in the case. [EC 5-10; Model Rule 3.7, comment 4; Restatement §108, comment h]

d. Testimony necessary to prevent miscarriage of justice [§690]

If the testimony of counsel is needed to prevent a miscarriage of justice, such testimony is proper. For example, a prosecutor may testify to refute the *unexpected denial* by defendant of a prior conversation with the prosecutor. Such testimony is required to rehabilitate the prosecutor's position before the jury. [**People v. Stokely,** 266 Cal. App. 2d 930 (1968)]

WHEN LAWYER MAY APPEAR AS WITNESS FOR CLIENT **gilbert**

GENERAL RULE: A LAWYER MAY NOT ACCEPT OR CONTINUE EMPLOYMENT WHEN HE KNOWS OR IT IS LIKELY THAT HE MAY BE CALLED AS A WITNESS.

EXCEPTIONS:

☑ When testimony relates only to an *uncontested matter*;

☑ When testimony pertains to the *nature and value of legal services*;

☑ To prevent a *substantial hardship to client*;

☑ To prevent a *miscarriage of justice.*

---

4. Lawyer Called as Witness by Opposing Party [§691]

A different problem is presented when the lawyer is called as a witness *other than* on behalf of the lawyer's client (*e.g.*, the adverse party calls the lawyer as a hostile witness to prove the content of the meeting between the client and the opposing party).

a. Possibility that testimony will create conflict of interest [§692]

If the lawyer's testimony would conflict with that of the client, the lawyer may act as counsel only with the informed consent of the client. [Model Rule 3.7, comment 6; DR 5-102(B); Restatement §108(3)]

b. Lawyer's firm sometimes also may not act as counsel [§693]

In such situations, the usual rule permitting another lawyer in the witness-lawyer's firm to act as counsel may not apply. Cross-examining and testing the credibility of one's own law partner would present a conflict requiring the client's informed consent, and in some cases may be too great a conflict to be waived at all. [Model Rule 3.6, comment 7; Restatement §108(3)]

G. Improper Contacts with Court Officials and Jurors

1. Introduction [§694]

Proper functioning of the adversary system depends on the *impartiality* of judges, court officials, and jurors and on the litigants' *equal access* to the tribunal. [EC 7-34, 7-35]

2. No Gifts or Loans to Court Personnel [§695]

A lawyer may not make a gift or loan to a judge, hearing officer, or other employee of a tribunal unless permitted by law (*e.g.,* a gift to a friend or relative that is appropriate for the occasion and the relationship). [Model Rule 3.5(a); DR 7-110(A); EC 7-34; Restatement §113(2); Cal. Rule 5-300]

a. Scope of prohibition [§696]

This prohibition extends not merely to monetary compensation but to *anything* of value. [DR 7-110(A)]

b. Exception—political contributions [§697]

A lawyer may contribute to the *campaign fund* of a candidate for judicial office, provided the contributions comply with all requirements of the ABA Code of Judicial Conduct. [Model Rule 8.4(f); DR 7-110(A)]

3. Communication with Judge or Hearing Officer [§698]

In an adversary proceeding, the lawyer may communicate with a judge or hearing officer regarding the *merits of the case* only in the course of the proceedings or under certain specified conditions. [Model Rule 3.5(b)]

a. Written communication [§699]

In most states, a lawyer may not communicate with the judge or hearing officer in writing without promptly delivering a *copy* of the writing to opposing counsel (or to the adverse party if she is not represented by counsel). [DR 7-110(B)(2)]

b. Oral communications [§700]

Traditionally, it is improper for a lawyer to speak to the judge or hearing officer regarding a pending matter, other than during the course of the proceeding, unless adequate *prior notice* has been given to the opposing party. [DR 7-110(B)(3)]

c. Communications "otherwise authorized by law" [§701]

Communication with the court is only permitted to the extent authorized by applicable federal or state law. [Model Rule 3.5(b); DR 7-110(B)(4)] The most frequent instance in which such communications are authorized is in connection with *ex parte* applications to the court.

4. Contacts with Jurors [§702]

To safeguard the impartiality of the judicial process, jurors and prospective jurors must be protected against extraneous influence. Therefore, a lawyer owes a duty to the legal system to avoid improper communications or contacts with jurors, and a duty to disclose to the appropriate court any such conduct by others. [Model Rule 3.5(a); DR 7-108; Cal. Rule 5-320; Restatement §115]

a. Communications before trial [§703]

Before the trial of a case, lawyers connected with the matter *must not communicate* (or cause anyone else to communicate) with any person known to be a member of the jury panel from which a jury for the case will be selected. Any investigation of members of the jury panel to determine their backgrounds and the existence of any factors that would be grounds for a challenge (*e.g.*, bias, relationship to party, etc.) must be conducted with "circumspection and restraint" so as not to discourage jury service. [EC 7-30; DR 7-108(E)]

b. Contacts during trial [§704]

Other than addressing the jurors as part of the official proceedings (*e.g.*, in closing argument), a lawyer who is connected with the case *may not communicate* (or cause another to communicate) with a member of the jury during the course of a trial. [DR 7-108(B)(1)]

EXAM TIP   **gilbert**

Note that this no contact with jurors rule is strict: There should be *no communications* with jurors or prospective jurors except as part of official proceedings *during and before trial*. Thus, for example, if the lawyer sees a juror in the elevator, she should not talk to the juror even about unrelated topics and regardless of who initiates the conversation.

---

c. Communications after trial [§705]

After the conclusion of a trial, a lawyer has somewhat more freedom to communicate with jurors regarding the case. [EC 7-29]

(1) To determine basis for challenging jury verdict [§706]

A jury verdict may be subject to challenge for certain kinds of irregularities in the jury deliberations, *e.g.*, improper influence from outsiders or a verdict arrived at by flipping a coin. (*See* Civil Procedure Summary.) To discover such irregularities, the lawyer may interview the jurors after the trial if not prohibited by law or court order. [Model Rule 3.5(c)(1); DR 7-108(D); Restatement §115(3)(b)]

(2) To improve advocacy skill [§707]

Another reason for permitting contact with jurors after trial is to inform lawyers of the factors that led to the jury verdict and thus enable the lawyers to improve their skill and efficiency for other clients. [ABA Opn. 319]

(3) Limitations [§708]

However, a lawyer may not interrogate any juror who does not wish to be interviewed. Moreover, in questioning those jurors willing to talk, the lawyer must take great care to avoid questions or comments that are calculated to *harass or embarrass* the jurors or to influence their conduct in future jury service. [Model Rule 3.5(c); DR 7-108(D); Restatement §115(3)(a)]

d. Communications with members of juror's family [§709]

The same restraints on communications with jurors and prospective jurors apply as well to contacts with members of their families. [DR 7-108(F); EC 7-31]

H. Special Duties of Prosecutors and Other Government Lawyers

1. Introduction [§710]

The "client" of the public prosecutor or government lawyer is the state, and the prosecutor's responsibility is to *seek justice* rather than to convict. As a result, the obligations of these lawyers are somewhat different from those of the private advocate.

2. Special Limitations on Prosecutorial Function [§711]

There are basic limitations that set the prosecutor apart from a lawyer representing a private client:

a. Restraint in exercise of governmental power [§712]

As a representative of the sovereign, the prosecutor is obliged to use *restraint* in the discretionary exercise of governmental powers, and particularly in the *selection of cases to prosecute.*

(1) Probable cause required [§713]

In this connection, a public prosecutor may not institute criminal charges when she knows (or it is obvious) that such charges are *not supported by probable cause.* [Model Rule 3.8(a); DR 7-103(A); Restatement §97(3)]

(2) Must not require waiver of rights [§714]

Similarly, a prosecutor may not seek to get an unrepresented accused to *waive important pretrial rights,* such as the right to a preliminary hearing. [Model Rule 3.8(c)]

b.   Must help accused obtain counsel [§715]

The prosecutor must also reasonably assure that the accused knows how to obtain counsel and has had a chance to do so. [Model Rule 3.8(b)]

c.   Dual role during trial [§716]

At trial, the prosecutor is both an advocate *and* a representative of the broad public interest. Thus, the prosecutor's decisions must be *fair to all*, rather than calculated merely to prevail in the pending action. [EC 7-13]

3.   Duties Respecting Witnesses and Evidence [§717]

In light of the special responsibility to see that justice is done, the prosecutor also has special duties with respect to witnesses and evidence in criminal proceedings.

a.   Obligation to disclose evidence beneficial to defense [§718]

The prosecutor has a constitutional as well as a professional obligation to make timely disclosure to the defense of any available evidence known to the prosecutor that may negate guilt, mitigate the degree of the offense, or reduce the appropriate punishment. [Model Rule 3.8(d); DR 7-103(B); Restatement §97(4); **Brady v. Maryland,** 373 U.S. 83 (1963)]

b.   Obligation to pursue "harmful" evidence [§719]

Similarly, a prosecutor may not intentionally fail to pursue evidence merely because such evidence may damage the prosecution's case or aid the accused. [EC 7-13]

c.   Access to government witnesses [§720]

The prosecutor ordinarily must also permit defense counsel to *interview* government witnesses and may not properly counsel such witnesses to refuse to talk to the defense. [**Gregory v. United States,** 369 F.2d 185 (D.C. Cir. 1966)]

d.   Use of subpoena to get defense records [§721]

A relatively new practice of United States Attorneys has been to subpoena defense lawyers' files or call the lawyers before a grand jury to testify about fee arrangements and other information about their clients. Model Rule 3.8(e) now *prohibits* such conduct unless the prosecutor reasonably believes:

(1)   The information is *not privileged*;

(2)   The evidence is *essential* to an ongoing investigation or prosecution; and

(3)   There is *no other feasible way* to get the information.

4.   Obligations of Government Lawyers Generally [§722]

Many of the above duties are incumbent upon *all* government lawyers, not merely public prosecutors.

> ### EXAMPLES OF SPECIAL RESPONSIBILITIES OF PROSECUTORS   gilbert
>
> #### TO ASSURE THAT A DEFENDANT IS TRIED BY FAIR PROCEDURES AND THAT GUILT IS DECIDED ON PROPER AND SUFFICIENT EVIDENCE, A PROSECUTOR:
>
> ☑ *Must make reasonable efforts* to assure that an accused is advised of the *right to counsel* and is given an opportunity to obtain counsel;
>
> ☑ *Must timely disclose* to the defense all evidence and information known to the prosecutor that tends to *negate guilt, mitigate the degree of an offense, or reduce the appropriate punishment*;
>
> ☑ *Must not* institute a criminal charge that is *not supported by probable cause*;
>
> ☑ *Must not seek a waiver of important pretrial rights* from an unrepresented accused;
>
> ☑ *Must not subpoena a lawyer* to give evidence about a client *unless* the information *is not privileged*, *is essential*, and *cannot be obtained* in any other way;
>
> ☑ *Must not make extrajudicial statements* that have a substantial likelihood of *heightening public condemnation* of the accused (except for statements necessary to inform the public of the nature and extent of the prosecutor's action and that serve a legitimate law enforcement purpose).

a. **Terminating actions [§723]**

Thus, a government lawyer with discretionary power relative to civil litigation should not institute or continue actions that are obviously unfair. [EC 7-14; *and see* **Freeport-McMoRan Oil & Gas Co. v. Federal Energy Regulatory Commission**, 962 F.2d 45 (D.C. Cir. 1992)—government should concede what is clearly true and not make private party prove point]

b. **Developing full record [§724]**

Even where litigation appears warranted, the government lawyer has a responsibility to develop a full and fair record; the lawyer must not use her position or the economic power of the government to harass parties or to force unjust settlements or results. [EC 7-14]

Chapter Seven:
The Business of Practicing Law

CONTENTS

Chapter Approach

This chapter covers the basic rules of running a modern law office. It is hard to think of most of the issues in this chapter as dealing with "ethics" at all, but they are the subject of professional rules that you will need to know and follow. The key issues relate to:

1. The variety of *ways that lawyers associate themselves* to practice law and the obligations of *supervisors* in those practice organizations;

2. The aggressive *marketing of law practice* and limits on that marketing;

3. Lawyer *specialization;* and

4. *Fee sharing.*

Finally, keep in mind that one of the most important aspects of the "business" of practicing law—the charging of legal fees—was addressed earlier in Chapter 2 of this Summary (*see supra,* §§210 *et seq.*).

A. Associations of Lawyers for the Practice of Law

1. Introduction [§725]

Much of the ABA Code was written as though law were practiced primarily by sole practitioners in a general practice. That, of course, is no longer true. The Model Rules better recognize that law firms, legal services agencies, legal clinics, and other groups, corporations, and government agencies are all settings for the practice of law. [Model Rules 5.1 - 5.3, 7.5; ABA Code DR 2-102] Some of these associations, and the rules of ethics that apply to them, are discussed below.

2. Law Firms and Professional Law Corporations

a. Roles in a traditional law firm [§726]

Partly as a result of the benefits to be derived from specialization and partly for economic reasons (*e.g.,* sharing overhead), partnerships and other associations of lawyers are common.

(1) Partners [§727]

Partners are the principals in a traditional firm.

(a) Normally share fees [§728]

Partners normally share the fees generated by the firm. This financial interest in each other's work is one of the justifications for imputation of conflicts of interest (*see supra*, §470).

(b) Holding out as partners [§729]

Lawyers may not hold themselves out as partners unless they in fact are partners. If they violate this rule, they will be treated as partners liable for each other's malpractice. [Model Rule 7.5(d); DR 2-102(C); **Gosselin v. Webb**, 242 F.3d 412 (1st Cir. 2001)]

EXAM TIP   gilbert

You may see a question that involves lawyers who are not associated with each other in a law practice but who share office space, secretarial help, a photocopier, etc. Remember that, although this is permitted, they *must not imply that they are associated* in a law firm (e.g., by sharing a firm name) or they risk being treated as partners when one gets sued for malpractice (*i.e.*, liable for damages).

---

(2) Associates [§730]

Reference to a lawyer as an "associate" is proper only where the lawyer has an ongoing relationship with a law firm (or another lawyer) other than as a partner. Normally, an associate performs legal services for the firm's clients as a salaried employee of the firm. [ABA Opn. 310]

(a) Rights of associates [§731]

In the past, little was said about the rights or status of associates. However, associates have been held entitled to: (i) *form a union* to bargain with their law firm under federal labor laws [**Foley, Hoag & Eliot**, 229 N.L.R.B. 456 (1977)]; and (ii) sue their law firms for *discrimination* under Title VII of the Civil Rights Act of 1964 [*see, e.g.,* **Lucido v. Cravath, Swaine & Moore**, 425 F. Supp. 123 (E.D. Va. 1977); *and see* **Hishon v. King & Spalding**, 467 U.S. 69 (1984)— failure to admit lawyer to *partnership* in a firm is a decision subject to the Civil Rights Act]

Example: In *Hishon, supra*, a female associate at a law firm filed a gender discrimination suit after she was rejected twice for promotion to the position of partner. She alleged that, when she accepted employment with the firm, she relied on the firm's representation that advancement to partnership was customary for associates with satisfactory evaluations and that partnership decisions were made on a "fair and equal basis." She further alleged that consideration for partnership was a provision of her employment contract and that the partnership decision was critical, because associates who were not promoted to partners were terminated. The

Court held that the opportunity to become a partner was a benefit of employment that could not be denied discriminatorily and that the plaintiff stated a claim under Title VII.

(3) "Of counsel" [§732]

The term "of counsel" signifies a lawyer's continuing relationship with a law firm, *other than as a partner or associate*. The term describes many kinds of relationships, but often the title is taken by a lawyer who formerly was a partner in the law firm and now has only occasional client responsibility. The lawyer may or may not maintain an office with the firm. [DR 2-102(A)(4)]

(4) Paralegals [§733]

The Model Rules expressly authorize the use of nonlawyer legal assistants (popularly called "paralegals"). This benefits the client through more efficient service at reduced cost, and the lawyer through increased income. [Model Rule 5.3; EC 3-6; ABA Opn. 320]

b. Practice through professional law corporations [§734]

In most states today, lawyers may form a corporation or limited liability company ("LLC") to carry on the practice of law by complying with special incorporation requirements. [*See, e.g.,* Cal. Bus. & Prof. Code §§6127.5, 6160 - 6172] The principals in some professional law corporations are called "shareholders," rather than partners.

c. Supervisory relationships [§735]

The Model Rules contain provisions on supervisory responsibilities in a law firm, law office, or professional corporation that have no direct counterparts in the ABA Code.

(1) Partner's responsibility to ensure conformity with professional standards [§736]

A law firm partner must make reasonable efforts to assure that the firm has measures in place to ensure that all lawyers in the firm will conform to professional standards. [Model Rule 5.1(a)]

(2) Direct supervisor of another lawyer [§737]

A lawyer who directly supervises another lawyer must make reasonable efforts to see that the other lawyer conforms to professional standards. [Model Rule 5.1(b)]

EXAM TIP   **gilbert**

Note that a supervisory lawyer who has *no knowledge* of a subordinate lawyer's misconduct may still be *subject to discipline* if he has not made *reasonable efforts* to ensure the subordinate lawyer's conformity to professional standards.

(3) Responsibility for another lawyer's ethical violation [§738]

A lawyer is *responsible for another lawyer's violation* of the Model Rules if the lawyer:

(i) *Ordered*, or with knowledge *ratified*, the other's conduct; or

(ii) Is a *partner* in the firm, or a *direct supervisor* of the other, and *fails to take reasonably available remedial action* to avoid or mitigate consequences of the action.

[Model Rule 5.1(c)]

(4) Responsibility of a subordinate lawyer [§739]

A lawyer is *bound by the Model Rules* even if directed to act contrary to them by another person. [Model Rule 5.2(a)]

(a) Exception [§740]

If the question of the subordinate lawyer's professional duty is *arguable*, the lawyer may rely on the *reasonable*, though incorrect, interpretation of that duty by a supervising lawyer. [Model Rule 5.2(b)]

EXAM TIP   **gilbert**

Although a subordinate lawyer will not be subject to discipline for following a supervisory lawyer's reasonable resolution of a *debatable ethics question*, keep in mind that this is *no excuse for clearly unethical conduct*. If a supervisory lawyer orders a subordinate lawyer to commit a clear ethics violation, the subordinate lawyer will be subject to discipline if he carries out the order.

---

(5) Responsibility concerning nonlawyer assistants [§741]

The duties of partners and supervising lawyers are the *same* with respect to nonlawyers under their supervision as with respect to lawyers. [Model Rule 5.3]

d. Name of firm or corporation [§742]

Traditionally, a firm name could not contain names other than those of persons who were, in fact, lawyers in the firm. Thus, neither a lawyer nor a law firm engaged in private practice could do business under a trade name (*e.g.,* "The Winners") or a misleading name (*e.g.,* "Associates of Perry Mason"). [DR 2-102(B)] The Model Rules now *permit* use of a trade name as long as it is *not misleading* and does *not imply connection with* a *government agency or a legal services organization* (*e.g.,* "City Legal Clinic"). [Model Rule 7.5(a)]

(1) Names of deceased or retired members [§743]

A firm name *may include* the names of *deceased or retired members*. [Model Rule 7.5, comment 1; DR 2-102(B)]

(2) Multi-state firms [§744]

A firm comprised of lawyers licensed in different jurisdictions may use the same firm name in each jurisdiction. However, the firm's letterhead and other listings *must make clear any jurisdictional limitations* of the members and associates. [Model Rule 7.5(b); DR 2-102(D)]

(3) Lawyers holding public office [§745]

The name of a lawyer who enters public service for a substantial period, and thus is not engaged in firm business, *must be removed* from the firm name. [Model Rule 7.5(c); DR 2-102(B)]

(4) Law corporations [§746]

A professional corporation or association may (and in some states must) include the abbreviation "P.C." or "P.A." in its name. [DR 2-102(B)]

e. Association with nonlawyers in practice [§747]

The restrictions on unauthorized practice of law by nonlawyers have already been discussed (*see supra*, §§85 *et seq.*). Similar concerns about nonlawyer practice *restrict* the extent to which a lawyer *may associate* in practice with nonlawyers.

(1) Partnerships with nonlawyers prohibited [§748]

The ABA Code and Model Rules flatly prohibit partnerships between lawyers and nonlawyers *if any* of the partnership *activities include the practice of law.* [Model Rule 5.4(b); DR 3-103(A)]

---

e.g. **Example:** A lawyer and an accountant may not form a partnership in which legal advice on tax matters is given to clients; this is true even if the *lawyer alone* furnishes such legal advice. [ABA Opn. 297]

(a) Distinguish—partnerships not involving practice of law [§749]

A lawyer is free to enter into a partnership with a nonlawyer if the partnership confines itself *solely to nonlegal activities* (*e.g.*, investments, operation of a restaurant, etc.).

EXAM TIP	gilbert

Whenever you see an exam question involving a lawyer and a nonlawyer forming a partnership, you should suspect trouble. Be sure to check the facts carefully to see if *any legal service* is provided by the partnership—even one that is only incidental to the main partnership activities. If so, the lawyer is subject to discipline, even if she alone provides the service and even if she does it only occasionally. Thus, if Lawyer and Nonlawyer form a partnership to sell life insurance policies, this is fine, but if every now and then Lawyer sets up a trust for a client purchasing life insurance, Lawyer is subject to discipline for associating with Nonlawyer for the practice of law.

(2) Law corporations [§750]

Law corporations are similarly *prohibited* from allowing a nonlawyer to (i) own an interest therein, (ii) act as a director or officer, or (iii) direct or control the practice of a lawyer. [Model Rule 5.4(d); DR 5-107(C)]

(3) Sharing fees with nonlawyer prohibited [§751]

Both the ABA Code and Model Rules also prohibit the division of legal fees with a nonlawyer, subject to the following *exceptions* [Model Rule 5.4(a); DR 3-102]:

(a) Employment on flat salary basis permitted [§752]

A lawyer is *permitted to employ* nonlawyers, as long as their compensation is *not tied to fees collected* for particular legal services. For example, an investigator can be paid by the hour but cannot be given 10% of the fee collected in a case.

(b) Profit sharing permissible in firm plans [§753]

A broad exception to the rule against "fee splitting" permits salaried employees of a lawyer or law firm to participate in a retirement or profit-sharing plan, even though the plan will inevitably be based upon sharing income with the lawyer-employer. [Model Rule 5.4(a)(3); DR 3-102(A)(3)]

(c) Payments to estate of deceased lawyer permissible [§754]

Another exception to the rule against fee sharing with nonlawyers permits the surviving members of a law firm to pay the estate of a deceased lawyer a sum of money for a reasonable period of time after his death. [Model Rule 5.4(a)(1); DR 3-102(A)(1)] Also, a lawyer who buys the practice of a dead, disabled, or missing lawyer may pay the purchase price to the lawyer's estate or representative. [Model Rule 5.4(a)(2)]

(d) Sharing court-awarded fee with nonprofit organization permitted [§755]

When a court awards attorney's fees to a lawyer, the lawyer may share the fees with a nonprofit organization that hired him or recommended him as counsel in the matter. [Model Rule 5.4(a)(4)]

f. Noncompetition agreements [§756]

To ensure that lawyers are not bound to their firms forever, both the ABA Code and Model Rules *forbid* agreements that *restrict* the right of a lawyer to practice after termination of the relationship, except as a condition for continued payment of retirement benefits. [Model Rule 5.6(a); DR 2-108(A)]

g. Law-related services [§757]

For many years, law firms have engaged in activities beyond the traditional practice of law. The Model Rules call these ancillary business activities "law-related services" and define them as services that "in substance are related to the provision of legal services, and that are not prohibited as unauthorized practice of law when provided by a nonlawyer." Such services might include providing title insurance, financial planning, lobbying, accounting, trust services, real estate counseling, economic analysis, social work, tax return preparation, and patent, medical, or environmental consulting. [Model Rule 5.7(b)]

(1) Model Rules presumed applicable [§758]

A lawyer is "subject to the Rules of Professional Conduct with respect to the provision of" law-related services if the services are rendered as part of the delivery of legal services to clients. The Rules are even applicable if the law-related services are provided to clients separately from the provision of legal services, unless the lawyer takes reasonable measures to make clear that the services are not legal services and that protections such as the attorney-client privilege do not apply. [Model Rule 5.7(a)]

EXAM TIP   **gilbert**

When answering a question involving *law-related services*, remember that even though law-related services are not legal services, a lawyer is *subject to the Rules of Professional Conduct* when providing law-related services to her clients in circumstances that are not distinct from her provision of legal services. The Rules also apply when the law-related services *are distinct* from her provision of legal services, *unless the lawyer takes reasonable steps* to assure that people who receive the law-related services understand that those services are not covered by the Rules of Professional Conduct.

---

3. Group and Prepaid Legal Services Plans [§759]

Group and prepaid legal services plans are designed to make legal services easily available to middle-income citizens who are union members or members of other voluntary associations.

a. Past opposition to group legal services plans [§760]

For many years, the bar argued that group legal services plans would interfere with a client's free choice of counsel and would divide the lawyer's loyalty between the individual client and the group from which future referrals might come. Thus, lawyers were largely prohibited from participating in group plans.

b. Constitutional right to provide group services [§761]

On four separate occasions, the United States Supreme Court held that, under certain circumstances, the right to furnish group legal services is protected under the "freedom of expression and association" guaranteed by the First and Fourteenth Amendments to the United States Constitution.

(1) Services necessary to further group's constitutional objectives [§762]

In **NAACP v. Button**, 371 U.S. 415 (1963), the Court struck down a Virginia statute that barred the NAACP from retaining lawyers for litigants challenging various forms of racial discrimination. Under the NAACP program, the lawyer (although paid by the NAACP) had complete control over the litigation, and the client could withdraw the case at any time. The Court held that such activity was a "mode of expression and association" which could not be prohibited by state regulation.

(2) Group legal services for union members [§763]

Three other Supreme Court decisions upheld labor union plans designed to furnish legal services to members bringing workers' compensation claims. The Court approved the plans on the ground that they were protected by First Amendment guarantees of free speech, assembly, and petition. The right to employ counsel was considered part of the union members' right to band together and express themselves on matters of common interest. [**Brotherhood of Railroad Trainmen v. Virginia**, 377 U.S. 1 (1964); **United Mine Workers v. Illinois State Bar Association**, 389 U.S. 217 (1967); **United Transportation Union v. State Bar of Michigan**, 401 U.S. 576 (1971)]

c. Present status [§764]

These Supreme Court decisions clearly required the organized bar and state courts to expand the opportunities for group plans to meet the increased need for legal services while still preserving professional standards. There are now two main types of group and prepaid legal services plans:

(1) Closed panel plans [§765]

Under a closed panel plan, an organizing group (*e.g.*, a trade union) hires a lawyer or group of lawyers to handle the members' legal work on an annual flat fee basis or according to an agreed schedule of fees for various types of work. The clients ordinarily may not choose which lawyer will represent them.

(2) Open panel plans [§766]

In an open panel plan, a number of lawyers practicing in a geographic area agree to do legal work for clients that is ordinarily wholly or partly paid for by legal insurance (*i.e.*, the client pays a periodic premium and thereby becomes entitled to a set amount of legal services during the policy period). This type of plan allows the client to select a lawyer from the panel of lawyers who have agreed to take work on this basis.

d. ABA Code treatment of group plans [§767]

In states still following the ABA Code, DR 2-103(D)(4) permits a lawyer to participate in such a plan, but only if it satisfies a number of conditions, including:

(1) *The sponsoring organization does not make a profit on the rendering of the legal services alone.* If the sponsoring organization is a profit-making body in other respects (*e.g.*, an insurance company), the plan may be used only in matters in which the organization is ultimately liable on claims against its members or beneficiaries.

(2) *The participating lawyers do not initiate or promote the formation of the sponsoring organization for the primary purpose of their own profit.*

(3) *The plan does not act as a "feeder"* of legal business to the participating lawyers, unrelated to the plan services.

(4) *The person to whom the legal services are rendered is recognized as the client* to whom the lawyer owes loyalty.

(5) *A person who does not want to use the lawyer furnished by the sponsoring organization is free to go to an outside lawyer, and an "appropriate procedure for relief" is furnished* by the sponsoring organization to a person who believes that the lawyer designated by the organization cannot handle the matter adequately, properly, or ethically.

e. Model Rules treatment of group plans [§768]

The Model Rules place *no specific limits* on lawyer participation in such plans, other than the generally applicable rule that a lawyer may not let a group that recommends employment direct or regulate the manner in which the lawyer represents her clients. [Model Rule 5.4(c), 7.3(d); DR 5-107(B)]

B. Regulation of the Manner of Lawyers Seeking Employment— Solicitation and Advertising

1. Traditional Position of Organized Bar—Passive Acceptance of Employment [§769]

The organized bar *traditionally* took the position that a lawyer was *not permitted to actively publicize his services*. In effect, it was presumed that every lawyer had an established clientele, or that a lawyer's reputation for good work would inevitably lead others to seek out the lawyer's services. Under this approach, *direct publicity* by lawyers was *strictly controlled*. [EC 2-6]

a. Criticisms of traditional approach [§770]

The traditional "passive" standard was criticized as:

(1) Unfair to lawyers without *established practices;*

(2) Inappropriate for lower- and middle-income clients who might be *unaware of their need for legal services* or who might have *no idea how to locate a competent lawyer;*

(3) In conflict with *consumers' need to receive information* about lawyers and their services; and

(4) *Anticompetitive.*

b. Beginnings of change [§771]

The above criticisms developed strength in the mid-1970s as consumer groups, the Antitrust Division of the Justice Department, and some lawyers combined to oppose the restrictions on lawyer advertising.

(1) Legal profession not exempt from antitrust laws [§772]

In **Goldfarb v. Virginia State Bar,** *see supra,* §237, a case involving minimum fee schedules, the Supreme Court added momentum to these efforts by *rejecting* the notions that lawyers are exempt from antitrust laws as members of a "learned profession," or that enforcement of minimum fee schedules was exempted state action.

(2) Consumers' First Amendment "right to know" [§773]

The critics' position was further strengthened by two subsequent Supreme Court decisions that, although not specifically concerned with advertising by lawyers, held that commercial advertising was entitled to First Amendment protection. [**Bigelow v. Virginia,** 421 U.S. 809 (1975); **Virginia State Board of Pharmacy v. Virginia Citizens Consumer Council,** 425 U.S. 748 (1976)]

2. Lawyer Advertising and Publicity—Current Status of the Law

a. Relaxation of traditional restraints—*Bates* [§774]

In 1977, the Supreme Court at last squarely confronted the issue of lawyer advertising. In **Bates v. State Bar of Arizona,** 433 U.S. 350 (1977), disciplinary action had been brought against a lawyer for placing a newspaper ad that listed his fees for routine, standardized legal services. In finding the lawyer *not* subject to discipline, the Supreme Court held that:

(1) Advertising by licensed lawyers may *not be "subjected to blanket suppression"*;

(2) *Truthful* advertising conveying the *availability and terms* (fees) for routine legal services is *protected* by the First Amendment; but

(3) *Reasonable restrictions may be imposed* on the time, place, and manner of legal advertising; and

(4) Advertising that is *"false, deceptive, or misleading"* is subject to *restraint.*

b. ABA reactions to *Bates*

(1) ABA Code provisions on advertising [§775]

Shortly after the *Bates* decision, the ABA hurriedly amended the Code section pertaining to lawyer advertising. These amendments *accommodated Bates,* but took advantage of the permissible *restrictions* left by the Court and ignored all related issues not covered by *Bates.* The Code as revised permits dignified *print* advertising and *radio and television* advertising that is distributed or broadcast only in the geographic areas: (i) in which the lawyer *resides,* (ii) where the lawyer *maintains offices,* or (iii) in which a significant part of her *clients reside.* [DR 2-101(B)] (There is no such limitation under the Model Rules.) The Code prohibits any public communication by a lawyer that contains a *false, deceptive, self-laudatory, or unfair* statement or claim. [DR 2-101(A)] It specifies 25 categories of information that *may be included* in advertising. [DR 2-101(B)] These may be grouped into three types: (i) *biographical* information, (ii) *office* information, and (iii) *fee* information.

(a) Note—ABA Code provisions not current [§776]

Because the Model Rules were under consideration in the years following *Bates,* the ABA did not amend the Code to conform to later cases. Thus, the *ABA Code is not now a reliable guide* to the law of lawyer advertising and solicitation.

(2) Model Rules approach to advertising [§777]

By the time the Model Rules were adopted, the ABA had time to come up with a better approach to advertising.

(a) Only false and misleading advertising prohibited [§778]

The Model Rules *permit all advertising except* that which is *"false and misleading,"* which is defined as *containing a material misrepresentation* of fact or law, or omitting a fact necessary to make the statement not materially misleading. [Model Rule 7.1] Such statements include those:

(i) *Likely to create an unjustified expectation* about the results the lawyer can achieve, or implying that the lawyer can achieve results by *improper means;* or

(ii) *Comparing the lawyer's services* with those of other lawyers in ways that cannot be factually substantiated.

[Model Rule 7.1, comments 2, 3]

> **EXAM TIP**   **gilbert**
>
> An important point to remember is that even truthful advertisements can be *misleading*. For example, if the lawyer states in her ad that in her last personal injury case the jury awarded a $200,000 verdict, even if true, this might create an *unjustified expectation* that the lawyer can obtain the same result for other clients. Qualifying language would be needed.

(b) Manner of dissemination [§779]

Under the Model Rules, advertising may be done through any public media, or in a written communication not involving "solicitation" (*see infra*, §787). [Model Rule 7.2(a)]

(c) Lawyer's name required [§780]

Lawyer advertising must include the name of at least one lawyer responsible for its content. [Model Rule 7.2(c)] Other permissible information is listed in the chart, *infra*. [Model Rule 7.2, comment 2]

EXAMPLES OF ACCEPTABLE ADVERTISING INFORMATION   **gilbert**

THE MODEL RULES PERMIT THE FOLLOWING INFORMATION IN ADVERTISEMENTS:

☑ The lawyer's *name* (*must be included*), address, and telephone number;

☑ The lawyer's area of *practice*;

☑ How the lawyer's *fees are determined*;

☑ The *cost of specific services* and *payment arrangements*;

☑ Names of *references*;

☑ Names of regular *clients* (*with their consent*).

---

c. Additional limits on state regulation—*Zauderer* [§781]

The Supreme Court appeared to confirm the Model Rules approach to lawyer advertising in **Zauderer v. Office of Disciplinary Counsel,** 471 U.S. 626 (1985). It specifically held both that illustrations in lawyer advertising are entitled to the same constitutional protections as text, and that an appeal may be made in an advertisement encouraging persons with a particular kind of injury to consult the lawyer.

(1) Permissible state regulation [§782]

More specifically, *Zauderer* held that a state *may*:

(a) *Prohibit* lawyer advertising that is *false, deceptive, or misleading,* or that proposes an *illegal transaction*; and

(b) ***Require a lawyer to include a reasonable disclaimer*** or other information in order to help assure that potential clients can make an informed choice among lawyers.

(2) Limitations on state regulation [§783]

However, a state *may not*:

(a) ***Require*** that lawyer advertising *be "dignified";* or

(b) ***Limit*** lawyer advertising *except* "in the service of a ***substantial government interest,***" and even then, "only through means that *directly affect that interest.*"

d. State limits upheld—the *Went For It* case [§784]

In 1995, for the first time since *Bates,* the Supreme Court ***upheld state limits*** on lawyer advertising in **Florida Bar v. Went For It, Inc.,** 515 U.S. 618 (1995). The majority opinion in *Went For It* said that it applied the substantial government interest standard discussed above but concluded that the state's limitation on direct mail advertising within 30 days of an accident or disaster was valid.

(1) Majority [§785]

The Court concluded that the state had a "substantial interest" that justified such a regulation—"to protect the flagging reputations of Florida lawyers" from conduct that was "universally regarded as deplorable and beneath common decency" because it invaded the privacy of potential clients in a time of grief. Also, the state showed that the regulation advanced its interests "in a direct and material way." Relying on newspaper editorials and a Bar survey of citizen attitudes, the Court concluded that the facts were sufficient to justify regulation of post-accident contact. Finally, it found that the regulation was a "reasonable fit" for the problem the Bar had identified, even if it was not the "least restrictive means" of addressing the concern, and that plenty of other ways exist for lawyers to make their availability known to potential clients, *e.g.,* television, newspapers, billboards, the Yellow Pages, or even untargeted direct mail.

(2) Dissent [§786]

Four Justices dissented, claiming the majority had departed from earlier precedents. The fact that advertising was "offensive" or "undignified" had not been sufficient in the past to ban it. Also, the Bar's "proof" that a problem existed was methodologically flawed and largely anecdotal. Finally, the dissenters thought that the flat ban on direct mail was too broad, because it applied no matter how serious the accident or disaster.

3. Direct Contact Solicitation [§787]

The term "solicitation" used to refer to any conduct on behalf of a lawyer designed to help obtain new clients. It thus traditionally included all advertising. However,

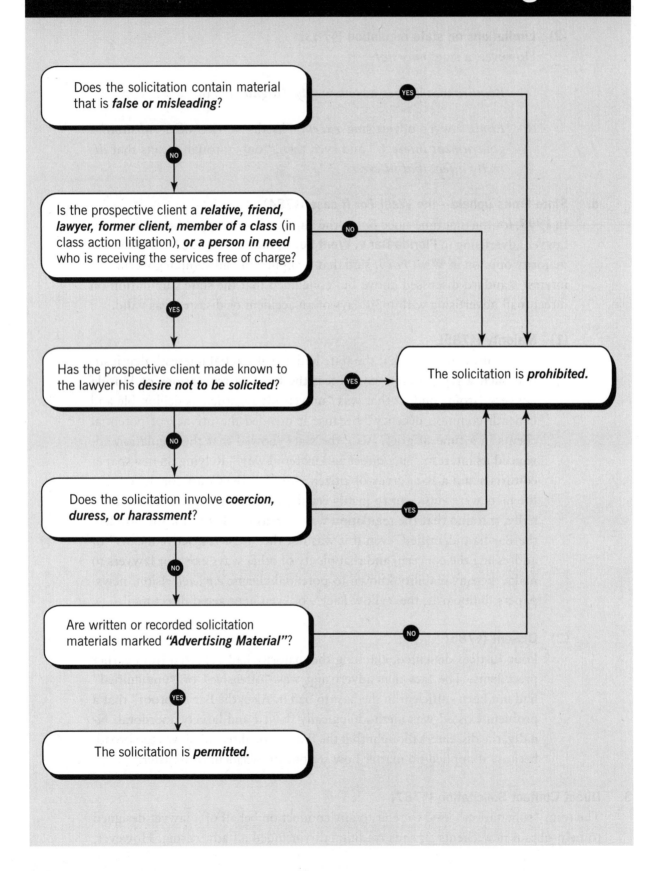

Does the solicitation contain material that is *false or misleading*?

YES → The solicitation is *prohibited.*

NO ↓

Is the prospective client a *relative, friend, lawyer, former client, member of a class* (in class action litigation), *or a person in need* who is receiving the services free of charge?

NO → The solicitation is *prohibited.*

YES ↓

Has the prospective client made known to the lawyer his *desire not to be solicited*?

YES → The solicitation is *prohibited.*

NO ↓

Does the solicitation involve *coercion, duress, or harassment*?

YES → The solicitation is *prohibited.*

NO ↓

Are written or recorded solicitation materials marked *"Advertising Material"*?

NO → The solicitation is *prohibited.*

YES ↓

The solicitation is *permitted.*

after *Bates*, "solicitation" has come to mean *in-person or other direct real-time contact with a potential client*, whether by the lawyer or the lawyer's agent, that is not protected as advertising. [Model Rule 7.3]

a. **Model Rules [§788]**

The Model Rules prohibit "in-person, live telephone or real-time electronic contact" with potential clients whom the lawyer has not previously served and where a *"significant motive"* for the contact is the *"lawyer's personal gain."* [Model Rule 7.3(a)]

(1) Duress prohibited [§789]

The Model Rules also prohibit contact with a prospective client if (i) the person has made known to the lawyer a *desire not to be solicited*; or (ii) the solicitation involves *coercion, duress, or harassment*. [Model Rule 7.3(b)]

(2) Warning to be affixed [§790]

All written or recorded communications with such a prospective client known to be in need of legal services in a particular matter must also say *"Advertising Material"* on the envelope or the recording. [Model Rule 7.3(c)]

b. **Constitutionality [§791]**

The United States Supreme Court has confirmed the validity of prohibiting in-person solicitation of clients for cases in which a fee will be charged, at least where the solicitation "in fact is misleading, overbearing, or involves other features of deception or improper influence." [**Ohralik v. Ohio State Bar Association**, 436 U.S. 447 (1978)]

c. **Exceptions to general prohibition on solicitation**

(1) Advice to close friend, relative, or present or former client [§792]

A lawyer may seek professional employment from a close friend, a relative, a current or former client, or another lawyer. [Model Rule 7.3(a); DR 2-104(A)(1)]

***

e.g. **Example:** A lawyer may send letters to persons for whom she has previously drafted wills, advising them of changes in tax laws affecting the tax treatment of the will provisions, and may accept employment to revise the wills accordingly. [ABA Opn. 213 (1941); *In re* **Madsen**, 370 N.E.2d 199 (Ill. 1977)]

***

(2) Request for referrals from lawyer referral service or legal aid organization [§793]

A lawyer may properly request referrals from a *lawyer referral service* in the lawyer's locality, and from *legal aid organizations*. [Model Rule 7.3(d); DR 2-103(C)]

(3) Services offered to persons in need [§794]

Traditionally, courts have refused to discipline lawyers who have offered their services *free of charge* to persons in need thereof. [*See* **In re Primus**, 436 U.S. 412 (1978)]

(a) Rationale

Such work is a means of "political expression and association" within the protection of the First Amendment. Furthermore, unlike solicitation of fee-generating business, the potential for overreaching is too slight. [**In re Primus**, *supra*; **NAACP v. Button**, *supra*, §762]

(4) Organizing prospective litigants—class action [§795]

It was also traditionally improper for lawyers to *initiate* the organization of prospective litigants as a means of providing employment for themselves, but the Supreme Court has held that it is improper for a court to set excessive limits on a lawyer's contact with prospective class members. [**Gulf Oil v. Bernard**, 450 U.S. 907 (1981)]

(a) But note [§796]

A court can constitutionally impose severe sanctions on a *defense lawyer* who counsels or personally tries to persuade class action plaintiffs to opt out of the class. [**Kleiner v. First National Bank of Atlanta**, 751 F.2d 1193 (11th Cir. 1985)]

4. Other Types of Permitted Personal Publicity [§797]

Forms of lawyer publicity other than advertising of legal services were not considered in *Bates*. The Code sets forth detailed regulation of a lawyer's business cards, letterhead, office sign, and announcements about a change in practice. Under the Code, a lawyer is permitted to be identified as such in political advertisements, public notices, legal documents and in reports of business, civic, professional, or political organizations in which the lawyer is a director or officer. [DR 2-101(H), 2-102(A)] However, the validity of the Code regulations seems highly questionable. The Model Rules, on the other hand, leave all of those matters *unregulated, except* for the general *prohibition against misleading communications* in Model Rule 7.1.

C. Specialization and Limitation of Practice

1. Introduction [§798]

In today's complicated legal structure, no lawyer can be thoroughly competent in every field of law. Large firms have traditionally been able to provide expert legal services in many fields of law by de facto specialization, but present rules regulate how the individual lawyer may tell potential clients the kinds of work she is qualified to do.

2. General Rule—No Designation of Specialty [§799]

As a general rule, it is *not proper* for lawyers to identify themselves as specialists or experts in any particular field of law in their advertising or on their business cards, letterheads, or office signs. [Model Rule 7.4(d); DR 2-105]

3. Exceptions to General Rule

a. Patent lawyers [§800]

Lawyers "admitted to engage in patent practice" are permitted to indicate this fact, because they have passed a special exam and have a recognized credential. [Model Rule 7.4(b); DR 2-105(A)(1)]

b. Admiralty lawyers [§801]

As a matter of tradition, the Model Rules permit a lawyer engaged in admiralty practice to designate this. [Model Rule 7.4(c)]

c. Certified specialists [§802]

Lawyers may hold themselves out as specialists if they have been certified by an appropriate authority.

(1) State certification programs [§803]

A number of states have programs to certify lawyers as specialists; *e.g.,* California certifies specialists in taxation, criminal law, family law, and workers' compensation. Such programs typically require proof of qualifying experience in the specialty field (such as five years of practice, more than 50% of which is devoted to the specialty) and/or the passing of a written examination.

(2) Certification by private organizations [§804]

Although the ABA Code requires certification by an authority *sanctioned by the state* [DR 2-105(A)(3)], the Supreme Court has held that a state may not limit speciality certification to state agencies, and a lawyer may not be disciplined for noting on a letterhead that the lawyer has been "certified" as a specialist by an independent private organization if the claim is both *verifiable* and *true*. [**Peel v. Attorney Registration & Disciplinary Commission of Illinois**, 496 U.S. 91 (1990)]

Example: In *Peel, supra,* disciplinary proceedings were brought against Peel, because his letterhead indicated that he was certified as a trial specialist by the National Board of Trial Advocacy (a private association). The Supreme Court found that a truthful reference to a lawyer's certification by a private lawyer association was not misleading, and the state's fear that potential clients would believe that the statement was a claim of special skill was insufficient to justify prohibiting it.

---

(3) Model Rules requirements [§805]

The ABA has amended the Model Rules to recognize private certification as well as state-sanctioned certification. However, a lawyer may not hold himself out as a specialist unless the certifying organization is identified and it has been approved by a state authority or the ABA. [Model Rule 7.4(d)]

EXCEPTIONS TO NO DESIGNATION OF SPECIALTY RULE   gilbert

THE GENERAL RULE IS THAT LAWYERS MAY *NOT* IDENTIFY THEMSELVES AS SPECIALISTS OR EXPERTS IN A FIELD, *EXCEPT FOR:*

☑ *Patent* lawyers

☑ *Admiralty* lawyers

☑ Lawyers *certified as specialists* by a certifying body *approved by the state or the ABA.*

---

4. Limitation of Practice [§806]

In contrast to specialization, both the ABA Code and Model Rules recognize the concept of "*limiting practice*" that describes what the lawyer is and is not prepared to undertake and carries with it *no implication of special skill.*

a. ABA Code approach [§807]

Under the ABA Code, the right to describe the categories in which one practices is limited to designations and definitions prescribed in state law. [DR 2-105(A)(2)] However, the Supreme Court *struck down* a state rule prescribing specific language to be used in advertisements listing lawyers' areas of practice (*e.g.,* allowing "property law" but not "real estate law"). Categories may only be as narrow as "furthers the state's substantial interest." [**Matter of RMJ,** 455 U.S. 191 (1982)]

b. Model Rules approach [§808]

The Model Rules, on the other hand, *do not limit* or prescribe the fields of law by which a lawyer may describe her practice except that the description may not be false or misleading. [Model Rule 7.4(a)]

EXAM TIP   gilbert

Keep in mind the different rules for *designating a specialty* and *limiting a practice* to certain areas of law: A lawyer *cannot call herself a specialist or an expert* except in the very limited areas of patent and admiralty law or when she has been certified by an appropriate authority, but she may *freely limit her practice* as long as her statements are truthful and not misleading. The reason for the difference is that calling oneself a specialist can mislead clients by indicating that the lawyer has special knowledge or skill, which she may or may not have. On the other hand, merely stating that one limits practice to certain areas, or does not handle certain types of cases, does not in and of itself imply special knowledge or skill.

D. Division of Fees with Lawyers Outside One's Firm

1. Introduction [§809]

Under certain circumstances, lawyers may share fees with lawyers outside their firms. Types of fee sharing, and the rules that pertain to them, are addressed below.

2. Fee Splitting—In General [§810]

When two or more lawyers from different firms associate on a case, they may submit a single bill to the client and split the fee if certain conditions are met. (*See infra,* §§815-816.)

a. Working on case together [§811]

Fee sharing is permitted when lawyers from different firms work together on a case that neither of them could handle as well alone.

b. Referral fees [§812]

If a solo practitioner or a lawyer in a small firm gets a matter outside his area of expertise, on which he does not plan to work at all, the question arises whether he must simply turn the matter down or whether it may be "forwarded" and the fee shared with a more competent lawyer.

(1) Concern about referral fees

The traditional concern about referral fees has been that a lawyer who receives compensation in return for referring a case or client may refer potential clients to the lawyer who pays the most, rather than to the lawyer who is most competent. [*See, e.g.,* **Ohio State Bar Association v. Kanter,** 715 N.E.2d 1140 (Ohio 1999)]

(2) Practice not prohibited [§813]

Nevertheless, the division of fees between lawyers is permitted in states that have adopted the ABA Code or the Model Rules if the arrangement is couched in terms of fee sharing with joint responsibility. (*See infra,* §§815-817.)

(3) Distinguish—reciprocal referral arrangements [§814]

A lawyer may receive referrals from other lawyers or even nonlawyers in exchange for referring some of the lawyer's clients to them if (i) the arrangement is *not exclusive*, and (ii) clients are informed of the *existence and nature* of the arrangement. [Model Rule 7.2(b)(4)]

3. ABA Code Approach [§815]

The general rule under the ABA Code is that fee splitting (either because of a referral or because of work done together) between lawyers who are not partners or associates is *prohibited unless*: (i) the client gives *informed consent*; (ii) the total fee is *reasonable*; and (iii) the division corresponds to the *services performed and responsibilities assumed* by each lawyer. [DR 2-107(A)] There has been confusion over the phrase "services performed and responsibilities assumed by each lawyer," as it relates to referral fees, but courts have often held that pure referral fee agreements are prohibited under the ABA Code. Thus, to avoid violating DR 2-107(A), a referring lawyer's participation must be more than merely referring the case to another lawyer.

4. Model Rules Approach—Joint Responsibility [§816]

The Model Rules preserve the Code standard, but ease the third requirement. Under the Model Rules, the client must consent and there must be a reasonable total fee, but lawyers who assume *joint responsibility* for a matter may share the fee in *whatever proportions they agree*, regardless of how much work each did. [Model Rule 1.5(e)(1)]

a. Joint responsibility as sharing malpractice liability [§817]

The meaning of joint responsibility is simple—the referring lawyer agrees to be jointly liable for any malpractice committed by the lawyer to whom the matter is referred. [**Elane v. St. Bernard Hospital**, 672 N.E.2d 820 (Ill. 1996)]

(1) Analogy to practice in a law firm [§818]

The rationale for this standard is that it encourages the referring lawyer to send the matter only to someone who will handle it competently. Furthermore, it is what a lawyer requires of partners in a law firm where it is common to refer work on a case to a lawyer other than the one to whom the client first came.

b. Client must consent in writing to terms of the referral [§819]

Unlike the practice in most law firms, however, the Model Rules require that the client be told "the *share each lawyer will receive*," and *an agreement* to the arrangement must be "*confirmed in writing*." [Model Rule 1.5(e)(2)]

5. Other Types of Fee Sharing [§820]

In two other situations, which do not present the same concerns as referral fees, a lawyer may share fees with someone outside the lawyer's firm.

a. Division of fees with former partners and associates [§821]

A firm may make payments to a *former partner or associate* pursuant to a separation or retirement agreement. [DR 2-107(B); Model Rule 1.5, comment 8]

b. Charges of a legal service plan or nonprofit referral service [§822]

A lawyer may pay the usual charges of an *organization* established to refer its members or inquirers to participating lawyers. [Model Rule 7.2(b)(2)]

6. Purchase of Lawyer's Practice [§823]

A lawyer who retires or otherwise leaves practice may wish to sell that practice to a

gilbert

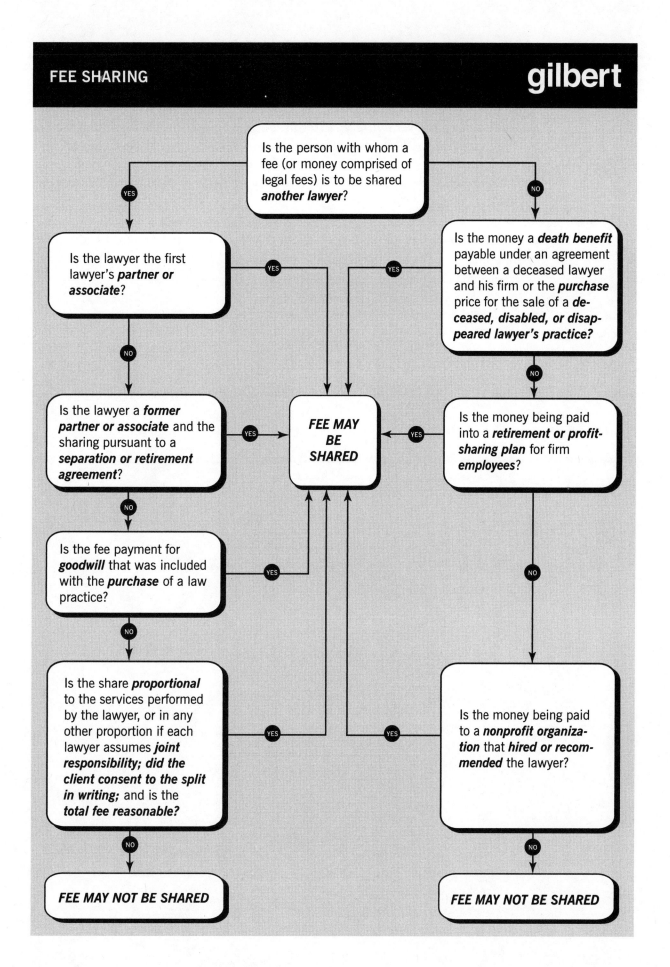

Is the person with whom a fee (or money comprised of legal fees) is to be shared **another lawyer**?

YES

NO

Is the lawyer the first lawyer's **partner or associate**?

Is the money a **death benefit** payable under an agreement between a deceased lawyer and his firm or the **purchase** price for the sale of a **deceased, disabled, or disappeared lawyer's practice?**

YES

YES

NO

NO

Is the lawyer a **former partner or associate** and the sharing pursuant to a **separation or retirement agreement**?

FEE MAY BE SHARED

Is the money being paid into a **retirement or profit-sharing plan** for firm **employees**?

YES

YES

NO

NO

Is the fee payment for **goodwill** that was included with the **purchase** of a law practice?

YES

NO

Is the share **proportional** to the services performed by the lawyer, or in any other proportion if each lawyer assumes **joint responsibility; did the client consent to the split in writing;** and is the **total fee reasonable?**

YES

Is the money being paid to a **nonprofit organization** that **hired or recommended** the lawyer?

YES

NO

NO

FEE MAY NOT BE SHARED

FEE MAY NOT BE SHARED

nonpartner for a price that reflects *"goodwill,"* *i.e.,* future fees the new lawyer will earn because of the firm's reputation. Sale of goodwill was once prohibited, but Model Rule 1.17 now *permits* the sale of a law practice to include goodwill *if:*

a. *The selling lawyer entirely ceases practice*, or ceases practicing in the *area of practice being sold*, in the jurisdiction where the practice has been conducted;

b. *The practice or area of practice is sold in its entirety* to one or more lawyers or law firms;

c. *Written notice is given to each client* that the client may retain other counsel and need not continue with the lawyer buying the practice (but the client's silence may be taken as consent to the sale); and

d. *Clients' fees are not increased* because of the sale.

Chapter Eight:
Enforcement of Lawyers' Professional Obligations

CONTENTS

Chapter Approach

The previous chapters have discussed the obligations a lawyer has to clients, the court, and others. This chapter considers what may happen to a lawyer who fails to meet those obligations.

Lawyer misconduct can result in:

1. *Professional discipline* by the state (*e.g.,* disbarment, suspension, and reprimand or censure);

2. *Malpractice liability* (*i.e.,* damages); and/or

3. *Contempt sanctions* (*i.e.,* fine or imprisonment).

Be sure you understand the differences between these concepts.

Professional discipline is not a criminal process, but it is analogous to it. It is designed to *protect the public* from "bad" lawyers—*i.e.*, those who violate the disciplinary rules or otherwise engage in dishonest or fraudulent conduct.

A *malpractice* action, on the other hand, is a tort claim that seeks to *compensate a victim* of the lawyer's negligence. Thus, to recover in a malpractice action, the client must show that the lawyer breached the standard of care, and in doing so, caused the client to suffer some harm.

Contempt sanctions, in turn, primarily enforce standards of *litigation* conduct.

A. The Formal Disciplinary Process

1. **General Grounds for Discipline [§824]**
   A lawyer may be disciplined on any of the following grounds:

   a. **Violation of professional ethics [§825]**
      Violating, or *attempting* to violate, a state version of the ABA Model Rules or a Disciplinary Rule, in states whose rules are still based on the ABA Code, is a ground for professional discipline. Furthermore, a lawyer must not knowingly *assist or induce* another person to violate professional rules of ethics nor *use the acts of another person* to commit a violation. [Model Rule 8.4(a); DR 1-102(A)(1), (2)]

      (1) **Disciplinary jurisdiction wherever lawyer practices or is licensed [§826]**
          A lawyer may be disciplined in each state in which the lawyer is licensed,

no matter where the conduct occurs. Indeed, if the conduct takes place in a state in which the lawyer is not licensed at all, discipline may be imposed there as well. [Model Rule 8.5(a)]

(2) Law to be applied [§827]

In principle, no matter where the lawyer is subject to discipline, the same conduct standard should be applied; *i.e.*, the choice of law rule in each state should yield the same result.

(a) Litigation matters [§828]

In cases seeking discipline for acts done in cases pending before a tribunal, the disciplinary standard applied is that of *the state in which the tribunal sits*. [Model Rule 8.5(b)]

(b) Nonlitigation matters [§829]

For all other acts, the law to be applied is that of *the state in which the conduct occurred*. But if the *predominant effect* of the act is in another state, the professional standards of *that state* are to govern. [Model Rule 8.5(b)]

(c) Lawyer's reasonable belief [§830]

If the lawyer's conduct conforms to the law of a jurisdiction in which the lawyer *reasonably believes* the predominant effect of the conduct will occur, the lawyer will not be subject to discipline. [Model Rule 8.5(b)]

EXAM TIP   **gilbert**

Choice of law questions involving litigation matters do not pose a problem—a lawyer is subject to the disciplinary rules of the forum state. In *nonlitigation* matters, the rules of the *jurisdiction in which the conduct occurred* usually should be applied, but remember the exceptions: If the *predominant effect* of the conduct is in another jurisdiction, *that jurisdiction's rules apply*. However, if a lawyer's conduct is *proper* in the jurisdiction which he *reasonably believes* is most affected by his conduct, he will *not* be subject to discipline.

---

b. Commission of a crime [§831]

In every state, a lawyer is subject to professional discipline for committing a crime that casts doubt on the lawyer's fitness to practice.

(1) Model Rules standard [§832]

Under Model Rule 8.4, a lawyer is subject to discipline for crimes that reflect adversely on the lawyer's *honesty, trustworthiness, or fitness as a lawyer*. The Model Rules state the principle in this way to avoid imposing discipline for matters of personal morality, such as adultery, that used to be reached under the heading of "crimes involving moral turpitude."

(2) Some jurisdictions—crimes of moral turpitude [§833]

The term "moral turpitude" is still used in the California rules and those of some other jurisdictions. It has been held to mean conduct that *"offends* the generally accepted *moral code* of mankind." [*In re* **Colson**, 412 A.2d 1160 (D.C. 1979)]

(3) Crime need not have been committed while acting as a lawyer [§834]

The crime need not have been connected with the lawyer's professional activities; criminal acts *wholly unrelated* thereto, such as fraud on a personal income tax return, assault, and murder, are proper grounds for discipline. [**People v. Musick**, 960 P.2d 89 (Colo. 1998)]

(4) Effect of appeal [§835]

Normally, disciplinary proceedings are deferred until criminal proceedings are final, giving the lawyer the opportunity to appeal the conviction. But this is discretionary with the court before which the disciplinary proceedings are brought, and the court has the power to order an immediate suspension. [*See, e.g.,* Cal. Bus. & Prof. Code §6102(a)—providing for immediate suspension upon conviction of any crime in which there is "probable cause to believe" that moral turpitude was involved]

(5) Effect of reversal of conviction or pardon [§836]

The fact that the conviction has been reversed on appeal, or even pardoned, does *not affect the power of the court* to proceed with the disciplinary hearing. Indeed, a lawyer may even be disciplined for conduct as to which he was *acquitted* in the criminal proceedings. [*See, e.g.,* **In re Segal**, 719 N.E.2d 480 (Mass. 1999)—acquittal; *and see* **In re Abrams**, 689 A.2d 6 (D.C. 1997)—pardon]

c. Engaging in conduct involving dishonesty, fraud, deceit, or misrepresentation [§837]

A lawyer may be disciplined for her involvement in conduct involving dishonesty, fraud, deceit, or misrepresentation. The act *need not even be a crime* to result in the lawyer's disbarment or other discipline. [Model Rule 8.4(c); DR 1-102(A)(4)]

---

e.g. **Example:** A lawyer who impersonated her husband and took the bar exam for him was disbarred. The lawyer had been under physical and emotional stress when she gave in to her husband's pleas to take the bar exam for him, and the court found no convincing evidence of the lawyer's complete recovery from her emotional difficulties. The court concluded that disbarment was warranted because the lawyer's dishonesty could have significantly harmed the public by enabling an unqualified person to practice law. [*In re* **Lamb**, 49 Cal. 3d 239 (1989)]

---

e.g. **Example:** A lawyer submitted a form to the Commission on Continuing Legal Education ("CLE"), falsely claiming to have attended a CLE seminar. The court found that this conduct involved dishonesty, fraud, deceit, and misrepresentation and warranted a 90-day suspension. [**Matter of Diggs,** 544 S.E.2d 628 (S.C. 2001)]

d. Engaging in conduct prejudicial to administration of justice [§838]

This basis for discipline most often involves dishonest dealings with a court. [Model Rule 8.4(d); DR 1-102(A)(5)]

Example: A lawyer formed co-counsel relationships with close relatives of two judges who were considered tough sentencing judges. The purpose of the co-counsel relationships was to keep those judges from hearing cases involving the lawyer's clients. Disciplinary panels dismissed the charges against the lawyers, but the court held that this method of obtaining the recusal of judges interfered with proper assignment of cases and was prejudicial to the administration of justice. Thus, the court remanded the case to the hearing panel. [**Grievance Administrator v. Fried,** 570 N.W.2d 262 (Mich. 1997)]

Example: In a fee petition, a lawyer claimed to have spent 80 hours working on a brief, much of which turned out to be plagiarized. The court found that the lawyer had deliberately attempted to defraud the court and suspended the lawyer for six months. [**Iowa Supreme Court Board of Professional Ethics and Conduct v. Lane,** 642 N.W.2d 296 (Iowa 2002)]

e. Stating or implying ability to improperly influence officials [§839]

A lawyer must not state or imply that he has the ability to improperly influence a government agency or official or to achieve results by means that violate the law or legal ethics rules. [Model Rule 8.4(e)]

f. Assisting a judge in violation of judicial code [§840]

A lawyer is subject to discipline for *knowingly* assisting a judge or judicial officer in conduct that violates the Code of Judicial Conduct or other law. [Model Rule 8.4(f)]

g. Specific statutory grounds for discipline [§841]

A number of state statutes also define specific acts that will subject a lawyer to discipline.

(1) California rule [§842]

A lawyer in California may be disbarred or suspended from practice for: (i) violating the attorney's oath [Cal. Bus. & Prof. Code §6103], (ii) appearing for another as attorney without authority [Cal. Bus. & Prof. Code §6104], (iii) advocating the violent overthrow of government [Cal. Bus. & Prof. Code §6106.1], or (iv) switching from prosecution to defense in a criminal case [Cal. Bus. & Prof. Code §6131(b)].

(2) New York rule—discipline of a law firm [§843]

Most states impose discipline only on individual lawyers, but in New York a law firm is subject to discipline, *e.g.,* for failure to supervise associates and for other institutional failings. [N.Y. Code of Professional Responsibility §§1200.3, 1200.5, 1200.24(e)]

CHECKLIST OF GROUNDS FOR DISCIPLINE   **gilbert**

A LAWYER MAY BE SUBJECT TO PROFESSIONAL DISCIPLINE FOR:

☑ *Violation of a professional ethics rule;*

☑ Commission of some *crimes;*

☑ Conduct involving *dishonesty, fraud, deceit, or misrepresentation;*

☑ Conduct *prejudicial to administration of justice;*

☑ Stating or implying *ability to improperly influence officials;*

☑ *Assisting a judge in violation of the judicial code;*

☑ *Violation of a specific state statute.*

---

2. Sanctions

a. Types

(1) Disbarment [§844]

Disbarment is a *permanent revocation* of the lawyer's license to practice, although in most states, a disbarred lawyer who has been rehabilitated may apply to the state bar for readmission (*see infra,* §874).

(2) Suspension from practice [§845]

Suspension is a *temporary revocation* of the right to practice. After the period of suspension has passed, the lawyer can return to practice. [*See In re* **Mackay,** 416 P.2d 823 (Alaska 1964)]

(3) Reprimand or admonition [§846]

Typically, a state bar may impose a reprimand or admonition either *publicly or privately.*

(4) Other sanctions [§847]

Other sanctions in some states include probation, restitution, costs of the disciplinary proceedings, and limitations on the lawyer's practice.

b. Factors affecting sanctions [§848]

The sanctions imposed in a given case depend upon all of the circumstances. Aside from the *seriousness of the offense* itself, factors that might affect the appropriate penalty include the *lawyer's mental state* at the time of the offense, the *injury* caused by the offense, any *aggravating or mitigating factors*, and any *evidence of rehabilitation*. [ABA Standards for Imposing Lawyer Sanctions (1986)]

(1) Mental illness or chronic alcoholism [§849]

Mental illness and chronic alcoholism are usually seen as affecting the culpability of a lawyer. Sanctions in such cases are often limited to *suspending* the lawyer from practice pending proof of recovery. [*See, e.g.,* **Matter of Walker,** 254 N.W.2d 452 (S.D. 1977); **Petition of Johnson,** 322 N.W.2d 616 (Minn. 1982)]

(a) Note

Alcoholism and mental illness are not only mitigating factors in discipline cases, but may also be a *basis for suspension* of a lawyer *before* wrongdoing. Although such a sanction has serious consequences in that it denies the lawyer a right to make a living, many states use summary procedures to suspend an impaired lawyer before too many clients' cases have been neglected or their interests damaged. [*See* ABA Model Rule for Lawyer Disciplinary Enforcement 23; *In re* **Kelley,** 52 Cal. 3d 487 (1990)—suspension from practice after two drunk driving convictions]

EXAM TIP gilbert

Note the possible effects a lawyer's *alcoholism or mental illness* may have on a disciplinary sanction. A court may consider the lawyer's alcoholism or mental illness a *mitigating factor* that calls for a lighter sentence (*e.g.,* suspension instead of disbarment). On the other hand, a court may regard the lawyer's alcoholism or mental illness as a danger to his clients' interests that is a *ground for disciplinary action*.

---

(2) But note—financial misfortune or economic necessity not mitigating factor [§850]

A lawyer's financial problems are *not* by themselves generally regarded as a *mitigating factor* in disciplinary proceedings. [**People v. Luhan,** 890 P.2d 109 (Colo. 1995)]

3. Stages in Disciplinary Proceedings

a. Complaint to state bar [§851]

Disciplinary proceedings against a lawyer are initiated by lodging a complaint with the state disciplinary authorities. While most complaints come from aggrieved

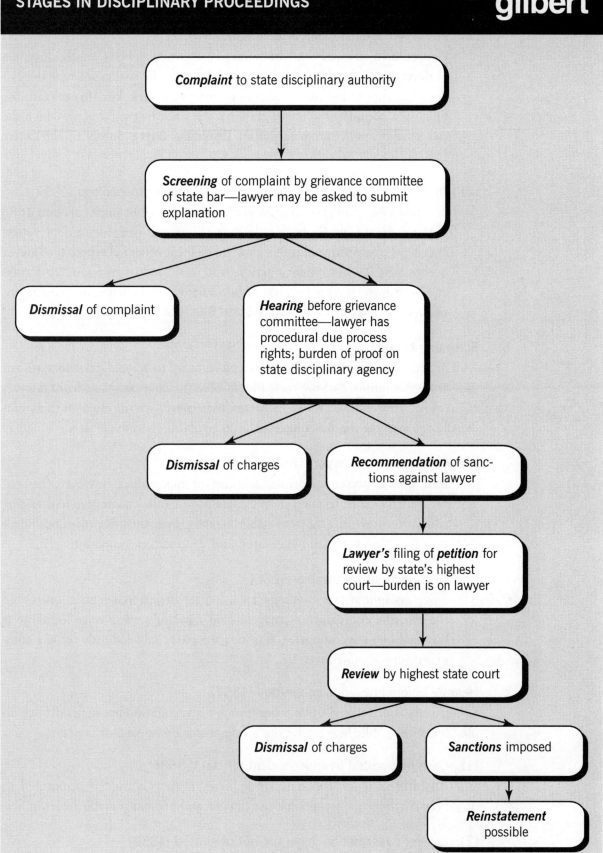

Complaint to state disciplinary authority

Screening of complaint by grievance committee of state bar—lawyer may be asked to submit explanation

Dismissal of complaint

Hearing before grievance committee—lawyer has procedural due process rights; burden of proof on state disciplinary agency

Dismissal of charges

Recommendation of sanctions against lawyer

Lawyer's filing of **petition** for review by state's highest court—burden is on lawyer

Review by highest state court

Dismissal of charges

Sanctions imposed

Reinstatement possible

clients, they may also be made by fellow lawyers, judges, or any other person with knowledge of the alleged misconduct.

(1) Privileged against claim of defamation [§852]

Courts have stressed that the ability to complain about misconduct is a "safety valve" for the public and is vital to public assurance that the bar does not shelter lawyers engaging in such activities. For this reason, the filing of a complaint with the state bar may not be the basis on which the lawyer may later claim defamation. [**Weber v. Cueto**, 568 N.E.2d 513 (Ill. 1991)]

(2) Distinguish—federal civil rights action to enjoin proceedings [§853]

In a few cases, lawyers have been allowed to file suit under section 1983 of the Federal Civil Rights Act (which allows suit to enjoin a deprivation of federal constitutional rights by state or local officials) where the lawyer alleges that the disciplinary action was instituted in bad faith to harass and punish the lawyer because of his controversial clients, unpopular positions, etc. [**Taylor v. Kentucky State Bar**, 424 F.2d 478 (6th Cir. 1970)]

b. Screening of complaint by state bar [§854]

As a general rule, complaints are referred initially to a local grievance or administrative committee of the state bar. Where the charges result from lawyer-client misunderstandings, an appropriate discussion with the client at this point usually resolves the matter, often without involving the lawyer at all.

(1) Explanation by lawyer [§855]

If the charge presents a prima facie case of misconduct, however, the lawyer may be asked to submit an explanation to the committee (either personally or in writing). After further investigation, the grievance committee may find the charges unwarranted and dismiss the complaint.

(2) Dismissal not reviewable [§856]

Since disciplinary proceedings are a matter of internal regulation within the bar, the complaining party has *no right of review* once a charge is dismissed by the committee, nor may the party subsequently refile a complaint on the same facts.

c. Hearing before grievance committee [§857]

Complaints not disposed of by a preliminary investigation are generally scheduled for a nonpublic hearing before a committee composed of lawyers.

(1) Case prosecuted by independent official [§858]

An attorney from the state disciplinary agency is usually appointed to prepare the evidence against the lawyer and present it at the hearing.

(2) Lawyer's resignation generally not permitted [§859]

A lawyer under disciplinary charges will generally *not* be permitted to resign, at least not without admitting the offenses in detail. Otherwise, if the lawyer later files a petition for reinstatement (*see infra*, §874), there would be no clear findings as to what the lawyer had done.

(3) Lawyer's right to procedural due process [§860]
The accused lawyer is entitled to procedural due process, which means a fair and impartial hearing.

(a) Due process required [§861]
The following rights are guaranteed by law:

(i) The right to *be heard* and to *introduce evidence*;

(ii) The right to *counsel*;

(iii) The right to *cross-examine* adverse witnesses; and

(iv) The right to *fair notice*, which also means that the hearing must be *limited to charges made in the complaint* [*In re* **Ruffalo**, 390 U.S. 544 (1968)].

[*See, e.g.,* Cal. Bus. & Prof. Code §6085; **Giddens v. State Bar,** 28 Cal. 3d 730 (1981)]

(b) But note—proceeding not given all due process of a criminal case [§862]
A disciplinary hearing is *not* treated as a *criminal proceeding* and does not provide all of the due process protections required in a criminal case. Thus, for example, evidence obtained by wiretap or even by unlawful search and seizure *may* be used against a lawyer in a disbarment proceeding. [**Emslie v. State Bar,** 11 Cal. 3d 210 (1974); **Kelly v. Greason,** 23 N.Y.2d 368 (1968)]

(c) No jury right [§863]
There is also *no right to a jury trial* in a disciplinary proceeding.

(d) Discovery procedures [§864]
Some states make usual discovery procedures—including depositions, requests for admission, and production of documents—available to the lawyer preparing for the disciplinary hearing. [*See, e.g.,* **Brotsky v. State Bar,** 57 Cal. 2d 287 (1962)]

(e) Privilege against self-incrimination applies [§865]
The lawyer has a constitutional right under the Fifth Amendment to refuse to answer questions in disciplinary proceedings concerning the lawyer's professional conduct, and *no disciplinary action can be taken*

against the lawyer based solely on such claim of privilege. [**Spevack v. Klein,** 385 U.S. 511 (1967)]

1) But note [§866]

If a lawyer *admits* misconduct pursuant to an order granting *immunity from criminal prosecution,* the admission *may* be used against the lawyer in a professional discipline case. [*In re Schwarz,* 282 N.E.2d 689 (Ill. 1972)]

CHECKLIST OF LAWYERS' RIGHTS AT DISCIPLINARY HEARINGS

LAWYERS ARE GUARANTEED THE FOLLOWING RIGHTS AT DISCIPLINARY HEARINGS:

☑ The right to *be heard* and to *introduce evidence;*

☑ The right to *counsel;*

☑ The right to *cross-examine* adverse witnesses;

☑ The right to *fair notice;* and

☑ The *Fifth Amendment privilege against self-incrimination*.

---

(4) Burden of proof [§867]

The burden of proof is *on the party presenting the charge (i.e.,* the state disciplinary agency). Most states permit only *legally sufficient evidence* to be considered (*e.g.,* inadmissible hearsay is excluded), and require proof *exceeding a preponderance of the evidence* (though allowing something less than proof beyond a reasonable doubt). [**State v. Neilssen,** 136 N.W.2d 355 (Neb. 1965)]

d. Decision by grievance committee [§868]

After the hearing, the grievance committee (or hearing panel) enters its decision—either dismissing the charges against the lawyer or recommending appropriate sanctions.

e. Review and determination by highest state court [§869]

All the early phases of the disciplinary process are only seen as preparing the case for action by the state's highest court. That is who granted the lawyer the right to practice in the first place, and it is typically the only body that can take away the right.

(1) Procedure [§870]

A lawyer who wishes to *challenge* the action or recommendations of the state bar *must file a timely petition for review* before the court. The *burden is on the lawyer* to show that the state bar's action or recommendation is not supported by the record or is otherwise unlawful. [*In re* **Bogart**, 9 Cal. 3d 743 (1973); Cal. Bus. & Prof. Code §6083]

EXAM TIP   **gilbert**

Remember that, although the **burden of proof in a disciplinary hearing** initially is on the **party prosecuting** the charge (*i.e.,* the state disciplinary agency), the **burden shifts when a lawyer challenges the decision** of the grievance committee. The burden is then on the lawyer to show that the recommended discipline decision was erroneous or unlawful.

---

(2) Scope of review [§871]

The court's review is limited to the record below, but the court is *not bound* by the state bar's findings of fact. The court may independently assess the evidence and pass on its sufficiency. Furthermore, the court may impose a greater or lesser sanction than that proposed by the state bar. [**Selznick v. State Bar,** 16 Cal. 3d 704 (1976)]

(3) Sanctions [§872]

The court can impose reprimand or admonition, suspension, disbarment, or other sanctions (*see supra,* §§844-847).

f. Original proceeding before state's highest court [§873]

The one instance in which the court often does not require use of the hearing process discussed above is *when a lawyer has been convicted of a crime.* The record of the lawyer's conviction is often filed directly with the court, which then may order a hearing or determine from the transcript whether the offense justifies imposing a disciplinary sanction directly. [*See* Cal. Bus. & Prof. Code §§6101, 6102]

g. Reinstatement [§874]

A lawyer suspended for a *fixed* period is deemed *reinstated at the expiration of the period* without any formal petition or order. Where a lawyer has been disbarred or suspended from practice for an *indefinite* period, the court may subsequently reinstate the lawyer by an *appropriate order*. The lawyer must petition the court for reinstatement and must present supporting evidence to convince the court of present fitness to practice law. [*In re* **Hiss,** 333 N.E.2d 429 (Mass. 1975)]

EXAM TIP   **gilbert**

Although a lawyer who has been suspended for a fixed period of time is considered reinstated at the end of that period, don't overlook the fact that a lawyer may also be suspended for an indefinite period. If the suspension is for an **indefinite** period, the lawyer **must petition the court for reinstatement** and **must prove his present fitness** to practice law. Similarly, a lawyer who has been disbarred must apply for readmission.

---

4. **Obligation to Disclose Misconduct by Other Lawyers [§875]**

The legal profession is largely self-policing, and the enforcement of professional rules requires assistance from its members. Thus, a lawyer is under an *affirmative duty* to disclose conduct by other lawyers that the lawyer believes to be a violation of the rules of professional conduct. Such disclosure must be made to the tribunal or authority empowered to act upon such violation. [Model Rule 8.3(a); DR 1-103(A)] A lawyer also has a duty to report a judge's violation of rules of judicial conduct. [Model Rule 8.3(b); DR 1-103(B)]

a. **Scope of obligation**

(1) **ABA Code obligation [§876]**

Under the ABA Code, a lawyer is required to disclose any and all unprivileged knowledge of lawyer conduct that violates the Code. [DR 1-103]

(2) **Model Rules obligation narrower [§877]**

The Code obligation is so broad that lawyers do not seem to take it seriously. Thus, under the Model Rules, a lawyer is required to report only misconduct that *"raises a substantial question"* as to the other lawyer's *"honesty, trustworthiness, or fitness as a lawyer."* [Model Rule 8.3(a)]

EXAM TIP   **gilbert**

Keep in mind that the *duty to report* professional violations *even applies* to violations discovered during activities and conversations *unrelated to the practice of law*. Thus, if two lawyers are complaining to each other about tax increases, and one of the lawyers admits that he underreports his income, the other lawyer has a duty to report the violation.

---

b. **Exception for confidential knowledge [§878]**

A lawyer may not disclose knowledge of misconduct by fellow lawyers where knowledge of such conduct is protected by the professional duty of confidentiality (Model Rule 1.6). [Model Rule 8.3(c)]

(1) **Distinguish—lawyer's partners [§879]**

The fact that a lawyer is a partner or associate of another lawyer *does not create any privilege* between them that would excuse either from the duty to disclose misconduct by the other. [**Attorney Grievance Commission v. Kahn**, 431 A.2d 1336 (Md. 1981)]

(2) **Information gained in Lawyer Assistance Program [§880]**

Most states have created Lawyer Assistance Programs ("LAP") designed to counsel and support the recovery of lawyers who have a problem with drugs or alcohol. Information learned in the course of such a program is treated as if it were *privileged* and need *not* be reported to disciplinary authorities. [Model Rule 8.3(c)]

c. **Sanctions for failure to disclose [§881]**

Failure of a lawyer to disclose the misconduct of another lawyer itself subjects the lawyer to appropriate sanctions. [Model Rule 8.3(a); DR 1-103(A); *In re* **Himmel,** 533 N.E.2d 790 (Ill. 1988)]

5. Effect of Disbarment or Suspension in Other Jurisdictions [§882]

A lawyer is subject to sanction in every state in which he is licensed, regardless of where the misconduct occurred, but disbarment or suspension in one state does not automatically affect a lawyer's standing in other jurisdictions. [Model Rule 8.5(a)]

a. Other states [§883]

Although in theory, two states applying the same professional standards should reach the same result, an order imposing discipline in one state is not inevitably binding in a sister state. Typically, the disciplinary action in one state will be accepted as *conclusive proof of the misconduct* alleged, but *not of the sanctions* warranted by such misconduct. [**Matter of Iulo,** 766 A.2d 335 (Pa. 2001)]

b. Federal courts [§884]

A federal court in the same state is *not obliged* to sanction a lawyer simply because a state has done so. The federal system is *entirely separate*, and therefore each federal court in which the lawyer has been admitted to practice must evaluate the lawyer's conduct. However, a federal court is likely to impose the same sanction unless the lawyer can show by clear and convincing evidence that it should not do so. [*In re* **Hoare,** 155 F.3d 937 (8th Cir. 1998); *In re* **Kramer,** 282 F.3d 721 (9th Cir. 2002)]

B. Personal Financial Liability of Lawyer (Malpractice)

1. Malpractice Action Compensates Injured Plaintiff [§885]

Most states in which the issue has arisen have held that disciplinary proceedings may not grant *private remedies* and that an injured client who wishes to seek recovery must do so in a separate malpractice action in a civil court. [*See, e.g.,* **Re Ackerman,** 330 N.E.2d 322 (Ind. 1975); *but see* **Yokozeki v. State Bar,** 11 Cal. 3d 436 (1974)— lawyer was suspended for five years and until he made full restitution]

COMPARISON OF DISCIPLINARY ACTION AND MALPRACTICE SUIT		**gilbert**
	DISCIPLINARY ACTION	MALPRACTICE SUIT
FORUM	• Disciplinary tribunal	• Civil court
ADVERSARY	• State bar	• Injured plaintiff
PURPOSE	• To protect the public and the legal profession from future misconduct	• To compensate injured plaintiff

2. **Relevance of Rules of Professional Conduct in a Malpractice Case [§886]**

Because lawyers are expected to conform to the state's rules of professional conduct in order to avoid professional discipline, the question naturally has arisen whether a breach of those rules constitutes a breach of the standard of care in a malpractice case.

   a. **Traditional view [§887]**

   The view under the ABA Code and, until recently, under the Model Rules has been a resounding "no." Professional rules were a "just basis for a lawyer's self-assessment or for sanctioning a lawyer," but not a basis for civil liability. [Model Rules (1983), Scope §18; *compare* ABA Code, Preliminary Statement—Code does not prescribe standards for civil liability]

   b. **Current view [§888]**

   However, in real life, courts accept testimony about the professional rules as a guide in determining what is expected of lawyers in particular situations. Thus, even though breach of such a rule is still not negligence per se, courts do consider an ethics violation as relevant evidence that a lawyer's conduct was below the appropriate standard of conduct. The Model Rules now acknowledge that reality. [Model Rules (2002), Scope §20; Restatement §52(2)]

3. **Negligence—Most Common Basis for Malpractice Action [§889]**

Although the plaintiff in a legal malpractice case may invoke a variety of legal theories, the most common theory used is the unintentional tort of **negligence**. Under this theory, the plaintiff must establish the usual elements of any negligence case: (i) a **duty of due care**, (ii) **breach** of that duty, (iii) legal **causation**, and (iv) **damages**.

   a. **General standard of care— "skill and knowledge in community" [§890]**

   The level of competency demanded of a lawyer in malpractice cases is the "*skill, prudence, and diligence*" possessed by lawyers of *ordinary skill and capacity* who perform *similar services*. [**Lucas v. Hamm**, 56 Cal. 2d 583 (1961)]

      (1) **Minimum duty owed [§891]**

      Thus, *at a minimum*, the lawyer is held to the standard of care exercised by lawyers generally, regardless of whether the lawyer personally possesses such skills.

      (2) **Higher standard of care owed by specialists [§892]**

      If a lawyer *has greater competence*, she is *bound to exercise it*; *i.e.,* lawyers who hold themselves out as specialists in a particular field (*e.g.,* tax, litigation, probate) will be held to the *standard of care* customarily exercised by *fellow specialists,* rather than merely that required of other members of the legal community generally. [**Wright v. Williams**, 47 Cal. App. 3d 802 (1975)]

(3) Appointed counsel [§893]

Appointed counsel also owes a duty of due care to her client and may be held liable to a client for malpractice. [**Ferry v. Ackerman,** 444 U.S. 193 (1979)]

(4) Application

(a) Knowledge and research ability [§894]

As part of the general standard of care, a lawyer is expected to possess knowledge of those *"plain and elementary principles* of law which are commonly known by well-informed attorneys" and to *discover* those additional rules of law which, even though not commonly known, may readily be found *by standard research techniques.* [**Smith v. Lewis,** 13 Cal. 3d 349 (1975)]

1) Ignorance of new laws no defense [§895]

Thus, it is *no defense* to a malpractice suit that the lawyer was *unaware* of recent changes in statutes or case law which affected the correctness of her advice.

2) Factual investigation [§896]

Also, the lawyer is obliged to make a reasonable investigation of the facts of the case. [**Woodruff v. Tomlin,** 616 F.2d 924 (6th Cir. 1980)]

3) Further research required [§897]

A lawyer has an *affirmative duty to investigate* upon receiving information that should reasonably put the lawyer on notice that further research or action is required. [*See, e.g.,* **Owen v. Neely,** 471 S.W.2d 705 (Ky. 1971)—notice of defect in title]

4) Foreign law [§898]

Normally, lawyers are expected to be familiar with rules of law and procedure in *their own states.* However, where in the exercise of reasonable care they should realize that the case involves an issue that must be decided under the law of some other state or country, lawyers *may* be under a duty to become familiar with appropriate *foreign law* (or associate competent counsel with such familiarity). [**Rekeweg v. Federal Mutual Insurance Co.,** 27 F.R.D. 431 (N.D. Ind. 1961)]

(b) No liability for errors in judgment [§899]

Lawyers are not, however, liable for every mistake they make in practice. They do not guarantee the soundness of their opinions or the validity of instruments they are engaged to draft. If the action or decision involved is one as to which there is *reasonable doubt* by well-informed lawyers, judgmental errors by a lawyer are *not malpractice.*

1) Trial tactics [§900]

This is especially true as to errors made in the course of *litigation,* where the decision made is often a matter of judgment or tactics (*e.g.,* whether or not to call a certain witness, demand a jury trial, etc.). [**Kirsch v. Duryea,** 21 Cal. 3d 303 (1978)]

2) Law uncertain [§901]

Likewise, where the area of law in question is *unsettled or unclear,* the fact that the lawyer's advice or interpretation of the law ultimately proves wrong is not enough by itself to establish malpractice. [**Lucas v. Hamm,** *supra,* §890]

---

e.g. **Example:** In *Lucas,* misinterpreting a complicated Rule Against Perpetuities problem in drafting a will was held *not* to constitute malpractice. The court found that the lawyer used the skill, prudence, and diligence commonly exercised by other lawyers.

---

cf. **Compare:** A lawyer was held liable for malpractice for giving possibly *correct advice* about the law but with insufficient research to protect the client when the advice proved wrong. [**Aloy v. Mash,** 38 Cal. 3d 413 (1985)]

EXAM TIP	gilbert

If a lawyer's mistake caused his client to lose a case, *do not automatically assume* that the lawyer committed *malpractice*. Look to see if the lawyer exercised *due care*. For example, if a lawyer decided not to take the pretrial deposition of a witness because it appeared that the witness's testimony was unimportant, but it later became evident that the witness's testimony could have helped the client, the lawyer did not necessarily commit malpractice if his decision was reasonable when made and the lawyer otherwise acted with due care.

b. Causation—harm to client must be shown [§902]

Failure to meet the general standard of care constitutes negligence, but traditionally there is *no malpractice liability unless harm* to the client has proximately resulted therefrom. Thus, the client must show that *"but for"* the lawyer's errors or omissions, the client would have avoided the complained of loss. [**Winskunas v. Birnbaum,** 23 F.3d 1264 (7th Cir. 1994)]

(1) "Case within a case" [§903]

In litigation matters, this has meant that the client *must in effect prove two cases:* (i) that the *lawyer was negligent* in handling the matter, and (ii) *that* the *client would otherwise have won* the lawsuit. This has often been a very difficult burden for the client—particularly where the case involved disputed facts or close liability issues.

---

e.g. Example: Lawyer is hired to defend Client in a contract action, but Lawyer fails to appear and the action is lost, resulting in a judgment against Client. Whether Client can recover damages against Lawyer for malpractice depends on whether Client had a *valid defense* to the action (*i.e.,* whether Client would have prevailed "but for" Lawyer's negligence).

(a) Distinguish—disciplinary action [§904]

Disciplinary sanctions can be invoked regardless of the "but for" test. Thus, technically, a lawyer could be disciplined for incompetence that does not constitute malpractice.

(2) "Substantial factor" test [§905]

In an effort to reduce the burden on a malpractice plaintiff, some courts have demanded only that the lawyer's conduct have been a "substantial factor" in the client's loss, *i.e.,* that the client need not prove with certainty that the client would have won the underlying case. [*See, e.g.,* **Conklin v. Hannock Weisman,** 678 A.2d 1060 (N.J. 1996)]

EXAM TIP   **gilbert**

Remember this important difference between proving a violation of professional conduct and proving malpractice—although a lawyer is subject to *professional discipline* for misconduct *even if harm to someone is not shown*, in a suit for *malpractice*, the plaintiff must prove that the lawyer's conduct was the cause of the plaintiff's injury. This means that the injury would not have happened *but for* the lawyer's negligence.

---

c. Damages [§906]

The plaintiff in a professional negligence case must prove damages—*e.g.,* the money paid out to discharge an adverse judgment, or the value of a lost cause of action. The plaintiff can recover for direct losses and also for losses that are indirect but foreseeable.

d. Liability for acts of others [§907]

The general standard of care may render lawyers liable not only for their own acts, but also for the acts of others:

(1) Co-counsel [§908]

Where several lawyers have been employed to represent a client concurrently, *each* owes the duty of care stated above. Ordinarily, *no delegation of responsibility* among counsel *excuses* one from malpractice liability for errors or omissions of the others, unless the client agrees to the division of responsibilities.

(2) Partners [§909]

Malpractice by a partner in a law firm generally renders *all other partners equally liable unless* the negligent partner had *no actual or apparent authority* to act on behalf of the firm in the matter. [*See, e.g.,* **Cook v. Lyon**, 522 S.W.2d 740 (Tex. 1975)—no liability for partner's faulty investment advice to client where investment was unrelated to matter firm was handling]

(a) But note—increased use of limited liability partnerships [§910]

In an effort to change the automatic imputation of liability to all law partners, many states have now adopted statutes that permit creation of limited liability partnerships ("LLP") or limited liability companies ("LLC") that expressly limit liability to the negligent partner and the entity itself, thus immunizing other partners from personal liability.

(3) Employees [§911]

A lawyer is generally liable on a theory of *respondeat superior* for losses caused to a client by negligent acts of the lawyer's employees or subordinates (*e.g.,* an administrative assistant or clerk carelessly loses a file, throws out a will, or destroys crucial evidence without which the client loses the case).

(4) Referring lawyer [§912]

In addition, a lawyer who refers a client to another lawyer whose negligence causes the client loss *may be held liable* for the other lawyer's negligence if the first lawyer made the referral *without reasonable care* (*i.e.,* without checking into the lawyer's reputation and skill). [*See, e.g.,* **Tormo v. Yormark**, 398 F. Supp. 1159 (D.N.J. 1975)—client's funds embezzled by lawyer to whom referred]

4. Other Theories for Malpractice Liability [§913]

In addition to the negligence theory for lawyer malpractice, other theories may be available:

a. Intentional tort [§914]

A lawyer is liable for fraud, misrepresentation, malicious prosecution, abuse of process, or misuse of funds.

b. Breach of contract [§915]

The lawyer-client relationship is ultimately based on a contract between the lawyer and client, and sometimes clients prefer to sue for breach of that contract in addition to, or instead of, suing under a tort theory. [Restatement §54]

(1) Different statute of limitations [§916]

In many states, the statute of limitations on contract actions is longer than that available for tort claims.

(2) Extra promises by lawyer [§917]

In other cases, the lawyer may have made particular claims of expertise or willingness to devote extra people to a matter, or may have otherwise assumed duties greater than those that would have been required under the usual standard of care under tort law.

c. Breach of fiduciary duty [§918]

Increasingly, clients are filing suit alleging that their lawyer breached a fiduciary duty owed to the client; *e.g.,* the lawyer misused confidential information or took the case while burdened by a conflict of interest. [Restatement §49]

(1) Remedy of fee forfeiture [§919]

The principal significance of a breach of fiduciary duty claim is that courts have increasingly been willing to sanction lawyers by partially or completely denying them the right to collect fees for the representation, regardless of whether the plaintiff can prove any actual damages. [*See, e.g.,* **Burrow v. Arce,** 997 S.W.2d 229 (Tex. 1999); Restatement §37]

(a) Extent of forfeiture—a matter for the court [§920]

Fee forfeiture is not automatic, and the amount of forfeiture ordinarily is a matter for the court, not the jury. [**Burrow v. Arce,** *supra*]

THEORIES OF MALPRACTICE　　　**gilbert**

A PLAINTIFF MAY INVOKE THE FOLLOWING THEORIES OF MALPRACTICE:

☑ *Negligence;*

☑ *Intentional tort* (*e.g.,* fraud, misrepresentation, misuse of funds);

☑ *Breach of contract*;

☑ *Breach of fiduciary duty.*

---

5. Malpractice Liability to Nonclients [§921]

Ordinarily, a lawyer is liable for malpractice *only to the lawyer's client*. However, there are important *exceptions* to that general principle:

a. Prospective client [§922]

A person consulting the lawyer for the purpose of becoming a client is not yet a client and may never become one (*e.g.,* because the lawyer has a conflict of interest). However, the lawyer *may be guilty of malpractice* to such a prospective client if the lawyer: (i) *misuses confidential information* of the prospective client, (ii) *fails to protect property* entrusted to the lawyer by the prospective client, or (iii) *fails to use reasonable care* in giving the prospective client legal advice (*e.g.,* saying "you don't have a good case" and causing the prospective client not to get further legal advice). [Model Rule 1.18; Restatement §§15, 51(1)]

b. Person lawyer invites to rely on lawyer's help [§923]

A lawyer may also be liable for malpractice if the lawyer invites a nonclient to rely on the lawyer's legal opinion (*e.g.,* advises the nonclient about the meaning of contract terms). [**Greycas v. Proud,** *supra,* §522; Restatement §51(2)]

c. Person the client expressly intended to benefit [§924]

If a lawyer is employed by the client to render services *intended to benefit an identified third person (e.g.,* draft a will to leave money to particular persons), the lawyer may be liable to the *intended beneficiary,* if the work is done negligently and the gift is not successfully made. [**Lucas v. Hamm,** *supra,* §901; Restatement §51(3)]

d. Person to whom a trustee-client owes duties [§925]

A lawyer representing a trustee or similar fiduciary may be held liable for *malpractice* to the *beneficiaries* to whom the trustee-client owes duties if the lawyer *knowingly assists* the trustee-client in the *breach of a fiduciary duty.* The lawyer may also be liable for malpractice if he does not try to prevent a breach of fiduciary duty by the trustee-client and preventing the breach would not significantly impair representation of the trustee. *But note:* Inaction is *not malpractice* if the *breach of duty is not clear* or if action would *violate the lawyer's duty to the trustee-client.* [**Fickett v. Superior Court,** 558 P.2d 988 (Ariz. 1976); Restatement §51(4)]

6. Attempts to Limit Malpractice Liability

a. ABA Code approach [§926]

The ABA Code *expressly prohibits any attempt* by lawyers to exculpate themselves or otherwise limit their liability to clients for malpractice. [DR 6-102; Restatement §54(2), (4)]

b. Model Rules approach [§927]

Under the Model Rules, a lawyer may not contract with a client to prospectively limit the lawyer's liability for malpractice *unless the client is separately represented* in making the agreement. [Model Rule 1.8(h)]

(1) Comment

It is likely to be a rare case when an individual client will get separate counsel to agree to such a limitation, but drafters of the Model Rules recognized that corporate clients often have in-house counsel who might so agree in order to get an outside specialist to review a particularly complex matter.

c. Settling a malpractice claim [§928]

A lawyer may not settle a claim for malpractice with an unrepresented client or former client without giving that person *written notice* that seeking *independent counsel* is desirable and giving the person *reasonable opportunity to consult such counsel*. [Model Rule 1.8(h); Restatement §54(3)]

d. Reimbursement of client [§929]

A lawyer who has breached a duty to his client with monetary effect *cannot escape discipline* by reimbursing the client for any loss. Thus, even if the lawyer pays the client back for any damage he caused, he is still subject to discipline.

C. Contempt Sanctions

1. Introduction [§930]

Although not often thought of as a device for keeping lawyers "ethical," the power of a court to punish a lawyer for contempt is one of the most direct and effective techniques for enforcing professional standards. Indeed, the contempt sanction may be the only practical way to enforce *proper standards of courtroom conduct*.

2. Direct Criminal Contempt [§931]

Direct criminal contempt consists of any conduct *within the personal knowledge of the judge* that tends to obstruct the court in the administration of justice or that brings the administration of justice into disrepute. [**People v. Sherwin**, 166 N.E. 513 (Ill. 1929)]

Examples: A lawyer's willful disruption of a trial [*In re* **Isserman**, 87 A.2d 903 (N.J. 1953)], or filing of briefs filled with scandalous language falsely accusing the court of improprieties, can result in a finding of direct criminal contempt.

---

a. Summary enforcement [§932]

An act of direct contempt in open court allows the trial judge to act on personal knowledge of the facts and punish the offender *summarily*, without a hearing. [*Ex parte* **Terry**, 128 U.S. 289 (1888)]

(1) Delay in acting [§933]

If the judge does not act summarily, she must refer the case to another judge (who will presumably be less personally involved) for a hearing. [**Mayberry v. Pennsylvania**, 400 U.S. 455 (1971)]

(2) Right to jury trial [§934]

If the judge proposes to sentence the contemnor to more than a six-month jail term, the accused is entitled to a jury trial. [**Bloom v. Illinois**, 391 U.S. 194 (1968)]

3. Indirect Criminal Contempt [§935]

When the relevant facts regarding the lawyer's alleged contempt are *not within the personal knowledge of the judge*, the contempt is said to be indirect.

Example: A prosecutor got into a physical altercation with opposing counsel, a public defender, in the courthouse hallway after court had recessed for the day. The next day, the public defender moved for dismissal of the case, mistrial, and sanctions against the prosecutor. Although the prosecutor's misconduct took place outside of the courtroom, the subsequent hearings on the public defender's motions interrupted the trial. Thus, the prosecutor was later found guilty of indirect criminal contempt because his actions caused the interruption of the administration of justice. [**Milian v. State**, 764 So. 2d 860 (Fla. 2000)]

---

a. Hearing required [§936]

Because the trial judge does not personally know the facts, a hearing must be held. If the trial judge is so personally involved with the case that the judge's impartiality might be questioned, the contempt case should be referred to another judge.

Chapter Nine:
The Special
Responsibilities of Judges

CONTENTS

Chapter Approach

Chapter Approach

Judges are lawyers first, and thus they are subject to the rules of ethical conduct for lawyers. On assuming the bench, they become subject to additional ethical norms. This chapter discusses those additional obligations of judges and the limitations on their activities both on and off the bench.

The obligations generally fall into the following groups:

1. The judge's *official actions;*

2. The judge's duty to *disqualify* herself if necessary;

3. The judge's *unofficial* and *money-making activities;* and

4. The judge's *political activities.*

Also note that state and federal judges are subject to rules that are similar, but not identical.

A. Introduction

1. **State Judges [§937]**
   The *ABA Model Code of Judicial Conduct ("CJC")* provides detailed rules to govern the conduct of judges so that the *independence* and *integrity* of the judiciary is preserved. As is true with the Model Rules relating to the conduct of lawyers, the CJC becomes legally binding on judges only as it is adopted by individual states.

   a. **Format of Code of Judicial Conduct [§938]**
      The CJC, as amended in 1990, is made up of five Canons. Like the Model Rules, it follows a Restatement-type format, with black-letter provisions and accompanying Commentary.

   b. **Relevance of Code to the MPRE [§939]**
      Also like the Model Rules, the content of the CJC is tested on the Multistate Professional Responsibility Examination ("MPRE").

2. **Federal Judges [§940]**
   The standards governing federal judges are prescribed by federal statute and are discussed at §§1042-1048, *infra.*

3. **Arbitrators and Other "Private" Judges [§941]**

Since 2002, the conduct of lawyers who sit as arbitrators, mediators, or other third-party neutrals has been regulated by ABA Model Rule 2.4, which requires them to make clear that they do not represent any of the parties before them. The conduct of such third-party neutrals has never been regulated by the CJC, however, and it will not be discussed further in this Summary.

B. General Norms

1. **Maintain High Standards of Conduct [§942]**

A judge must establish, maintain, enforce, and observe *high standards of personal conduct* at all times. [CJC Canon 1]

---

e.g. **Example:** Upon discovering his estranged wife in a car with another man, a judge struck the car, breaking the car window and causing the other man to be cut with broken glass. The judge also slapped his estranged wife, but she did not sustain injuries. Misdemeanor charges of reckless endangerment and assault were dismissed after the parties resolved the matter out of court. However, in the subsequent disciplinary proceeding, the court held that discipline is not limited to sanctions for conduct associated with the performance of judicial duties. Thus, although the judge's conduct was not related to his judicial duties, the court found that his failure to respect and comply with the law warranted censure. [*In re* **Roth**, 645 P.2d 1064 (Or. 1982)]

---

2. **Promote Public Confidence in Judiciary [§943]**

A judge must *obey the law* and behave in a manner that promotes public confidence in the *integrity and impartiality* of the judiciary. [CJC Canon 2A]

3. **Avoid Using Influence or Being Influenced [§944]**

A judge must not let family, social, or other relationships influence judicial acts, or let it appear that they could. [CJC Canon 2B]

a. **May not advance the judge's or others' interests [§945]**

The judge may not use the prestige of the office to advance the private (usually business) interests of the judge or others. [CJC Canon 2B]

b. **May not give impression that others can influence [§946]**

The judge may not convey, or permit others to convey, the impression that others are in a special position to influence the judge. [CJC Canon 2B]

c. **May not act as witness [§947]**

The judge may not testify as a character witness *unless subpoenaed* to do so; the judge may not testify voluntarily. [CJC Canon 2B]

4. **Avoid Membership in Discriminatory Organizations [§948]**

A judge *may not be a member* of any organization that "practices *invidious discrimination* on the basis of race, sex, religion, or national origin" or that engages in any form of discrimination that violates the law of the judge's jurisdiction. [CJC Canon 2C and Commentary]

a. Distinguish—permissible organizations [§949]

A judge may be a member of a *completely private* organization whose membership limitations could not be constitutionally prohibited *or* an organization that is "*dedicated to the preservation of religious, ethnic, or cultural values* of legitimate common interest to its members." [CJC Canon 2C, Commentary]

Example: Judge Jones belongs to the Lansing Library Reading Group, open only to Lansing citizens, who meet each month to talk about a specific work. Judge Brant belongs to the American Indian Society, whose members promote cross-cultural awareness and are descendants of Native Americans. Judge Connors is a member of the alumni association of Heathmoor Women's College and assists in planning fund-raising activities (but does not actually participate in the fund-raising activities). None of these organizations practices invidious discrimination, and the judges' memberships are permissible.

---

b. Appropriate responses [§950]

If a judge learns that an organization to which she belongs practices discrimination, she must either *resign promptly or work to end the discriminatory practice.* She must not participate in the organization until the situation is remedied, and if it is not remedied within one year of the judge's learning of it, she must resign. [CJC Canon 2C, Commentary]

EXAM TIP   **gilbert**

Whenever an exam question involves a judge's conduct *off the bench* that is completely separate from her judicial duties, be sure to remember that a judge is the subject of constant public scrutiny and should manifest integrity and impartiality in *all of her activities*, whether official or personal, to preserve public confidence in the judiciary.

JUDGE'S MEMBERSHIP IN DISCRIMINATORY ORGANIZATIONS—EXAMPLES   **gilbert**

PERMISSIBLE	IMPERMISSIBLE
Monday night men-only poker club consisting of judge and his college chums	Men-only social club with 6,000 members and dining and health club facilities
Women's support group for breastfeeding mothers	Women's bar association that refuses to admit male members
Talmudic study group that limits membership to members of the judge's temple	Country club that excludes members on the basis of race or religion

C. Judge's Official Actions

1. **Priority of Judicial Duties [§951]**

   A judge must put her judicial duties ahead of all other activities. [CJC Canon 3A]

2. **Behavior on the Bench [§952]**

   A judge must be *faithful to the law, remain competent,* and be *unswayed by outside pressures.* [CJC Canon 3B(2)]

   ---

   e.g. **Example:** A judge who was an outspoken opponent of laws against prostitution and gun control routinely dismissed these cases, despite contrary court orders entered by superior courts. The judge was charged with disobeying court orders, refusing to follow decisions of higher courts, abusing his contempt powers, and improperly excluding lawyers from the courtroom. In the judicial disciplinary proceeding, the court found that the judge's misconduct was prejudicial to the administration of justice and eroded public confidence in the impartiality of the judiciary. The court suspended the judge for 60 days without pay. [*In re* **Hague,** 315 N.W.2d 524 (Mich. 1982)]

   ---

   a. **Hear all cases [§953]**

      A judge must hear and decide all assigned cases *unless disqualified* from a case. [CJC Canon 3B(1)]

   b. **Right to be heard [§954]**

      A judge must give every person who has a legal interest in a proceeding (or that person's lawyer) the right to be heard in accordance with the law. [CJC Canon 3B(7)]

   c. **Order and decorum in court [§955]**

      The judge must maintain order and decorum in the courtroom. [CJC Canon 3B(3)]

   d. **Relations with others [§956]**

      A judge must be *patient, dignified, and courteous* to litigants, lawyers, jurors, witnesses, and others with whom the judge deals in an official capacity, and must require the same of lawyers appearing in the court, court staff, and any other persons subject to the judge's direction and control. [CJC Canon 3B(4)]

   e. **Perform duties without bias or prejudice [§957]**

      A judge and other court officials *must not exhibit bias or prejudice* based on race, sex, religion, national origin, disability, age, sexual orientation, or socio-economic status. The judge must be alert even to body language that may suggest judicial bias. [CJC Canon 3B(5) and Commentary]

   f. **Not allow lawyers to manifest bias [§958]**

      A judge must also require that lawyers appearing before her do not manifest prohibited bias, but she *may not preclude* lawyers from engaging in *legitimate advocacy* when issues of bias or prejudice are involved in contested proceedings. [CJC Canon 3B(6)]

3. Ex Parte Contacts [§959]

The judge *may not initiate or consider* ex parte contacts with parties or their lawyers, *except* as otherwise authorized by law, and in the following specific situations [CJC Canon 3B(7)]:

a. Scheduling matters and emergency situations [§960]

The judge may speak with parties ex parte when necessary for administrative purposes, to schedule matters, or to deal with emergency situations that *do not affect the merits of a matter,* provided that (i) the judge reasonably believes that *no party will be advantaged* thereby, and (ii) the judge *arranges to notify the other parties* promptly of the substance of the communication and *gives them a chance to respond.* [CJC Canon 3B(7)(a)]

b. Discussions in the context of settling cases [§961]

With the *consent of the parties*, the judge *may meet individually* with the parties in an effort to *mediate or settle* a matter. [CJC Canon 3B(7)(d)]

c. Findings of fact and conclusions of law [§962]

If a judge asks the lawyers for one side to propose findings of fact and conclusions of law, the lawyers for the other parties must be told of the request and given a chance to respond to the proposed findings and conclusions. [CJC Canon 3B(7), Commentary]

4. Communications Outside Presence of Parties and Their Lawyers [§963]

a. Consultation with disinterested expert on the law [§964]

The judge may, without prior notice to the parties, *consult with a disinterested expert* on the law applicable to a case before the court. But the judge *must* later *tell the parties* the *name* of the person consulted and the *substance* of the advice obtained, and must *give the parties an opportunity to respond.* [CJC Canon 3B(7)(b)]

b. Consultation with clerks or other judges [§965]

The judge may, of course, talk about a case with fellow judges and with court personnel who assist the judge with her responsibilities (*e.g.,* the judge's law clerk). [CJC Canon 3B(7)(c)]

5. Independent Investigation of Facts [§966]

A judge *must not* independently investigate the facts in a case and must consider only the evidence presented. [CJC Canon 3B(7), Commentary]

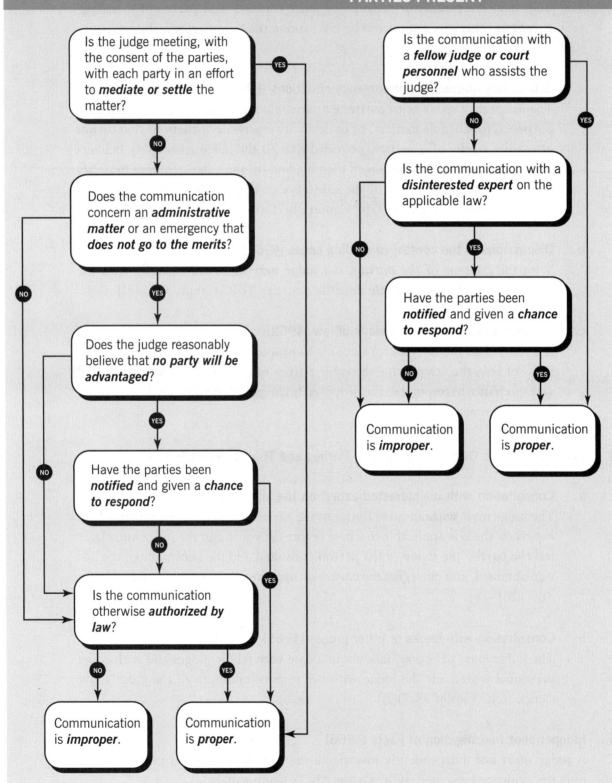

EX PARTE COMMUNICATIONS

Is the judge meeting, with the consent of the parties, with each party in an effort to *mediate or settle* the matter?

— NO →

Does the communication concern an *administrative matter* or an emergency that *does not go to the merits*?

— YES ↓ / NO →

Does the judge reasonably believe that *no party will be advantaged*?

— YES ↓ / NO →

Have the parties been *notified* and given a *chance to respond*?

— NO ↓ / YES →

Is the communication otherwise *authorized by law*?

— NO → Communication is *improper*.
— YES → Communication is *proper*.

(YES from mediate/settle → Communication is *proper*.)

COMMUNICATIONS WITHOUT PARTIES PRESENT

Is the communication with a *fellow judge or court personnel* who assists the judge?

— NO ↓ / YES →

Is the communication with a *disinterested expert* on the applicable law?

— YES ↓ / NO →

Have the parties been *notified* and given a *chance to respond*?

— NO → Communication is *improper*.
— YES → Communication is *proper*.

6. Disposition of Matters [§967]

The judge must dispose of matters *promptly, efficiently, and fairly.* [CJC Canon 3B(8)]

7. Comments About Jurors [§968]

A judge *may not commend or criticize* jurors for their verdict other than in a court order or opinion, but the judge may thank them for their service. [CJC Canon 3B(11)]

8. Relations with News Media [§969]

The judge and other court personnel *may not make comments* to the news media about a pending or impending matter that might reasonably be expected to *affect its outcome or impair its fairness.* [CJC Canon 3B(9)]

a. No pledges or promises about cases or issues [§970]

A judge must not make public pledges, promises, or commitments about cases or issues "likely to come before the court" that are *inconsistent with impartial performance* of the judge's duties. [CJC Canon 3B(10)]

b. Distinguish—permitted public statements [§971]

A judge may make other public statements, such as *explanations of the status* of proceedings *or court procedures.* [CJC Canon 3B(9)]

c. Rules pertaining to lawyers [§972]

The Code of Judicial Conduct only governs the judges' duties. Rules on pre-trial comments by lawyers are found in DR 7-107 of the ABA Code and Rule 3.6 of the Model Rules. [CJC Canon 3B(9) and Commentary]

9. Nonpublic Information [§973]

A judge *may not use or disclose* nonpublic information learned in a judicial capacity. [CJC Canon 3B(12)]

10. Administrative Duties of the Judge [§974]

The judge must manage the court's administration *diligently, competently, cooperatively,* and *without discrimination* and must insist that court staff do the same. [CJC Canon 3C(1)-(3)]

a. No unnecessary appointments [§975]

A judge appointing receivers, trustees, and the like may not do so unnecessarily and *must base appointments on merit.* Furthermore, compensation for appointees may not be set at excessive levels. [CJC Canon 3C(4)]

b. No reward for campaign contributions [§976]

A judge *may not appoint a lawyer* to such a paid position if the judge knows or learns that the lawyer *contributed more than a sum prescribed* by state law to the judge's campaign, unless no other lawyer can be found willing, competent, and able to accept the position. [CJC Canon 3C(5)]

11. Disciplinary Duties of the Judge [§977]

The judge must take or initiate appropriate disciplinary action against a judge or lawyer when the judge "receives information indicating a substantial likelihood" of misconduct. Such action taken by the judge is absolutely *privileged against a retaliatory action* by the judge or lawyer who is accused. [CJC Canon 3D)]

D. Judicial Disqualification

1. Bases for Disqualification [§978]

A judge is disqualified to act in any proceeding in which the judge's *"impartiality might reasonably be questioned."* The CJC lists several such situations, but says there may be others. [CJC Canon 3E]

a. Personal bias concerning a party [§979]

The judge is disqualified if she "has a personal bias or prejudice concerning a party or a party's lawyer." [CJC Canon 3E(1)(a)]

(1) Distinguish—policy issue [§980]

A judge is *not necessarily disqualified* where the bias is with respect to a *policy issue.* Thus, an African-American judge is not ordinarily disqualified to sit in a civil rights case, and either a male or female judge may hear a sex discrimination case. However, the judge is disqualified if she "has made a public statement that commits, or appears to commit" her as to "an issue" or " the controversy" in the case. [CJC Canon 3E(1)(f)]

(2) Extrajudicial source factor and pervasive bias exception [§981]

Normally, to be disqualified for bias, the judge's alleged bias also must come from an *"extrajudicial source"*; what the judge learns in a courtroom inevitably is a part of the judge's decision and is ordinarily not "bias or prejudice." However, a *"pervasive bias"* exception applies even to the extrajudicial source doctrine. Whenever the judge has a *"clear inability to render fair judgment,"* the judge's recusal is required. [**Liteky v. United States**, 510 U.S. 540 (1994); **United States v. Microsoft Corp.**, 253 F.3d 34 (D.C. Cir. 2001)]

EXAM TIP	gilbert

Although a judge may be disqualified because of a bias acquired from an *extrajudicial* source, remember these caveats:

(i) *Not every* opinion derived from a source outside of judicial proceedings is cause for disqualification (*e.g.,* bias concerning a policy issue).

(ii) A judge's opinions based on facts introduced during the proceedings may be *so extreme* and undeserved that disqualification is necessary because a *fair judgment is impossible* (pervasive bias exception).

---

b. Knowledge of disputed evidentiary facts [§982]

The judge may take judicial notice of some facts, of course, but if the judge has knowledge as to the facts in dispute, she is disqualified. [CJC Canon 3E(1)(a)]

c. Prior involvement in the matter [§983]

A judge may not hear a case in which the judge *served as a lawyer* before coming on the bench. Also, a judge may not hear a case if she was *associated* in law practice with a lawyer who handled the case at the time they practiced together or if the judge served as a *material witness* in the case. [CJC Canon 3E(1)(b)]

d. Financial interest in party or subject matter of litigation [§984]

A judge is disqualified if she knows that she or a family member has an *economic interest* in a party or in the subject matter of the proceeding *or any interest* that is *more than de minimis* that could be affected by the proceeding. [CJC Canon 3E(1)(c)]

(1) Whose interest can be disqualifying [§985]

The disqualifying interest may be that of the judge's *spouse, parent, child, or any other family member residing in the household.* An interest that the judge has acting as a *fiduciary* (*i.e.,* an executor, administrator, trustee, or guardian) is also disqualifying.

(2) Economic interest defined [§986]

A judge has an economic interest if she has more than de minimis legal or equitable interest, or is a director, advisor, or active participant in the affairs of a party. However, the following are *not disqualifying* interests:

(a) Mutual fund [§987]

Ownership of a mutual fund does not constitute a financial interest in the firms whose securities are held by the fund, unless the judge is a manager of the fund or the case could substantially affect the value of the fund.

(b) Nonprofit organization [§988]

An office in an educational, charitable, fraternal, or civic organization does not constitute an interest in the securities held by the organization.

(c) Policyholder or depositor [§989]

The judge's interest as a policyholder in a mutual insurance company or depositor in a mutual savings association is not disqualifying unless the value of the judge's interest could be substantially affected by the result of the case.

(d) Government securities [§990]

Finally, a judge who holds government securities is not disqualified from hearing cases involving the government unless the value of the securities could be substantially affected. [CJC Terminology]

e. Cases in which judge's relatives involved [§991]

A judge is also disqualified by the roles or interests of the judge's *spouse,* or someone within the *third degree of relationship* to either of them, or the *spouse of such a relative.* [CJC Canon 3E(1)(d)] The "third degree of relationship" is calculated according to the civil law system and includes parents, grandparents, great-grandparents, siblings, aunts and uncles, nieces and nephews, children, grandchildren, and great-grandchildren. [CJC Terminology]

(1) Relevant disqualifying interests [§992]

Disqualification is required when such a person is:

(a) A *party,* or *officer, director, or trustee* of a party;

(b) Acting as a *lawyer* in the proceeding;

(c) Known by the judge to have an *interest* that could be substantially affected by the outcome of the case; or

(d) Known by the judge to likely be a *material witness* in the case.

(2) Scope of obligation [§993]

The judge must keep informed about her own economic interests, and she must make *reasonable efforts* to be informed about financial interests of her spouse and minor children residing in her household. [CJC Canon 3E(2)]

f. Persons making contributions to judge's election campaign [§994]

A judge who is subject to public election must disqualify herself if she knows, or learns through a timely motion, that a party or a party's lawyer has, within a designated number of prior years, made contributions to the judge's election campaign that *exceed* the jurisdiction's specified amount. [CJC Canon 3E(1)(e)]

2. Disclosure by Judge [§995]

The judge should disclose on the record any information the judge believes that the parties or their lawyers might consider relevant to the question of disqualification, even if the judge believes there is no reasonable basis for disqualification. [CJC Canon 3E(1), Commentary]

3. Remittal of Disqualification [§996]

If the judge is disqualified for any reason *"other than personal bias or prejudice* concerning a party," the parties may consider whether to *waive* the judge's disqualification. [CJC Canon 3F]

a. Procedure [§997]

The judge, instead of immediately withdrawing, may disclose on the record the basis of the disqualification and ask the parties and their lawyers to consider whether to waive the disqualification.

b. Judge not to participate [§998]

The judge may not solicit or hear comments about the possible disqualification. If, outside the presence of the judge, all parties and lawyers agree that the problem is insubstantial and want to waive the disqualification, *each party and each lawyer* should so indicate in writing. The writing is then incorporated in the record. [CJC Canon 3F]

4. Rule of Necessity [§999]

Case law has created a *rule of necessity* that *overrides the rules of disqualification.* Under this rule, a judge who would otherwise be disqualified because of a conflict of interest may hear a case if there is no other way for the case to be heard (*i.e.,* no other judge is able to hear the case or every judge who might be assigned would also be disqualified). The judge must make reasonable efforts to transfer the matter to a judge who is not disqualifed as soon as possible. [CJC Canon 3E(1), Commentary]

CHECKLIST OF BASES FOR DISQUALIFICATION OF A JUDGE **gilbert**

A JUDGE MAY BE DISQUALIFIED FOR:

- ☑ Having a *personal bias or prejudice* against a party or his lawyer

- ☑ Having *knowledge of facts in dispute*

- ☑ Having a *prior involvement* in the matter

- ☑ Having an *economic interest in a party or the subject matter* of the proceeding or having a family member with such an interest

- ☑ Having a *relative involved in the case* (as a likely witness, a party, or an officer or director of a party; as a lawyer in the case; or having an interest that could be substantially affected)

- ☑ Receiving *excessive campaign contributions* from a party or his lawyer

---

E. Extrajudicial Activities of the Judge

1. In General [§1000]

A judge may engage in nonjudicial activities, whether or not associated with law, but all such activities are subject to the qualification that the activities *may not:* (i) *cast doubt on the judge's impartiality,* (ii) *demean* the judicial office, or (iii) *interfere with proper performance* of judicial duties. [CJC Canon 4A]

2. May Speak, Write, Lecture, and Teach [§1001]

The judge may speak, write, lecture, and teach on *both legal and nonlegal subjects,* as long as the activities do not violate any other judicial standards. [CJC Canon 4B]

3. **May Consult with Legislators and Executive Officials [§1002]**

The judge may appear in a public hearing or otherwise consult with legislators and executive officials, but *only* on matters concerning *the law, the legal system, and the administration of justice,* or when appearing *pro se* on the judge's own behalf. [CJC Canon 4C(1)]

4. **May Not Serve on Government Commissions [§1003]**

A judge *may not serve* on a government commission concerned with factual or legal issues other than the law, the legal system, or the administration of justice, but a judge *may serve* as an official *representative* at ceremonies or in connection with *historical, educational, or cultural activities.* [CJC Canon 4C(2)]

5. **Officer of Organizations [§1004]**

The judge *may be a member* of, and *serve* as an officer, director, trustee, or nonlegal advisor to, *nonprofit* agencies or educational, religious, charitable, fraternal, or civic organizations. [CJC Canon 4C(3)]

   a. **Note—public/private school distinction**

   Service on the board of a *public* educational institution other than a law school is prohibited, but service on the board of a *private* educational institution is generally permitted. [CJC Canon 4C(2), Commentary]

EXAM TIP	gilbert
Be wary of questions where a judge is appointed to the board of a school. Recall the limitations here: A judge may serve on the board of a public *law* school and *any* private school.	

   b. **Distinguish—organization that often litigates [§1005]**

   A judge *may not serve* as an officer, director, trustee, or advisor of an organization: (i) engaged in litigation that would ordinarily come before the judge, or (ii) engaged frequently in litigation in the court on which the judge serves or in a court subject to the judge's appellate jurisdiction. [CJC Canon 4C(3)(a)]

   c. **Distinguish—may not raise money [§1006]**

   Likewise, the judge *may not personally solicit memberships* in *or raise money* for such organizations, or permit the prestige of the judicial office to be so used. The judge should *not be a speaker or guest of honor* at a *fund-raising* event, although she may attend such events and may seek contributions to the organizations from other judges over whom the judge does not exercise supervisory or appellate authority. [CJC Canon 4C(3)(b)]

   d. **May participate in investment decisions [§1007]**

   The judge may participate on boards that make investment decisions for such organizations. [CJC Canon 4C(3)(b)(i)]

ACTIVITY	ALLOWABLE ONLY IF:		
JUDGE'S ACTIVITIES INVOLVING THE GOVERNMENT—EXAMPLES			**gilbert**
APPEAR AT HEARING BEFORE OR CONSULTATION WITH EXECUTIVE OR LEGISLATIVE OFFICIAL(S)	*Relates to the law, legal system, or administration of justice*	*Or*	Pro se to *protect judge's own interests*
SERVE ON GOVERNMENTAL COMMISSION	*Relates to the law, legal system, or administration of justice*	*Or*	Representing governmental unit on *purely ceremonial grounds* or for a historical, educational, or cultural activity
ACT AS OFFICER, DIRECTOR, TRUSTEE, OR NONLEGAL ADVISOR TO PUBLIC SCHOOL	*The public school is a law school*	*And*	School not likely to be in proceedings in the judge's court (or court under judge's appellate jurisdiction), and judge not personally involved in fund-raising or membership solicitation

F. Money-Making Activities of the Judge

1. In General [§1008]

As with other "outside" activities of the judge, all financial activities are subject to the requirements that they *do not:* (i) *reflect on the judge's impartiality,* (ii) *interfere with judicial duties,* (iii) *exploit the office, or* (iv) *involve the judge in dealings with persons likely to come before the court.* [CJC Canon 4D(1)]

2. Investments [§1009]

With the above qualifications, the judge *may* hold and manage financial investments, including real estate. [CJC Canon 4D(2)] However, the judge must manage investments so as to minimize circumstances in which she would be disqualified and divest herself of investments that might require frequent disqualification. [CJC Canon 4D(4)]

3. Participation in a Business [§1010]

The judge *may not* serve as officer, director, manager, advisor, or employee of any business *except a closely-held family business or investment trust.* [CJC Canon 4D(3)]

4. Gifts, Bequests, Favors, or Loans [§1011]

The judge and members of her family residing in the household must be careful about accepting gifts, bequests, favors, or loans, but the *following may be accepted:*

a. A *gift incident to a public testimonial* to the judge or *books* from a publisher for *official use* [CJC Canon 4D(5)(a)];

b. *Complimentary tickets to a bar-related function* [CJC Canon 4D(5)(a)];

c. A *gift to the judge's spouse or relative that could not reasonably be perceived to influence* the judge [CJC Canon 4D(5)(b)];

d. *Ordinary social hospitality* [CJC Canon 4D(5)(c)];

e. A *gift from a relative or friend* fairly commensurate with the occasion and the relationship [CJC Canon 4D(5)(d)];

f. A *gift from someone whose relationship with the judge would already require disqualification* [CJC Canon 4D(5)(e)];

g. A *loan from a lending institution* in the ordinary course of business [CJC Canon 4D(5)(f)];

h. A *scholarship* awarded on the same terms as for others [CJC Canon 4D(5)(g)];

i. A *gift from someone unlikely to come before the court,* provided the gift is reported as if it were compensation if its value exceeds $150 [CJC Canon 4D(5)(h)].

5. Fiduciary Activities [§1012]

A judge *may not* act as executor, administrator, trustee, guardian, or other fiduciary *except for a member of the family,* and, even then, only if the work *will not interfere* with the judge's official duties. [CJC Canon 4E(1)]

a. "Member of the family" [§1013]

A member of the family includes any person related to the judge by blood or marriage or who is treated by the judge as a member of the family and resides in the judge's household. [CJC Terminology]

b. Limitation—not if matter might come before the judge [§1014]

The judge may not act if it is likely that proceedings in the matter would come before the court on which the judge serves or under its appellate jurisdiction. [CJC Canon 4E(2)]

6. Arbitrator or Mediator [§1015]

A judge *may not* act as an *arbitrator or mediator* unless expressly authorized by law. [CJC Canon 4F]

7. **Practice of Law [§1016]**

A judge *may not practice law,* but she may act pro se and give legal advice to family members without compensation. [CJC Canon 4G]

8. **Receiving and Reporting Compensation [§1017]**

A judge *must report* compensation and reimbursement of expenses for her extrajudicial activities to the extent required by law. [CJC Canon 4H(1)]

    a. **Compensation reasonable in amount [§1018]**

    A judge *may not accept* compensation for services that is *excessive* or greater than what someone who is not a judge would be paid for the same activity. [CJC Canon 4H(1)(a)]

    b. **Expense reimbursement [§1019]**

    Reimbursed expenses *must be limited* to actual expenses of the judge and, where appropriate, the judge's spouse or guest. Any excess reimbursement is compensation. [CJC Canon 4H(1)(b)]

    c. **Public reporting [§1020]**

    The *CJC requires public reporting* of compensation and expenses at least annually. Income earned by the judge's spouse but attributed to the judge in community property states need not be reported. [CJC Canon 4H(2)]

    d. **Disclosure of other assets and debts [§1021]**

    Other disclosure of a judge's assets and debts need only be made as required by law or by a specific portion of the Code of Judicial Conduct. [CJC Canon 4I]

G. Involvement of Judges and Judicial Candidates in Political Activities

1. **General Principles Applicable to Judges and Judicial Candidates [§1022]**

With only a few exceptions, the following rules on political activity of judges apply as well to lawyers running for judicial office. [CJC Canon 5E; Model Rule 8.2(b); DR 8-103]

    a. **No office in political organization [§1023]**

    A judge or judicial candidate may not hold office or act as a leader in a political party or organization (*but see infra,* §1039). [CJC Canon 5A(1)(a)]

    b. **No endorsements of political candidates [§1024]**

    A judge or judicial candidate may not speak for or publicly endorse a political candidate (*but see infra,* §1034). [CJC Canon 5A(1)(b)]

c.   No speeches for political organizations [§1025]

A judge or candidate may not make speeches on behalf of political organizations. [CJC Canon 5A(1)(c)]

d.   No political fund-raising [§1026]

A judge or judicial candidate *may not raise money* for others. Furthermore, a judge *may not attend political gatherings, contribute* to a political organization, or *buy tickets* for political functions (*but see infra,* §1033). [CJC Canon 5A(1)(d), (e)]

e.   No running for nonjudicial office [§1027]

A judge is required to *resign* as judge when seeking any nonjudicial office other than delegate to a state constitutional convention. [CJC Canon 5A(2)]

f.   No other political activity [§1028]

An incumbent judge (but not a judicial candidate) must avoid all other political activities *except* those:

(i)   *Designed to improve the law,* the legal system, or the administration of justice;

(ii) *Specifically authorized by law;* or

(iii) *Permitted under the CJC.*

[CJC Canon 5D]

g.   Dignified campaign [§1029]

A judge or judicial candidate must personally act, and see that the campaign is conducted, in a dignified manner that is consistent with the impartiality and independence expected of a judge. [CJC Canon 5A(3)(a) - (c)]

h.   Statements and promises

(1) No misrepresentations or campaign promises [§1030]

A judge or judicial candidate may not misrepresent her own or the opponents' qualifications to hold office, and she may not make "campaign promises" (other than to do a good job as judge). [CJC Canon 5A(3)(d)]

(2) Statements of personal views [§1031]

CJC Canon 5A(3)(d) used to prohibit a judge or other candidate for judicial office from publicly announcing her personal views about disputed legal or political issues. *But note:* The Supreme Court has held that this provision "unnecessarily circumscribe[s] protected expression" and thus is unconstitutional. [**Republican Party of Minnesota v. White,** 536 U.S. 765 (2002)]

(3) Response to attacks [§1032]

A judge or other judicial candidate may respond to attacks on herself or her record. [CJC Canon 5A(3)(e)]

2. Judicial Candidates Subject to Public Election

a. All judicial candidates subject to public election [§1033]

A judicial candidate subject to public election (or a judge subject to election for a nonjudicial position) *may*, at any time, unless prohibited by law:

(i) *Buy tickets* for political functions;

(ii) *Attend* political events;

(iii) *Identify* her political party; and

(iv) *Contribute* to a political organization.

[CJC Canon 5C(1)(a)]

b. Judicial candidates running for public election [§1034]

When actually running for public election, a judge or candidate *may* also:

(i) *Speak* to gatherings on her own behalf;

(ii) *Appear in media advertising and distribute promotional literature* supporting her candidacy;

(iii) *Publicly endorse or oppose other candidates* for the same judicial office.

[CJC Canon 5C(1)(b)]

c. Solicitation of campaign contributions [§1035]

It is *improper* for a candidate for judicial office *personally* to solicit campaign contributions or endorsements. Such solicitation is considered to raise doubts about the judge's future impartiality. [CJC Canon 5C(2) and Commentary]

(1) Distinguish—committees to raise campaign money [§1036]

Properly constituted *committees may solicit* reasonable financial contributions and public statements of support on behalf of the candidate, including contributions and statements from lawyers. [CJC Canon 5C(2)]

(2) Time periods for raising money [§1037]

Committee fund-raising is limited by the CJC to a period *one year before and up to 90 days after* the election in which the candidate is running. Thus, this creates a questionable situation of lawyers sending contributions after they know who will be their judge for the next multi-year term. [CJC Canon 5C(2)]

3. Candidates Seeking Appointment to Judicial Office

a. No personal solicitation of funds [§1038]

A person seeking appointment to a judicial office *may not solicit* or accept funds, *whether personally or through a committee,* to support that candidacy. [CJC Canon 5B(1)]

b. **Other political activity [§1039]**

Neither may such a person engage in political activity to secure the appointment, except that the person *may:*

(i) *Communicate with the nominating authority* or committee designated to screen candidates;

(ii) *Seek endorsement from organizations that regularly make recommendations* for such appointments or from *individuals, if requested* by the appointing authority;

(iii) *Provide information* about her qualifications to the appointing authority and to supporting organizations; and

(iv) *If the candidate is not currently a judge,* buy tickets for political functions, attend political gatherings, make political contributions, and retain an office in a political party.

[CJC Canon 5B(2)]

c. **Judge seeking other government office [§1040]**

The *same rules* apply to an incumbent judge who is seeking appointment to another government office. [CJC Canon 5B]

EXAM TIP   **gilbert**

When answering a question dealing with the political involvement of a judicial candidate, remember the reasons for the *limitations* imposed and the *exceptions* to the limitations:

(i) All judicial candidates *must avoid* political activity that may create the appearance of *political bias* or *impropriety*, and because the impartiality of judges is essential to the preservation of public confidence in the judiciary, incumbent judges are subject to additional restrictions;

(ii) Judicial candidates subject to *public election* need support for their candidacies, and, therefore, there are *exceptions* allowing both judge and nonjudge candidates to speak on their own behalf and *establish campaign committees* to solicit public support and financial contributions;

(iii) Judicial candidates *seeking appointment* or reappointment need to apprise the appointing authority of their qualifications, and *exceptions* permit these candidates to communicate with and *provide information to the appointing authority* and *seek endorsement from organizations* that regularly make recommendations for appointments.

RULES FOR JUDGES AND CANDIDATES FOR JUDICIAL ELECTION

MAY A JUDGE OR CANDIDATE BE INVOLVED IN POLITICAL ACTIVITY?

POLITICAL ACTIVITY	NONCANDIDATE JUDGE	CANDIDATE SUBJECT TO PUBLIC ELECTION	CANDIDATE SEEKING APPOINTMENT OR REAPPOINTMENT	
			JUDGE	NONJUDGE
Act as leader or hold office in political organization?	NO	NO	NO	YES (may retain office)
Publicly endorse or oppose candidate?	NO	YES (if running for the same judicial office)	NO	NO
Make speeches on behalf of political organization?	NO	NO	NO	NO
Solicit funds for political organization?	NO	NO	NO	NO
Buy tickets for political party function?	NO	YES	NO	YES
Attend political gatherings?	NO	YES	NO	YES
Identify herself as a member of political party?	NO	YES	NO	YES
Contribute to political organization?	NO	YES	NO	YES
Speak to gatherings on her own behalf?	NO	YES (when running for judicial office)	NO	YES
Appear in advertising and distribute campaign literature supporting her candidacy?	NO	YES (when running for judicial office)	NO	NO
Personally solicit campaign contributions or endorsements?	NO	NO	NO	NO
Accept funds raised by a properly constituted committee to support her candidacy?	NO	YES (when running for judicial office)	NO	NO

gilbert

4. Sanctions for Violating Rules on Political Activity [§1041]

A *successful* judicial candidate who violates the rules on political activity is subject to *judical discipline*. An *unsuccessful* candidate who is a lawyer and who violates the rules is subject to *lawyer discipline*. [CJC Canon 5E]

H. Standards Applicable to Federal Judges

1. No Practice of Law [§1042]

A federal judge or justice may not practice law; one who engages in the practice of law is guilty of a "high misdemeanor." [28 U.S.C. §454]

2. Circumstances in Which Disqualification Required [§1043]

Most of the standards for disqualification of a federal judge—*e.g.*, personal bias toward a party, having served as a lawyer in the matter, and financial interest in the outcome—are *substantially the same* as the standards under the CJC and will not be repeated here. A few disqualification standards, however, are *different* or are stated differently:

a. Litigant's right to file an affidavit of bias or prejudice [§1044]

A federal district judge must recuse himself upon a litigant's filing of a "timely and sufficient affidavit" asserting that the judge "has a personal bias or prejudice either against him or in favor of any adverse party." The affidavit must be accompanied by a certificate of counsel that the affidavit is made in good faith. [28 U.S.C. §144]

b. Impartiality subject to question [§1045]

A federal judge, including a Supreme Court justice, must recuse himself whenever his "impartiality might reasonably be questioned." [28 U.S.C. §455(a)]

c. Anticipation in case or views expressed while in government service [§1046]

Disqualification is also required whenever the judge or justice, while in other government service, "participated as counsel, adviser or material witness" concerning the case or "expressed an opinion concerning the merits of the particular case in controversy." [28 U.S.C. §455(b)(3)]

d. Divesting a disqualifying financial interest [§1047]

If a disqualifying financial interest is discovered only after substantial time has been devoted to a case, the judge may avoid disqualification by disposing of the interest. [28 U.S.C. §455(f)]

3. Discipline of Federal Judges [§1048]

Federal judges are appointed by the President and hold office for life, during good behavior. A federal judge can be removed from office through impeachment by the House of Representatives and conviction by the Senate. Also, the judicial council of each circuit may impose discipline in less drastic ways (*e.g.,* by admonishing the judge or by temporarily suspending the assignment of cases to the judge). [28 U.S.C. §354]

Review Questions
and Answers

Review Questions
& Answers

Review Questions

1. Indicate whether the following statements are true or false:

   a. While the courts generally administer regulations governing the legal profession, the inherent power of regulation lies with the legislative branch. _____

   b. Under an "integrated" bar system, membership in the state bar association is voluntary, but all local bar groups are members of the state association. _____

   c. The ABA Model Rules of Professional Conduct directly regulate the conduct of all practicing lawyers. _____

   d. A lawyer can be disciplined for violating either an ABA Code Ethical Consideration or a Disciplinary Rule, provided these have been adopted by the state bar in question. _____

2. State X requires that applicants for admission to practice law be residents of the state in which they are applying at least six months prior to admission. Is the requirement constitutional? _____

3. May State X insist upon graduation from an accredited law school as a condition for practicing law? _____

4. If a question is raised regarding an applicant's moral character, the burden of establishing good character rests with the applicant. True or false? _____

5. An adverse determination on moral character by the state bar is final and may not be reviewed by the courts. True or false? _____

6. Wylie applies for admission to practice in State Y. On his application, Wylie notes that he was once arrested for shoplifting but was subsequently acquitted. May the State Y Bar Association consider these charges in assessing Wylie's moral fitness? _____

7. Zelda likewise applies for admission in State Y and notes that she was convicted of petty theft at age 14. Could this be enough to bar Zelda's admission to practice? _____

8. Stanley, an applicant for admission in State Y, was once arrested for indecent exposure, but the charges were immediately dropped when the complaining party was adjudged mentally disturbed. Stanley's record is otherwise impeccable, and he is embarrassed to raise the exposure incident on his application. May he properly omit it? _____

9. Carol seeks admission in State A. She is a member of the Communist Party and acknowledges this fact. Is this enough to bar her admission? _____

10. State X admits lawyers from State W without a bar examination, but requires an examination for State Y lawyers seeking to practice within State X. Does the State X policy have constitutional defects? _____

11. State A requires that any out-of-state lawyer seeking admission pro hac vice associate local counsel and have at least two years of trial experience in her home state. Are these requirements enforceable? _____

12. Admission to the bar of a state entitles a lawyer to practice in the federal courts of that state. True or false? _____

13. Smith, a lawyer licensed to practice in State X, opens an office in State Y for the purpose of advising clients solely on matters of patent law. Can State Y prevent Smith from practicing in the state? _____

14. Professor Canon tells his students that "the ABA Code places great reliance on history and custom in determining what constitutes the practice of law." Is he correct? _____

15. Harry, a local grocer, is sued by a patron allegedly injured by a protruding nail on a display shelf. Can Harry appear personally to defend himself in court? _____

16. Would the result be different if Harry were appearing as president of his grocery? _____

17. Scam-O Title Company, without assistance from a lawyer, completes a standardized mortgage form for the sale of a house to Arthur (who is also unrepresented by counsel). Is this permissible? _____

18. Samantha, an enterprising local businesswoman and recent divorcee, opens a "divorce clinic" in which she advises spouses considering divorce on their property rights and obligations. Is Samantha guilty of the unauthorized practice of law? _____

19. Might the result be different if Samantha instead had written a book on the subject and advertised it for sale? _____

20. Lawyer Jones is appointed to the federal district court bench. Thereafter, Jones continues to appear in state court from time to time on behalf of clients. Is Jones's conduct proper? _____

21. Might the result be different if Jones were a law student rather than a federal judge? _____

22. Lawyer Ling is asked to represent Zeke, an itinerant worker charged with the rape-slayings of six women in the local community. If Ling has strong feelings on the subject of rape, can she properly refuse to represent Zeke? _____

23. Orville files a lawsuit for his client, Wilbur. Shortly thereafter, defense counsel asks that the case be dismissed. May Orville proceed to execute the necessary documents without Wilbur's authorization? _____

24. In discussing a pending lawsuit with opposing counsel, Lawyer admits that her client was "partially at fault" in the matter at issue. Can opposing counsel introduce this admission at trial? _____

25. Would the result be different if the response were made by Lawyer in written answers to interrogatories propounded by opposing counsel? _____

26. Client asks Lawyer to represent her in a tax dispute with the I.R.S. Lawyer has never handled tax matters but is presently enrolled in a continuing education course on the subject. May he properly take the case? _____

27. Lawyer Winston is assigned to represent Zach, an indigent accused of manslaughter. At trial, the prosecution seeks to introduce evidence obtained in a search of Zach's hotel room. Winston objects but fails to cite a recent case which would have supported exclusion. If the evidence is admitted and a conviction results, should it be set aside? _____

28. Lawyer's failure to answer a civil complaint results in a default judgment against her client. If the failure was due to Lawyer's inexcusable negligence, should the default be set aside? _____

29. To insure zealous representation, must a lawyer personally share the viewpoints of her client? _____

30. Lawyer Anita represents her client Boris in negotiating the purchase of an apartment complex. Boris gives Anita $50,000 to be applied toward purchase of the property. Can Anita deposit the funds in her personal bank account? _____

31. David hires Ted to represent him as a plaintiff in a products liability case at the rate of $100 per hour. After a brief review of the facts and one phone call to the defendant, Ted realizes he can settle the case immediately for a substantial sum. May Ted properly change his arrangement with David to a contingent fee? _____

32. Assume instead that the original agreement called for a flat fee of $10,000. Ted settles the case with 10 hours of work, and David refuses to pay the full fee. Can Ted successfully sue for the $10,000? _____

33. If the court finds the $10,000 fee to be unreasonable and clearly excessive, is Ted subject to disciplinary action? _____

34. Amore, a leading divorce lawyer, is asked by Stella to represent her in an action for increased alimony from her husband. Amore agrees to do so for 20% of the increase obtained for the following two years. Is this a proper fee arrangement? _____

35. Elwood agrees to handle the probate of an estate in State X which imposes a maximum statutory attorney's fee of 3% of the estate assets. During the probate, Elwood handles a number of tax problems for the estate and arranges the sale of certain assets therein. May he properly bill the estate for a fee in excess of the statutory maximum? _____

36. Bob represents Ted in a State Y breach of contract suit, obtaining a judgment in Ted's favor. Ted subsequently refuses to pay the agreed fee for Bob's services. State Y recognizes charging liens but not retaining liens. May Bob enforce a lien on the judgment to satisfy his fees in the matter? _____

37. Can Bob foreclose on the judgment for unpaid fees on a business reorganization he previously performed for Ted? _____

38. Client asks Lawyer to file suit against Client's neighbor, Gladys, for breach of contract. After reviewing the facts, Lawyer decides that the case has no merit and is being brought solely to pressure Gladys regarding a boundary dispute. Despite Lawyer's advice, Client refuses to drop the matter. May Lawyer continue to represent Client in the lawsuit? _____

39. If a lawyer wants to withdraw from a case, must she obtain court permission to do so? _____

40. If a client consents to his lawyer's withdrawal, must the lawyer return any unearned portion of the client's original retainer fee? _____

41. Lawyer Jones is retained by Smith to represent him in a contract dispute with Williams. The retainer agreement specifies that Jones will be paid $2,000 for her work and will have Smith's authority to conduct the matter as Jones sees fit. Shortly thereafter, Smith decides that he wants another lawyer.

   a. May Smith discharge Jones if there is no cause shown for the discharge? _____

   b. If Jones is discharged without cause, can she represent Williams in the dispute? _____

42. Suppose that Jones and Smith had agreed to a 30% contingency fee on Smith's recovery, whereupon Jones is discharged without cause. Smith retains Lawyer Brown, who ultimately obtains $30,000 for Smith. Is Jones entitled to $9,000 from Smith? _____

43. Colleen consults Lawyer Able regarding a potential lawsuit against Baker. In the initial interview, Colleen gives Able sensitive information regarding her business strategies and sales. Colleen then decides to employ David as her lawyer in the matter.

   a. The Better Business Bureau subsequently contacts Able regarding Colleen's business operations. May Able disclose the information presented in the prior interview? _____

b.   Able's administrative assistant, Rosemary, types up notes on the Able-Colleen discussion. Thereafter, she tells her boyfriend Tom about Colleen's operations. If Tom is one of Baker's employees, is Able subject to discipline? _____

c.   If there are friends of Colleen present when her business operations are discussed, may Able disclose such discussions at a later time? _____

44. Max is the lawyer for Blimpo Corporation. Blimpo's president asks Max to prepare a memorandum discussing the business and legal ramifications of a proposed merger. Can Max be compelled to disclose the memorandum in a subsequent lawsuit against Blimpo? _____

45. Lawyer Jafar is retained by Stanley to defend him on an indictment for income tax evasion. While reviewing the facts, Stanley admits to Jafar that he previously lied under oath in a civil case regarding his income and disbursements. Is this information privileged? _____

46. At Stanley's trial, the court asks Jafar whether he has any information regarding prior crimes committed by the client. Jafar asserts the attorney-client privilege, whereupon the court orders him to respond. May Jafar reveal his previous discussions with Stanley? _____

47. Wallace contacts his lawyer, Xavier, by telephone and tells him that he is fleeing to another state to avoid prosecution for embezzlement. Xavier cannot persuade Wallace to change his mind. Is Xavier under a duty to disclose this information if sought by the proper authorities? _____

48. Arthur asks his lawyer, Roger, to represent him in negotiating for the lease of an office complex. After contacting the present owners of the building, but without telling Arthur, Roger decides to purchase a 10% ownership interest in the property as a personal investment. Thereafter, Roger consummates a lease on office space for Arthur. Has Roger engaged in improper conduct? _____

49. Suppose instead that Arthur owns the office building and asks Roger to represent him in litigation with certain of his tenants. While the matter is in progress, Roger offers to purchase a 10% interest in the building. Arthur agrees and signs the contract drawn up by Roger. Has Roger breached his professional duties? _____

50. Yolanda asks her lawyer, Yasmin, to draft a will leaving one-half of her total estate to Yasmin. May Yasmin proceed to prepare the document? _____

51. Might the result be different if Yasmin were Yolanda's granddaughter and sole heir? _____

52. Professor Canon tells his class that "a lawyer may properly represent clients with potentially different interests in a nonlitigation matter as long as the lawyer is satisfied that no actual conflict exists." Is the professor correct? _____

53. Frank and Jesse are indicted for armed robbery, and Lawyer Earp is appointed to defend them at trial. Although Frank is a convicted felon and Jesse is not, Earp believes she can properly represent both, and the two defendants acquiesce. Should the court nevertheless appoint separate counsel for each? _____

54. Would the result be different if Frank and Jesse jointly retained Earp to represent them? _____

55. Sergio represents Acme Finance, a secured creditor of Fido Corporation. Fido institutes bankruptcy proceedings, and one of its other creditors asks Sergio to handle its claim against Fido. Should he do so? _____

56. Edgar represents Charlie in a breach of contract suit against Candice. While the matter is pending, Candice asks Edgar to handle her alimony claim against David. If the two matters are unsettled, may Edgar take the alimony case? _____

57. Jorge is asked to negotiate a lease for client Lessee. May he also represent Landlord in the matter if both Lessee and Landlord consent to dual representation? _____

58. Would the result be different if the matter involved a dispute between Lessee and Landlord over the terms of an existing lease? _____

59. X is general counsel for Flim-Flam Brokerage Co., which is under investigation for securities fraud. The president of Flim-Flam is subpoenaed to testify before a grand jury about his knowledge of the matter and asks X to advise him. Should X do so? _____

60. Lawyer Willis is retained by Tightwad Insurance to represent its insured, Baker, in a personal injury suit brought by Able. Prior to trial, Able offers to settle the case for $10,000. Realizing that Baker's policy limit is $12,000, Willis adamantly refuses to discuss any settlement. At trial, Able receives a judgment of $75,000. Is Willis subject to discipline? _____

61. When a lawyer is retained by parents to represent their minor child in juvenile court proceedings, the lawyer has a client responsibility to both the minor and the parents and so should honor the parents' decisions about the case. True or false? _____

62. Lawyer Ellen formerly served as general counsel for Widget Corp. As a member of a new law firm, she is now asked to represent the plaintiff in an antitrust case against Widget. May she do so? _____

63. Would the result be different if another lawyer in the firm was then asked to represent the plaintiff and Ellen took no part whatever in the case? _____

64. Mary and Ted are married lawyers who work at different firms. Mary is lead counsel for a client in a case against a client represented by Ted's firm, but Ted is doing no work on the case. Does this situation present a conflict of interest? _____

65. Lawyer Bigwig has joined Law Firm after serving as general counsel of the U.S. Department of Energy. Law Firm has been representing several clients in cases against the Department of Energy. May Bigwig work on those cases at Law Firm? _____

66. In a negotiation with opposing counsel, Lawyer says that his client's property lies in the path of "absolutely certain development" that will make it worth millions in a few years. Lawyer has no reason to believe that it is nearly that valuable. Is Lawyer subject to discipline for his excessive claim?

67. Lawyer Tom files a lawsuit for client P against D, who is represented by lawyer Ralph. Shortly thereafter, Tom calls D to discuss D's willingness to settle the case at the onset. Is Tom subject to discipline?

68. Lawyer calls her opposing counsel in a case and tells him that she will institute disbarment proceedings for misappropriation of funds unless he agrees to a settlement with Lawyer's client. If the settlement terms are fair to both parties, is Lawyer subject to discipline?

69. Blimpo Corporation retains Lawyer Helen to appear before a Food and Drug Administration hearing in support of new drugs that Blimpo wants to place on the market. As a public relations matter, Blimpo asks Helen not to reveal that she is representing the corporation. Must Helen nevertheless disclose her capacity at the hearing?

70. Lawyer is elected to the state senate but continues to maintain a private, part-time law practice. May Lawyer properly represent a client before a state administrative board?

71. Following a trial in which a judgment was entered against his client, Lawyer Mason is asked to analyze the case for news reporters. Mason replies that "the case was clear to most people—but apparently it was a little too complicated for the court." Is Mason subject to discipline for his remarks?

72. Attorney files a lawsuit for her client, Mei. The opposing party fails to respond to the complaint or request additional time to answer. Is Attorney obligated to seek a default judgment in favor of her client?

73. Assume instead that the defendant answers and the case proceeds. The court orders both parties to appear for a pretrial conference at a specific time and date. Attorney fails to appear. Is she subject to sanctions?

74. Lawyer Clark knows that if she can prolong a case for six more months, her opponent will be so damaged economically that he will settle for much less. She files a motion in the appellate court for mandamus to have the trial judge recuse himself in the case. She knows there is no basis for the motion, but she also knows it will take six months for the court to act. Has she done anything that would subject her to discipline?

75. Able is appointed to represent an indigent defendant, Baker, on an appeal requested by Baker. Able examines the record and all the facts, and concludes that the appeal is frivolous. May Able withdraw by advising the client that he finds no merit in the appeal?

76. Attorney Alma files an antitrust case for her client, Sam, against Z Corp., alleging damages due to Z's market restraints. In his deposition, Sam testified that the damages were very high, but Sam later told Alma that his injuries resulted from ineffective sales personnel during the period in question. Should Alma disclose this information to anyone? _____

77. Attorney Alma files an antitrust suit for her client, Sam, against Z Corp. Z Corp. files a motion for summary judgment. In preparing an opposing brief, Alma discovers that there are several cases adverse to Sam's position. By construing the facts favorably to Sam, Alma believes the cases are distinguishable from the present action. Should Alma disclose the cases in her brief? _____

78. Lawyer is appointed to defend D on a charge of selling narcotics. On the stand at trial, D testifies that he has never used narcotics in his life. During a recess, D admits to Lawyer that he has used cocaine for several years. Should Lawyer disclose this to the court? _____

79. Albert, the lawyer for a plaintiff in a products liability case, hires Bert as an expert witness on the defects in a defendant's product. Albert tells Bert that his client is presently short of funds but will pay Bert 5% of any recovery he obtains in the case. Is this arrangement improper? _____

80. Roscoe, a flamboyant trial lawyer, comments in his closing statement to the jury that "the defendant's chief witness, Smith, is just as crooked as the defendant himself, and his perjury on the stand proves it. I think his testimony is preposterous." Is this proper? _____

81. In her closing statement, Lawyer Jones tells the jury that "my client is poor and an innocent victim in this case—treat him as you would want to be treated if you were in his shoes." Is this improper? _____

82. Lawyer Dan is contacted by opposing counsel, who requests an extension of time to answer the complaint filed by Dan's client. Dan orally agrees to the extension, but no written stipulation is entered. Thereafter, Dan notices the defendant's default for failure to answer within the statutory period. Is Dan subject to discipline? _____

83. During the trial of his client's personal injury claim, Attorney Smith attempts to introduce certain evidence helpful to the claim. Defense counsel objects, and the court refuses to admit the evidence. Smith asks the court to reconsider its ruling "because Your Honor is totally wrong." Is Smith subject to discipline? _____

84. During a trial, the local newspaper publishes an editorial attacking the defendant's lawyer, Quickly, as "a known opportunist who would say anything to gain publicity for himself and his client." Quickly appears on a television show and refers to the editorial as "totally false and an obvious attempt to injure my reputation." Is Quickly subject to discipline for his statement? _____

85. Perry Prosecutor has filed multiple murder charges against Barry Bumm. Perry calls a press conference and announces the facts of the charges and the name and address of the accused. Has the prosecutor acted properly? _____

86. Lawyer Irving is asked by Clyde to handle his securities fraud claim on a contingency arrangement. May Irving properly advance the costs of litigation to Clyde while the case is in progress? _____

87. Helen is a lawyer for Baker Corporation, which is sued in a products liability case. By chance, Helen was present when the accident in question occurred. Can she properly represent Baker in the litigation? _____

88. Lawyer anticipates that she may be called as a witness concerning a minor dispute involving service of process in a lawsuit she has filed. This fact becomes known after Lawyer has already done substantial work on the case (for which she has been paid). May she continue to represent the client in the litigation? _____

89. During a trial, Judge Hangem calls opposing counsel A and B into chambers for a conference. As they are leaving, B decides to ask the judge about expediting discovery in another case B has before the court. Is this proper? _____

90. Lawyer Marvin represents the defendant in a personal injury lawsuit. Prior to the trial in his case, Marvin encounters a member of the jury panel outside the courthouse and asks him if he has ever been a plaintiff in a personal injury case. If Marvin does not otherwise discuss the case, is his communication proper? _____

91. Shortly after a verdict for plaintiff is returned, Marvin decides to call several of the jurors and discuss the factors they found significant in the case. May he properly do so? _____

92. Prosecutor Allen is preparing to try an accused for first degree murder. While interviewing a prospective witness, Allen learns that the accused may not have been present at the scene of the crime. Is he obligated to disclose this information to defense counsel? _____

93. Allen decides that Charlie will be his chief witness. Can Allen properly instruct Charlie not to discuss the case with defense counsel unless Allen is present? _____

94. Felix and Oscar are lawyers sharing offices and secretarial help. Occasionally, Oscar refers tax matters to Felix. May the two use a letterhead reading "Law Offices of Felix and Oscar"? _____

95. Civil rights legislation and the federal labor laws do not apply to the relationship between an associate and her law firm. True or false? _____

96. Indicate whether the following statements are true or false:

a. The original opposition to group services plans was based on the fact that the intermediary obtained a profit from the provision of legal services. _____

b. "Open panel" group plans are now permissible, but "closed panel" plans are still prohibited. _____

c. The ABA Code and Model Rules permit partnerships between lawyers and nonlawyers as long as the practice of law is merely incidental to the primary partnership activities. _____

d. In certain situations, it may be permissible for a lawyer to share legal fees with a nonlawyer. _____

97. Attorney Melina wants to list certain biographical information, including her educational background and publications, in a local directory. Does it matter whether she chooses the city directory or a bar directory of lawyers for this purpose? _____

98. Lawyer Eager files an antitrust class action with two named plaintiffs. Thereafter, Eager sends a letter to a trade association of similar business entities, informing them of the lawsuit and his willingness to "discuss the case" with any interested party. Is Eager guilty of solicitation? _____

99. Block is a lawyer who is state-certified as a tax specialist. May she properly list this tax specialty on her business cards? _____

100. May a lawyer leaving one law firm to join a new one inform the clients for whom he has done work that the clients may follow the lawyer to the new firm? _____

101. Nancy, a tax lawyer in River City, systematically refers all personal injury matters involving her clients to Alice, a trial lawyer. Alice then pays Nancy 30% of whatever fee she collects in each such case. Is this arrangement proper? _____

102. Lawyer Jones suspects her partner, Smith, of misappropriating certain funds of his clients. Does Jones have an obligation to report Smith's misconduct to disciplinary authorities? _____

103. At the disciplinary hearing, Smith pleads that he was faced with enormous medical expenses incurred by his sick child and would not otherwise have borrowed the money. Should the state bar consider this plea in assessing sanctions against Smith? _____

104. During the hearing, the examining lawyer seeks to introduce a taped telephone conversation between Smith and a friend, made via a wiretap set by Jones. Should this evidence be admitted? _____

105. Assuming the state supreme court imposes a one-year suspension on Smith, can the local federal court disbar Smith? _____

106. Paolo asks his lawyer, Luther, for an opinion on the tax effects of a complicated leasing transaction. Paolo follows Luther's opinion and is later held to have violated certain regulations applicable to the transaction. Can Paolo hold Luther liable for malpractice? _____

107. Lawyer Smith agrees to represent Jones, the defendant in a personal injury lawsuit. In responding to plaintiff's motion for summary judgment, Smith fails to note a recent case favorable to Jones. If summary judgment is entered against Jones, is Smith liable for the amount of the damages? _____

108. Arthur asks Lawyer Leonard to defend him in a large lawsuit. Leonard explains that the legal issues are extremely complicated, and that he must have Arthur's agreement not to sue for malpractice before he will take the case. In return, Leonard agrees to charge only 80% of his normal hourly fee. Provided Arthur consents after full disclosure, is the agreement enforceable? _____

109. During the trial of her client's case, Lawyer Jones blurts out to the judge, "You are the stupidest judge I've ever known. This trial is a charade." The judge says nothing but the next morning announces that she is sentencing Jones to 10 days in jail for contempt. Does the judge have authority to act in this way? _____

110. Judge Smith gives a speech at a dinner for a local labor union whose members frequently appear before her. She also has her picture taken with the union president, knowing that it will be posted in the union hall with a "we have a friend at court" caption. Are Judge Smith's actions proper? _____

111. Judge Quashem, a candidate for reelection to the bench, appears at a fund-raising dinner to exchange endorsements with the party's candidates for nonjudicial offices. Is the judge's conduct proper? _____

Answers to Review Questions

1.a. **FALSE**   Ultimate regulatory power lies with the *judicial branch*, since the practice of law is intimately connected with the administration of justice. [§2]

  b. **FALSE**   An integrated bar system involves *compulsory* membership by all lawyers in the state bar association. [§6]

  c. **FALSE**   The Model Rules are not directly binding on lawyers. However, over 30 states have adopted the Rules, so they form an *indirect* basis for regulation of much of the legal profession. [§21]

  d. **FALSE**   Only *Disciplinary Rules* are *mandatory* and carry disciplinary sanctions for their violation. The Ethical Considerations are aspirational and constitute guides to proper conduct. [§18]

2. **NO**   The Supreme Court has held that residency requirements for admission to the bar violate the Privileges and Immunities Clause. [§32]

3. **YES**   Such a requirement has been deemed to meet the test of a "rational relationship" to fitness to practice law. [§34]

4. **TRUE**   The reasoning is that the applicant is in the best position to supply the facts about himself. [§43]

5. **FALSE**   An applicant is entitled to judicial review, usually by the highest state court. [§45]

6. **YES**   *Any* past conduct—including charges on which there is a subsequent acquittal or dismissal—may be deemed relevant to a character investigation. [§47]

7. **YES**   Theft is often considered conduct that reflects upon the ability to practice law. However, it could be argued that (due to Zelda's age at the time) this was mere "adolescent misbehavior," and hence not sufficient per se to block her admission. [§§48, 50]

8. **DEPENDS**   Stanley was not convicted of a crime, and the conduct did not involve dishonesty, but if he is asked about arrests, this must be disclosed—and failure to do so *would* be sufficient to bar Stanley's admission. [§52]

9. **NO**   Membership in the Communist Party is not sufficient per se to exclude an applicant from practicing law. [§56]

10. **NOT NECESSARILY**   If the State X policy is based on *reciprocity* (*i.e.,* State W automatically admits State X lawyers, but State Y does not), the policy does not violate equal protection. [§60]

11.	**YES**	Limitations on admission pro hac vice are generally valid, unless applied to block adequate representation in civil rights cases. [§§66-68]
12.	**FALSE**	While no separate examination is required, admission to practice in the federal courts is *distinct*, and a separate application must be made. (A few federal courts also require completion of certain courses prior to admission.) [§§74-76]
13.	**NO**	A state ordinarily may prevent an out-of-state lawyer from maintaining a continuous practice of law in the state, but here, *federal regulations* govern Smith's practice, and State Y cannot prevent her from maintaining an office for that purpose. [§78]
14.	**NO**	While some courts still follow the "history and custom" test, the ABA Code has emphasized the *need for professional judgment* as the relevant criterion. [§§90-91]
15.	**YES**	Representation "in propria persona" is always available to an individual in court proceedings. [§85]
16.	**YES**	A corporation *cannot* appear for itself in court (through its *nonlawyer* officers or directors). [§109]
17.	**SPLIT OF AUTHORITY**	Most courts permit title companies to complete standardized mortgage or deed forms according to information furnished by the parties. Others, however, find this impermissible, on the ground that this is "drafting"—requiring a lawyer's expertise on choice of forms—rather than "scrivening." [§§94-97]
18.	**YES**	Giving individualized advice about legal rights and obligations is usually regarded as the practice of law. [§100]
19.	**YES**	Courts have held that publication of such a book by a layperson is not the practice of law. [§101]
20.	**NO**	Full-time judges may not practice law even though they are also licensed attorneys. [§105]
21.	**YES**	Ordinarily, law students are also prohibited from appearing in court for clients. However, an exception is made where the student does so in connection with an *authorized law school training program.* [§§106-107]
22.	**YES**	Although she has a moral obligation to accept the case unless there is a valid *professional reason* not to do so, a lawyer is *not obliged* to take any case. [§§126-128, 132-133]
23.	**DEPENDS**	If the dismissal is with prejudice, it must be authorized by Wilbur. However, Orville probably has implied authority to execute a dismissal *without prejudice* if he considers it to be *in Wilbur's interests.* [§164]

24. **DEPENDS** If Lawyer was *authorized* to make the statement, it would be admissible; otherwise, it is not admissible. In either event, it is probably not conclusive on the issue. [§171]

25. **YES** This is a *judicial admission*, which is binding upon the client unless the court permits an amendment or withdrawal. [§170]

26. **YES** A lawyer may accept employment where he expects in good faith to become qualified to perform the necessary services. However, Lawyer should not accept the retainer if there will be unnecessary expense or delay to Client in gaining such competence. [§§177-178]

27. **PROBABLY NOT** Unless failure to cite the case would amount to shocking incompetence, there is no basis for setting aside the conviction. A mere mistake is not enough. [§185]

28. **SPLIT OF AUTHORITY** Many courts require a reasonable excuse for the failure to answer in order to set aside a default. Others, however, will not charge a client with his lawyer's gross negligence if doing so denies justice in the particular case. [§186]

29. **NO** A lawyer has no obligation to approve or adopt a client's viewpoints, though she is encouraged to be circumspect in expressing an opposing position. [§193]

30. **NO** The funds must be deposited in a *separately identified* trust (or other bank) account. [§§200-202]

31. **PROBABLY NOT** Certainly the change would be improper if Ted did not inform David of the prospects for a quick settlement. And even with disclosure, Ted would have the burden of proving that the new agreement was a reasonable one. [§215]

32. **DEPENDS** Courts will review a fee agreement to determine its reasonableness. Whether Ted can collect the full $10,000 depends on *all the circumstances* (*i.e.*, skill, experience, etc.). [§§216-218]

33. **YES** The charging of unreasonable and clearly excessive fees may subject a lawyer to discipline. [§216]

34. **PROBABLY** Courts increasingly permit contingent fees in domestic relations matters *after* a divorce has been granted, *i.e.*, for collecting or renegotiating alimony. However, the law changes slowly in this area and the propriety of a contingent fee is thus not completely clear. [§229]

35. **PROBABLY** Elwood has apparently performed extraordinary services for the estate and is therefore entitled to an additional reasonable fee for that work. [§241]

36. **YES** A charging lien can be affirmatively enforced against a judgment awarded to the client for fees in that matter. [§261]

37.	**NO**	Charging liens are *limited* to fees and costs incurred in the particular matter in which recovery is obtained. Note that if State Y recognized retaining liens, Bob could withhold documents or other items he received as lawyer for the reorganization—and use this as "leverage" in obtaining any fees unpaid by Ted. [§§262, 252-256]
38.	**NO**	Lawyer has an obligation to withdraw under these circumstances, and she is subject to disciplinary action if she continues with the lawsuit. [§271]
39.	**DEPENDS**	If the matter is *pending* before the court (*i.e.,* a complaint on file), permission of the court must be obtained for withdrawal. [§282]
40.	**YES**	Whatever the basis for withdrawal, the lawyer is not entitled to retain any unearned portion of fees paid in advance—unless paid solely to insure the laywer's availability for the case. [§§284-285]
41.a.	**YES**	A client has the unilateral right to discharge his lawyer at any time, without cause, and despite any agreement for an "irrevocable" retainer. [§§287-288]
b.	**NO**	Despite the discharge without cause, Jones's fiduciary duties to Smith continue—including the duty not to represent conflicting interests. [§290]
42.	**SPLIT OF AUTHORITY**	Some courts would allow Jones the full 30% contingency (*i.e.,* $9,000), while others would limit recovery to the reasonable value of her services (quantum meruit). [§§294-297]
43.a.	**NO**	The attorney-client privilege and the professional duty of confidentiality apply to information obtained from a *prospective* client, even though the lawyer is not subsequently employed. [§§136-138, 302]
b.	**PERHAPS**	Able may disclose such information to his office staff, but he has a duty to prevent such employees from disseminating it to others. If Able has not exercised reasonable care in this regard (*e.g.,* by careful hiring and proper warnings), he is subject to sanctions. [§§306, 308, 741]
c.	**NO**	The presence of others may waive the "confidentiality" requirement so that the attorney-client privilege would not apply. However, Able's professional duty of nondisclosure is broader, and is *not* affected by the fact that others were present at the interview. [§§313, 349]
44.	**NO**	*Mixed communications* between a corporation and its counsel are within the attorney-client privilege, although discussion of business issues alone are not. [§§318-319]
45.	**YES**	A client's confidential admission to counsel that he perjured himself in a prior proceeding is privileged information. [§326]
46.	**SPLIT OF AUTHORITY**	Some courts hold that a lawyer must refuse to disclose privileged information, whatever the personal consequences to him may be (*e.g.,* citation for contempt).

However, the ABA Code allows disclosure of such information in response to a *court order*, and the Comments to the Model Rules state that a lawyer may comply with a final order of a court requiring such information. [§§331-332]

47. **DEPENDS**   As a general matter, the whereabouts of a client is privileged information. Note, however, that if the violation of a court order is involved (*e.g.,* Wallace was previously released on bail upon Xavier's motion), Xavier *must* advise the court of his client's whereabouts. [§§344-346]

48. **YES**   It is improper for a lawyer to acquire an adverse interest in the subject matter of his employment, since there is at least the potential for a conflict of interest (*e.g.,* Roger's interest as part owner may conflict with his negotiating the most favorable lease terms for Arthur). [§375]

49. **DEPENDS**   Because of the opportunities for overreaching by counsel, such transactions with a client are subject to a *presumption of undue influence* by the lawyer and are examined very closely by the court. Hence, under the Model Rules, the terms of the purchase must be objectively fair to Arthur, he must have had a chance to consult with outside counsel in the matter, and he must have consented in writing. [§§379-382]

50. **NO**   Yasmin must insist that Yolanda obtain the assistance of another lawyer in drafting the will, since Yasmin is named as a beneficiary. Also, she should urge Yolanda to obtain the disinterested advice of a competent third person. [§§387-388]

51. **YES**   Most courts permit a lawyer to prepare wills for relatives, provided that any bequest therein to the lawyer is *reasonable under the circumstances* and that there is no hint of overreaching. Here, Yolanda's bequest appears to be less than Yasmin's intestate share and hence a reasonable gift. [§389]

52. **NO**   A lawyer may undertake such representation only after he has the *written consent* of all the clients concerned, upon *full disclosure* of the risks and advantages of joint representation. And a client's refusal to consent is binding, regardless of the lawyer's conclusions on the propriety of multiple representation. [§404]

53. **YES**   The court has a duty to see whether differing interests appear and to appoint separate counsel if they do. Here, Frank's previous record may indicate differences in the strength of the case against each defendant, and, if so, separate counsel should be appointed. [§§406, 408]

54. **YES**   In this situation, the duty is on Earp (as retained counsel) to consider and disclose any potential conflicts. [§409]

55. **DEPENDS**   The propriety of representing both creditors depends on whether there are conflicts of interest involved. If the second client is not a secured creditor, and/or if Fido's assets cannot satisfy the claims of both, dual representation would be improper. [§§417-419]

56.	**DEPENDS**	Even though Candice's success on her alimony claim might benefit Charlie, it is a conflict of interest to represent opposing clients in unrelated matters. The conflict may be waived, however, with the informed, written consent of each client. [§§397, 420]
57.	**DEPENDS**	Jorge must *fully disclose* to Lessee and Landlord the possible conflicts in representing both parties to the lease negotiations. If this done, and *informed, written* consent is given by the parties, dual representation is probably permissible. [§§428]
58.	**YES**	Once the matter goes to court, the conflict between adversaries is not subject to waiver, even with the informed consent of each client. [§401]
59.	**NO**	As general counsel, X owes his loyalty to Flim-Flam. Since the company may have a potential action against the president in this matter, he should retain independent counsel for the grand jury appearance. [§432]
60.	**YES**	A lawyer who rejects a settlement proposal without letting the client make the final decision may be guilty of both unethical conduct and civil malpractice. The lawyer must inform the insurer of its duty to the insured regarding settlement, and must use her best efforts to see that the interests of the insured are protected. Willis's adamant refusal to discuss any settlement was improper. [§§449-451]
61.	**FALSE**	The client responsibility is owed solely to the *child*, regardless of who pays the lawyer's fees. The lawyer should consult with the child and let the child make most of the decisions. [§§455-458]
62.	**PROBABLY NOT**	A lawyer is prohibited from representing someone where the lawyer would be taking a position materially adverse to a former client in a matter closely related factually or legally to the prior one, or where there is some other substantial risk that the lawyer will use confidential information obtained in the prior representation against the former client. Unless it can be shown that this antitrust case is unrelated to any matter handled by Ellen at Widget and that the case does not involve confidential information she received while employed by the company, Ellen may not take the case. [§462]
63.	**NO**	The prohibitions applicable to Ellen apply as well to any lawyer affiliated with her—*i.e.,* if there is a conflict as to her representation, it applies to the firm as well. [§§469-470]
64.	**NO**	While the relationship between husband and wife is obviously close, it does not present a disqualifying conflict unless Mary and Ted are personally representing the opposing clients. [§479]
65.	**POSSIBLY**	Bigwig may not work on any matter in which she was *personally and substantially* involved while in the government. However, even an agency counsel is not involved in every matter in the office, so Bigwig's involvement would have

to be determined case by case. Furthermore, even if Bigwig would be personally disqualified from working on some matters at Law Firm, the firm itself would not be disqualified by imputation if Bigwig is screened against involvement in those matters. [§§490-492]

66. **PROBABLY NOT**   A lawyer may not knowingly make a false statement of material fact even in the course of a negotiation. However, some statements are obviously puffing and would be taken as such by the other side. Thus, they are not deemed to be a violation of the general rule. [§517]

67. **YES**   If a lawyer knows the opposing party is represented by counsel, the lawyer *must not* communicate directly with that party on any matter in controversy without the consent of opposing counsel. [§534]

68. **DEPENDS**   Zealous representation does not permit the threat of criminal or other charges (including disbarment) to gain advantages for a lawyer's client. This is an improper use of the legal process regardless of whether the final results are reasonable, but the ABA Code's explicit prohibition of it was left out of the Model Rules. [§§552-554]

69. **YES**   Unless the identity of the client is privileged information (which is not the case here), Helen has a duty to reveal her representative capacity at administrative proceedings. [§558]

70. **DEPENDS**   Lawyer must avoid any foreseeable conflict between his private interests and his public duties as legislator. In practice, the issue will probably be decided as a matter of state legislation, not legal ethics rules. [§§565-567]

71. **POSSIBLY**   While snide or petty comments might be considered simply bad manners, intemperate criticism of a court can be disciplined as a threat to public confidence in the judicial system. [§570]

72. **NO**   Attorney may feel it is in Mei's best interest *not* to seek a default, and Attorney will not be disciplined or held liable for civil malpractice if she does not seek a default judgment. [§581]

73. **YES**   Failure to appear at a court-ordered hearing, particularly without advance notice to the court, is punishable as contempt of court and possibly as neglect of the client's case. [§588]

74. **YES**   The ABA Code prohibits a lawyer from delaying a trial merely to harass or maliciously injure another, and the Model Rules impose a requirement to expedite litigation. Benefits to the client from *improper delay* may not be taken into account by a lawyer. [§§584-587]

75. **NO**   The lawyer must seek permission to withdraw, accompanied by a written brief to the court citing any grounds that might arguably support an appeal. [§580]

76.	**YES**	In a matter pending before a tribunal, a lawyer must, under the Model Rules, take *reasonable remedial measures* when the lawyer becomes aware that a witness has made a false statement of material fact to the tribunal, including a statement made in a deposition. This duty continues up to the conclusion of the proceedings, and it applies even to otherwise protected confidential information. Unless the client agrees to rectify the situation himself, the lawyer must reveal the deceit to the court or the other party. [§602]
77.	**PROBABLY**	A lawyer must disclose *directly adverse* legal authority in the *controlling jurisdiction*. Exactly how relevant the cases are is unclear in this question, but doubts involving the applicability of adverse decisions usually should be resolved in favor of disclosure. The lawyer may then go on to distinguish the cases or otherwise attempt to avoid the result suggested by the cases. [§§596-600]
78.	**PROBABLY**	Assuming this is a material fact, Lawyer must, under the Model Rules, attempt to persuade D to correct his testimony. If D refuses, Lawyer should seek to withdraw. If the court will not permit withdrawal, there is a strong argument that Lawyer must disclose the perjury to the court. The opposite result is reached under the ABA Code, which prohibits the lawyer from revealing the perjury because of the duty of confidentiality. [§§603-611]
79.	**YES**	Fees for any witness contingent on the outcome of the case or the substance of the testimony are prohibited. [§629]
80.	**NO**	Expressions of a lawyer's personal opinion on testimony by witnesses are improper. [§633]
81.	**YES**	Jurors are expected to decide the case as objective triers of fact, and appeals to personal feelings or sympathy are improper (but common). [§645]
82.	**DEPENDS**	Dan is obligated to follow *local customs* on extensions of time unless he notifies opposing counsel to the contrary. If oral agreements to extend time *are accepted* local practice, Dan could be sanctioned for attempting to take a default. In any case, Dan should abstain from offensive conduct, should treat opposing counsel with courtesy, and should comply with opposing counsel's reasonable requests. [§§654-656]
83.	**NO**	A lawyer may properly challenge a court ruling by asking for reconsideration. While Smith's statement is strong, it is probably not disrespectful. [§653]
84.	**NO**	The restrictions on publicity regarding criminal proceedings do not preclude a defense lawyer from replying publicly to charges of misconduct that may unduly prejudice the lawyer's client. [§668]
85.	**YES**	Each of these items of information is permitted under the ABA Code and Model Rules. [§664]

86.	**YES**	Where litigation is pending or contemplated, the ABA Code permits a lawyer to lend the client money for litigation expenses, provided the client remains ultimately liable for such expenses. Under the Model Rules, a lawyer may make the obligation to repay contingent on the outcome of the case, or may make no provision for repayment where the client is indigent. Thus, if Irving complies with the applicable provisions of the Code or the Model Rules, he may properly advance litigation costs to Clyde. [§§672-677]
87.	**NO**	A lawyer may not handle litigation in which it is apparent that she may be called as a *witness* during the proceedings. [§682]
88.	**PROBABLY**	Since the matter for testimony appears to be an *insubstantial* one, and since there may be *hardship* to the client in substituting new counsel at this juncture, Lawyer probably may remain as counsel. [§§686, 688]
89.	**MAYBE**	It is ordinarily improper for B to communicate with the court ex parte on a pending matter without notifying opposing counsel so that she could be present. However, since this is a mere administrative matter not going to the merits, it may be allowed. [§698]
90.	**NO**	Such out-of-court communications are *not permitted*, although Marvin might try to obtain such information by means of a proper investigation. (The question itself is a proper one for voir dire examination in open court.) [§703]
91.	**PROBABLY**	Most courts would permit such communications (*e.g.*, as a means of improving the lawyer's advocacy skills), as long as there is no harassment of jurors. [§§705-708]
92.	**YES**	Government prosecutors are *required* to make timely disclosure to the defense of any available evidence that might negate guilt or otherwise bear upon the accused's position (*e.g.*, mitigation of offense). [§718]
93.	**NO**	A prosecutor *must permit* defense counsel to interview government witnesses and may not properly advise government witnesses not to talk to the defense. [§720]
94.	**PROBABLY NOT**	This designation implies that Felix and Oscar are partners. Lawyers may not hold themselves out as partners unless they in fact are partners. [§729]
95.	**FALSE**	Both sets of laws protect law firm associates. [§731]
96.a.	**FALSE**	Nonprofit intermediaries were also prohibited from providing such services on the ground that the necessary relationship of trust and confidence between lawyer and client was lacking. [§760]
b.	**FALSE**	"Closed panel" plans are constitutionally protected in at least some situations (*e.g.*, union retaining counsel for its members in workers' compensation disputes).

And the ABA now imposes the same requirements on both open and closed panel plans. [§§761-768]

c. **FALSE**   Such partnerships are prohibited where *any* of the activities include the practice of law. [§748]

d. **TRUE**   However, these situations are limited to profit-sharing retirement plans, payment of accrued fees to the estate of a deceased attorney, or sharing court-awarded fees with the nonprofit organization that hired the lawyer or recommended him as counsel in the matter. The general rule prohibits fee sharing with nonlawyers. [§§751-755]

97. **NO**   Under the ABA Code and Model Rules, material of this kind may be published for the public generally, not simply lawyers. [§§775-779]

98. **PROBABLY NOT**   Under both the ABA Code and the Model Rules, Eager's conduct could be considered as prohibited direct contact with a potential client. However, with regard to class action litigation, the Supreme Court has held that it is improper for a court to set excessive limits on a lawyer's contact with prospective class members. Under this line of reasoning, it is not likely that Eager's conduct will be deemed to be prohibited solicitation. [§795]

99. **YES**   Under the ABA Code and Model Rules, state-certified specialties may be noted on professional cards if permitted by state rules. [§803]

100. **PROBABLY**   It has been held improper for former associates to *encourage* clients to follow them to their new firm. However, simple announcements merely *informing* former clients of the change of practice are proper. [§792]

101. **DEPENDS**   Fee sharing with lawyers is permitted, but only where the client knows and consents and the total fee is reasonable. Under the ABA Code, the division (here 70-30) must correspond to the *services performed,* but under the Model Rules, lawyers who *assume joint responsibility* for a matter may share the fee in whatever proportions they agree and to which the client approves. If these conditions are met, the Nancy-Alice fee arrangement is permissible. [§§815-819]

102. **YES**   At minimum, a lawyer is required to disclose any acts that violate professional standards and raise a substantial question about another lawyer's honesty. The fact that Smith and Jones are partners is no exception. [§§875, 879]

103. **POSSIBLY**   The factor of his child's illness probably warrants consideration of the unusual pressure Smith was under in this case. [§848]

104. **YES**   The normal exclusionary rules of criminal procedure (*e.g.,* as to illegal wiretaps) *do not apply* to disciplinary hearings. [§862]

105. **YES**   The federal court is not bound by the state proceedings but will often follow a state's decision in such a case. [§884]

106. **DEPENDS**   Luther owes Paolo a duty to exercise the *skill and knowledge normally possessed* by lawyers in the area. If Luther is a tax specialist, the duty is to exercise the care of other such specialists; if he is not, the duty is to associate such a specialist (with the client's consent), develop the necessary expertise, or decline the matter. If Luther has breached the applicable duty, he can be held liable for malpractice. [§§890-892]

107. **DEPENDS**   Smith owes a duty to discover recent developments in the law available through standard research techniques. Before civil malpractice can be proved, however, Jones must usually show that summary judgment would have been avoided had Smith cited the case in question. [§§894, 902]

108. **DEPENDS**   Traditionally, a lawyer could not exculpate himself in advance from liability for malpractice. However, the Model Rules provide that the agreement could be enforceable if Arthur was separately represented in making the agreement. [§927]

109. **NO**   If the judge had acted immediately, the summary procedure would have been proper. But since she waited until the next day, the case must be sent to another judge to hold a hearing. [§927]

110. **NO**   A judge may participate in community affairs but *may not* give the impression that persons are in a special position to *influence* her. [§946]

111. **NO**   A judge may not contribute to a political organization, buy tickets to political dinners, and the like, unless she is subject to public election. Even when actually running for public election, a judge may publicly endorse or oppose only other candidates for the same judicial office, not the party's candidates generally. [§§1024, 1033-1034]

Exam Questions
and Answers

QUESTION I

Sarah Smart has just graduated from law school and wants to go into practice on her own.

1. Sarah's first potential client is an inventor who wants to issue stock in a company he has formed. Sarah talks to him for two hours and takes good notes, but she realizes she is not competent to handle a public issue of securities. She calls a friend in a well-regarded securities firm in the city and sends the client, plus a written summary of their discussion, to that firm. A week later, Sarah receives a check for $1,000 from the firm as "a down payment on your one-third of our fee in this matter." What should she do with the check? Discuss.

2. A local television station invites Sarah to appear on a talk show about "women's issues in the law." She expects to be asked questions by the host and telephone callers about child support, abortion, rape, etc. Do you have any advice as to the way she should respond to questions? May she offer to have viewers come to her office for further advice? Explain.

QUESTION II

Harry Johnson was an associate at Black & White in New York. He worked on prospectuses for securities issues, one of which was for G & E, a national manufacturer of electrical items. After three years in the firm, he took a position as Assistant U.S. Attorney for the Southern District of New York. One of his first assignments was to help prosecute G & E for tax fraud. In the middle of that case, he left the U.S. Attorney's office to become a partner in a Philadelphia firm. That firm was defending the G & E tax fraud case, but Harry was assigned to work on other cases exclusively.

Does anyone have a right to complain about Harry's career path? What relief could they obtain, if any? Explain.

QUESTION III

"Mister Tax" is the newest addition to the tax advisory firms springing up around the country. It has one difference—it purports to do tax planning as well as fill out tax returns. Mary Adams has been hired as general counsel and has been made a full partner in the firm. The other partners are accountants and financial analysts. Adams's job will be to write booklets explaining tax planning to clients. She will also give seminars for the CPAs who will actually fill in the blanks on the clients' preprinted wills. If Mister Tax can get itself named executor of clients' estates, Mary will act as counsel for the executor.

Mary describes this plan to you. After you recover your composure, what will you tell her about the propriety of the plan and her role in it? Explain.

QUESTION IV

Bob Brilliant became a busy barrister. He had plenty of time to talk to prospective clients and obtain retainers, but little time to follow up his cases. One day an inventor brought a great invention to Bob's office and asked him to apply for a patent. Bob did not know anything about patent law but accepted a $500 retainer and agreed to do the necessary work. He put the file in his "IN" basket, where it stayed until nine months later, when the inventor stormed into Bob's office. A competitor had applied for a patent on the same idea so that the inventor's claim was now worthless.

Does Bob have reason to be worried? What options does the inventor have? Explain.

QUESTION V

Jones and Yates have been partners for 12 years. They have a personal injury and probate practice, and each has worked on issues brought into the office by the other. Now they have decided to split up, although they will both remain in the same city. Each is concerned about keeping "his" cases.

1.   Describe what they should tell their clients and in what way.

2.   What are the rights and duties of each partner with respect to firm files?

QUESTION VI

Mary and Bill have come to you and say they want a divorce. They have two children but little money and want a "clean break." Neither one wants the children, but Mary says she will take them. Mary tells you privately that she will inherit a large sum of money soon. Publicly, Mary is asking for one-third of Bill's salary as alimony and another one-third as child support.

1.   Can you take this case? After Mary has confided in you, are your obligations any different?

2.   May you charge one month's child support as your fee in this case? Explain.

QUESTION VII

Mark Russell represented Pat Novak in a divorce. Pat was ordered to pay child support. He has fallen behind. Mark is subpoenaed and asked Pat's address. He refuses to give it, citing both the evidentiary privilege and his professional obligation. The court overrules both grounds and orders Mark to answer.

1. What should Mark do? How will the issue arise? Explain.

2. The court asks Mark, "Is Novak a drug addict?" Mark believes the answer is yes because, while handling Pat's case, Mark had overheard Pat and a friend discussing Pat's use of narcotics. What should Mark's answer be? Explain.

QUESTION VIII

Doris Dash represents Mavis Martin, a local building contractor. Mavis asserts that she has not been paid for materials used on a job she is doing for a larger firm. Doris has filed suit on Mavis's behalf. As Doris investigates, however, she hears that Mavis may actually have sold the materials to another contractor and may be trying to recover twice. She looks at Mavis's files more closely and sees a letter from the other contractor thanking Mavis for her help. Doris obliquely asks Mavis what is going on, and Mavis tells her to mind her own business.

What should Doris do? Explain.

QUESTION IX

Claudia Carns has finished law school and seeks admission to the bar. She had been a member of a radical environmental protection group in the 1980s. Arrested for 21 counts of arson at a manufacturing plant, she pleaded guilty to three counts of malicious damage to property and spent four months in jail. She was also charged with perjury for her testimony in a friend's trial on the same charges, but the perjury charges were later dropped in order to reduce the prosecutor's backlog of cases. She has refused "on principle" to fill out the required character and fitness committee form.

Will Claudia be denied admission to the bar for any of this? Explain.

QUESTION X

Former Governor Don Runner has filed a lawsuit accusing the current secretary of state of illegally overcharging for automobile license plates. Don called a press conference to charge the secretary with mismanagement and the present governor with lax supervision. Don issued a general call for citizens to send $10 and join his class action. During his press conference and later TV interviews, Don posed under a large sign reading "Don (The People's Lawyer) Runner: Law for the Little Guy."

Is there any basis for subjecting Don to professional discipline? Explain.

ANSWER TO QUESTION I

1. Sarah should hold on to the check until she informs the client of the fee division.

    Sarah has behaved properly in this case. She listened to the client's story, understood the limits of her own ability, and put the client in touch with a firm that would be able to serve his needs. She prepared a basic memorandum of the facts and is entitled to be paid for that effort.

    Under the Model Rules, if the client consents in writing to the terms of the fee division, and the total fee is reasonable, lawyers who assume joint responsibility for a matter may share the fee in whatever proportions they agree, regardless of how much work each did.

    Note that under the ABA Code, Sarah would have to return the check. The Code required the division of fees to correspond to the services performed and responsibilities assumed by each lawyer. The value of Sarah's services would not likely amount to $1,000.

2. Sarah may appear on the program and provide general information about the law. However, she should not try to solve individual problems of viewers over the telephone, and she should not offer to have viewers come into her office for further advice.

    The public needs information about legal issues, and lawyers are often in the best position to provide that information. Sarah should certainly try to do a good job of communicating valuable information on the issues that viewers raise. However, each actual case is unique, and a lawyer should not try to solve an actual case without a detailed and careful understanding of the facts. This would violate the lawyer's duty of competence, and the public nature of a television talk show interferes with the confidentiality of the lawyer-client relationship, which is designed to give clients a chance to provide the facts candidly and fully. Thus, Sarah should refuse to give advice in specific cases.

    Sarah should not offer to have viewers come to her office. While a lawyer may advertise her services generally on television, under the Model Rules, all "in-person or live telephone contact" with potential clients whom the lawyer has not previously served is prohibited where a "significant motive" for the contact is the lawyer's personal gain. Sarah may (and sometimes should) recommend that callers seek advice of a lawyer, and if a viewer later turns up at her office seeking personal advice, Sarah is not forbidden to deal with the client's problem. She may not, however, solicit the person's business on the television show.

ANSWER TO QUESTION II

G & E can object to Harry's work while in government, and the Justice Department can complain about Harry's firm's participation in the tax fraud case.

The problem here is that of representation contrary to the interest of a former client. The first such problem arose when Harry went to work for the government and was assigned a case prosecuting a firm he had formerly represented. This was potentially a serious conflict of interest, and G & E could have filed a motion to have Harry reassigned. However, the kind of information Harry received in his work on the securities cases was probably not the kind of information involved in this alleged tax fraud; indeed, what he learned in the securities work may have been made public in the prospectuses anyway, so that G & E's interest in confidentiality would probably not have been great enough to cause Harry to be ineligible to prosecute the later tax case. Even if Harry were ineligible, however, other U.S. Attorneys could prosecute the case, as a court would be reluctant to attribute the knowledge of one Assistant U.S. Attorney to the whole office.

After Harry left government, he clearly could not defend the case he formerly prosecuted. That would run directly afoul of Model Rule 1.11(a), which prohibits a former government lawyer from representing a private client in a matter in which the lawyer participated personally and substantially while in government. ABA Code DR 9-101(B) also forbids a lawyer to work on a matter for which he had "substantial responsibility" as a government lawyer. However, Harry's assignment by his new firm to work exclusively on other cases would make it possible to effectively screen him from any participation in the tax fraud case. Under Model Rule 1.11(a)(1) and case law, a former government lawyer's firm is not necessarily disqualified if the lawyer is screened and he shares no fees earned from the case. Thus, it is probable that the government could not have Harry's firm disqualified as defense counsel for G & E.

ANSWER TO QUESTION III

Mary's new venture has a series of problems, the most basic of which is that she is practicing law with nonlawyers and helping persons engage in the unauthorized practice of law.

No problem is presented by Mary's writing booklets explaining tax planning to clients. Some activities of lay firms (*e.g.,* divorce clinics) have been held to be unauthorized practice, but the writing of booklets has generally been held not to constitute unauthorized practice, even booklets on subjects traditionally practiced by lawyers.

Giving seminars for CPAs is likewise not a problem, but having the CPAs fill in blanks on preprinted wills may constitute the unauthorized practice of law. There are cases holding that allowing real estate agents to fill in blanks for routine items on certain standard contracts is not unauthorized practice, but wills are sufficiently individualized so that it is unlikely that a CPA would be permitted to supply missing terms. Mary's assisting in this process would cause her to be in violation of Model Rule 5.5(b) and DR 3-101(A), which forbid aiding others in the unauthorized practice of law.

Furthermore, Model Rule 5.4(a) and DR 3-103 prohibit a lawyer from forming a partnership with nonlawyers where any of the activities involve the practice of law. Mary's involvement in the Mister Tax partnership would violate these rules. The nature of the tax planning activities is such that Mary, if not the entire company, would be deemed to be engaging in the practice of law, and thus Mary's role as a partner is improper. Many persons believe that this is an uncalled-for ethical prohibition because the work of firms such as this may well be of value to the public, but the Model Rules and the ABA Code clearly prohibit this type of arrangement.

Finally, Mary's acting as counsel when her company is named executor of clients' estates might also involve Mary in assisting improper solicitation. When a lawyer seeks to encourage a client to name her executor or counsel to the executor, there is a potential problem of overreaching, and Mister Tax seems to be heavily involved in that here.

ANSWER TO QUESTION IV

Neglect by busy lawyers is an all too common situation, and Bob should indeed be worried. The inventor may file a complaint with the state's discipline commission and almost certainly has a viable malpractice claim against Bob.

Although Bob was not familiar with patent law, it was not improper for him to take the inventor's case. However, upon doing so, Bob had an obligation to promptly become familiar with that area of law and to proceed to prosecute the patent claim. Alternatively, Bob had an obligation to involve a more experienced lawyer in the process and require him to get the patent on file. The failure to do either of these things constituted neglect on Bob's part, and the inventor could file a complaint with the state's discipline commission.

To succeed in a malpractice claim against Bob, the inventor would have to demonstrate that Bob breached a duty to him and that he was harmed by the breach. Bob clearly breached his duty of care. If the inventor could show that he would have received the patent if Bob had proceeded expeditiously, he can successfully sue Bob. The damages might be the royalties the inventor would have received from the patent.

ANSWER TO QUESTION V

1. Each client should be sent a letter explaining that the firm is breaking up and informing the client that his file may be sent to the lawyer or law firm of the client's choice. Clients are not the property of either lawyer, and there is no proper way for Jones or Yates to compel or even properly encourage a client to remain with one of them.

2. Each partner may keep a copy of whatever material is necessary to protect that partner's interest. As indicated above, the clients are free to go with either partner or with another law firm, and their files must be sent to the selected lawyer or firm.

However, if a client has not paid his fees, the partners may have a lien for those fees that will allow them to retain some of the files. Likewise, either or both partners may be liable for malpractice with respect to any of the cases that they have been working on, and thus it may be in each partner's interest to retain copies of some or all of the files.

ANSWER TO QUESTION VI

1. Although the ABA does not specifically prohibit a lawyer's taking this kind of case, some state statutes do, and most lawyers would not try to represent both sides in a case like this.

   A lawyer may take a case involving conflicting interests where both parties understand the potential conflict and consent to the dual representation *and* the lawyer believes that she can adequately represent the interests of each client. Moreover, the lawyer may counsel Mary and Bill in an uncontested, nonlitigation situation, and it would be proper to draw up an agreement concerning child custody and property settlement. However, the lawyer can act for both clients only after full disclosure of the conflicting interests of Mary and Bill and with the express consent of both of them, confirmed in writing.

   Here, even if a lawyer believed at the outset that adequate representation of both Mary and Bill was possible, it would be hard to maintain that belief after Mary's confidence. Once the lawyer knows that Mary's needs are not likely to continue to be as they appear, the lawyer is forced to take a position that will in some sense constitute taking advantage of Bill. As Mary's private counsel, the lawyer probably could seek to get Mary a large alimony payment as long as no affirmative misrepresentations were made. However, as Bill's lawyer, she would presumably also be trying to make those payments as low as possible and would be obliged to use Mary's information on Bill's behalf. Absent Mary's consent, the lawyer cannot disclose confidential information elicited from Mary in preliminary discussions. The lawyer owes a professional duty under the Model Rules and the ABA Code to preserve all client confidences. This obligation is not limited to legal proceedings but applies to any client confidence gained in the course of the lawyer-client relationship. Thus, the lawyer could not make a full disclosure to Bill and so is prohibited from representing him.

   Furthermore, a clear conflict of interests is apparent after Mary's disclosure, and Mary will certainly not let the lawyer reveal her secret as would be necessary to get Bill's informed consent. When a conflict of interest becomes apparent after employment, the lawyer must withdraw from representing one of the clients pursuant to Model Rule 1.7. At a minimum, the lawyer should suggest that Bill get other counsel. It may be that Bill's interest will not be prejudiced if the lawyer continues to represent Mary.

2. A fee based on the amount of child support awarded would not be proper. Under the Model Rules, a fee contingent on obtaining a divorce or on the amount of alimony

or support would be prohibited. Particularly in a case in which the lawyer is representing both sides, such a fee might even encourage the lawyer to try to increase the amount of child support (to the disadvantage of one party) so as to increase her own fee.

ANSWER TO QUESTION VII

1. Mark should probably continue to refuse to answer, at least until the court's order is tested on appeal.

    Mark is probably correct in citing the evidentiary attorney-client privilege as a reason not to disclose Pat's address. A communication made in confidence by a client to his lawyer in obtaining legal assistance is generally protected under the privilege. Here, Pat himself "communicated" the address to Mark, and disclosure of the address would clearly not be in Pat's interest. Pat has not waived the privilege. Thus, Mark should not disclose the information.

    Also, the information certainly qualifies as a "secret" protected by the professional obligation of confidentiality (under both the ABA Code and Model Rules). Thus, it is information Mark should not reveal.

    If Mark refuses to disclose the information when the court orders him to answer, Mark will probably be sentenced for contempt of court. Mark will then be in a position to appeal the court's order to disclose, which is about the only way that he can get a judicial test of the privilege question. If the appellate court sustains the trial court, then presumably Mark has an obligation to disclose and should do so.

    It should be noted that the ABA Code and Model Rules would *permit* Mark to reveal the client's secret when ordered to do so by the trial court, but he is *not required* to do so, and most lawyers believe their duty to their client is somewhat higher than the Code standard.

2. Mark should attempt to avoid being ordered to tell the court what he heard. The information about Pat's drug habit is not protected by the attorney-client privilege since the information was not communicated to Mark by the client, but the information was something Mark heard in the course of representation that could be embarrassing or harmful to Pat. That puts the information again into the category of a "secret." A lawyer must reveal such information when ordered by the court to do so, but Mark should assert his professional obligation as a basis for trying to get the court not to issue such an order.

ANSWER TO QUESTION VIII

Doris should look into this situation more fully to assure herself that she is not perpetrating a fraud.

A lawyer is the client's representative, not her judge. However, the lawyer is neither required nor permitted to assist a client in perpetrating a fraud on someone else. In this situation, Doris has become aware of the possibility that her client may be making a false claim. Doris would not be required to go to the prosecutor and accuse her client of fraud or perjury, but she is under an obligation to try to prevent more damage from being done. Doris should not conduct a further search of Mavis's files; she is not permitted to use her role as a trusted advisor to become a self-appointed investigator. However, she should confront Mavis directly about the issue and try to get satisfactory answers. If she is not satisfied that Mavis's claim is legitimate, she should advise Mavis to drop it. If Mavis refuses, Doris must withdraw from the representation to avoid assisting in a crime or fraud.

ANSWER TO QUESTION IX

Claudia is likely to be denied admission to the bar.

Conviction of a crime such as arson is often sufficient to deny an applicant admission to the bar. The bar admissions committee is not limited by the label of an offense but may investigate all of the surrounding facts. A finding that Claudia consciously engaged in setting fires so as to do damage might be considered to make her a sufficiently "bad person" that admission would be denied, even if she were engaged in a form of political protest at the time.

The charge of perjury would be even more serious. Offenses involving deceit are thought to be particularly serious for potential lawyers. Although the charges were dropped, the bar admissions committee would again be entitled to look into the evidence that the prosecutor had and would not be bound by the fact that the charges were never brought to trial.

Finally, the refusal to fill out the required character and fitness form would probably itself cause denial of admission to the bar. The burden of supplying relevant information is on the applicant for admission. The Supreme Court has held that failure to supply information can be the basis for denial of admission. There may be substantive limits on the criteria that the bar admissions committee can consider in actually ruling on the applicant's case, but there is no excuse for not supplying relevant information.

Since all of Claudia's criminal behavior took place many years ago, it is possible that Claudia has been rehabilitated. However, since Claudia did not bother to fill out the form, she did not raise the rehabilitation argument, so it would probably not be considered by the committee.

ANSWER TO QUESTION X

Runner might be subject to discipline for improper pretrial publicity.

Lawsuits are to be tried in the courts and not in the media. The Model Rules and ABA Code allow a lawyer to reveal certain basic information about a case that has been filed, but they do not permit the lawyer to argue that case in the media. This problem presents a somewhat closer case because Don is obviously mixing politics with litigation. Some of his remarks are presumably partisan and possibly designed to aid a political comeback. The Model Rules and ABA Code do not prohibit political activity, but they may be read to require Don to do his politicking in some way other than by publicizing a litigated case.

Calling for citizens to join a class action and send in cash also might be prohibited. Soliciting clients for fee-generating work by an announcement on television could be considered improper solicitation, although Runner should be able to get court approval for his broadcasting notice to get more clients into his class action once the case is actually filed.

Advertising on television no longer violates the ABA Code and is acceptable under Model Rules 7.1 and 7.2, but posing under a large sign extolling one's own talents might violate even the fairly narrow prohibition of false or misleading advertising.

Tables of Citations

CITATIONS TO ABA CODE OF PROFESSIONAL RESPONSIBILITY

Citation	Text Reference	Citation	Text Reference	Citation	Text Reference
EC 1-2	§39	DR 2-107(A)	§815	EC 5-10	§§683, 689
EC 1-6	§39	DR 2-107(B)	§821	EC 5-11	§441
DR 1-101	§52	DR 2-108(A)	§756	EC 5-14	§394
DR 1-101(B)	§39	DR 2-108(B)	§659	EC 5-17	§410
DR 1-102(A)(1), (2)	§825	DR 2-109(A)(1)	§149	EC 5-18	§432
DR 1-102(A)(4)	§§511, 837	DR 2-109(A)(2)	§150	EC 5-19	§370
DR 1-102(A)(5)	§838	DR 2-110(A)(2)	§§283, 286	DR 5-101(A)	§§367, 374, 375
DR 1-103	§876	DR 2-110(A)(3)	§284	DR 5-101(B)	§682
DR 1-103(A)	§§875, 881	DR 2-110(B)(1)	§271	DR 5-101(B)(1)	§686
EC 2-6	§769	DR 2-110(B)(2)	§269	DR 5-101(B)(2)	§686
EC 2-17	§217	DR 2-110(B)(3)	§270	DR 5-101(B)(3)	§687
EC 2-18	§217	DR 2-110(B)(4)	§§272, 287	DR 5-101(B)(4)	§688
EC 2-19	§213	DR 2-110(C)(1)(d)	§278	DR 5-102(A)	§682
EC 2-20	§§221, 227, 231	DR 2-110(C)(5)	§279	DR 5-102(B)	§692
EC 2-23	§248	DR 2-110(C)(6)	§280	DR 5-103(A)	§376
EC 2-25	§128	EC 3-1	§87	DR 5-103(A)(2)	§221
EC 2-26	§126	EC 3-5	§§87, 88, 91	DR 5-103(B)	§672
EC 2-29	§132	EC 3-6	§733	DR 5-104(A)	§§379, 381
EC 2-30	§§146, 147, 148	EC 3-7	§85	DR 5-104(B)	§378
EC 2-32	§267	DR 3-101(A)	§114	DR 5-105	§§371, 399
DR 2-101(A)	§775	DR 3-102	§§115, 751	DR 5-105(A)	§§367, 369
DR 2-101(B)	§775	DR 3-102(A)(1)	§754	DR 5-105(B)	§367
DR 2-101(H)	§797	DR 3-102(A)(3)	§753	DR 5-105(C)	§§369, 404
DR 2-102	§725	DR 3-103	§116	DR 5-105(D)	§§469, 684
DR 2-102(A)	§797	DR 3-103(A)	§748	DR 5-106	§425
DR 2-102(A)(4)	§732	EC 4-2	§§306, 308	DR 5-107(A)	§442
DR 2-102(B)	§§742, 743, 745, 746	EC 4-3	§307	DR 5-107(B)	§§441, 443, 768
		EC 4-4	§329		
DR 2-102(C)	§729	EC 4-5	§308	DR 5-107(C)	§750
DR 2-102(D)	§744	EC 4-6	§304	EC 6-3	§§178, 179
DR 2-103(C)	§793	DR 4-101	§592	EC 6-4	§178
DR 2-103(D)(4)	§767	DR 4-101(A)	§§299, 339	EC 6-5	§183
DR 2-104(A)(1)	§792	DR 4-101(A)(2)	§354	DR 6-101	§176
DR 2-105	§799	DR 4-101(C)(2)	§332	DR 6-101(A)(1)	§177
DR 2-105(A)(1)	§800	DR 4-101(C)(3)	§362	DR 6-102	§926
DR 2-105(A)(2)	§807	DR 4-101(D)	§308	EC 7-3	§191
DR 2-105(A)(3)	§804	EC 5-4	§378	EC 7-4	§191
DR 2-106(A)	§216	EC 5-5	§§385, 386	EC 7-5	§§192, 509
DR 2-106(B)	§218	EC 5-6	§390	EC 7-7	§§158, 159
DR 2-106(C)	§231	EC 5-9	§681	EC 7-8	§503

Citation	Text Reference	Citation	Text Reference	Citation	Text Reference
EC 7-12	§172	DR 7-102(A)(7)	§505	DR 7-108(E)	§703
EC 7-13	§§716, 719	DR 7-102(A)(8)	§505	DR 7-108(F)	§709
EC 7-14	§§723, 724	DR 7-102(B)(1)	§607	DR 7-109(A)	§624
EC 7-15	§§557, 558	DR 7-102(B)(2)	§606	DR 7-109(B)	§625
EC 7-16	§§557, 558	DR 7-102(B)(3), (5)	§590	DR 7-109(C)	§§627, 628, 629
EC 7-17	§193	DR 7-103(A)	§713	DR 7-110(A)	§§695, 696, 697
EC 7-21	§552	DR 7-103(B)	§718	DR 7-110(B)(2)	§699
EC 7-23	§599	DR 7-104(A)(1)	§§534, 543	DR 7-110(B)(3)	§700
EC 7-25	§§637, 639, 647	DR 7-104(A)(2)	§§547, 548	DR 7-110(B)(4)	§701
EC 7-28	§626	DR 7-105(A)	§552	EC 8-1	§561
EC 7-29	§705	DR 7-106(A)	§§508, 653	EC 8-2	§560
EC 7-30	§703	DR 7-106(B)(1)	§597	EC 8-6	§§568, 569, 570
EC 7-31	§709	DR 7-106(C)(1)	§§638, 643	EC 8-8	§565
EC 7-34	§§694, 695	DR 7-106(C)(2)	§632	EC 8-9	§560
EC 7-35	§694	DR 7-106(C)(3)	§642	DR 8-101(A)(1)	§566
EC 7-36	§658	DR 7-106(C)(4)	§§633, 642	DR 8-101(A)(2)	§566
EC 7-37	§654	DR 7-106(C)(5)	§655	DR 8-102(B)	§570
EC 7-38	§656	DR 7-106(C)(6)	§651	DR 8-103	§1022
DR 7-101(A)	§190	DR 7-106(C)(7)	§646	DR 8-103(A)	§573
DR 7-101(A)(1)	§152	DR 7-107	§660	DR 9-101(B)	§§486, 490
DR 7-101(B)(1)	§581	DR 7-107(A)	§664	DR 9-101(C)	§488
DR 7-101(B)(2)	§510	DR 7-107(B)	§§665, 666	DR 9-102	§200
DR 7-102(A)(1)	§584	DR 7-107(F)	§669	DR 9-102(A)	§§201, 204
DR 7-102(A)(2)	§575	DR 7-108	§702	DR 9-102(A)(1)	§§202, 203
DR 7-102(A)(3)	§§512, 514, 590	DR 7-108(B)(1)	§704	DR 9-102(A)(2)	§207
DR 7-102(A)(5)	§§511, 590	DR 7-108(D)	§§706, 708	DR 9-102(B)	§209

CITATIONS TO ABA MODEL RULES OF PROFESSIONAL CONDUCT

Citation	Text Reference	Citation	Text Reference	Citation	Text Reference
1.0(c)	§§476, 478	1.8(i)	§§376, 490	2.3	§§520, 529
1.0(e)	§§369, 404	1.9(a)	§§461, 468	2.3(a)	§521
1.0(k)	§§473, 483	1.9(b)	§§462, 475	2.3(b)	§523
1.1	§§146, 176, 177, 178, 180, 181, 182	1.9(c)	§359	2.3(c)	§524
		1.10	§473	2.4	§941
1.2	§152	1.10(a)	§§469, 476	3.1	§§150, 191, 575, 576, 577
1.2(a)	§§158, 159, 160, 165, 167, 169	1.10(b)	§ 474		
		1.11(a)	§490	3.2	§§585, 656
1.2(b)	§193	1.11(b)	§492	3.3	§§609, 610, 611, 613, 617
1.2(c)	§§153, 156	1.11(c)	§§493, 494, 495		
1.2(d)	§§505, 508, 509	1.11(d)	§478	3.3(a)	§620
1.3	§§187, 188	1.11(d)(1)	§496	3.3(a)(1)	§§590, 594, 595
1.4	§197	1.11(d)(2)(i)	§496	3.3(a)(2)	§597
1.4(a)	§196	1.11(d)(2)(ii)	§497	3.3(a)(3)	§§602, 608, 615, 616
1.4(b)	§195	1.11(e)	§§491, 494	3.3(b)	§§619, 620
1.5	§§219, 221, 821	1.12(a)	§490	3.3(c)	§§621, 622
1.5(a)	§§216, 218	1.12(b)	§§392, 497	3.3(d)	§623
1.5(b)	§§159, 211, 212, 213	1.12(c)	§492	3.4(a)	§624
1.5(c)	§223	1.13(a)	§432	3.4(b)	§§626, 627, 628
1.5(d)(1)	§228	1.13(b)	§435	3.4(c)	§§646, 647, 653
1.5(d)(2)	§231	1.13(c)	§436	3.4(d)	§589
1.5(e)(1)	§816	1.13(d)	§437	3.4(e)	§§633, 638, 642, 643
1.5(e)(2)	§819	1.13(g)	§433	3.4(f)	§625
1.6	§§300, 333, 365, 513, 515, 524, 592, 622, 878	1.14	§456	3.5(a)	§§695, 702
		1.14(a)	§172	3.5(b)	§§698, 701
1.6(a)	§§304, 306, 307, 340	1.14(b)	§173	3.5(c)	§708
1.6(b)	§357	1.15	§200	3.5(c)(1)	§706
1.6(b)(1)	§363	1.15(a)	§§141, 201, 203, 209	3.5(d)	§651
1.6(b)(2)	§§364, 365	1.15(b)	§202	3.6	§§660, 665, 669, 693
1.6(b)(3)	§§364, 365	1.15(c)	§204	3.6(a)	§§661, 666
1.6(b)(4)	§360	1.15(d)	§§206, 207	3.6(b)	§664
1.6(b)(5)	§350	1.15(e)	§208	3.6(c)	§668
1.6(b)(6)	§332	1.16(a)	§515	3.6(d)	§666
1.7	§§371, 390, 399, 422, 423, 479, 480, 481	1.16(a)(1)	§§144, 269	3.7	§§682, 689, 692
		1.16(a)(2)	§§145, 270	3.7(a)	§683
1.7(a)	§368	1.16(a)(3)	§§272, 287	3.7(a)(1)	§686
1.7(a)(2)	§375	1.16(b)(1)	§274	3.7(a)(2)	§687
1.7(b)	§§369, 374, 441	1.16(b)(2)	§§275, 453, 510	3.7(a)(3)	§688
1.7(b)(1)	§402	1.16(b)(3)	§275	3.7(b)	§684
1.7(b)(2)	§403	1.16(b)(4)	§276	3.8(a)	§713
1.7(b)(3)	§401	1.16(b)(5)	§277	3.8(b)	§715
1.7(b)(4)	§404	1.16(b)(6)	§§278, 280, 332	3.8(c)	§714
1.8	§386	1.16(c)	§§282, 454	3.8(d)	§718
1.8(a)	§§379, 382	1.16(d)	§§267, 283, 284, 286, 454	3.8(e)	§721
1.8(b)	§355			3.8(f)	§667
1.8(c)	§§384, 385, 387, 389, 390	1.17	§823	3.9	§558
		1.18	§922	4.1(a)	§511
1.8(d)	§378	1.18(a)	§136	4.1(b)	§§365, 512, 513
1.8(e)	§§676, 677	1.18(b)	§§137, 302	4.2	§§534, 536, 537, 539, 540, 541, 542, 543, 545
1.8(f)	§442	1.18(c)	§§138, 303		
1.8(g)	§§425, 427	1.18(d)	§140	4.3	§§547, 548
1.8(h)	§§927, 928	2.1	§§192, 502, 503, 504	4.4	§§149, 542, 632

Citation	Text Reference	Citation	Text Reference	Citation	Text Reference
4.4(a)	§549	5.5(d)(1)	§72	7.4(a)	§808
4.4(b)	§§336, 636	5.5(d)(2)	§78	7.4(b)	§800
5.1	§§308, 725	5.6(a)	§756	7.4(c)	§801
5.1(a)	§736	5.6(b)	§659	7.4(d)	§§799, 805
5.1(b)	§737	5.7(a)	§758	7.5	§§725, 743
5.1(c)	§738	5.7(b)	§757	7.5(a)	§742
5.2	§725	6.1	§128	7.5(b)	§744
5.2(a)	§739	6.1(a)	§129	7.5(c)	§745
5.2(b)	§740	6.1(b)	§130	7.5(d)	§729
5.3	§§725, 733, 741	6.2	§132	7.6	§572
5.3(a)	§308	6.2(c)	§147	8.1	§§39, 52, 57
5.4(a)	§§115, 751	6.3	§§459, 562	8.2	§570
5.4(a)(1)	§754	6.3(a)	§563	8.2(b)	§§573, 1022
5.4(a)(2)	§754	6.4	§564	8.3(a)	§§875, 877, 881
5.4(a)(3)	§753	6.5(a)	§439	8.3(b)	§875
5.4(a)(4)	§755	6.5(b)	§440	8.3(c)	§§878, 880
5.4(b)	§§116, 748	7.1	§§778, 797	8.4	§§566, 832
5.4(c)	§§443, 768	7.2	§780	8.4(a)	§825
5.4(d)	§750	7.2(a)	§779	8.4(c)	§§511, 837
5.5	§§63, 88	7.2(b)(2)	§822	8.4(d)	§§506, 838
5.5(a)	§§62, 114	7.2(b)(4)	§814	8.4(e)	§839
5.5(b)(1)	§71	7.3	§787	8.4(f)	§§697, 840
5.5(b)(2)	§73	7.3(a)	§§788, 792	8.5(a)	§§9, 826, 882
5.5(c)(1)	§64	7.3(b)	§789	8.5(b)	§§828, 829, 830
5.5(c)(2)	§65	7.3(c)	§790		
5.5(c)(3)	§§69, 70	7.3(d)	§§768, 793		

Table of Cases

Dombey v. Detroit, Toledo & Ironton Railroad - **§295**
DuPont v. Southern Pacific Co. - **§412**

E

Eisenberg v. Gagnon - **§321**
Elane v. St. Bernard Hospital - **§817**
Emslie v. State Bar - **§862**
Evans v. Jeff D. - **§247**
Ex parte - *see* name of party

F

Fambo v. Smith - **§519**
Faretta v. California - **§86**
Fellerman v. Bradley - **§358**
Ferry v. Ackerman - **§893**
Fickett v. Superior Court - **§925**
Firestone Tire & Rubber Co. v. Risjord - **§482**
First Wisconsin Mortgage Trust v. First Wisconsin Corp. -
§484
Flanagan v. United States - **§482**
Florida Bar v. McLawhorn - **§511**
Florida Bar v. Went For It, Inc. - **§§784, 785, 786**
Foley, Hoag & Eliot - **§731**
Fracasse v. Brent - **§296**
Freeport-McMoRan Oil & Gas Co. v. Federal Energy
Regulatory Commission - **§723**
Fund of Funds, Ltd. v. Arthur Andersen & Co. - **§472**

G

G.W.L., *Re* - **§47**
Gardner v. North Carolina State Bar - **§110**
Gentile v. Nevada State Bar - **§663**
Giddens v. State Bar - **§861**
Goldfarb v. Virginia State Bar - **§§237, 772**
Gosselin v. Webb - **§729**
Greenberg, *In re* - **§429**
Gregory v. United States - **§720**
Greycas, Inc. v. Proud - **§§522, 923**
Grievance Administrator v. Fried - **§838**
Grievance Committee v. Rottner - **§420**
Griffiths, *In re* - **§31**
Grimes, *In re* - **§571**
Gulbankian, State v. - **§390**
Gulf Oil v. Bernard - **§795**
Gullo v. Hirst - **§582**

H

Haack v. Great Atlantic & Pacific Tea Co. - **§686**
Haddad, United States v. - **§347**
Hague, *In re* - **§952**
Hallinan v. Committee of Bar Examiners - **§§42, 50, 51**

Harris, People v. - **§313**
Hawk v. Superior Court - **§642**
Hay v. Erwin - **§234**
Hendry v. Pelland - **§373**
Hensley v. Eckerhart - **§243**
Herron v. Jones - **§473**
Himmel, *In re* - **§881**
Hirschkop v. Snead - **§670**
Hishon v. King & Spalding - **§731**
Hiss, *In re* - **§874**
Hoare, *In re* - **§884**
Holloway v. Arkansas - **§406**
Hoover v. Ronwin - **§4**
Horan, State v. - **§387**
Horne v. Peckham - **§179**
Hunydee v. United States - **§322**

I

In re - *see* name of party
Iorizzo, United States v. - **§465**
Iowa Supreme Court Board of Professional Ethics and
Conduct v. Lane - **§838**
Isserman, *In re* - **§931**
Iulo, Matter of - **§883**

J

Jackson v. State Bar - **§208**
Jedwabny v. Philadelphia Trust Co. - **§411**
Jeffry v. Pounds - **§421**
Johns v. Smyth - **§579**
Johnson, Petition of - **§849**
Jonathan Corp. v. Prime Computers, Inc. - **§314**
Jones, State v. - **§478**
Jones v. Barnes - **§580**
Jones v. Board of Commissioners of Alabama State Bar -
§37

K

Kala v. Aluminum Smelting & Refining Co. - **§392**
Kandel v. State - **§588**
Kaplan, *In re* - **§343**
Katris v. Immigration & Naturalization Service - **§598**
Keller v. State Bar of California - **§8**
Kelley, *In re* - **§849**
Kelly v. Greason - **§862**
Kentucky Bar Association v. Heleringer - **§570**
Kirsch v. Duryea - **§900**
Kleiner v. First National Bank of Atlanta - **§796**
Klemm v. Superior Court - **§416**
Konigsberg v. Board of Bar Examiners - **§46**
Kor, People v. - **§331**
Kramer, *In re* - **§884**

Krieger v. Bulpitt - **§229**
Krule, *In re* - **§48**

L

Lamb, *In re* - **§837**
Lathrop v. Donahue - **§7**
Law Students Research Council v. Wadmond - **§55**
Lawline v. American Bar Association - **§87**
Lewis v. State Bar of California - **§177**
Lindsey, *In re* **§320**
Liteky v. United States - **§981**
Lopez, v. United States - **§544**
Lowery v. Cardwell - **§617**
Lucas v. Hamm - **§§890, 901, 924**
Lucido v. Cravath, Swaine & Moore - **§731**
Luethke v. Suhr - **§161**
Luhan, People v. - **§850**

M

McGuirk, People v. - **§630**
McMann v. Richardson - **§185**
Mackay, *In re* - **§845**
Madsen, *In re* - **§792**
Mallard v. United States District Court - **§135**
Maness v. Meyers - **§649**
March v. Committee of Bar Examiners - **§53**
Massachusetts School of Law at Andover v. American
    Bar Association - **§34**
Matter of - *see* name of party
Maunus v. State Ethics Commission - **§5**
Maxwell v. Superior Court - **§378**
Mayberry v. Pennsylvania - **§933**
Mayes, State v. - **§249**
Meyerhofer v. Empire Fire & Marine Insurance Co. -
    §328
Microsoft Corp., United States v. - **§981**
Miku v. Almen - **§645**
Milian v. State - **§935**
Mitton v. State Bar - **§535**
Morrell v. State - **§311**
Musick, People v. - **§834**

N

NAACP v. Button - **§§762, 794**
NCK Organization Ltd. v. Bregman - **§464**
Neilssen, State v. - **§867**
Newby v. Enron Corp. - **§3**
New York County Lawyers Association v. Dacey - **§101**
News America Publishing, Inc., *In re* - **§537**
Nix v. Whiteside - **§613**

O

Office of Disciplinary Counsel v. Eilberg - **§567**

Ohio-Sealy Mattress Manufacturing Co. v. Kaplan - **§323**
Ohio State Bar Assocation v. Kanter - **§812**
Ohralik v. Ohio State Bar Association - **§791**
Oklahoma, State of, v. Smolen - **§678**
Olwell, State v. - **§352**
Oregon State Bar v. Miller & Co. - **§100**
Osprey v. Cabana Limited Partnership - **§680**
Owen v. Neely - **§897**

PQ

Parsons v. Continental National American Group - **§448**
Peel v. Attorney Registration & Disciplinary Commission -
    §804
Pennsylvania v. Delaware Valley Citizens' Council for
    Clean Air - **§243**
People *ex rel.* Clancy v. Superior Court - **§232**
People *ex rel.* Gallagher v. Hertz - **§552**
People v. - *see* opposing party
Person v. Association of the Bar of the City of New York -
    §629
Petition of - *see* name of party
Plaza Shoe Store v. Hermel - **§297**
Primus, *In re* - **§794**

R

R.M.J., Matter of - **§807**
Radiant Burners v. American Gas Association - **§§315,
    317**
Radtke v. Board of Bar Examiners - **§52**
Raney v. Federal Bureau of Prisons - **§244**
Re - *see* name of party
Rekeweg v. Federal Mutual Insurance Co. - **§898**
Remole Soil Service v. Benson - **§109**
Republican Party of Minnesota v. White - **§1031**
Richardson Merrill, Inc. v. Koller - **§482**
Richardson, State v. - **§132**
Richette v. Solomon - **§288**
Riverside, City of, v. Rivera - **§245**
Roadway Express, Inc. v. Piper - **§589**
Robinson, *In re* - **§506**
Rock v. Arkansas - **§613**
Roth, *In re* - **§942**
Ruffalo, *In re* - **§861**

S

Sanders v. Russell - **§68**
Satcom International Group, PLC v. Orbcomm Interna-
    tional Partners, L.P. - **§319**
Schneider, *Ex parte* - **§344**
Schultheis, People v. - **§614**
Schumacher v. Nix - **§60**

Schware v. Board of Bar Examiners - **§§30, 56**

Schwarz, *In re* - **§866**

Sealed Case, *In re* - **§335**

Securities and Exchange Commission v. National Student
Marketing Corp. - **§526**

Segal, *In re* - **§836**

Selznick v. State Bar - **§871**

Shaulis v. Pennsylvania State Ethics Commission - **§2**

Sheppard v. Maxwell - **§662**

Sherwin, People v. - **§931**

Smith v. Lewis - **§894**

Sperry v. State of Florida *ex rel.* Florida Bar - **§78**

Spevack v. Klein - **§865**

Stanley v. Richmond - **§393**

State v. - *see* name of party

State Bar v. Arizona Land Title & Trust Co. - **§90**

Stephan v. Smith - **§134**

Stokely, People v. - **§690**

Strickland v. Washington - **§185**

Supreme Court of New Hampshire v. Piper - **§32**

Swidler & Berlin v. United States - **§305**

T

T.C. Theater Corp. v. Warner Bros. Pictures, Inc. - **§466**

Taylor v. Kentucky State Bar - **§853**

Taylor v. Sheldon - **§302**

Terry, *Ex parte* - **§932**

Thomas, United States v. - **§551**

Thomas v. Douglas - **§454**

Togstad v. Vesely, Otto, Miller & Keefe - **§124**

Tormo v. Yormak - **§912**

Trist v. Child - **§233**

U

Unauthorized Practice of Law Committee v. Parsons
Technology - **§102**

United Mine Workers v. Illinois State Bar Association -
§763

United States v. - *see* opposing party

United Transportation Union v. State Bar of Michigan -
§763

Upjohn Co. v. United States - **§§309, 315**

V

Venegas v. Mitchell - **§247**

Virginia State Board of Pharmacy v. Virginia Citizens
Consumer Council - **§773**

Virzi v. Grand Trunk Warehouse - **§519**

Vizcaino v. Microsoft Corp. - **§246**

WX

Walker, Matter of - **§849**

Weber v. Cueto - **§852**

Wellner v. Committee - **§44**

West Virginia State Bar Association v. Hart - **§505**

Westbrook, Commonwealth v. - **§407**

Westinghouse Electric Corp. v. Kerr-McGee Corp. - **§471**

White v. United States - **§407**

White, United States v. - **§482**

Winskunas v. Birnbaum - **§902**

Wolff v. McDonnell - **§103**

Woodruff v. Tomlin - **§896**

Woods v. City National Bank - **§419**

Wright v. Williams - **§892**

Y

Yokozeki v. State Bar - **§885**

Z

Zauderer v. Office of Disciplinary Counsel - **§§781, 782**

Index

Subject	Model Rules	ABA Code
education, §§33-35		
examination, §§36-38		
Americans with Disabilities Act, §38		
residency, §32		
unauthorized practice, §62	5.5(a)	
ADVANCING FUNDS TO CLIENTS		
client obligation to repay, §§674, 677		
indigent client, §677	1.8(e)	
law may be changing, §680		
litigation expenses, §§673, 676	1.8(e)	DR 5-103(b)
no other financial support, §§678-680		
pending or contemplated litigation, §§671-677	1.8(e)	DR 5-103(b)
ADVERSE LEGAL AUTHORITY, DUTY TO REVEAL,		
§§596-600	3.3(a)(2)	EC 7-23; DR 7-106(B)(1)
ADVERSE PARTY, COMMUNICATION WITH,		
§§534-548		
See also Communication with		
persons represented by counsel, §§534-545	4.2	DR 7-104(A)(1)
persons unrepresented by counsel, §§546-548	4.3	DR 7-104(A)(2)
ADVERTISING		
See also Law firms, name of; Solicitation of business		
ABA Code restrictions, §§775-776		DR 2-101
provisions not current, §776		
antitrust laws, §772		
Bates liberalization, §774		
limitation of practice, §§806-808	7.4(a)	DR 2-105(A)(2)
Model Rules approach, §§777-783		
confirmed by *Zauderer*, §781		
copy of ad required, §797	7.2(b), (d)	
dissemination methods, §779	7.2(a)	
false and misleading ads prohibited, §777	7.1	
illustrations protected, §781		
lawyer's name required, §780	7.2(c)	
personal publicity, §797	7.1	DR 2-101(H), 2-102(A)
specialization, §799. *See also* Specialization	7.4(d)	DR 2-105
substantial government interest for state		
limitations, §§784-786		
traditional approach, §§769-770		
Zauderer expansion, §§781-783		
ADVICE BY LAWYER		
See also Candor, duty of; Solicitation of business		
client, former or regular, §792	7.3(a)	DR 2-104(A)(1)
close friend, §792	7.3(a)	DR 2-104(A)(1)
employment resulting from, §§813-814	7.3(a)	DR 2-104(A)(1)-(5)
must be candid, §§502-504	2.1	EC 7-8
nonlegal matters, §504	2.1	
relative, §792	7.3(a)	DR 2-104(A)(1)
unrepresented person, §548	4.3	DR 7-104(A)(2)
AGENT, LAWYER AS, §120		
AIDING UNAUTHORIZED PRACTICE OF LAW,		
§§114-116	5.5(a), (b)	DR 3-101(A), 3-102, 3-103

Subject	Model Rules	ABA Code
AMERICAN BAR ASSOCIATION		
See also Regulation of legal profession		
Model Code, §§14-18, 21-22, 25		
Model Rules, §§19-26		
revised in 2002-2003, §20		
ANTITRUST LAWS		
lawyer advertising, §772		
minimum fee schedules, §§237, 772		
APPOINTED COUNSEL, DUTY OF IN GENERAL,	6.2	
§§132-135		
ARGUMENT		
See Litigation duties of lawyer		
ASSOCIATES		
See Law firms		
ASSOCIATES OF LAWYER, DUTY TO CONTROL,		
§§735-738	5.1(a)-(c)	DR 3-101(A), 4-101(D), 7-107(J)
ASSOCIATION OF COUNSEL		
See also Fees for legal services; Fee splitting		
duty to associate another lawyer, §§177-180	1.1	EC 6-3; DR 6-101
ATTEMPTS TO EXERT PERSONAL INFLUENCE	3.5(a), (b)	EC 7-29 to 32, EC 7-34, 35;
ON TRIBUNAL, §§572, 695-701		DR 7-108, (B)(1), (2), (D)-(G)
ATTORNEY-CLIENT PRIVILEGE		
attorney duty to assert, §329		
client's whereabouts, §344		
co-clients, §§321-323		
confidential communications, §§300, 310-314		
eavesdroppers, §313		
incriminating evidence, §311		
physical evidence, §311		
privileged vs. unprivileged in courts, §300		
waiver by client disclosure, §314		
corporation or government as client, §§315-320		
disclosures within law firm, §§306-308	1.6(a)	EC 4-2, 4-3
doctrine of, §§299, 309		DR 4-101(A)
duty to safeguard, §308	5.1, 5.3(a)	EC 4-2, 4-5; DR 4-101(D)
exceptions to privilege		
court order, §332	1.6(b)(6)	DR 4-101(C)(2)
disclosures within law firm, §§306-308	1.6(a)	EC 4-2, 4-3
future crime or fraud, §§325-327		
lawyer conduct or fee collection, §328		
identity of client, §§341-342		
necessary elements, §310		
professional duty of confidentiality		DR 4-101(a)
compared, §§299, 338, 341-353		
waiver, §§314, 334-337		
client's subsequent disclosure, §314		
communication in issue, §337		
inadvertent disclosure, §336	4.4(b)	
when privilege applies, §§301-305		
after client's death, §305		
after employment ends, §304	1.6(a)	EC 4-6

Subject	Model Rules	ABA Code
potential client, §§302-303	1.18(b), (c)	EC 4-1
wrongful order to disclose, §§330-333	1.6(b)(6)	DR 4-101(C)(2)

ATTORNEY'S OATH, §55

AUTHORITY OF LAWYER
admissions, §§170-171
dismissal without prejudice, §164
procedural matters, §169   1.2(a)
settlement or compromise, §§160-162

B

BAR ADMISSION
See Admission to practice

BAR ASSOCIATIONS
See American Bar Association

BAR EXAMINATION, §§36-38, 61

BEQUEST BY CLIENT TO LAWYER, §§384-390
See also Conflicts of interest   1.8(c)

C

CANDOR, DUTY OF
See also Honesty in communication with others;
     Litigation duties of lawyer

Subject	Model Rules	ABA Code
advice to client, §§502-504	2.1	EC 7-8
as evaluator, §§520-533	2.3	
in general, §590	3.3(a)(1)	DR 7-102(B)
legal consequences of client's conduct, §509	1.2(d)	EC 7-5
nonlegal considerations, §504	2.1	
to court, §§591-623	3.3	
adverse authority, duty to disclose, §§596-600	3.3(a)(2)	EC 7-25; DR 7-106(B)(1)
client's false testimony, §§604, 607, 611	3.3(a)(3)	DR 7-102(B)(1)
correcting material misstatements, §594	3.3(a)(1)	
disclosing fraud upon the court, §619	3.3(b)	
discovery, §593		
false testimony of witness, §§604-606, 608-611	3.3(a)(3)	DR 7-102(B)(2)
harmful facts need not be disclosed, §§592-594	1.6	DR 4-101
intent to commit perjury, §§612-618	3.3(b)	
knowing mistatement of law, §595	3.3(a)(1)	
pleadings, §591		

CANONS, PURPOSE AND FUNCTION OF, §§15-18

CARE, DUTY OF
See Competence, duty of

CHARACTER REQUIREMENTS FOR ADMISSION,

Subject	Model Rules	ABA Code
§§39-56	8.1	EC 1-2, 1-6; DR 1-101
concealment or false statements, §52	8.1	DR 1-101
crimes, §§48-51		
investigation of, §§40-47		
moral turpitude, crimes involving, §48		
past conduct, §47		
political activity, §§54-56		
references from lawyers, §57	1.6	

Subject	Model Rules	ABA Code
rehabilitation, **§53**		
CITIZENSHIP AS REQUIREMENT FOR ADMISSION, §31		
CLIENT'S TRUST ACCOUNT, §§201-204	1.15(a)-(c)	DR 9-102(A)
CLIENTS		
See also Employment; Fee for legal services; Funds of client; Indigent parties, representation of		
attorney-client privilege, **§§299-337**	1.18(a)-(c), 6.1	EC 4-1 to 4-5; DR 4-101
authority of		
appeals, **§166**		
criminal cases, **§165**		
discharge of lawyer, **§§287-298**	1.16(a)(3)	DR 2-110(B)(4)
client liability for fees, **§§291-297**. *See also* Fee for legal services		
continuing duties of lawyer, **§290**		
court refusal of, **§289**		
irrevocable clause void, **§288**		
unconditional right, **§287**		
settlement or compromise, **§§160-164**	1.2(a)	
dismissal of case, **§§160, 163-164**		
ratification, **§162**		
ultimate decisions, **§§158-159**	1.2(a)	EC 7-7
commingling of funds of, **§202**	1.5(b)	DR 9-102(A)(1)
confidences of		
diminished capacity of, **§§172-174**	1.14(a), (b)	EC 7-12
perjury of, **§§601-619**	3.3(a), (b)	DR 7-102(B)(1)
property, protection of, **§209**	1.15(a)	DR 9-102(B)
secrets of. *See* Confidentiality, professional duty of	1.6	DR 1-101
CO-COUNSEL		
See Association of counsel		
CODE OF PROFESSIONAL RESPONSIBILITY, §§14-18, 25		
COMMINGLING OF FUNDS, §202	1.15(b)	DR 9-102(A)(1)
COMMUNICATION, DUTY OF, §§195-197	1.4	
COMMUNICATION WITH		
corporations, **§§539-542**		
former employees, **§542**		
government agencies, **§§541, 543-545**	4.2	DR 7-104(A)(1)
judicial officers, **§§698-701, 959-961**	3.5(b)	DR 7-110(B)(1)-(4); CJC 3B(7)(a), (d)
jurors, **§§702-709**	3.5(a), (c)	EC 7-25, 7-29 to 7-31
one of adverse interests, **§§534-538**	4.2, 4.3	DR 7-104
opposing party, threatening criminal prosecution, **§§552-555**		DR 7-105(A)
persons represented by counsel prohibition, **§§534-545**	4.2	DR 7-104(A)(1)
persons unrepresented by counsel, **§§546-548**	4.3	DR 7-104(A)(2)
represented criminal defendant, **§544**		
Justice Department efforts, **§545**		
third party, **§§549-551**	4.4	
witnesses, **§§626-633**	3.4(b), (e), 4.4	EC 7-28; 7-106(C); DR 7-109
COMMUNIST PARTY MEMBERSHIP, §56		

Subject	Model Rules	ABA Code
COMPENSATION		
See also Fee for legal services; Fee splitting		
for recommendation of employment, prohibition against,		
§§816-817	1.5(e)(1)	DR 2-107(A)
from third person, §442	1.8(f)	DR 5-107(A)
COMPETENCE, DUTY OF, §§175-186, 889-898	1.1	EC 6-3 to-6-5; DR 6-101
ability to represent client, §§177-180	1.1	DR 6-101(A)(1); EC 6-3, EC 6-4
association of counsel, §179	1.1	EC 6-3
duty of care	1.1	EC 6-5
adequate preparation, §§181-183	1.1	DR 6-101(A)(2)
more than "nonnegligence," §183		EC 6-5
limitation on liability, prohibition against, §§184, 926-928	1.8(h)	DR 6-102
malpractice, §§184, 889-898		.
setting aside judgments, §§185-186		
CONFIDENTIALITY, PROFESSIONAL DUTY OF		
attorney-client privilege compared, §§299, 338		
client's whereabouts, §§344-346		
doctrine, §§299, 339-340	1.6(a)	DR 4-101(A)
exceptions to duty		
client consent, §357	1.6(b)	
co-clients, §357	1.6(b)	
court-compelled testimony, §358		
fee collection, §§350, 357	1.6(b)(5)	
future crime or fraud, §§361-365	1.6(b)(1)	DR 4-101(C)(3)
possible mandatory disclosure, §365	4.1(b)	
substantial financial injury, §364	1.6(b)(2), (3)	
generally known information, §359		
lawyer self-protection, §§350, 357	1.6(b)(5)	
securing advice about duties, §360	1.6(b)(4)	
fee arrangements, §§347-348		
identity of client, §§341-343		
knowledge of criminal physical evidence, §353		
Lawyer Assistance Program, §880	8.3(c)	
lawyer's possession of physical evidence, §352		
lawyer's self-protection or fee collection, §350	1.6(b)(5)	
lawyer's use of confidential information, §§354-356	1.8(b)	
third parties' presence, §349		
CONFLICTS OF INTEREST		
See also Imputed disqualification of affiliated lawyers;		
Multiple clients		
basic principles, §§366-368		
concurrent conflicting interests of clients, §§394-440.		
See also Multiple clients, representation of	1.7	EC 5-14; DR 5-105
consequences of, §§371-373		
current and former clients, §§460-468	1.9(a), (b)	
identification of, §§366-367	1.7(a)	DR 5-101(A), (B)
imputed disqualification, §§469-501	1.10(a)	DR 5-105(D)
informed consent, §§369-370	1.0(e), 1.7(b)	DR 5-105(A), (C)
lawyer's personal interests affecting loyalty, §§374-393	1.7(b)	DR 5-101(A)
third persons, interests of, §§441-459		
CONSENT OF CLIENT, REQUIREMENT OF		
See also Conflicts of interest		

Subject	Model Rules	ABA Code
acceptance of employment though interests conflict, §§369-370, 399, 404, 468	1.0(e), 1.7(b), 1.9(a)	DR 5-101(A), 5-105(A), (C)
association of lawyer, §179	1.1	EC 6-3
compensation from third party, §442	1.8(f)	
corporate clients, §433	1.13(g)	
criminal defendants, §427	1.8(g)	
evaluations, §524	2.3(b)	
former government employment, §493	1.11	
limiting scope of representation, §155		
lump sum settlement, §425	1.8(g)	
personal injury litigation, §410		EC 5-17
referral fees, §820	1.5(e)(2)	
revelation of client's confidences, §357	1.6(b)	
withdrawal from employment, §279	1.16	DR 2-110(C)(5)

CONSENT OF TRIBUNAL TO LAWYER'S WITHDRAWAL, REQUIREMENT OF, §282	1.16(c)	

CONTEMPT SANCTIONS
See Discipline of lawyers

CONTINGENT FEE

advantages, §222		
discharge of lawyer, §§294-297		
maximum limits, §225		
minors' claims, §226		
prohibited		
criminal cases, §§230-232	1.5(d)(2)	DR 2-106(C)
domestic relations, §§227-229	1.5(d)(1)	EC 2-20
quantum meruit recovery, §234		
securing favorable legislation, §233		
reasonableness, §224		
requirements, §223		
witness's testimony, §629		

CONTRACT OF EMPLOYMENT

accepting employment. *See* Accepting employment; Conflicts of Interest		
fees. *See* Fee for legal services		
formal contractual duties, §§175-209		
client property, §§200-209	1.15	DR 9-102
communication, §§195-197	1.4(a), (b)	
competence, §§176-186	1.1	DR 6-101
confidentiality, §198. *See also* Confidentiality, professional duty of		
diligence, §§187-189	1.3	EC 6-4
loyalty, §199		
zealous representation, §§190-194	3.1	EC 7-3, 7-4; DR 7-101(A)
limitation on liability, §§184, 926-928	1.8(h)	DR 6-102
noncompetition agreement, §756	5.6(a)	DR 2-108(A)
scope of representation. *See* Scope and objectives of representation		
spheres of authority. *See* Authority of lawyer		

CONTROVERSY OVER FEE, AVOIDING, §§211-215, 248-250	1.5(b)	EC 2-19, 2-23

CORPORATE LAW FIRM
See Law firms

Subject	Model Rules	ABA Code
CORPORATIONS		
See also Multiple clients, representation of		
counsel for, §§431-437	1.13(a)-(d), (g)	EC 5-18
unauthorized practice, §§108-112		
COUNSEL, DESIGNATION AS		
See Law firms		
COURTESY		
obligation, in general, §650	3.5(d)	EC 7-10; DR 7-106(C)(6)
toward court, §§651-653, 657-658	3.5(c), (d)	EC 7-36; DR 7-106(C)(6), 7-106(A)
toward opposing counsel, §§654-656	3.2, 3.4(c)	EC 7-37, 7-38; DR 7-106(C)(5)
COURTS		
See also Judicial conduct of state judges, Judicial conduct		
of federal judges		
appointment of lawyer as counsel, §§132-135	6.2	EC 2-29
courtesy, known customs of, §655	3.4(c)	DR 7-106(C)(5); 9-101(C)
personal influence, prohibitions against exerting,		
§§488, 566, 658, 695-701	3.5(a), (b)	DR 7-110(A), (B)(2)-(4),
		DR 8-101(A)(1), (2)
CRIMINAL CONDUCT		
as basis for discipline of lawyer, §§831-836	8.4	
duty to reveal information as to, §§325, 361-365	1.6(b)(1)-(3), 4.1(b)	DR 4-101(C)(3)
providing counsel for those accused of, §132	6.2	EC 2-29
CRIMINAL DEFENDANT, REPRESENTATION OF		
appointment as counsel, §132	6.2	EC 2-29
contingency fees prohibited, §§230-232	1.5(d)(2)	EC 2-20; DR 2-106(C)
important decisions by client, §§165-166	1.2(a)	
ineffective assistance of counsel, §185		
multiple clients' consent, §427	1.8(g)	
plea bargains, §165	1.2(a)	
zealous representation, §§577-580	3.1	
CRITICISM OF JUDGES AND ADMINISTRATIVE		
OFFICIALS, §§570-571	8.2	EC 8-6; DR 8-102(B)

D

Subject	Model Rules	ABA Code
DECEASED LAWYER		
payment to estate of, §754	5.4(a)(1), (2)	DR 3-102(A)(1)
use of name by law firm, §743	7.5	DR 2-102(B)
DEFENSE AGAINST ACCUSATION BY CLIENT; MAY		
DISCLOSE CONFIDENCES,		
§§328, 357	1.6(b)	
DELAYING ADMINISTRATION OF JUSTICE, §§574,		
584-588	3.2	DR 7-102(A)(1)
DELEGATION BY LAWYER OF TASKS, §§730-738, 741	5.1(a)-(c), 5.3	
DIFFERING INTERESTS		
See Conflicts of interest; Multiple clients, representation of		
DILIGENCE, DUTY OF, §§187-189	1.3	EC 6-4
DISBARMENT		
as disciplinary sanction, §844		
effect of in other jurisdictions, §§882-884	8.5(a)	

Subject	Model Rules	ABA Code

Subject	Model Rules	ABA Code

E

EDUCATION
required for bar applicant, §§33-35

EMPLOYEES OF LAWYER

Subject	Model Rules	ABA Code
delegation of tasks, §§735-738	5.1(a)-(c)	
duty of lawyer to control, §§737-738, 741	5.1(b), (c), 5.3	
engaging in "solicitation," prohibition against, §§787-788	7.3	
payment to, §§752-753	5.4(a)	DR 3-102(A)

EMPLOYMENT

See also Accepting employment; Imputed disqualification
of affiliated lawyers
acceptance of. *See* Accepting employment
contract of. *See* Contract of employment
duty to accept. *See* Accepting employment

Subject	Model Rules	ABA Code
frivolous claims, §§150, 575-580	3.1	DR 2-109(A)(2)
manner of seeking. *See also* Advertising		
passive standard, §§769-773		EC 2-6
solicitation. *See* Solicitation of business		
public, retirement from, §§486-501	1.11	DR 9-101
rejection of. *See also* Accepting employment		
impairment of lawyer, §145	1.16(a)(2)	
lawyer not competent in matter, §146	1.1	EC 2-30
when client already represented, §148		EC 2-30
when purpose is harassment, §149	1.16	DR 2-109(A)(1)
when violation of law involved, §144	1.16(a)(1)	
withdrawal from. *See* Termination of attorney-client		
relationship		

ENFORCEMENT OF PROFESSIONAL RESPONSIBILITY
See Misconduct; Discipline of lawyers

**ETHICAL CONSIDERATIONS, PURPOSE AND
        FUNCTIONS OF, §17**

EVALUATOR, LAWYER AS, §§520-533   2.3
See also Honesty in communication with others

EXPENSES OF CLIENT, ADVANCING OR GUARANTEEING

Subject	Model Rules	ABA Code
PAYMENT OF	1.8(e)	DR 5-103(B)

See Advancing funds to clients

F

FEDERAL CONFLICT OF INTEREST ACT, §§498-501

FEDERAL PRACTICE
See Admission to practice

FEE FOR LEGAL SERVICES

Subject	Model Rules	ABA Code
agreement as to, §§211-215	1.5(b)	EC 2-19
ambiguities, §215		
presumption of undue influence, §214		
required subjects of, §212	1.5(b)	
time of, §211	1.5(b)	
writing preferable, §213	1.5(b)	EC 2-19
amount of		
arbitration, §219	1.5	

Subject	Model Rules	ABA Code
FRAUD		
attorney-client privilege, effect on, **§§325-327**		
confidentiality exception, **§§361-365**	**1.6(b), 4.1(b)**	
duty to reveal, **§§365, 519, 619**	**3.3(b), 4.1(b)**	
termination of attorney-client relationship, grounds for, **§275**	**1.16(b)(2), (3)**	
FRIVOLOUS POSITION, AVOIDING, §§150, 575-580	**3.1**	**DR 2-109(A)(2), DR 7-102(A)(2)**
FUNDS OF CLIENT		**DR 9-102(A), (B)**
commingling, prohibition against, **§§201-204**	**1.15**	**DR 9-102(A)(1)**
deposit in separate bank account, **§201**	**1.15(a)**	**DR 9-102(A)**
disputed, **§207**	**1.15(d)**	**DR 9-102(A)(2)**
expenses advanced, **§204**	**1.15(c)**	
funds belonging to both client and attorney, receipt of, **§§205-208**	**1.15(d)**	**DR 9-102(A)(2)**
lawyer as fiduciary of, **§208**	**1.15(e)**	
location of accounts, **§203**	**1.15(a)**	**DR 9-102(A)(1)**
protection of, in general, **§200**	**1.15**	**DR 9-102**
record keeping, duty of, **§201**	**1.15(a)**	**DR 9-102(A)**
third party, potentially belonging to, **§208**	**1.15(e)**	
undisputed fee, **§206**	**1.15(d)**	

G

Subject	Model Rules	ABA Code
GIFT TO LAWYER BY CLIENT, §§384-389	**1.8(c)**	**EC 5-5**
GIFT TO TRIBUNAL OFFICER OR EMPLOYEE, §§695-697	**3.5(a)**	**EC 7-34, DR 7-110(A)**
See also Judicial conduct of state judges		
GOODWILL, SALE OF, §823	**1.7**	
GOVERNMENT ATTORNEY, §§485-501		
See also Imputed disqualification of affiliated lawyers; Prosecutors, duties of		
GROUP AND PREPAID LEGAL SERVICES		
ABA Code limitations, **§767**		**DR 2-103(D)(4)**
constitutional protection of, **§§761-763**		
Model Rules—no limitations, **§764**		
types of		
closed panel, **§765**		
open panel, **§766**		
GUARDIAN, APPOINTMENT OF, §173	**1.14(b)**	

H

Subject	Model Rules	ABA Code
HARASSMENT, DUTY TO AVOID LITIGATION INVOLVING, §§149, 271	**3.1**	**DR 2-109(A)(1), 2-110(B)(1)**
HOLDING OUT		
as limiting practice, **§§806-808**	**7.4(a)**	**DR 2-105(A)(2)**
as partners, **§729**	**7.5(d)**	**DR 2-102(C)**
as specialist, **§§799-805**	**7.4(b)-(d)**	**DR 2-105(A)(1), (3)**
HONESTY IN COMMUNICATION WITH OTHERS		
See also Candor, duty of		
basic obligation, **§511**	**4.1(a)**	**DR 7-102(A)(5)**

Subject	Model Rules	ABA Code
communications with others, §§511-519	4.1(a)	DR 7-102(A)
duty to come forward, §§512-515	4.1(b)	DR 7-102(A)(3)
confidential information exception—substantial		
financial harm, §515	1.6	
evaluator, lawyer as,	2.3	
audit letters, §§529-533	2.3	
confidential information, §524	2.3(c)	
duty of care, §522		
opinions to nonclients, §§520-524	2.3	
when opinion adversely affects client, §523	2.3(b)	
negotiations, §§516-519	4.1	
widely disseminated information, §§525-528		
due diligence required, §527		
securities cases, §§526-527		
tax shelters, §528		

HUSBAND AND WIFE ATTORNEYS, §§479-481
See also Imputed disqualification of affiliated lawyers

I

IDENTITY OF CLIENT
duty not to disclose, §§341-343

Subject	Model Rules	ABA Code
ILLEGAL CONDUCT, AS CAUSE FOR DISCIPLINE,		
§§831-837	8.4	DR 1-102(A)(4)

IMPROPER INFLUENCES
See also Judicial conduct of state judges

Subject	Model Rules	ABA Code
gift or loan to judicial officer, §§695-697	3.5(a)	EC 7-34; DR 7-110(A)

IMPROPER PURPOSE, USE OF LEGAL PROCESS FOR

Subject	Model Rules	ABA Code
delay, §§584-588	3.2	
threatening criminal prosecution, §§552-555		EC 7-21; DR 7-105(A)
unfounded case, §§575-580	3.1	DR 7-102(A)(2)

IMPROVEMENT OF LEGAL SYSTEM, §§556-573

Subject	Model Rules	ABA Code
judicial office, running for, §573	8.2(b)	DR 8-103(A)
legal services or law reform organizations, §§562-564	6.3, 6.4	
selection of judges, involvement in, §§568-572	7.6, 8.2	EC 8-6; DR 8-102(B)
service in public office, §§565-567	3.5(a)	EC 8-8; DR 8-101(A)(1), (2)
supporting legislation, §§556-561	3.9	EC 7-15, 7-16, 8-2, 8-9

IMPUTED DISQUALIFICATION OF AFFILIATED LAWYERS

Subject	Model Rules	ABA Code
appeals, §482		
Federal Conflict of Interest Act, §§498-501		
criminal sanctions, §498		
no imputation to firm, §501		
general rule, §469	1.10(a)	DR 5-105
government legal offices, §478	1.0(c), 1.11(d)	
lawyers related as spouses, §§479-481	1.7	
legal aid clinics, §440	6.5(b)	
present and former government lawyers, §§485-501		
ABA Code—substantial responsibility, §§486-488		DR 9-101(B), (C)
coming from private practice, §496	1.11(d)(1), (2), (i)	
confidential government information, §§493-495	1.11(b), (c), (e)	
Model Rules, §489		
negotiating for private employment, §497	1.11(b)(2)(ii)	

Subject	Model Rules	ABA Code
settlement discussions ex parte, §961		CJC 3B(7)(d)
political activity		
all judicial candidates, §§1029-1032		CJC 5A(3)
ban on personal views unconstitutional, §1031		CJC 5A(3)(d)
appointed office, §§1038-1040		CJC 5B
judges and judicial candidates, §§1022-1028		
nonjudicial office, running for, §1027		CJC 5A(2)
political endorsements, §1024		CJC 5A(1)(b)
permitted activities, §1028		CJC 5D
political fund raising, §1026		CJC 5A(1)(d), (e)
political offices, §1023		CJC 5A(1)(a)
speeches for political organizations, §1025		CJC 5A(1)(c)
judicial candidates for public elections, §§1033-1037		CJC 5C(1)
permissible activities, §§1033-1034		CJC 5(C)(1)(a), (b)
solicitation of campaign contributions, §§1035-1037		CJC 5(C)(2)
JURORS AND COURT OFFICIALS		
arguments before, §§643-645	3.4(e)	DR 7-106(C)
communications with judge, §§698-701	3.5(b)	DR 7-110(B)(2)-(4)
communications with juror, §§702-709	3.5(a)	EC 7-29; DR 7-108
after trial, §§705-709	3.5(c)	DR 7-108(D)
before trial, §703		EC 7-30; DR 7-108(E)
during trial, §704		DR 7-108(b)(1)
juror's family, §709		EC 7-31; DR 7-108(F)
gifts or loans, §§695-697	3.5(a)	EC 7-34; DR 7-110(A)
political contribution exception, §697	8.4(f)	DR 7-110(A)
improper contacts by lawyer, §§694-709		
jury tampering, duty to reveal, §619	3.3(b)	
JUVENILE COURT PROCEEDINGS, §669		

K

Subject	Model Rules	ABA Code
"KICKBACKS," §390	1.8(f)	DR 5-107(A)(2)
KNOWLEDGE OF INTENDED CRIME, REVEALING, §§361-365		
See also Confidentiality, professional duty of	1.6(b)(1)	DR 4-101(C)(3)

L

Subject	Model Rules	ABA Code
LAW FIRMS		
associates, §§730-731		
law-related services, §§757-758	5.7(a), (b)	
name of, §§742-746		
deceased or retired members, §743	7.5	DR 2-102(B)
law corporations, §746		DR 2-102(B)
lawyers holding public office, §745	7.5(c)	DR 2-102(B)
multistate firms, §744	7.5(b)	DR 2-102(D)
noncompetition agreements prohibited, §756	5.6(a)	DR 2-108(A)
nonlawyers, association with, §§747-750		
prohibited if law is practiced, §§748-750	5.4(b), (d)	DR 3-103(A), DR 5-107(C)
of counsel, §732		DR 2-102(A)(4)
paralegals, §733	5.3	EC 3-6
partners, §§727-729		
professional law corporations, §734		
sale of goodwill with practice, §823	1.17	

Subject	Model Rules	ABA Code
sharing fees with nonlawyer, §§751-755	5.4(a)	DR 3-102
exceptions, §§752-755	5.4(a)(2)-(4)	
subordinate lawyer, duties of, §§739-740	5.2(a), (b), 5.3	
supervisory duties, §§735-738, 741	5.1(a)-(c), 5.3	
nonlawyer assistants, §741	5.3	

LAW-RELATED SERVICES, §§757-758	5.7(a), (b)	

LAW SCHOOLS, ACCREDITATION, §34		

LAW STUDENTS ENGAGED IN LIMITED PRACTICE, §107		

LAWYER-CLIENT EMPLOYMENT RELATIONSHIP

Subject	Model Rules	ABA Code
See also Contract of Employment		
accepting court appointments, §§132-135	6.2	EC 2-29
valid rejections, §133		
as agent, §120		
as fiduciary, §121		
contract basis, §119		
duty to reject cases, §§143-150		
client already represented, §148		EC 2-30
disciplinary violation, §144	1.16(a)(1)	
harassment motive, §149	4.4	DR 2-109(A)(1)
impaired physical/mental condition, §145	1.16(a)(2)	
lacks competency in matter, §146	1.1	EC 2-30
personal feelings, §147	6.2(c)	EC 2-30
unsupportable legal position, §150	3.1	DR 2-109(a)(2)
ethical duty of pro bono services, §§127-131		EC 2-26
ABA standards, §§128-130	6.1	EC 2-25
state standards, §131		
methods of formation, §§122-125		
by consent, §123		
client's reasonable belief, §124		
court appointment, §125		
no duty to accept, §126		
prospective clients, duties to, §§136-142		
competent legal advice, §142		
confidential information, §§137-140	1.18(b)-(d)	
protect client's property, §114	1.15(a)	
scope of representation, §§151-157. *See also* Scope and objectives of representation		

LAY INTERMEDIARY, EMPLOYMENT BY, §443	5.4(C)	DR 2-107(B)

LEGAL AID OFFICES, WORKING WITH, §§763-766	5.4(c)	EC 2-25, 2-33; DR 2-103 (D)(1)(a)-(d)
conflicts of interest special rule, §§438-440	6.5(a), (b)	
lawyer's membership in, §§562-564	6.3, 6.4	
referrals from, §§793, 822	7.3(d)	DR 2-103(c)

LEGAL ASSISTANCE PROGRAMS, §880	8.3(c)	

LEGAL DOCUMENTS OF CLIENT, DUTY TO SAFEGUARD, §209	1.15(a)	DR 9-102(B)

LEGAL SERVICES, FORM OF		
association with nonlawyers, §§747-755. *See also* Fee splitting, with nonlawyer; Employment; Law firms; Partnership	5.4(a), (b), (d)	DR 3-102(A)(1), (3), 3-103(A), 5-107(C)

Subject	Model Rules	ABA Code
group legal services, in general, §§755-764		
See also Group and prepaid legal services		
legal aid offices. *See* Legal aid offices, working with		
prepaid legal services. *See* Group and prepaid legal		
services	5.4(c), 7.3(d)	DR 2-103(D)(4), 5-107(B)
specialization. *See* Specialization		

Subject	Model Rules	ABA Code
LEGAL SYSTEM, DUTY TO IMPROVE, §§556-573		
client seeking legislation, §§556-558	3.9	EC 7-15, 7-16
judicial office, running for, §573. *See also* Judicial		
conduct of state judges	8.2(b)	DR 8-103(A)
lawyers in public service, §§565-567	3.5(a)	EC 8-8; DR 8-101(A)(1), (2)
legal services or law reform organizations, §§568-572	6.3, 6.4	
selection of judges, participation in, §§568-572	7.6, 8.2	EC 8-6; DR 8-102(B)
support of public interest legislation, §§559-561		EC 8-1, 8-2, 8-9

Subject	Model Rules	ABA Code
LEGISLATURE		
improper influence upon, §§565-566	3.5(a)	EC 8-8; DR 8-101(A)(1), (2)
proposal of public interest laws, §§559-561		EC 8-1, 8-2, 8-9
regulation of fees, §§239-241		
regulation of practice, §5		
representation of client before, §§556-558	3.9	EC 7-15, 7-16
securing favorable legislation, contingency fee for, §233		
serving as member of, §§565-567	3.5(a)	EC 8-8; DR 8-101(A)(1), (2)

Subject	Model Rules	ABA Code
LIABILITY TO CLIENT		
See Malpractice		

Subject	Model Rules	ABA Code
LIENS, ATTORNEY'S, §§252-265		

Subject	Model Rules	ABA Code
LIMITED PRACTICE, HOLDING OUT AS HAVING,		
§§806-808	7.4(a)	DR 2-105(A)(2)

Subject	Model Rules	ABA Code
LITIGATION DUTIES OF LAWYER		
See also Advancing funds to clients; Jurors and court		
officials; Prosecutors, duties of;		
Witness, lawyer acting as		
abuse of discovery, §589	3.4(d)	
assert only meritorious claims, §§574-583	3.1	DR 7-102(A)(2)
criminal cases distinguished, §§577-580	3.1	
duty to assert "technicalities," §581		DR 7-101(B)(1)
sanctions, §§582-583		
coaching witnesses, §630		
dignity requirement, §650		
disruption of tribunal, §§651-653	3.5(d)	DR 7-106(A), (C)(6)
evidence, suppression of, §624	3.4(a)	DR 7-109(A)
expedite, duty to, §§584-588	3.2	DR 7-102(A)(1)
Federal Rule 11, §586		
government lawyers, §§723-724		EC 7-14
honesty, duty of, §§590-623. *See also* Candor, duty of	3.3(a)(1)	DR 7-102(B)(3), (5)
adverse legal authority—affirmative duty, §§596-600		
confidential information, disclosure of, §§611, 616,		
622	3.3(b), (c)	
disclosure of crime or fraud upon court, §619	3.3(b)	
ex parte proceedings, §623	3.3(d)	
false evidence of client or witness, §§601-618	3.3(a)(2)	EC 7-23; DR 7-106(B)(1)
civil case, §602	3.3(a)(3)	

Subject	Model Rules	ABA Code
criminal case, §§603-611	3.3(a)(3)	DR 7-101(B)(1), (2)
general rule, §590	3.3(a)(1)	DR 7-102(B)(3), (5)
harmful facts, no disclosure duty, §§592-594	1.6, 3.3(a)(1)	DR 4-101
pleadings, §591		
when duty ends, §621	3.3(c)	
inadvertently sent document, receipt of, §§634-636	4.4(b)	
inducing favorable testimony, §§626-629	3.4(b)	EC 7-28; DR 7-109(C)
expert witnesses, §628		
local customs and practice, notice of noncompliance, §655	3.4(c)	DR 7-106(C)(5)
obstruction of access to potential witnesses, §625	3.4(f)	DR 7-109(B)
opposing counsel, conduct toward, §654	3.2, 3.4(d)	EC 7-37, 7-38
physical appearance, §657		
settlement restricting right to practice, §659	5.6(b)	DR 2-108(B)
treatment of adverse witnesses at trial, §§631-633	3.4(e), 4.4	DR 7-106(C)(2), (4)
trial publicity limitations, §§660-670	3.6	DR 7-107
constitutional issues, §§662-663		
criminal proceedings, §§664-669		
disciplinary or juvenile proceedings, §669	3.6	DR 7-107(F)
general rule, §§661-663	3.6(a)	
prosecutors, special duty of, §667	3.8(f)	
purpose, §660		
trial strategy and tactics, §§637-649		EC 7-25
appeal to emotion or prejudice, §§643-645	3.4(e)	DR 7-106(E)(1)
lawyer's personal knowledge or opinion, §642	3.4(e)	DR 7-106(C)(3), (4)
unsubstantiated matters, reference to, §§638-641	3.4(e)	DR 7-106(C)(1)
violation of procedural and evidentiary rules, §§646-649	3.4(c)	DR 7-106(C)(7)
constitutional limitation, §649		
sanctions, §648		
test validity of, §647	3.4(c)	EC 7-25
undue solicitude toward court, §658		EC 7-36

LIVING EXPENSES OF CLIENT, ADVANCES TO CLIENT OF, §§678-680

LOAN TO CLIENT BY ATTORNEY
See Advancing funds to client

LOAN TO JUDICIAL OFFICER
See Judicial conduct of state judges; Gift to tribunal officer or employee

LOYALTY, DUTY OF
See Conflicts of interest

LUMP-SUM SETTLEMENTS, §§424-426	1.8(g)	DR 5-106

See also Multiple clients, representation of

M

MALPRACTICE		
attempts to limit liability generally prohibited, §§926-929	1.8(h)	DR 6-102

breach of contract, §§915-917

breach of fiduciary duty, §§918-920

intentional torts, §914

negligence, §§889-912

nonclients, liability to, §§921-925

purpose, §885

reimbursement of client, §929

Subject	Model Rules	ABA Code
settling malpractice claim, **§928**		
violation of professional rules, effect of, **§§886-888**		
MEDICAL EXPENSES, §673	1.8(e)	DR 5-103(B)
MENTAL COMPETENCE OF CLIENT, EFFECT ON **REPRESENTATION, §§172-173**	1.14(a)	EC 7-12
MISCONDUCT		
See also Discipline of lawyers		
of lawyer, duty to reveal to proper officials, **§§875-881**	8.3(a)-(c)	DR 1-103(A), (B)
MODEL RULES OF PROFESSIONAL CONDUCT		
admiralty practice, **§801**	7.4(c)	
advancing funds to client, **§§671-680**	1.8(e)	
advertising, **§§769-786, 797, 806, 808**	7.1, 7.2(a), 7.4(a)-(d)	
appointed counsel, **§§132, 157**	1.5(c), 6.2	
arbitration, **§219**	1.5	
attorney-client privilege, **§§798-805**	1.6	
bar admissions, **§§52, 57**	8.1	
board member of legal services organization, **§459**	6.3	
client's property, protection of, **§§141, 200**	1.15	
communication with client, **§§195-196**	1.4(a), (b)	
competent legal advice, **§176**	1.1	
confidences and secrets, **§§299-300, 338, 340**	1.6, 4.1	
contingent fees, **§221**	1.5	
contributions to obtain favoritism, **§542**	7.6	
corporate counsel, **§§431-438**	1.13(a)-(d), (g)	
delaying litigation, **§585**	3.2	
diligence, **§187**	1.3	
disqualification of partners, **§476**	1.10	
disrupting tribunal, **§651**	3.5(d)	
embarrassing a witness, **§632**	4.4	
employment, contract of, **§152**	1.2	
evaluator, lawyer as, **§§520-521**	2.3	
fee agreements, **§§211-218, 221-226**	1.5	
government attorneys, **§§478, 490-501, 722**	1.11	
group plans, **§764**	5.4(c), 7.3(d)	
judicial office, running for, **§573**	8.2(b)	
law reform, **§562**	6.3, 6.4	
lawyer as witness, **§§682, 691**	3.6, 3.7	
lawyer's interests adverse to client, **§§374-391**	1.7(b), 1.8	
malpractice liability, **§§888, 921, 927**	1.8(h), 1.18	
misconduct by other attorneys, **§881**	8.3(a)	
multiple clients, **§§368, 395-398, 433**	1.7, 1.13	
payments to witnesses, **§§627-628**	3.4(b)	
perjured testimony, **§§601, 608, 613**	3.3	
pro bono work, **§129**	6.1(a)	
prosecutors, special duty of, **§§711-721**	3.8(a)-(e)	
prospective client, duties to, **§136**	1.18	
publication rights, **§378**	1.8(d)	
publicity, **§§660-661, 777-780, 799, 805**	3.6, 7.1, 7.2(a), (c)	
reasonable fee, **§§216, 224**	1.5(a)	
represented person, communication with, **§534**	4.2	
solicitation, **§788**	7.3	
specialized practice, **§§798-805**	7.4(a)-(d)	
successive clients, **§462**	1.9	

Subject	Model Rules	ABA Code
trade names, §742	7.5(a)	
unauthorized practice, §114	5.5	
unrepresented person, communication with, §§546-548	4.3	

MORAL CHARACTER, REQUIREMENT OF, §39

See also Character requirements for admission	8.1	EC 1-2, 1.6; DR 1-101(B)

MORAL TURPITUDE, CRIME OF AS GROUND FOR DISCIPLINE, §833

See also Character requirements for admission

MULTI-JURISDICTIONAL PRACTICE, §§63-70

See also Pro hac vice appearance	5.5(c)(1)-(3)	

MULTIPLE CLIENTS, REPRESENTATION OF

See also Conflicts of interest; Imputed disqualification of affiliated lawyers

Subject	Model Rules	ABA Code
clients with concurrent conflicting interests, §§394-440	1.7	EC 5-14; DR 5-105
informed consent, §404	1.0(e), 1.7(b)(4)	DR 5-105(C)
nonconsentable conflicts, §§400-403		
adverse parties—same litigation, §401	1.7(b)(3)	
when withdrawal mandatory, §§396-399	1.7	DR 5-105
current and former clients' conflicting interests	1.9(a), (b)	
same litigation, §461	1.9(e)	
substantially related matters, §§462-467	1.9(b)	
waiver by informed consent, §468	1.9(a)	
duty to decline or withdraw, §§399-403	1.7	DR 5-105
informed consent, §§399, 404	1.0(e), 1.7(b)(4)	DR 5-105(C)
litigation matters		
criminal, §§406-409, 427	1.8(g)	
divorce, §§413-417		
insurer and insured, §§447-448, 452-454		
liquidation and reorganization, §§417-419		
lump sum settlements, §§424-426	1.8(g)	DR 5-106
personal injury, §§410-412		EC 5-17
unrelated adversary proceedings, §§420-423	1.7	
inconsistent legal positions, §423		
nonlitigation matters, §§428-440		
borrower and lender, §429		
corporate counsel, §§431-437	1.13(a)-(d), (g)	EC 5-18
insurance settlements, §§449-451. See also Conflicts of interest		
legal aid work, §§438-440	6.5(a), (b)	
testator and fiduciary, §430		

MULTIPLE STATES, REGULATION BY, §9

	8.5(a)	

MULTISTATE LAW FIRMS, §744

	7.5(b)	DR 2-102(D)

MULTISTATE PROFESSIONAL RESPONSIBILITY EXAMINATION, §§26, 36-38

Americans with Disabilities Act, effect of, §38

Model Rules, as amended, tested, §26

N

NAME, USE OF

See Law firms

Subject	Model Rules	ABA Code
NEGLIGENCE OF LAWYER		
See Malpractice		
NEGOTIATIONS, DUTIES IN, §§516-519		
NONMERITORIOUS POSITION, DUTY TO AVOID,	3.1	DR 7-102(A)(2)
§§150, 575-583		
See also Litigation duties of lawyer		

O

Subject	Model Rules	ABA Code
OBJECTIVES OF CLIENT, DUTY TO SEEK		
See Scope and objectives of representation		
"OF COUNSEL" DESIGNATION, §732		DR 2-102(A)(4)
OFFENSIVE TACTICS BY LAWYER		
See Litigation duties of lawyer, trial strategy and tactics		
OPPOSING PARTY, COMMUNICATIONS WITH		
See Adverse party, communications with		

PQ

Subject	Model Rules	ABA Code
"PARTNER," §§727-729		
PARTNERSHIP		
advertising. *See* Advertising		
conflict of interest, §§470-475	1.9(b), 1.10	DR 5-105(D)
deceased member		
payments to estate of, §754	5.4(a)(1), (2)	DR 3-102(A)(1), (2)
use of name, §743	7.5	DR 2-102(B)
holding out as, falsely, §729	7.5(d)	DR 2-102(C)
members licensed in different jurisdictions, §744	7.5(b)	DR 2-102(D)
name, §§742-746	7.5(a)	DR 2-102(B)
noncompetition agreements, §756	5.6(a)	DR 2-108(A)
nonlawyer, with, §§747-755	5.4(b), (d)	DR 3-103(A), 5-107(C)
supervisory duties, §§735, 741	5.1(a), 5.3	
PATENT PRACTITIONER		
admission to practice, §77		
advertising by, §800	7.4(b)	DR 2-105(A)(1)
PAYMENT TO OBTAIN RECOMMENDATION OF		
EMPLOYMENT, PROHIBITION		
AGAINST, §§813, 816-817	1.5(e)(1), (2)	DR 2-107(A)
See also Fee splitting		
PENDING LITIGATION, DISCUSSION OF IN		
MEDIA, §§661-669	3.6	DR 7-107
See also Litigation duties of lawyer		
PERJURY, §§601-618, 622	3.3(a)(3), (b)	DR 7-102(B)(1), (2)
PERSONAL OPINION OF CLIENT'S CAUSE, §642	3.4(e)	DR 7-106(C)(3)
PHYSICAL APPEARANCE OF ATTORNEY		
IN COURT, §657		
PLEA BARGAINING		
and contingent fee prohibition, §231	1.5(d)(2)	EC 2-20; DR 2-106(C)
client's decision, §165	1.2(a)	
multiple clients' consent, §427	1.8(g)	

Subject	Model Rules	ABA Code
POLITICAL ACTIVITY		
See also Judicial conduct of state judges		
candidates for judgeship, **§573**	**8.2(b)**	
contributions to obtain favoritism, **§572**	**7.6**	
effect on admission to practice of law, **§§54-56**		
evaluation of judicial candidates, **§568**		EC 8-6
lawyers in public service, **§§565-567**	**3.5(a)**	EC 8-8; DR 8-101(A)(1), (2)
support of legislation, **§§559-561**		EC 8-1, 8-2, 8-9
PRACTICE OF LAW		
defined		
in general, **§§88-91**		EC 3-5
judicial determinations, **§§92-107**		
unauthorized. See Unauthorized practice of law		
PRESSURE ON LAWYER BY THIRD PERSON		
See Conflicts of interest		
PRIVILEGE, ATTORNEY-CLIENT		
See Attorney-client privilege		
PRO BONO SERVICES, §129	**6.1(a)**	
PRO HAC VICE APPEARANCE		
federal courts, **§80**		
foreign lawyers and Supreme Court, **§84**		
state courts, **§§66-68**		
PROFESSIONAL LAW CORPORATIONS, §§734, 746		
See also Law firms		
PROFESSIONAL NOTICES		
See Advertising		
PROFIT SHARING WITH LAY EMPLOYEES,		
AUTHORIZATION OF, §753	**5.4(a)(3)**	DR 3-102(A)(3)
PROPERTY OF CLIENT, HANDLING		EC 9-5; DR 9-102(A), (B)(2)-(4)
See also Funds of client		
identification and labeling, **§209**	**1.15(a)**	DR 9-102(B)
PROSECUTORS, DUTIES OF		
See also Litigation duties of lawyer		
communications with represented defendant, **§§544-545**	**4.2**	
duty to supervise police, **§551**		
limitations on trial publicity, **§§665-667**	**3.6(a), (d), 3.8(f)**	DR 7-107(B)
special duties, **§§710-716**		
dual role during trial, **§716**		
must help accused obtain counsel, **§715**	**3.8(b)**	
no waiver of pretrial rights, **§714**	**3.8(c)**	
probable cause required, **§713**	**3.8(a)**	DR 7-103(A)
restraint in exercising power, **§712**		
witnesses and evidence, duties towards, **§§717-721**		
defense access to government witnesses, **§720**		
disclose beneficial defense evidence, **§718**	**3.8(d)**	DR 7-103(B)
prohibition of subpoena for defense records, **§721**	**3.8(e)**	
pursue evidence, **§719**		EC 7-13
PUBLIC EMPLOYMENT, RETIREMENT FROM,		
§§485-495, 498-501	**1.11(a)-(c), (e)**	DR 9-101(B)

Subject	Model Rules	ABA Code
PUBLIC OFFICE, DUTY OF HOLDER, §§565-567	3.5(a)	EC 8-8; DR 8-101(A)(1), (2)
PUBLIC PROSECUTOR *See* Prosecutors, duties of		
PUBLIC STATEMENTS *See also* Advertising; Trial publicity criticizing judiciary, **§570**	8.2	EC 8-6; DR 8-102(B)
PUBLICATION RIGHTS CONCERNING EMPLOY- MENT, **§378**		
PUBLICITY, COMMERCIAL *See* Advertising		
PUBLICITY, TRIAL *See* Trial publicity		

R

Subject	Model Rules	ABA Code
RADIO BROADCASTING *See* Advertising		
REASONABLE FEE *See* Fee for legal services		/
RECOMMENDATION OF BAR APPLICANT BY LAWYER	8.1	
REFUND OF UNEARNED FEE WHEN WITHDRAWING, **§§284-285**	1.16(d)	DR 2-110(A)(3)
REGULATION OF LEGAL PROFESSION *See also* Unauthorized practice of law; Admission to practice; Enforcement of professional responsibility American Bar Association, role of, **§§11-26**. *See also* American Bar Association contempt sanctions, **§28** federal, **§10** malpractice liability, **§27** multiple states, **§9** state regulation—judicial, legislative, state bar association, **§§1-10**		EC 3-1, 3-3, 3-4, 3-5, 3-9; DR 3-101(B)
REHABILITATION OF BAR APPLICANT, §53		
RELATIONSHIPS BETWEEN ATTORNEYS *See* Imputed disqualification of affiliated lawyers; Law firms		
REPRESENTATION OF MULTIPLE CLIENTS *See* Conflicts of interest; Multiple clients, representation of		
REQUIREMENTS FOR BAR ADMISSION *See* Admission to practice		
RESIDENCY AS REQUIREMENT FOR ADMISSION, §32		
RETIREMENT *See also* Law firms, name of from public employment, **§§485-495, 498-501** plan for lay employees, **§753**	1.11(a)-(c), (e) 5.4(a)(3)	DR 9-101(B) DR 3-102(A)(3)
REVEALING OF CONFIDENCES *See* Confidentiality, professional duty of		

Subject	Model Rules	ABA Code
REVEALING TO TRIBUNAL		
fraud, §§365, 519, 619	1.6, 3.3(b), 4.1(b)	
representative capacity in which appearing, §558	3.9	EC 7-15, 7-16
RULES OF PROFESSIONAL CONDUCT		
See Model Rules of Professional Conduct		
S		
SALE OF LAW PRACTICE, §823	1.7	
SANCTION FOR VIOLATING DISCIPLINARY RULES, IN GENERAL, §§844-850		
See also Discipline of lawyers		
SCOPE AND OBJECTIVES OF REPRESENTATION		
definition, §§152-154	1.2(c)	DR 7-101(A)(1)
in general, §151		
informed consent, §§155-156	1.2(c), 1.5(c)	
limitation of, §§153-154		
SECRETS OF CLIENT		
See Confidentiality, duty of		
SELECTION OF JUDGES, DUTY OF LAWYERS, §568		EC 8-6
SELF-INTEREST OF LAWYER		
See Conflicts of interest		
SELF-REPRESENTATION, PRIVILEGE OF, §§85-86		EC 3-7
SETTLEMENT AGREEMENT, §§424-427	1.8(g)	EC 7-7; DR 5-106(A)
SOLICITATION OF BUSINESS		
See also Employment, manner of seeking	7.4	
by attorney or agent, §787	7.3	
constitutionality of prohibition, §791		
definition, §787	7.3	
exceptions to prohibition, §§792-796		
advice to friends, relatives, §792	7.3(a)	DR 2-104(A)(1)
advice to present or former client, §792	7.3(a)	DR 2-104(A)(1)
free services, §794		
lawyer referral service, §793	7.3(d)	DR 2-103(C)
legal aid groups, §793	7.3(d)	DR 2-103(C)
prospective class action members, §§795-796		
Model Rules, §§788-790	7.3	
"Advertising Material" affixed, §790	7.3(c)	
duress prohibited, §789	7.3(b)	
personal gain as significant motive, §788	7.3(a)	
mutual referral service, §822		
other types of publicity prohibited, §797	7.1	DR 2-101(H), 2-102(A)
payment for, §822		DR 2-103(B)
sale of "goodwill," §823	1.7	
scope of prohibition, §§787-791		
Model Rules, §§788-790	7.3	
SPECIALIZATION		
general rule—no designation of, §799	7.4(d)	DR 2-105
exceptions to rule, §§800-805		
admiralty practice, §801	7.4(c)	

Subject	Model Rules	ABA Code
certification by private organization, §804		DR 2-105(A)(3)
Model Rules certification requirements, §805	7.4(d)	
patent practice, §800	7.4(b)	DR 2-105(A)(1)
state certification, §803		DR 2-105(A)(3)
limitation on practice permitted, §§806-808	7.4(a)	DR 2-105(A)(2)
publicity of. *See* Advertising		

SPHERES OF AUTHORITY
See Authority of lawyer

STATE'S ATTORNEY
See Prosecutors, duties of

"STIRRING UP LITIGATION"
See Advertising; Advice by lawyer

Subject	Model Rules	ABA Code
STOCKHOLDERS OF CORPORATION, CORPORATE COUNSEL'S ALLEGIANCE TO, §§431-433	1.13(a), (g)	EC 5-18

See also Multiple clients, representation of

SUCCESSIVE CLIENTS, REPRESENTATION OF
See Multiple clients, representation of

SUGGESTED FEE SCHEDULE
See Fee for legal services, determination of, factors
to consider

SUGGESTION OF NEED FOR LEGAL SERVICES
See Advice by lawyer

Subject	Model Rules	ABA Code
SUIT TO HARASS OR MALICIOUSLY HARM ANOTHER §§149, 271, 632	4.4	DR 2-109(A)(1), 2-110(B)(1), 7-102(C)(2)

Subject	Model Rules	ABA Code
SUPPRESSION OF EVIDENCE		
confidentiality and physical evidence of crime, §§351-353		
incriminating documents, §311		
obstruction of access to evidence, §624	3.4(a)	DR 7-109(A)

Subject	Model Rules	ABA Code
SUSPENSION FROM PRACTICE		
as disciplinary sanction, §845		
effect of on other jurisdictions, §§882-884	8.5(a)	
temporary, §845		

T

Subject	Model Rules	ABA Code
TAX RETURNS		
and unauthorized practice, §99		
false, §505	1.2(d)	DR 7-102(A)(7), (8)

TELEVISION AND RADIO PROGRAMS
See Advertising

Subject	Model Rules	ABA Code
TERMINATION OF ATTORNEY-CLIENT RELATIONSHIP		
discharge by client, §§287-298	1.16(a)(3)	DR 2-110(B)(4)
agreement prohibiting, invalid, §288		
continuing fiduciary duty, §290		
court's refusal to allow, §289		
fees, effect upon, §§291-297		
third party liability for inducing, §298		
unconditional right, §287	1.16(a)(3)	DR 2-110(B)(4)

Subject	Model Rules	ABA Code
discretion of court to deny withdrawal, §307		DR 2-110(A)(1)
liability for fees, §§291-297		
contingent fees, §§294-297		
fixed fee, §292		
retainer fee, §293		
mandatory withdrawal, §§268-272		
discharge by client, §272	1.16(a)(3)	DR 2-110(B)(4)
employment violative of Disciplinary Rule, §269	1.16(a)(1)	DR 2-110(B)(2)
personal inability to continue, §270	1.16(a)(2)	DR 2-110(B)(3)
where services used to harass, §271	1.16(a)(3)	DR 2-110(B)(4)
obligations of attorney upon withdrawal, §§281-286		
court approval, §282	1.16(c)	
notice to client, §283	1.16(d)	DR 2-110(A)(2)
refund of unearned fees, §§284-285	1.16(d)	DR 2-110(A)(2)
return of client's materials, §286	1.16(d)	DR 2-110(A)(2)
permissive withdrawal, §§273-280		
client involves lawyer in illegality, §275	1.16(b)(2), (3)	
consent of client, §279		DR 2-110(C)(5)
court determination of good cause, §282	1.16(c)	
failure to pay or fulfill obligation, §277	1.16(b)(5)	
no material adverse effect on client, §274	1.16(b)(1)	
repugnant demands, §276	1.16(b)(4)	
unreasonably difficult relationship, §278	1.16(b)(c)	DR 2-110(C)(1)(d)
THREATENING CRIMINAL PROCESS, §§552-555		EC 7-21; DR 7-105(A)
TRADE NAME		
See Law firms, name of		
TRANSACTIONS, BUSINESS OR FINANCIAL, **WITH CLIENT**		
effect on duty of loyalty. *See* Conflicts of interest		
formalities required, §§379-383	1.8(a)	DR 5-104(A)
presumption of undue influence, §380		
TRIAL PUBLICITY, §§660-670	3.6, 5.3(c)	DR 7-107
See also Litigation duties of lawyer		
TRUSTEE, CLIENT NAMING LAWYER AS, §390	1.7, 1.8(c)	EC 5-6
U		
UNAUTHORIZED PRACTICE OF LAW		
activities constituting, §§88-103	5.5	EC 3-5
administrative proceedings, §93		
aiding a layperson in the, prohibited, §114	5.5(a)	DR 3-101(A)
attorney duty to prevent, §§114-116	5.5(a)	DR 3-101(A)
bar opinions, §117		
basic considerations, §§85-87		
corporations, §§108-112		
"do-it-yourself" clinics and kits, §§101-102		
drafting documents, §§94-97		
insurance companies, §110		
judges, §105		
law clerks, §106		
law students, §§106-107		
out-of-state lawyers. *See* Admission to practice		
partnership with nonlawyer, §116. *See also* Partnership	5.4(b)	DR 3-103

Subject	Model Rules	ABA Code
persons prohibited from, §§104-112		
prisoner legal assistance, §103		
real estate brokers, §96		
"scrivening," §95		
self-representation by layperson not included in, §§85-86		EC 3-7
sharing of fees with nonlawyer, §115. See also Fee for		
legal services, division of	5.4(a)	DR 3-102
tax advice, §§98-99		
tests for, §§89-91		EC 3-5
title insurance companies, §97		

UNREASONABLE FEES
See Fee for legal services, amount of

UNSOLICITED ADVICE
See Advice by lawyer

V

VARYING INTERESTS OF CLIENTS
See Conflicts of interest; Multiple clients, representation of

VENIREMEN
See Jurors and court officials

Subject	Model Rules	ABA Code
VIOLATION OF DISCIPLINARY RULES AS CAUSE FOR DISCIPLINE, §§825-830	8.4(a)	DR 1-102(A)(1), (2)
VIOLATION OF LAW AS CAUSE FOR DISCIPLINE, §831-837	8.4	DR 1-102(A)(4)
VOLUNTARY GIFTS BY CLIENT TO LAWYER, §§384-389	1.8(c)	EC 5-5

VOLUNTEERED ADVICE TO SECURE LEGAL SERVICES
See Advice by lawyer

WXY

Subject	Model Rules	ABA Code
WILL OF CLIENT		
gift to lawyer in, §§384, 387-389	1.8(c)	EC 5-5
lawyer named as executor, §390	1.7, 1.8(c)	EC 5-6

WITHDRAWAL
See Termination of attorney-client relationship

Subject	Model Rules	ABA Code
WITNESS		
coaching, §§628-630	3.4	
communication with, in general, §§626-628	3.4(a), (b), (e), 4.4	EC 7-28; DR 7-109(C)
false testimony by, §§601-611	3.3(a)(3)	DR 7-102(B)(2)
inducing favorable testimony of, §§626-628	3.4(b)	EC 7-28
lawyer acting as	3.7	EC 5-9, 5-10; DR 5-101(B), 5-102(A)
advocate and witness—generally prohibited, §§682-684	3.7	DR 5-101(B), 5-102(A)
imputation to firm, §684		DR 5-105(D)
no imputation to firm, §684	3.7(b)	
withdrawal as lawyer, §683	3.7(a)	EC 5-10
called by opposing party, §§691-693	3.6	DR 5-102(B)
conflict of interests, possibility of, §681		EC 5-9
duty to withdraw from case, §683	3.7(a)	EC 5-10

Subject	Model Rules	ABA Code
permissible appearance as witness		
avoid miscarriage of justice, §690		
legal services in issue, §687	3.7(a)(2)	DR 5-101(B)(3)
to prevent hardship to client, §§688-689	3.7(a)(3)	EC 5-10; DR 5-101(B)(4)
uncontested matters, §685	3.1(a)(1)	DR 5-101(B)(1), (2)
members of lawyer's firm acting as, §684	3.7(b)	DR 5-101(D)
obstructing access to, §625	3.4(f)	DR 7-109(B)
payment to, §§627-629	3.4(b)	DR 7-109(C)
perjury, intent to commit, §§612-618	3.3(a)(3)	
treatment of		
examining to degrade or harass, §632	4.4	DR 7-106(C)(2)
opinion as to credibility, §633	3.4(e)	DR 7-106(C)(4)

WORK PRODUCT, §484

Z

ZEAL

See also Competence, duty of; Diligence, duty of		
asserting "technicalities," §581		DR 7-101(B)(1)
criminal defendants, §§201-207		
general duty of, §§190, 557	3.1	EC 7-15, 7-16; DR 7-101(A)
lawyer's views contrary to client's, §195	1.2(b)	EC 7-17
legislative and administrative proceedings, §§556-558	3.9	EC 7-15, 7-16
litigation matters, §191	3.1	EC 7-3, 7-4
nonadversarial matters, §192	2.1	EC 7-5
trial limitations. *See* Litigation duties of lawyer		

Notes

Notes

Notes

Notes

Notes

Notes

Notes

Notes

Notes

Notes

Notes

Notes